CONTENTS

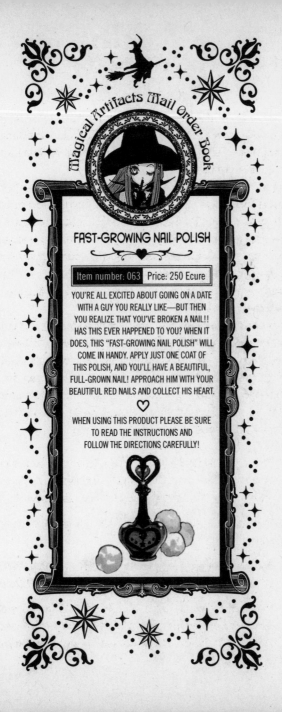

Magical Artifacts Mail Order Book

FAST-GROWING NAIL POLISH
♥

Item number: 063 | **Price: 250 Ecure**

YOU'RE ALL EXCITED ABOUT GOING ON A DATE WITH A GUY YOU REALLY LIKE—BUT THEN YOU REALIZE THAT YOU'VE BROKEN A NAIL!! HAS THIS EVER HAPPENED TO YOU? WHEN IT DOES, THIS "FAST-GROWING NAIL POLISH" WILL COME IN HANDY. APPLY JUST ONE COAT OF THIS POLISH, AND YOU'LL HAVE A BEAUTIFUL, FULL-GROWN NAIL! APPROACH HIM WITH YOUR BEAUTIFUL RED NAILS AND COLLECT HIS HEART.

♡

WHEN USING THIS PRODUCT PLEASE BE SURE TO READ THE INSTRUCTIONS AND FOLLOW THE DIRECTIONS CAREFULLY!

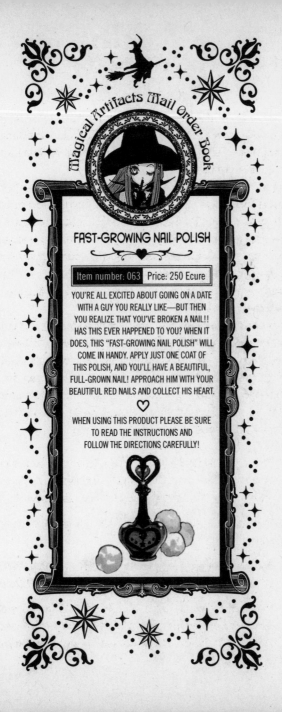

HONORIFICS EXPLAINED

Throughout the Del Rey Manga books, you will find Japanese honorifics left intact in the translations. For those not familiar with how the Japanese use honorifics and, more important, how they differ from American honorifics, we present this brief overview.

Politeness has always been a critical facet of Japanese culture. Ever since the feudal era, when Japan was a highly stratified society, use of honorifics–which can be defined as polite speech that indicates relationship or status–has played an essential role in the Japanese language. When addressing someone in Japanese, an honorific usually takes the form of a suffix attached to one's name (e.g., "Asuna-san"), is used as a title at the end of one's name, or appears in place of the name itself (e.g., "Negi-sensei," or simply "Sensei!").

Honorifics can be expressions of respect or endearment. In the context of manga and anime, honorifics give insight into the nature of the relationship between characters. Many translations into English leave out these important honorifics and therefore distort the feel of the original Japanese. Because Japanese honorifics contain nuances that English honorifics lack, it is our policy at Del Rey not to translate them. Here, instead, is a guide to some of the honorifics you may encounter in Del Rey Manga.

-SAN: This is the most common honorific and is equivalent to Mr., Miss, Ms., Mrs., etc. It is the all-purpose honorific and can be used in any situation where politeness is required.

-SAMA: This is one level higher than "-san." It is used to confer great respect.

-DONO: This comes from the word "tono," which means "lord." It is an even higher level than -sama and confers utmost respect.

-KUN: This suffix is used at the end of boys' names to express familiarity or endearment. It is also sometimes used by men among friends, or when addressing someone younger or of lower station.

-CHAN: This is used to express endearment, mostly toward girls. It is also used for little boys, pets, and among lovers. It gives a sense of childish cuteness.

BOZU: This is an informal way to refer to a boy, similar to the English terms "kid" and "squirt."

SEMPAI/

SENPAI: This title suggests that the addressee is one's senior in a group or organization. It is most often used in a school setting, where underclassmen refer to their upperclassmen as "sempai." It can also be used in the workplace, such as when a newer employee addresses an employee who has seniority in the company.

KOHAI: This is the opposite of "sempai" and is used toward underclassmen in school or newcomers in the workplace. It connotes that the addressee is of a lower station.

SENSEI: Literally meaning "one who has come before," this title is used for teachers, doctors, or masters of any profession or art.

-[BLANK]: This is usually forgotten on these lists, but it's perhaps the most significant difference between Japanese and English. The lack of honorific means that the speaker has permission to address the person in a very intimate way. Usually, only family, spouses, or very close friends have this kind of license. Known as *yobisute*, it can be gratifying when someone who has earned the intimacy starts to call one by one's name without an honorific. But when that intimacy hasn't been earned, it can also be insulting.

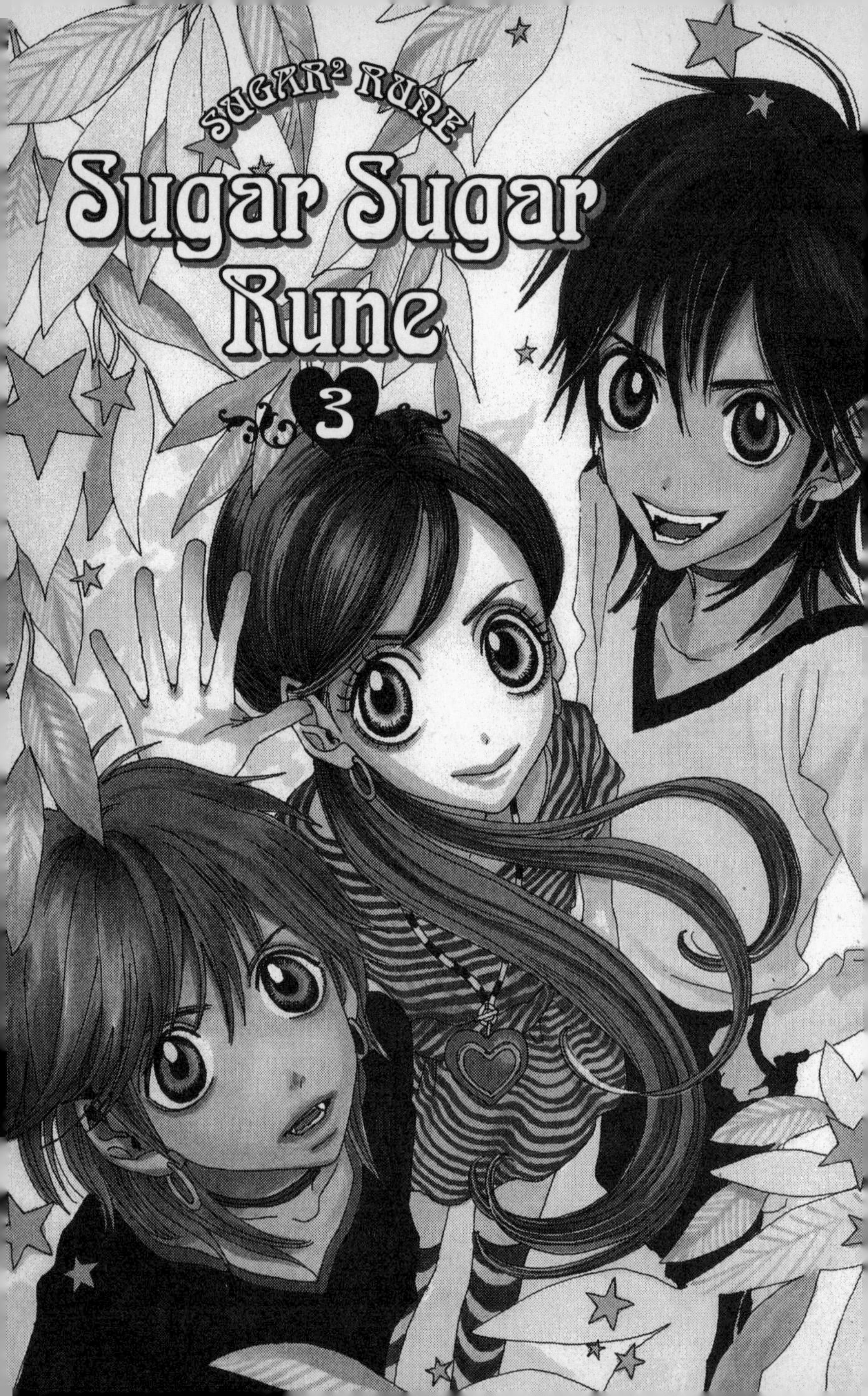
SUGAR² RUNE
Sugar Sugar Rune
3

CONTENTS

もくじ

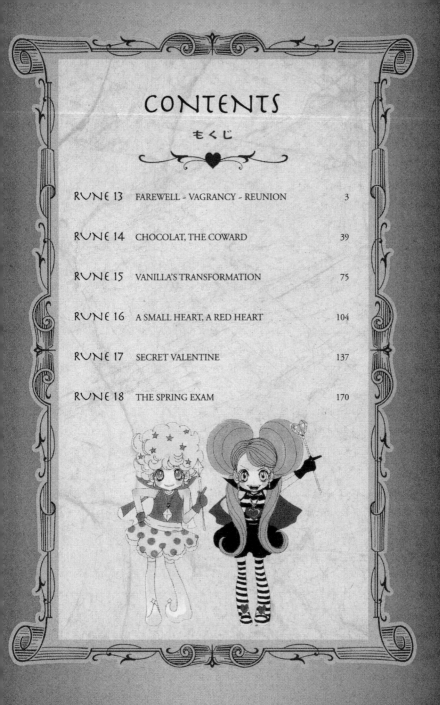

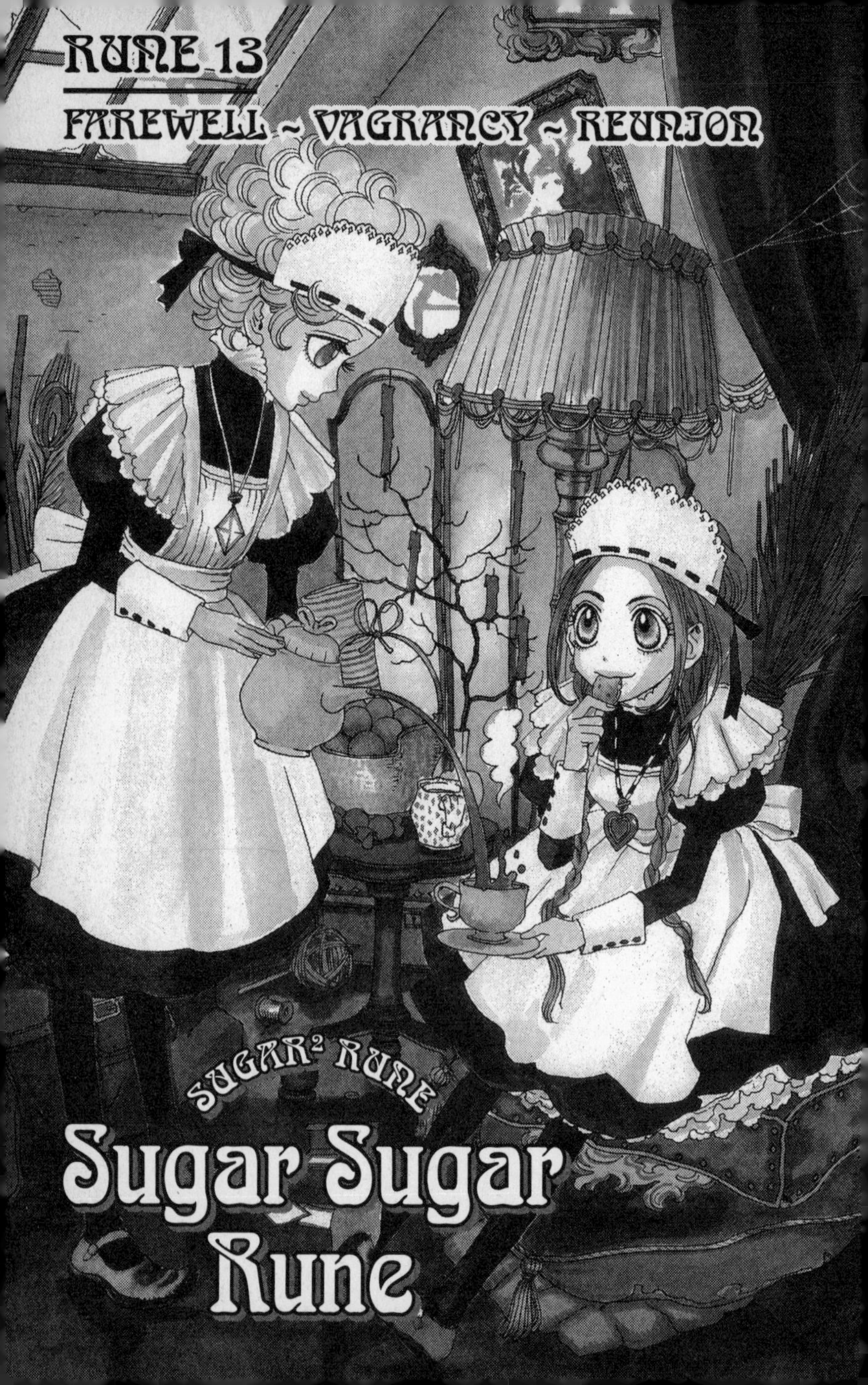
RUNE 13
FAREWELL ~ VAGRANCY ~ REUNION
SUGAR² RUNE
Sugar Sugar Rune

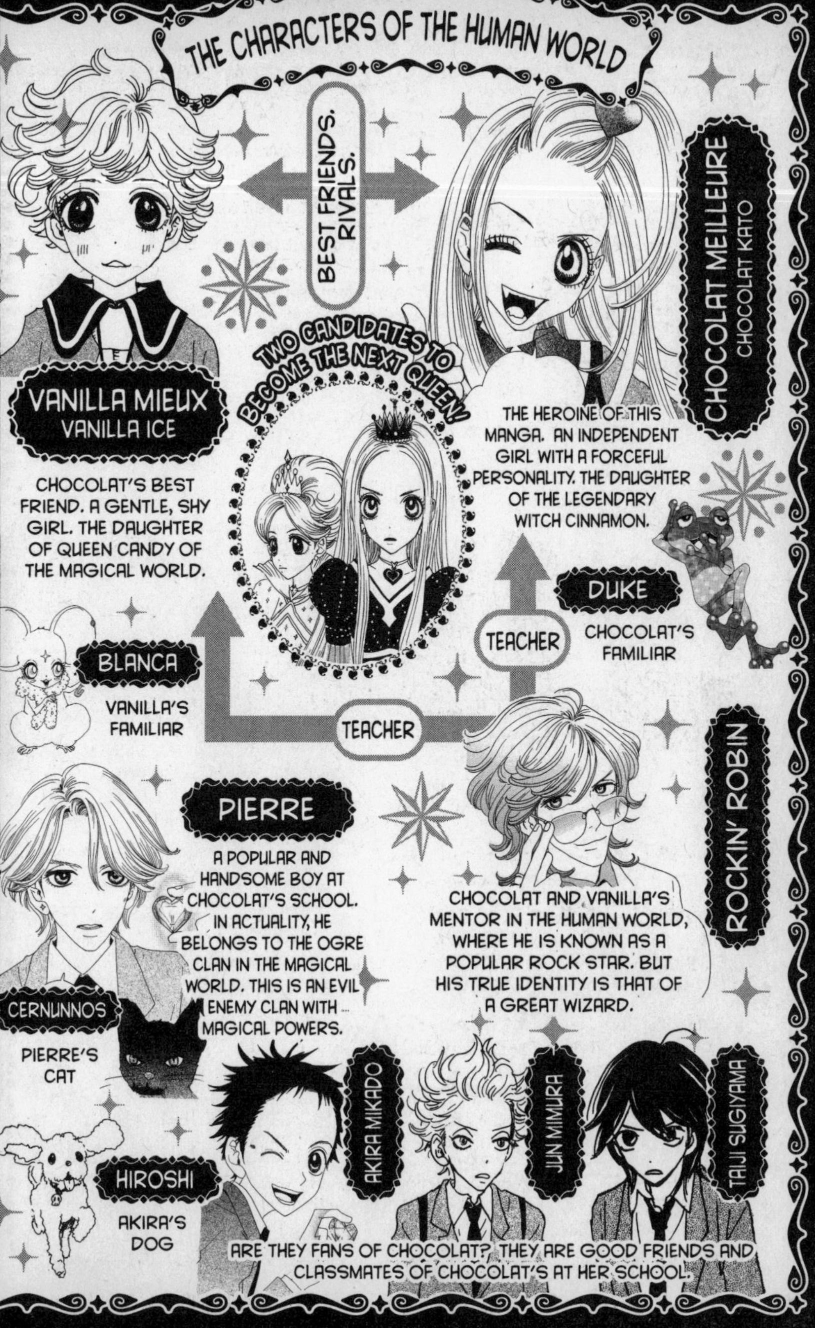
THE CHARACTERS OF THE HUMAN WORLD
CHOCOLAT MEILLEURE
CHOCOLAT KATO
THE HEROINE OF THIS MANGA. AN INDEPENDENT GIRL WITH A FORCEFUL PERSONALITY. THE DAUGHTER OF THE LEGENDARY WITCH CINNAMON.
BEST FRIENDS. RIVALS.
VANILLA MIEUX
VANILLA ICE
CHOCOLAT'S BEST FRIEND. A GENTLE, SHY GIRL. THE DAUGHTER OF QUEEN CANDY OF THE MAGICAL WORLD.
TWO CANDIDATES TO BECOME THE NEXT QUEEN!
DUKE
CHOCOLAT'S FAMILIAR
TEACHER
BLANCA
VANILLA'S FAMILIAR
TEACHER
ROCKIN' ROBIN
CHOCOLAT AND VANILLA'S MENTOR IN THE HUMAN WORLD, WHERE HE IS KNOWN AS A POPULAR ROCK STAR. BUT HIS TRUE IDENTITY IS THAT OF A GREAT WIZARD.
PIERRE
A POPULAR AND HANDSOME BOY AT CHOCOLAT'S SCHOOL. IN ACTUALITY, HE BELONGS TO THE OGRE CLAN IN THE MAGICAL WORLD. THIS IS AN EVIL ENEMY CLAN WITH MAGICAL POWERS.
CERNUNNOS
PIERRE'S CAT
TAIJI SUGIYAMA
JUN MIMURA
AKIRA MIKADO
HIROSHI
AKIRA'S DOG
ARE THEY FANS OF CHOCOLAT? THEY ARE GOOD FRIENDS AND CLASSMATES OF CHOCOLAT'S AT HER SCHOOL.

CHARACTERS OF THE MAGICAL WORLD

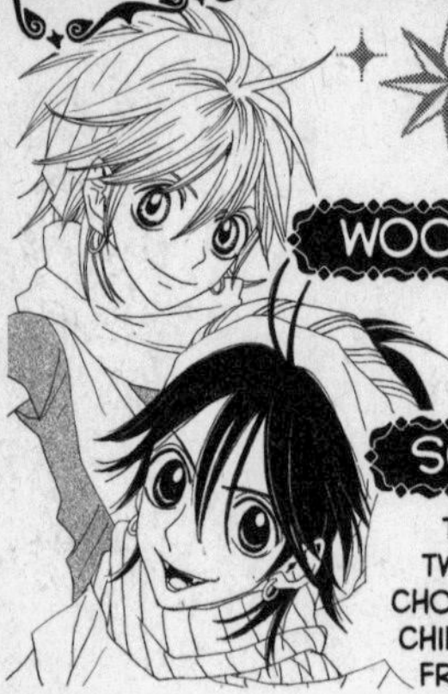

WOO

SOUL

THESE TWO ARE CHOCOLAT'S CHILDHOOD FRIENDS.

MAGICAL WORLD PRIMER

WAND

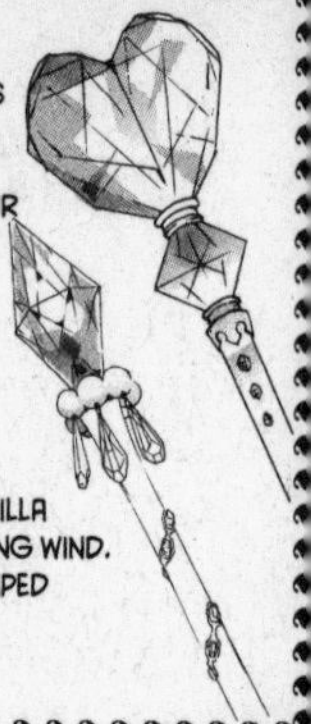

YOU CAN PURCHASE ACCESSORIES (CALLED "OPTIONS") WITH THE HEARTS YOU COLLECT AND MAKE YOUR WAND MORE PERSONAL. DEPENDING ON THE TYPES OF OPTIONS YOU GET FOR YOUR WAND, YOU'LL GAIN DIFFERENT TYPES OF MAGICAL POWERS.

♥ THE HEART-SHAPED OPTION CHOCOLAT HAS ON HER WAND IS CALLED "LA ÉTOILE BRILLANT." IT MAKES HER HAIR AND LIPS SHINE.

◆ THE DIAMOND-SHAPED OPTION VANILLA HAS ON HER WAND CAN BRING A SPRING WIND. THE PEARLS BELOW THE DIAMOND-SHAPED OPTION ARE CALLED "BUBBLE BATH." THEY PRODUCE BUBBLES.

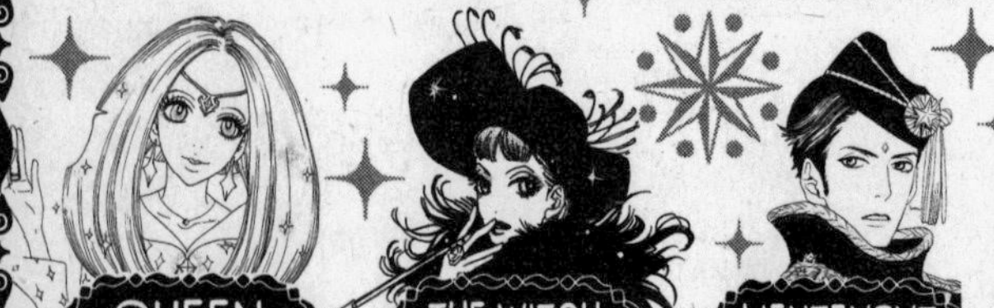

QUEEN CANDY

VANILLA'S MOTHER

THE WITCH CINNAMON

CHOCOLAT'S MOTHER. SHE HAS PASSED AWAY.

LIEUTENANT GLACIER

LIEUTENANT AT THE PALACE

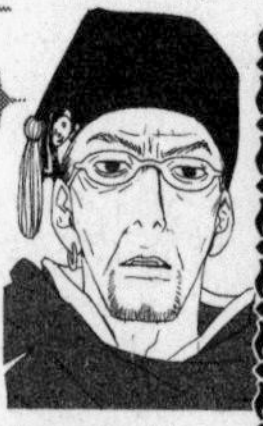

CORNE MEILLEURE (GRANDPA)

CHOCOLAT'S GRANDPA

THE STORY SO FAR

★MY NAME IS CHOCOLAT. MY BEST FRIEND, VANILLA, AND I ARE CANDIDATES TO BE THE NEXT QUEEN OF THE MAGICAL WORLD. WE'VE COME TO THE HUMAN WORLD FOR A TEST TO SEE WHO WILL BE THE NEXT QUEEN. THE TEST IS TO SEE WHICH ONE OF US CAN COLLECT THE MOST HEARTS.

★HUMANS HAVE MANY EMOTIONS, SO THERE ARE MANY DIFFERENT COLORED HEARTS: RED, PINK, ORANGE, VIOLET, ETC. BASED ON THE HEART'S COLOR, THE AMOUNT OF ECURE YOU CAN EARN WILL VARY. IF YOU EARN ECURE, YOU'LL BE ABLE TO PURCHASE VARIOUS OPTIONS FOR YOUR WAND AND MAGICAL ITEMS FROM THE MAGICAL ARTIFACTS MAIL ORDER BOOK.

★THE OTHER DAY PIERRE ASKED ME OUT SO I FIGURED I COULD DISCOVER HIS TRUE CHARACTER WHEN WE WERE TOGETHER. BUT THEN AN UNEXPECTED INCIDENT HAPPENED ON OUR DATE!! NOT ONLY THAT, PIERRE HAS APPROACHED VANILLA...

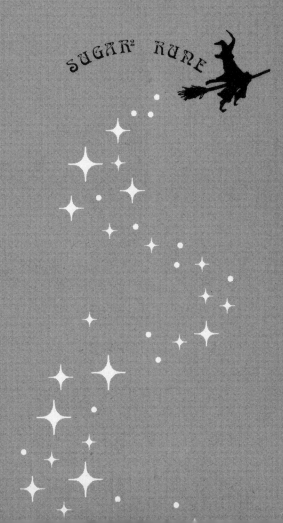

SUGAR RUNE

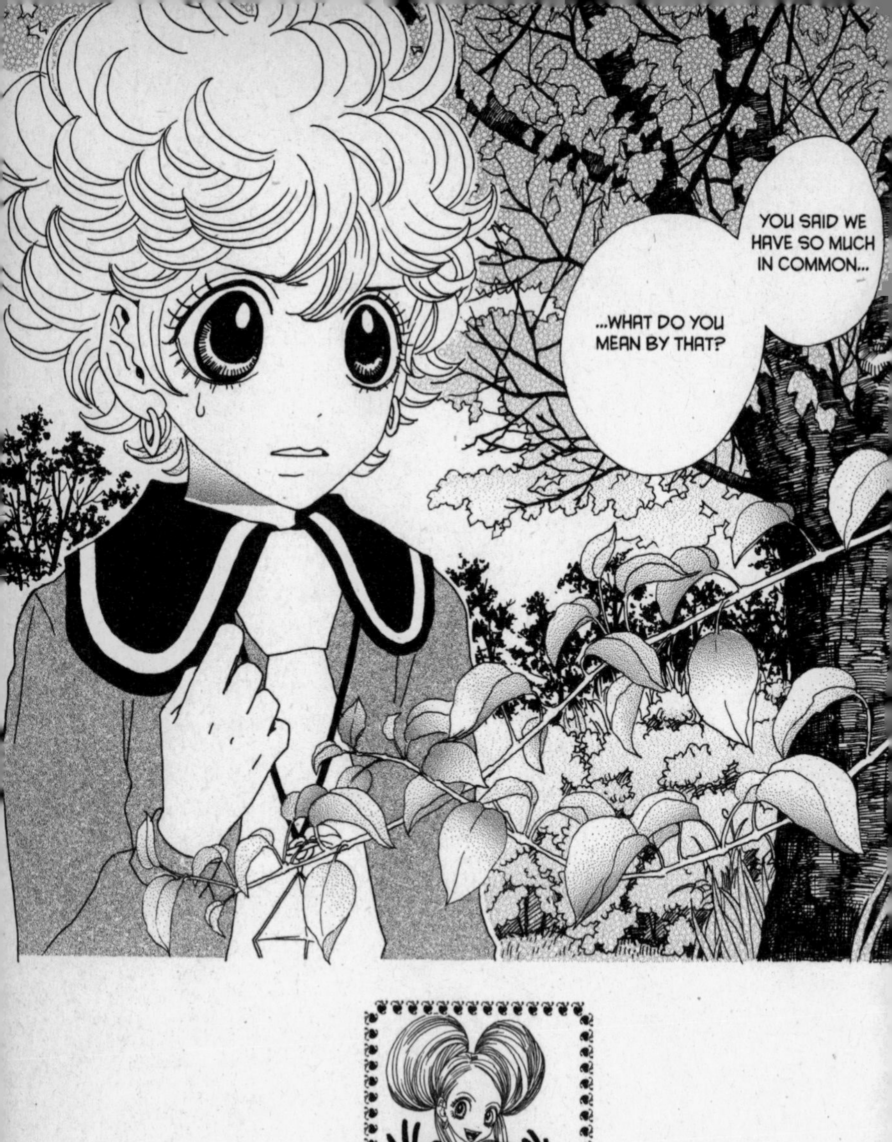
YOU SAID WE HAVE SO MUCH IN COMMON...
...WHAT DO YOU MEAN BY THAT?

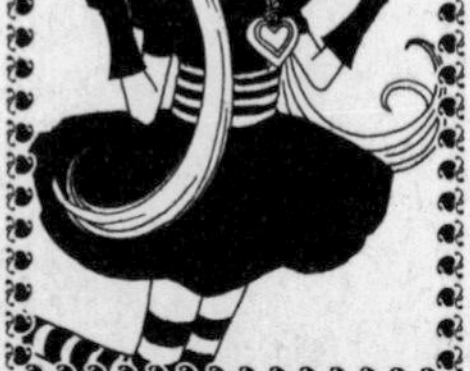

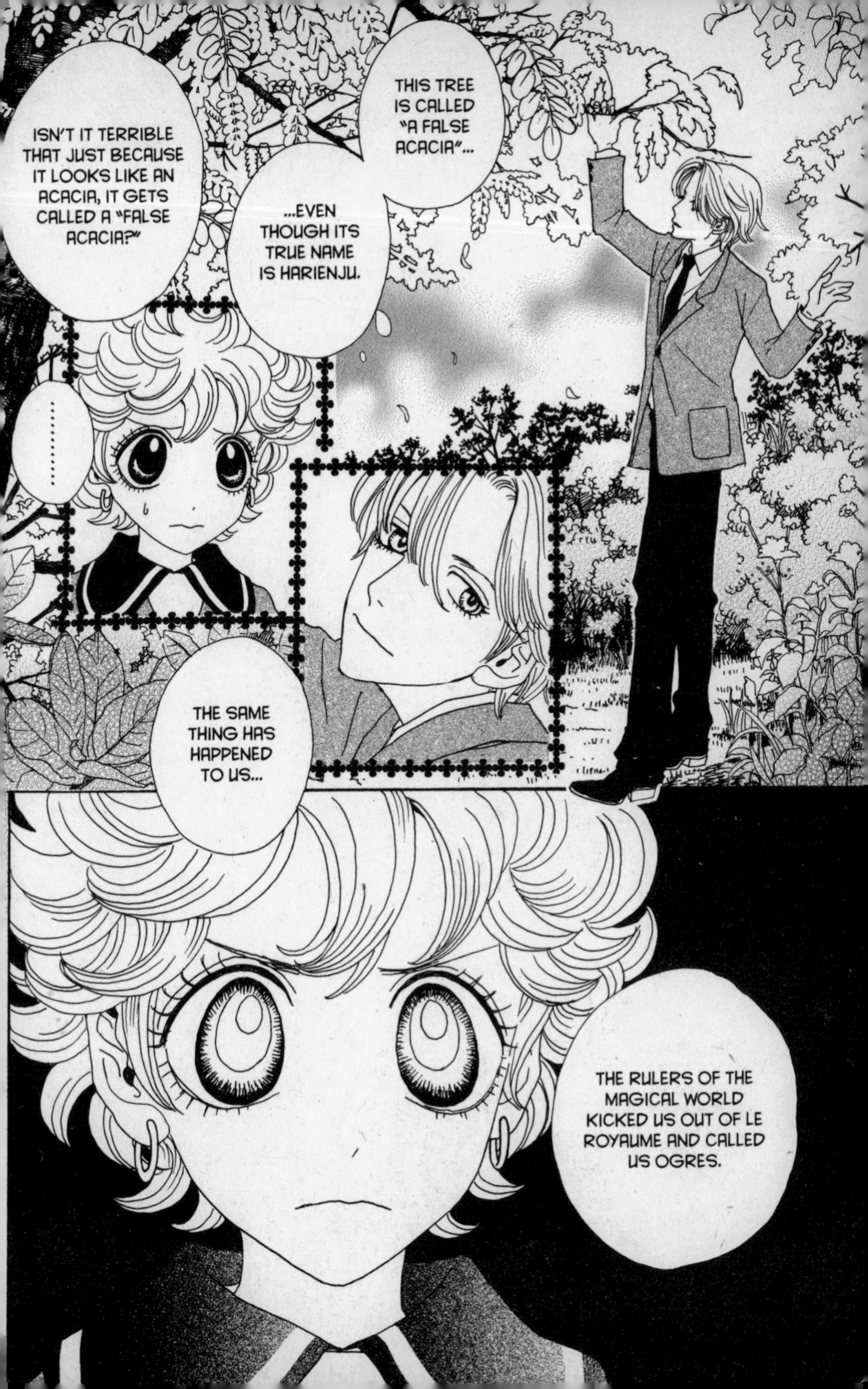
THIS TREE IS CALLED "A FALSE ACACIA"...
...EVEN THOUGH ITS TRUE NAME IS HARIENJU.
ISN'T IT TERRIBLE THAT JUST BECAUSE IT LOOKS LIKE AN ACACIA, IT GETS CALLED A "FALSE ACACIA?"
......
THE SAME THING HAS HAPPENED TO US...
THE RULERS OF THE MAGICAL WORLD KICKED US OUT OF LE ROYAUME AND CALLED US OGRES.

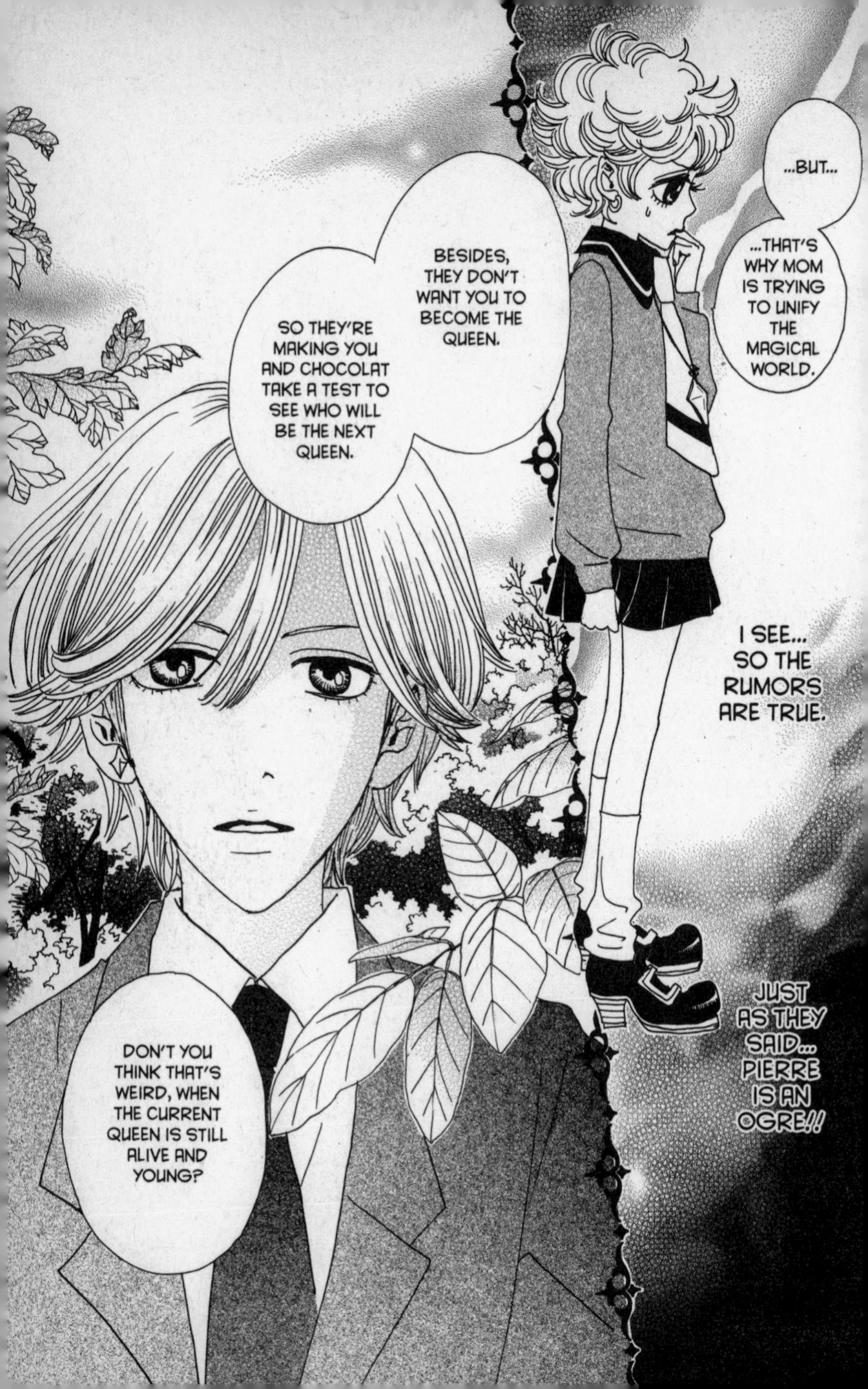
...BUT...
...THAT'S WHY MOM IS TRYING TO UNIFY THE MAGICAL WORLD.
BESIDES, THEY DON'T WANT YOU TO BECOME THE QUEEN.
SO THEY'RE MAKING YOU AND CHOCOLAT TAKE A TEST TO SEE WHO WILL BE THE NEXT QUEEN.
I SEE... SO THE RUMORS ARE TRUE.
JUST AS THEY SAID... PIERRE IS AN OGRE!!
DON'T YOU THINK THAT'S WEIRD, WHEN THE CURRENT QUEEN IS STILL ALIVE AND YOUNG?

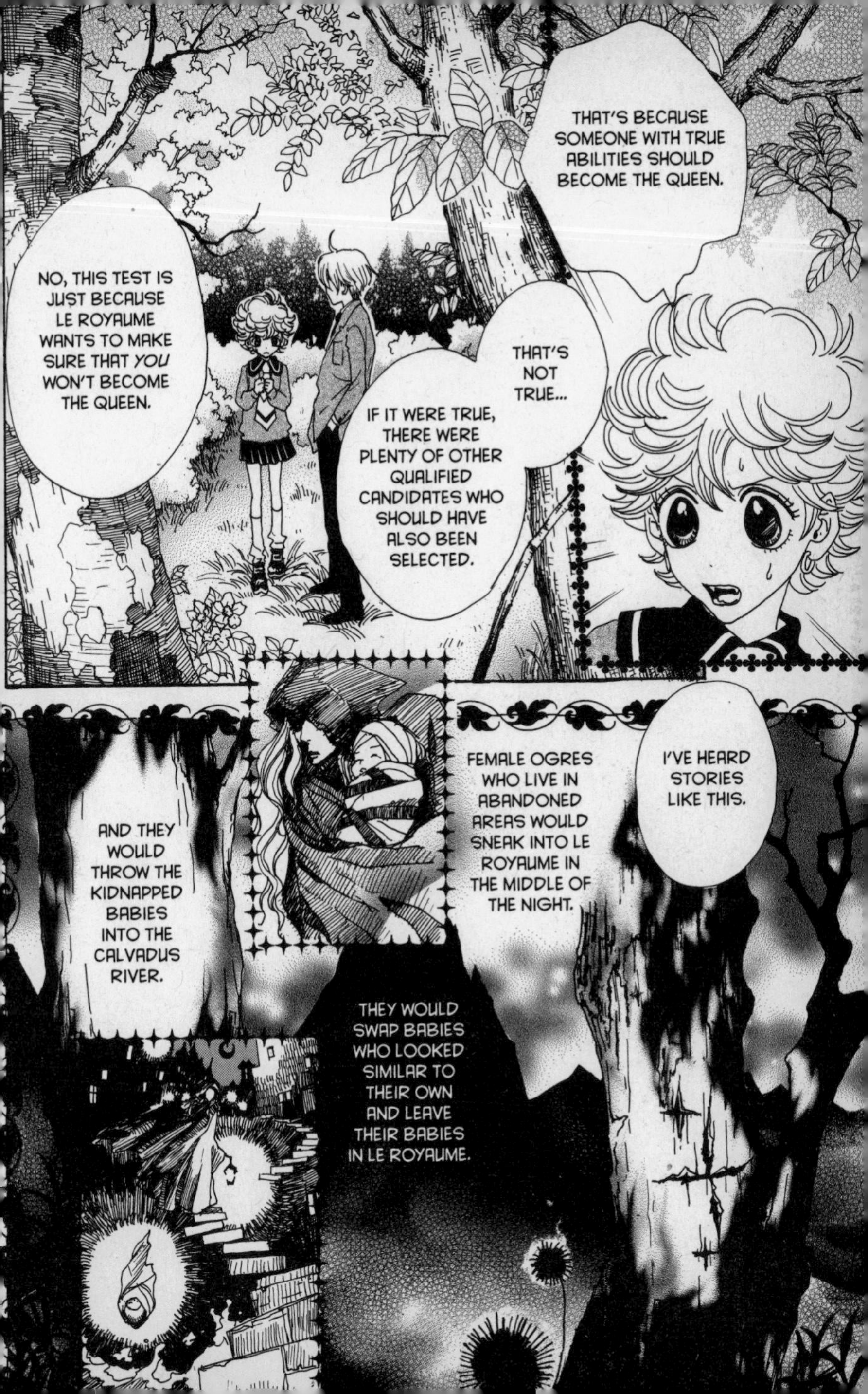
THAT'S BECAUSE SOMEONE WITH TRUE ABILITIES SHOULD BECOME THE QUEEN.
NO, THIS TEST IS JUST BECAUSE LE ROYAUME WANTS TO MAKE SURE THAT *YOU* WON'T BECOME THE QUEEN.
THAT'S NOT TRUE...
IF IT WERE TRUE, THERE WERE PLENTY OF OTHER QUALIFIED CANDIDATES WHO SHOULD HAVE ALSO BEEN SELECTED.
I'VE HEARD STORIES LIKE THIS.
FEMALE OGRES WHO LIVE IN ABANDONED AREAS WOULD SNEAK INTO LE ROYAUME IN THE MIDDLE OF THE NIGHT.
THEY WOULD SWAP BABIES WHO LOOKED SIMILAR TO THEIR OWN AND LEAVE THEIR BABIES IN LE ROYAUME.
AND THEY WOULD THROW THE KIDNAPPED BABIES INTO THE CALVADUS RIVER.

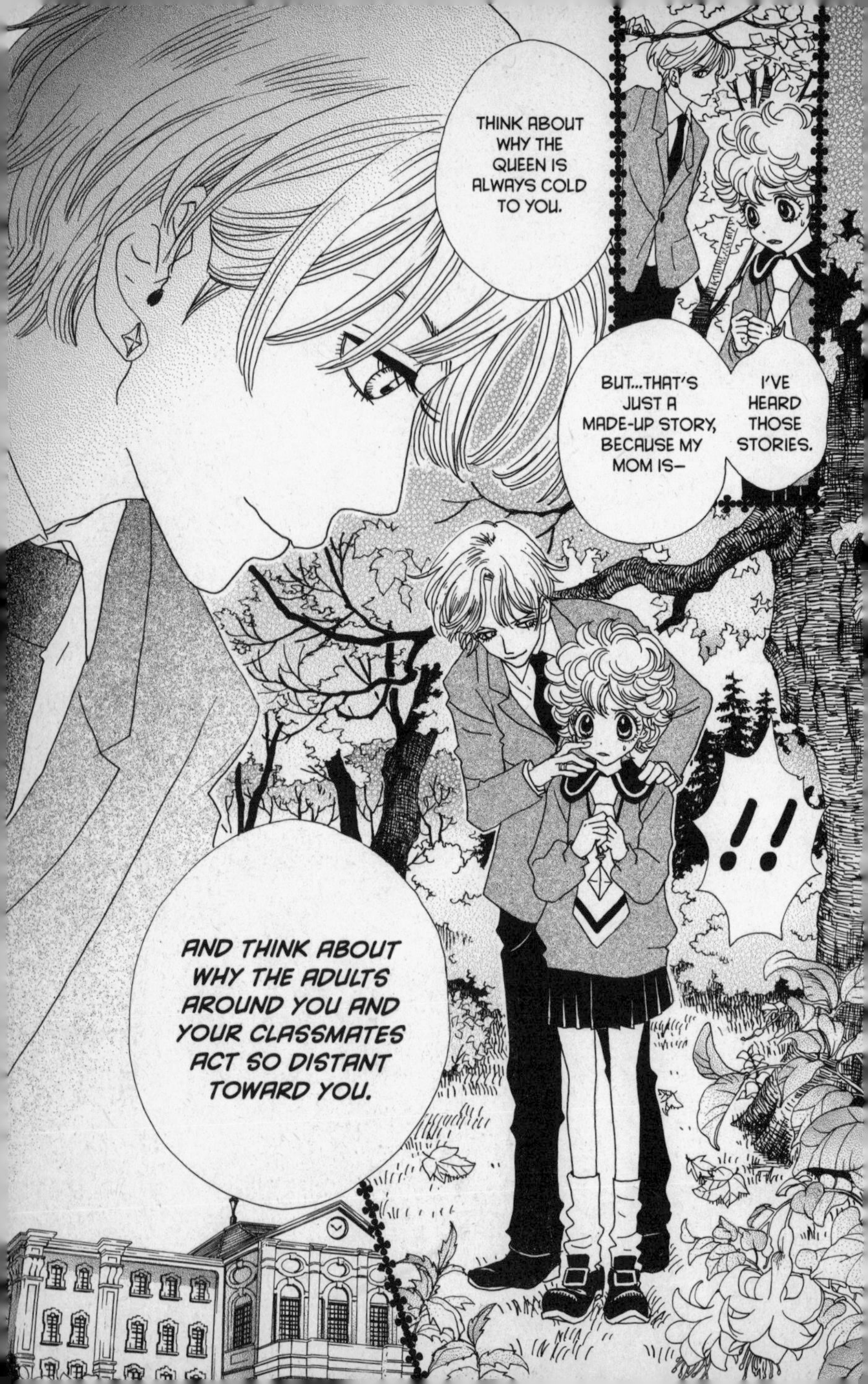
THINK ABOUT WHY THE QUEEN IS ALWAYS COLD TO YOU.
I'VE HEARD THOSE STORIES.
BUT...THAT'S JUST A MADE-UP STORY, BECAUSE MY MOM IS—
!!
AND THINK ABOUT WHY THE ADULTS AROUND YOU AND YOUR CLASSMATES ACT SO DISTANT TOWARD YOU.

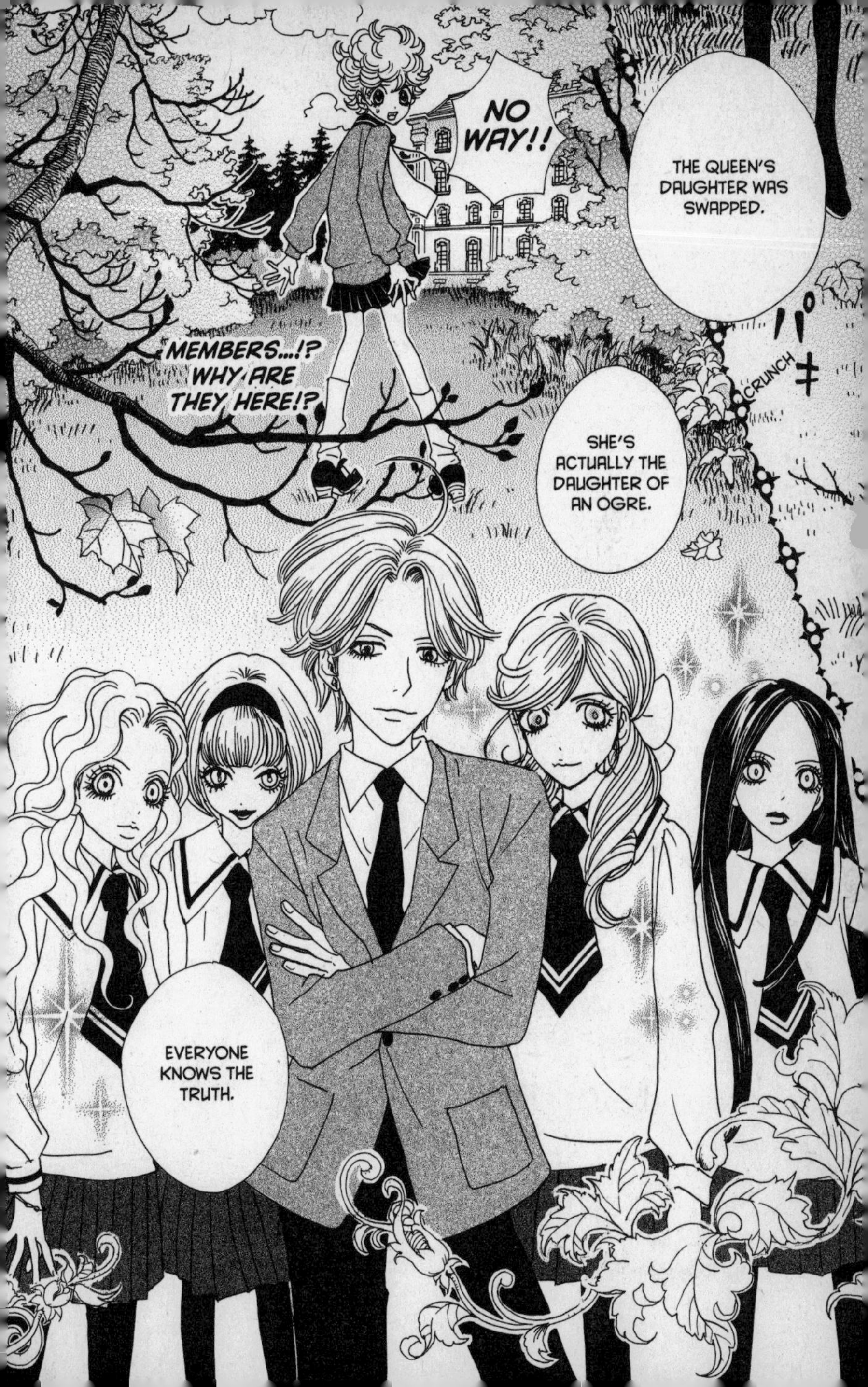
THE QUEEN'S DAUGHTER WAS SWAPPED.
NO WAY!!
パキ
CRUNCH
SHE'S ACTUALLY THE DAUGHTER OF AN OGRE.
MEMBERS...!? WHY ARE THEY HERE!?
EVERYONE KNOWS THE TRUTH.

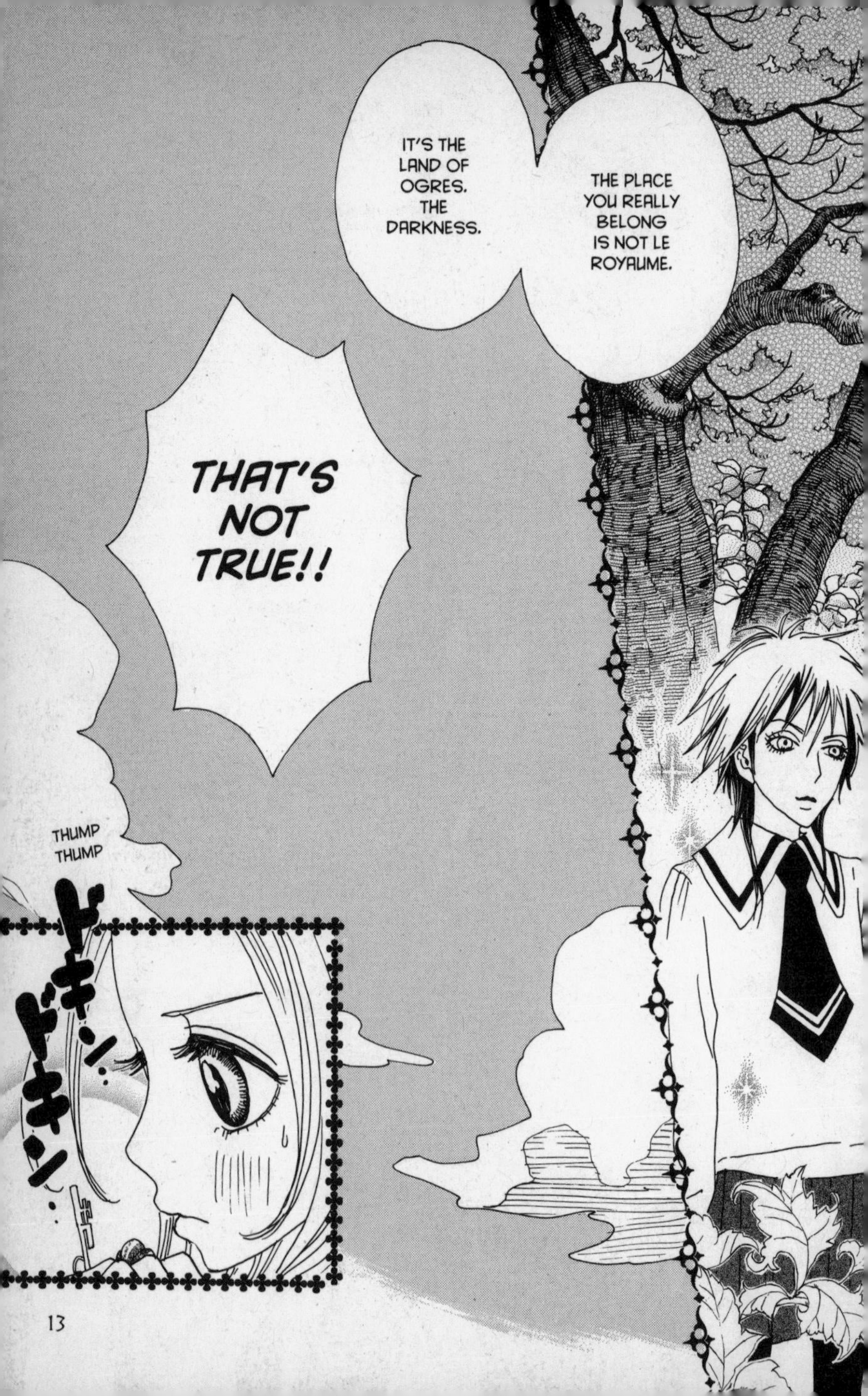
THE PLACE YOU REALLY BELONG IS NOT LE ROYAUME.
IT'S THE LAND OF OGRES. THE DARKNESS.
THAT'S NOT TRUE!!
THUMP THUMP

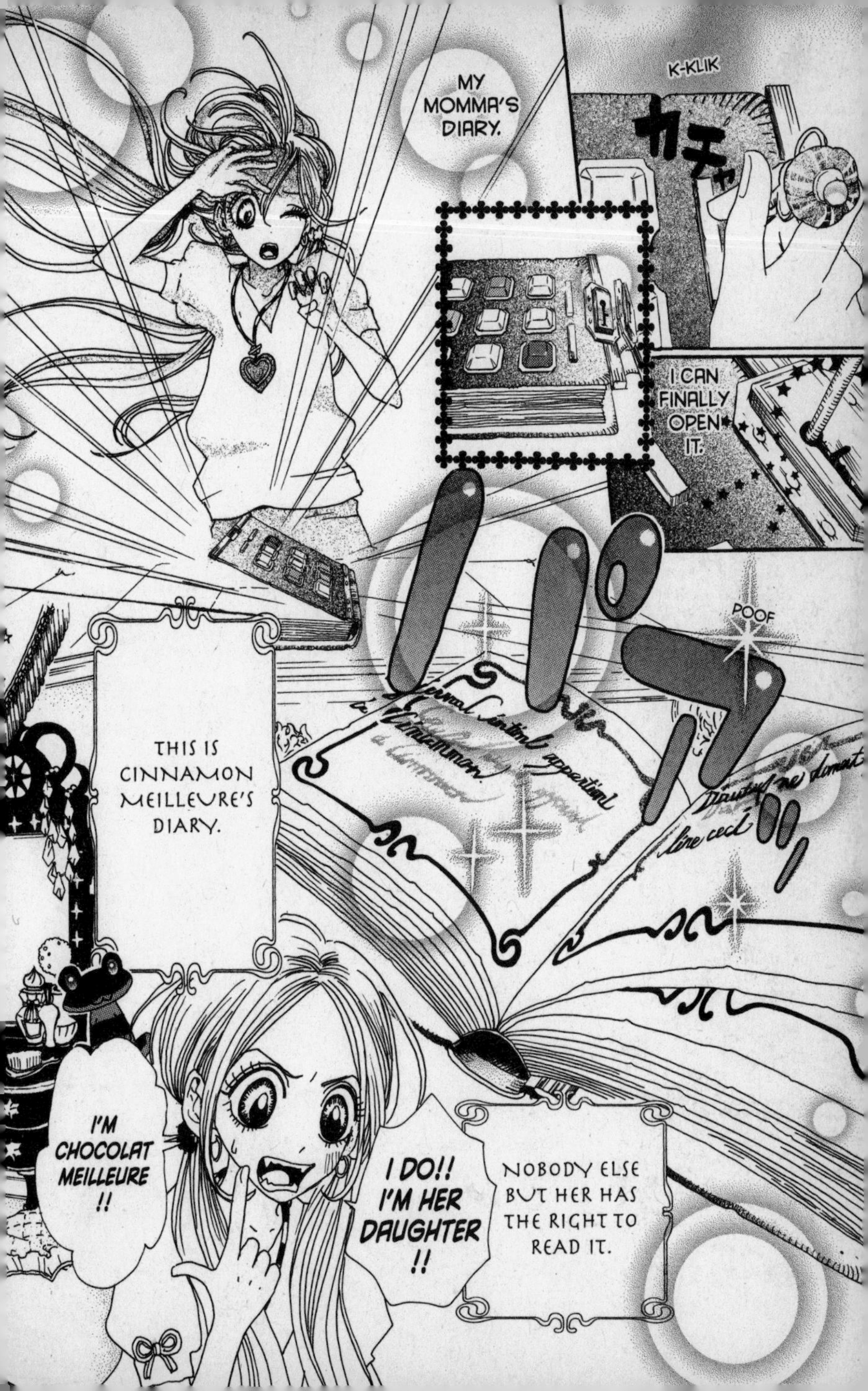
K-KLIK
カチャ
I CAN FINALLY OPEN IT.
MY MOMMA'S DIARY.
POOF
THIS IS CINNAMON MEILLEURE'S DIARY.
NOBODY ELSE BUT HER HAS THE RIGHT TO READ IT.
I DO!! I'M HER DAUGHTER!!
I'M CHOCOLAT MEILLEURE!!

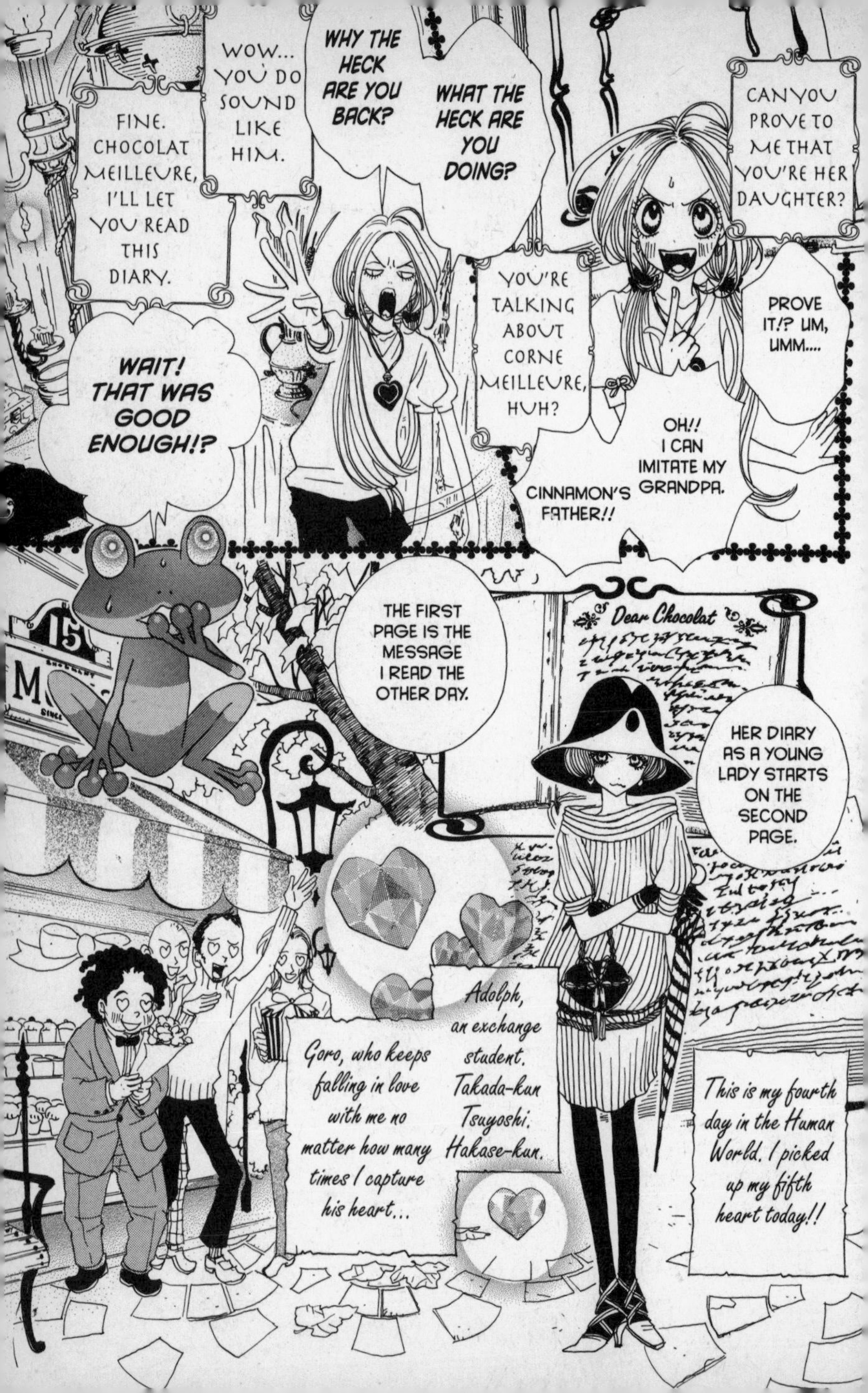
CAN YOU PROVE TO ME THAT YOU'RE HER DAUGHTER?
PROVE IT!? UM, UMM....
OH!! I CAN IMITATE MY GRANDPA.
CINNAMON'S FATHER!!
YOU'RE TALKING ABOUT CORNE MEILLEURE, HUH?
WHAT THE HECK ARE YOU DOING?
WHY THE HECK ARE YOU BACK?
WOW... YOU DO SOUND LIKE HIM.
FINE. CHOCOLAT MEILLEURE, I'LL LET YOU READ THIS DIARY.
WAIT! THAT WAS GOOD ENOUGH!?
Dear Chocolat
HER DIARY AS A YOUNG LADY STARTS ON THE SECOND PAGE.
THE FIRST PAGE IS THE MESSAGE I READ THE OTHER DAY.
This is my fourth day in the Human World. I picked up my fifth heart today!!
Adolph, an exchange student. Takada-kun Tsuyoshi. Hakase-kun.
Goro, who keeps falling in love with me no matter how many times I capture his heart...

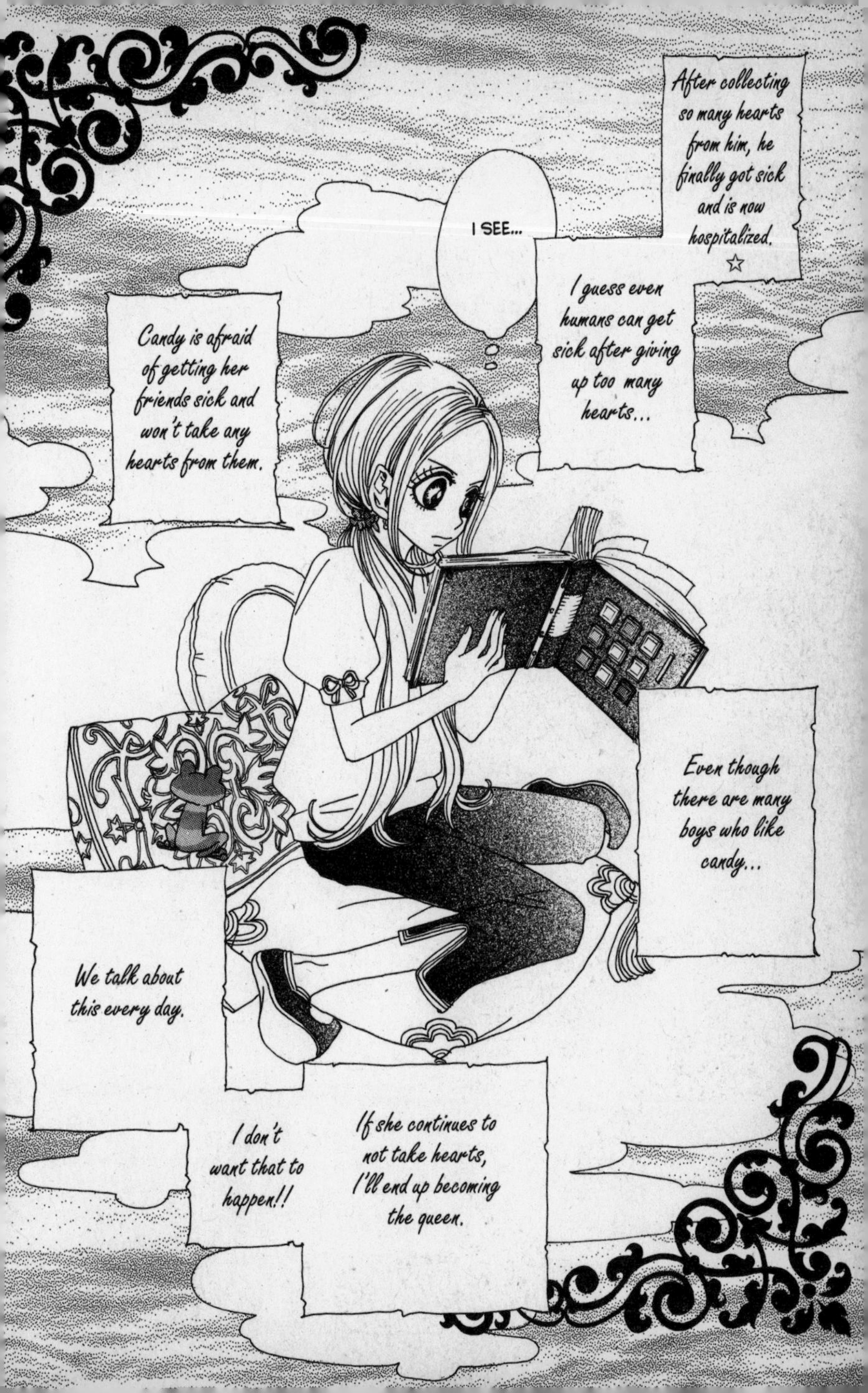
After collecting so many hearts from him, he finally got sick and is now hospitalized. ☆
I SEE...
I guess even humans can get sick after giving up too many hearts...
Candy is afraid of getting her friends sick and won't take any hearts from them.
Even though there are many boys who like candy...
We talk about this every day.
If she continues to not take hearts, I'll end up becoming the queen.
I don't want that to happen!!

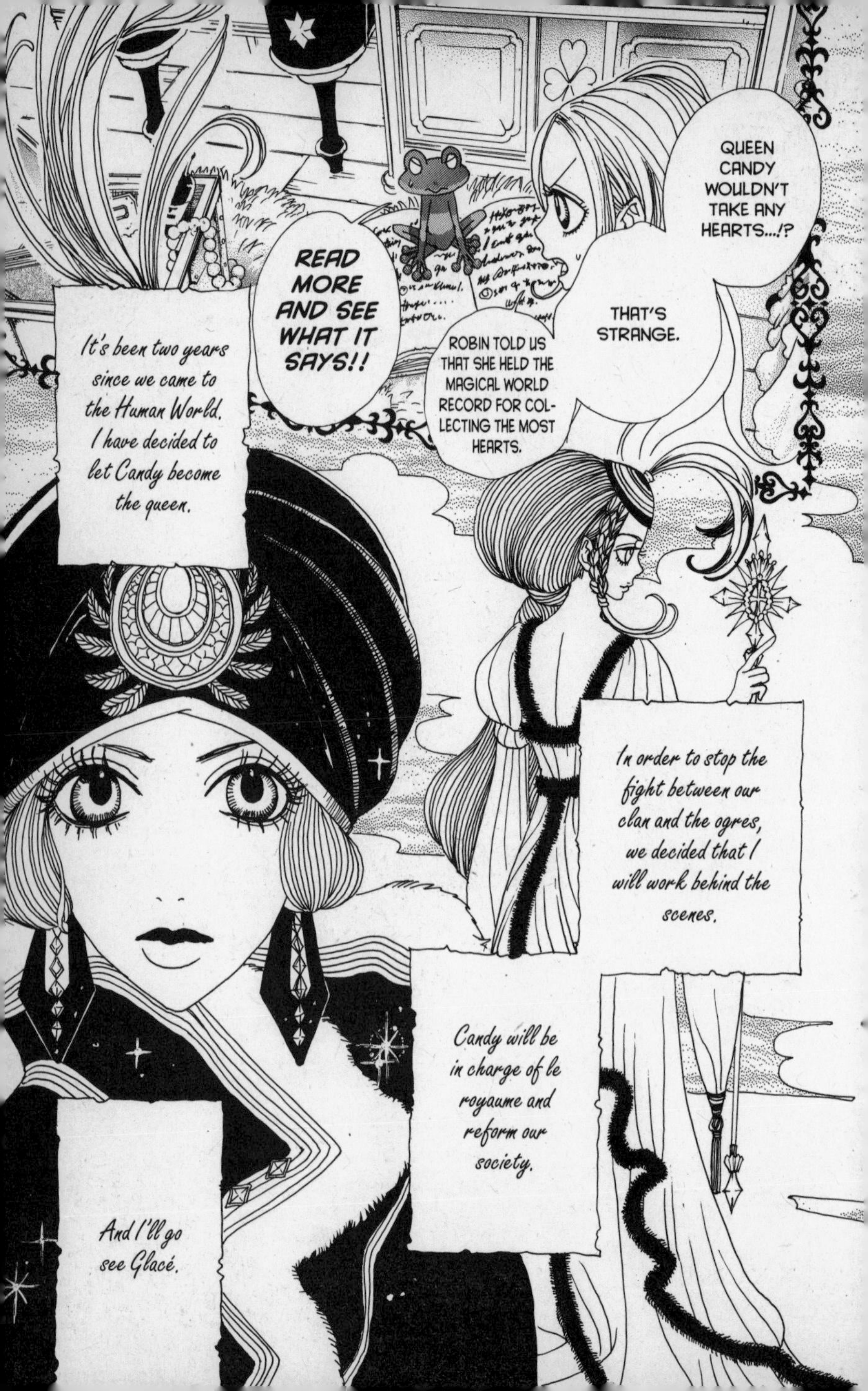
QUEEN CANDY WOULDN'T TAKE ANY HEARTS...!?
THAT'S STRANGE.
ROBIN TOLD US THAT SHE HELD THE MAGICAL WORLD RECORD FOR COL-LECTING THE MOST HEARTS.
READ MORE AND SEE WHAT IT SAYS!!
It's been two years since we came to the Human World. I have decided to let Candy become the queen.
In order to stop the fight between our clan and the ogres, we decided that I will work behind the scenes.
Candy will be in charge of le royaume and reform our society.
And I'll go see Glacé.

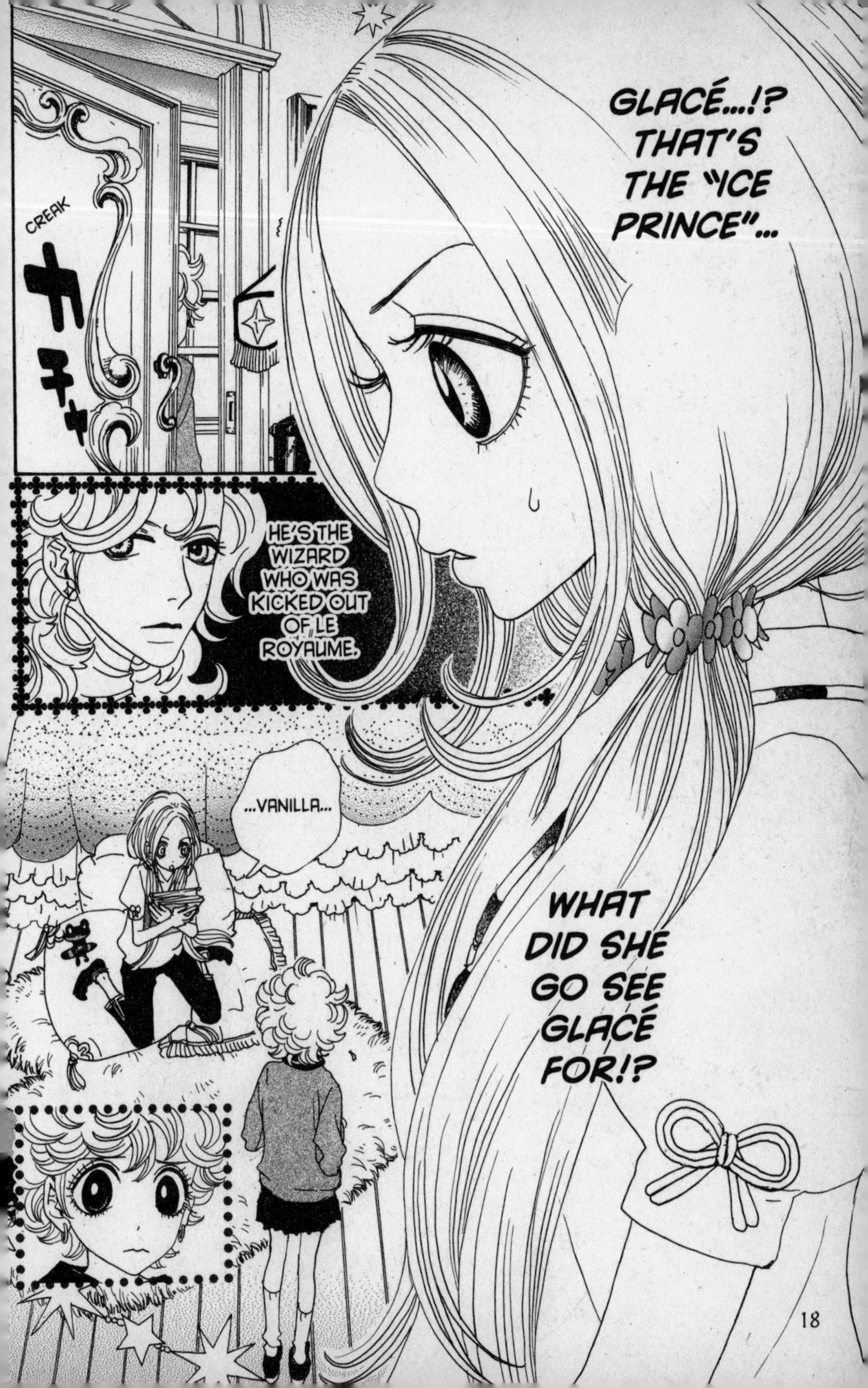
GLACÉ...!? THAT'S THE "ICE PRINCE"...
WHAT DID SHE GO SEE GLACÉ FOR!?
CREAK
カチャ
HE'S THE WIZARD WHO WAS KICKED OUT OF LE ROYAUME.
...VANILLA...

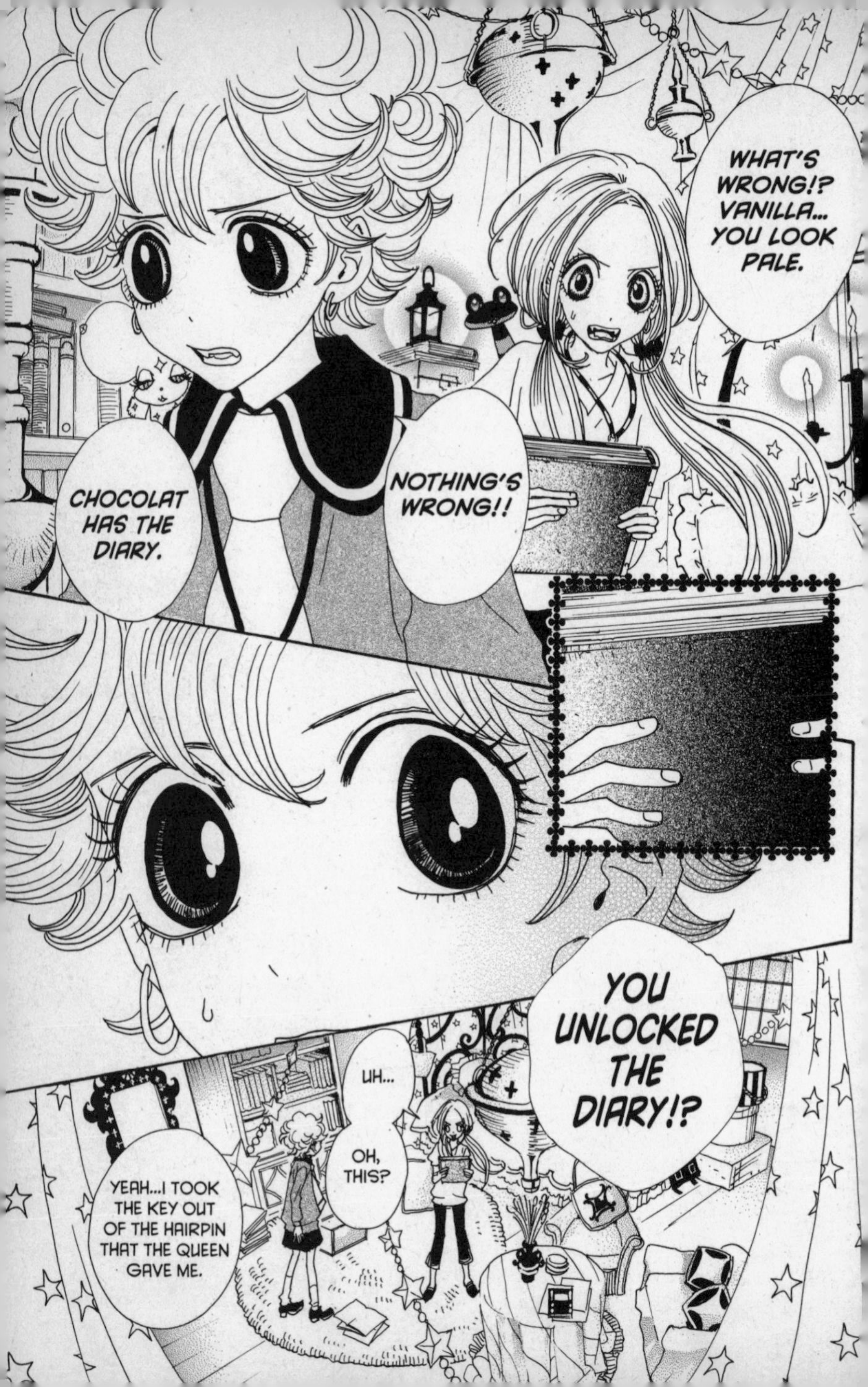
WHAT'S WRONG!? VANILLA... YOU LOOK PALE.
NOTHING'S WRONG!!
CHOCOLAT HAS THE DIARY.
YOU UNLOCKED THE DIARY!?
UH...
OH, THIS?
YEAH...I TOOK THE KEY OUT OF THE HAIRPIN THAT THE QUEEN GAVE ME.

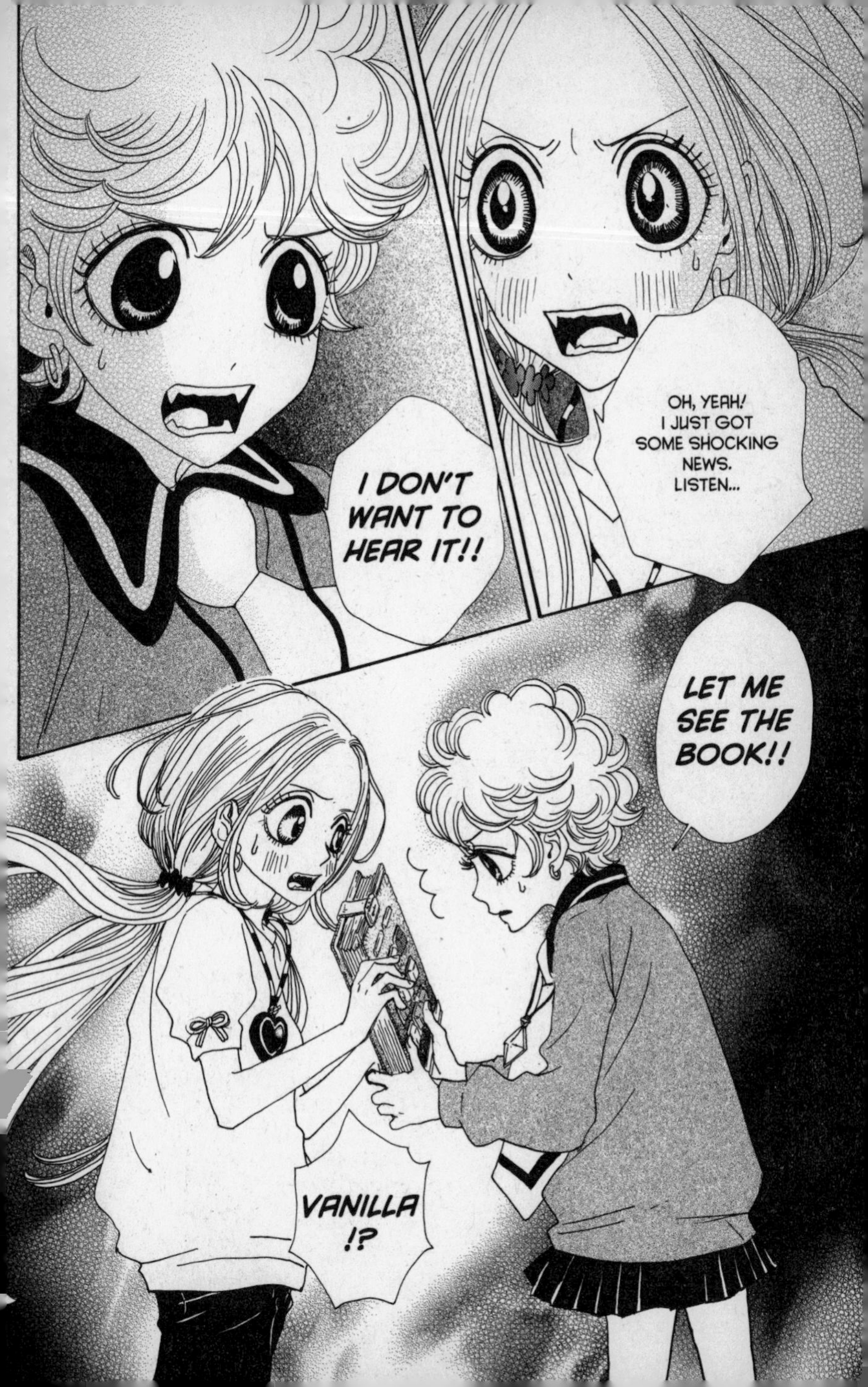
OH, YEAH! I JUST GOT SOME SHOCKING NEWS. LISTEN...
I DON'T WANT TO HEAR IT!!
LET ME SEE THE BOOK!!
VANILLA !?

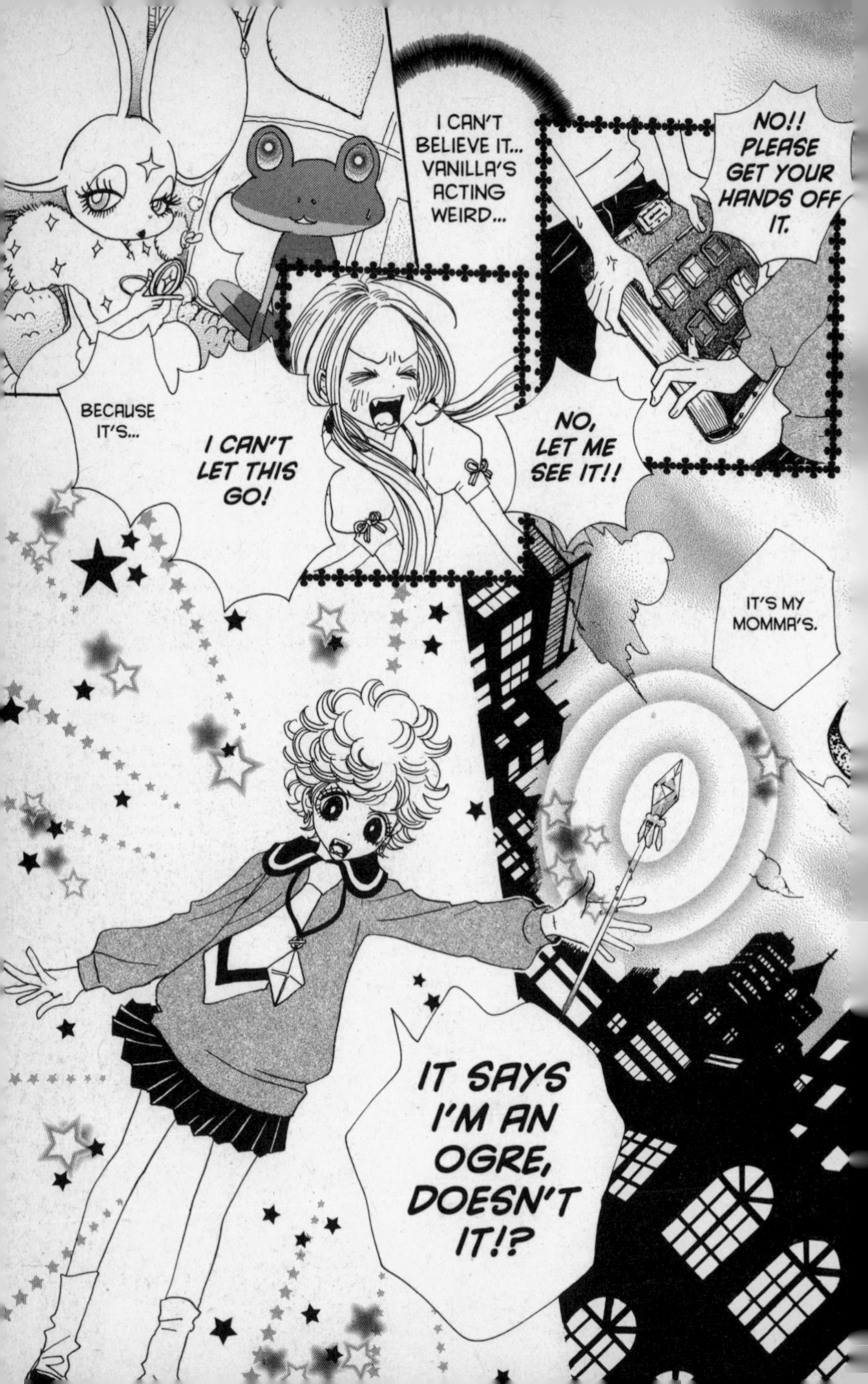
NO!! PLEASE GET YOUR HANDS OFF IT.
I CAN'T BELIEVE IT... VANILLA'S ACTING WEIRD...
NO, LET ME SEE IT!!
I CAN'T LET THIS GO!
BECAUSE IT'S...
IT'S MY MOMMA'S.
IT SAYS I'M AN OGRE, DOESN'T IT!?

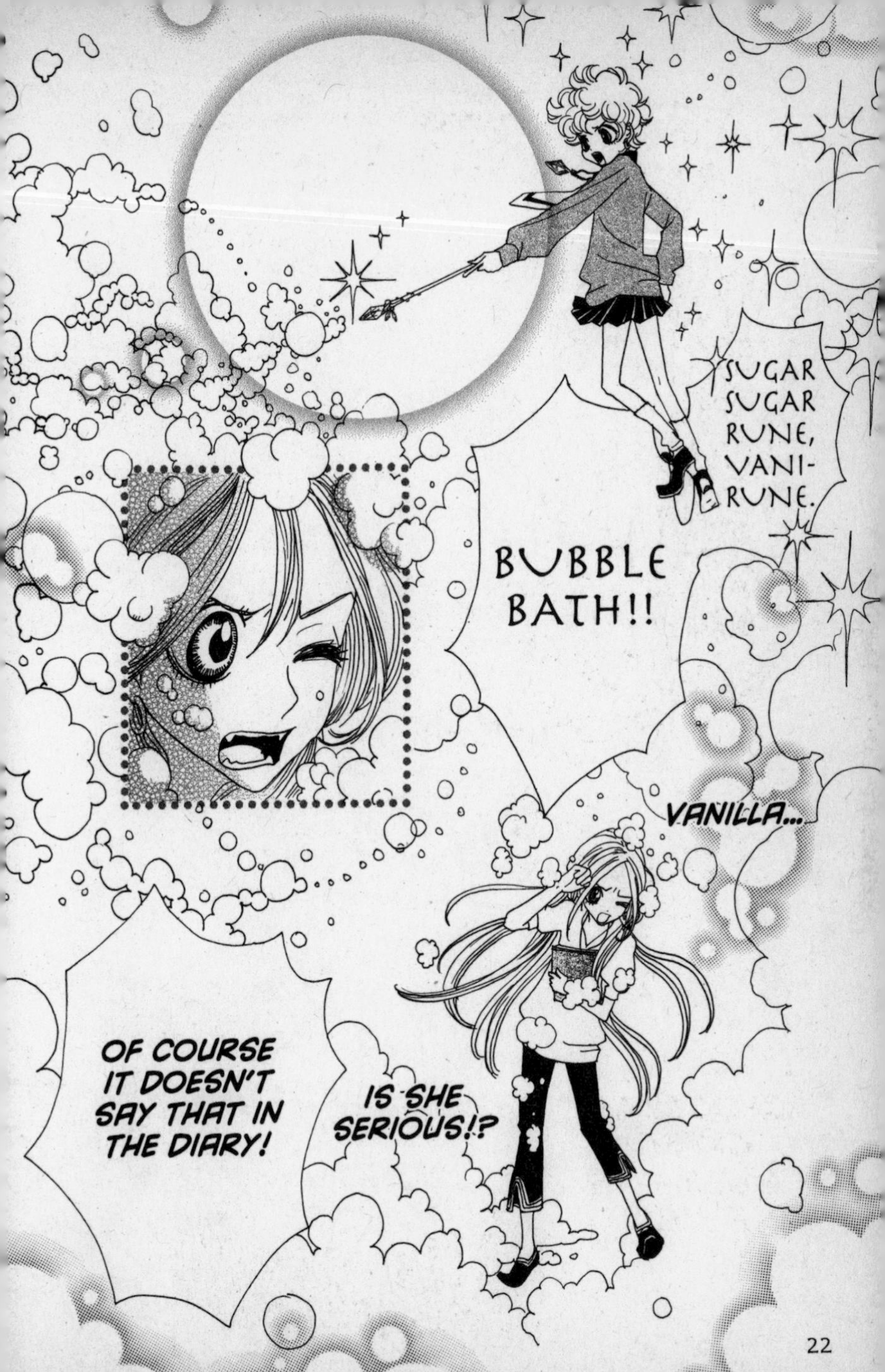
SUGAR SUGAR RUNE, VANI-RUNE.
BUBBLE BATH!!
VANILLA...
IS SHE SERIOUS!?
OF COURSE IT DOESN'T SAY THAT IN THE DIARY!

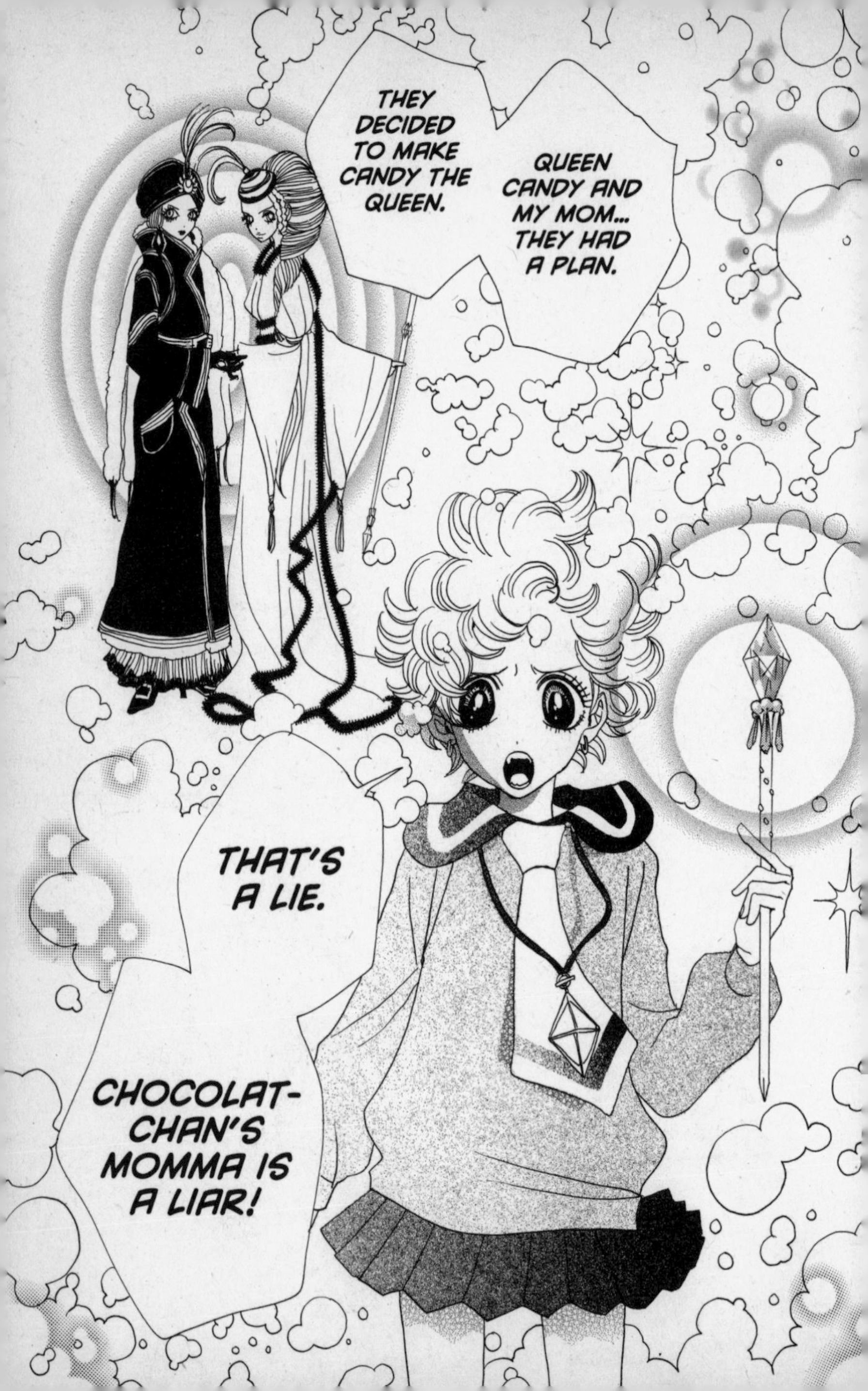
THEY DECIDED TO MAKE CANDY THE QUEEN.
QUEEN CANDY AND MY MOM... THEY HAD A PLAN.
THAT'S A LIE.
CHOCOLAT-CHAN'S MOMMA IS A LIAR!

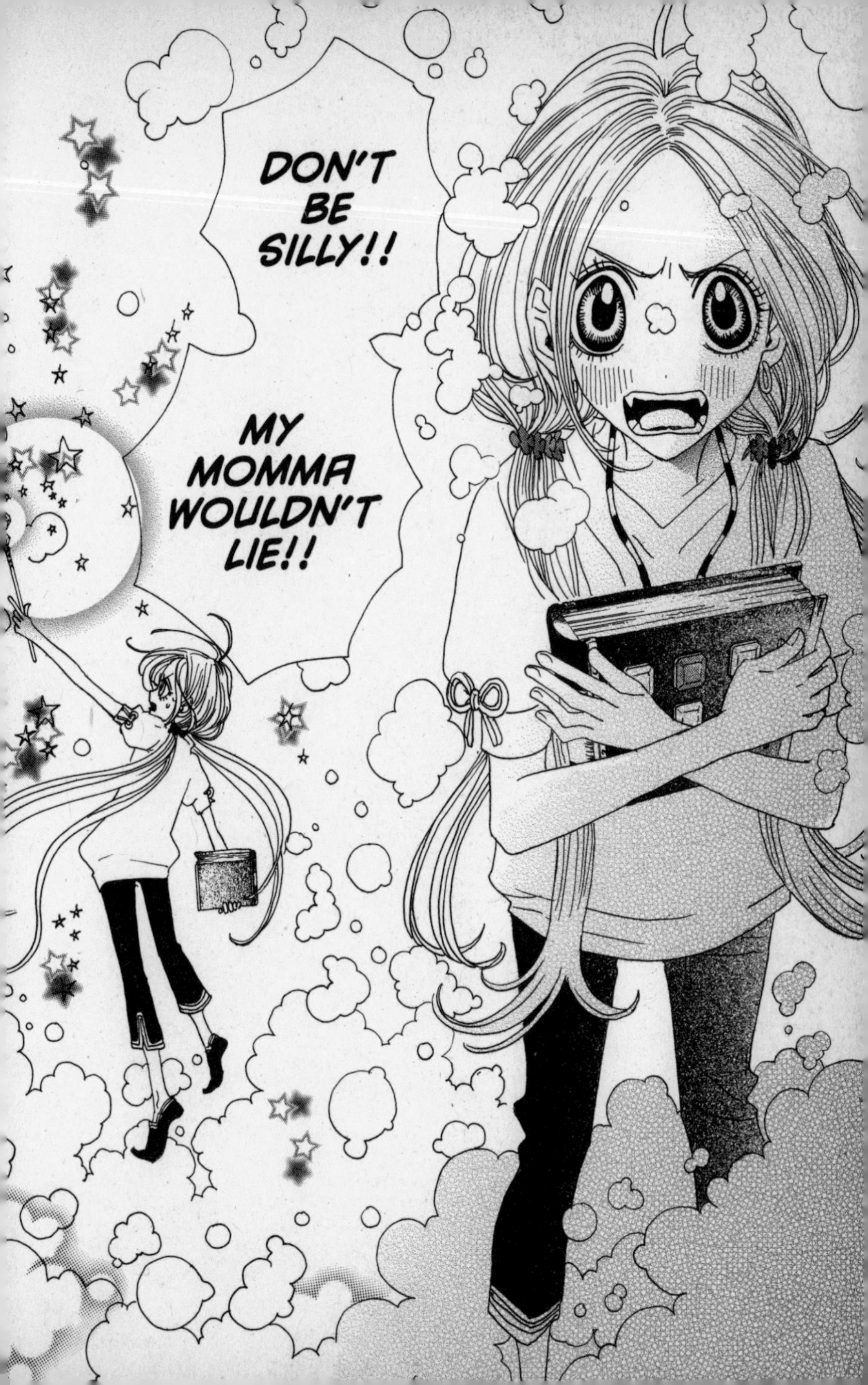
DON'T BE SILLY!!
MY MOMMA WOULDN'T LIE!!

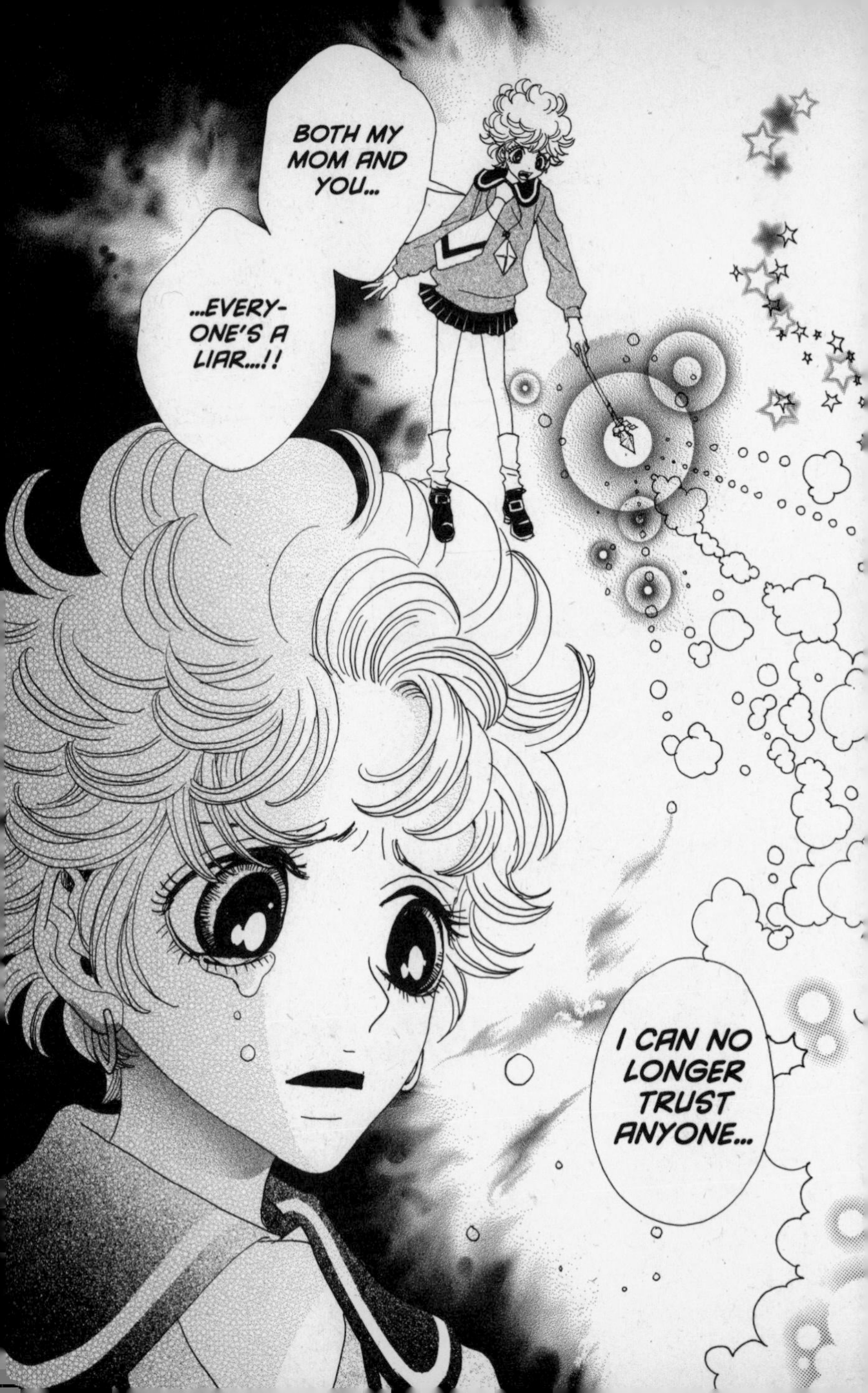
BOTH MY MOM AND YOU...
...EVERY-ONE'S A LIAR...!!
I CAN NO LONGER TRUST ANYONE...

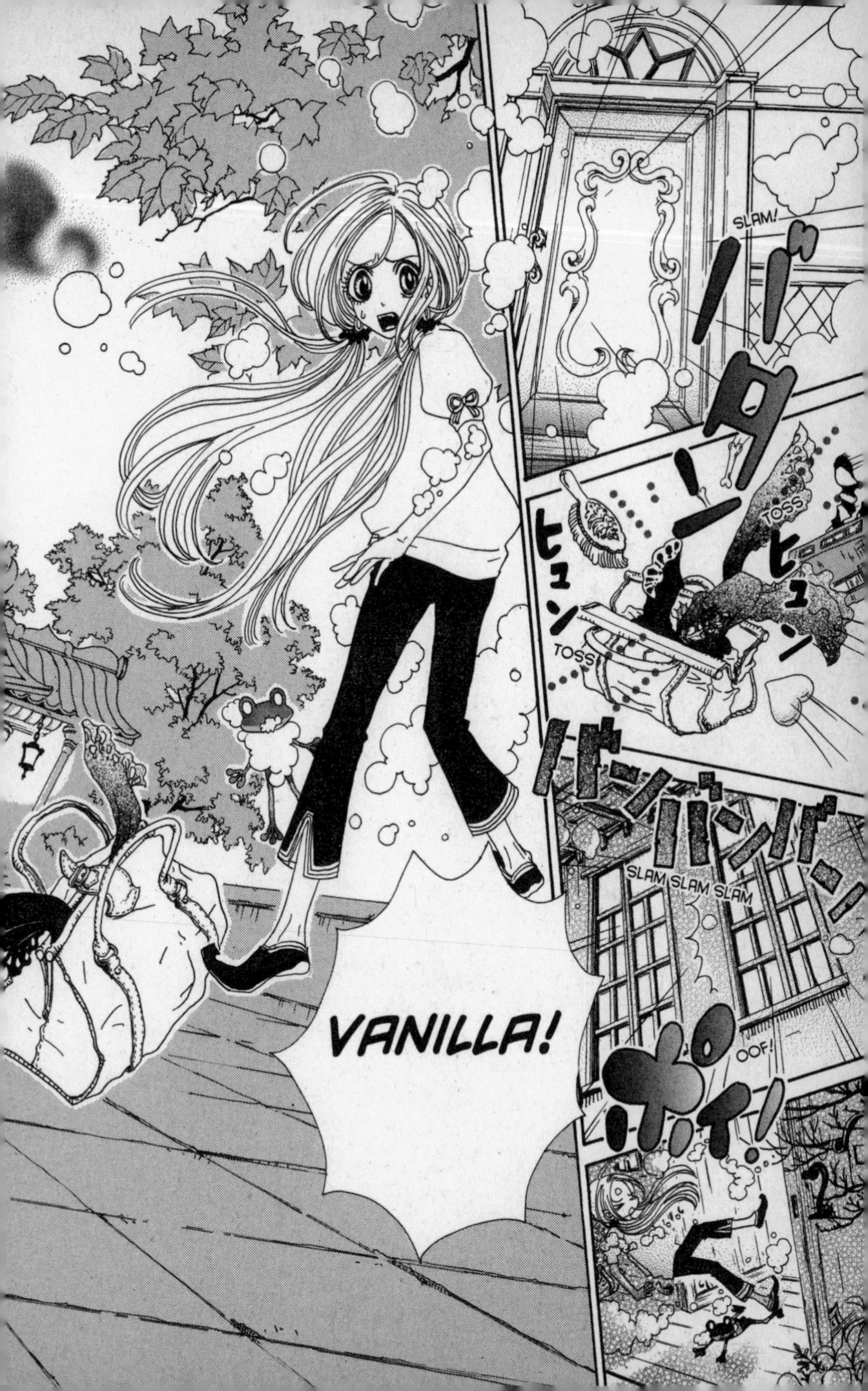
SLAM!
バターン
TOSS
ヒュン
ヒュン
TOSS
バンバンバン
SLAM SLAM SLAM
OOF!
ポイ!
VANILLA!

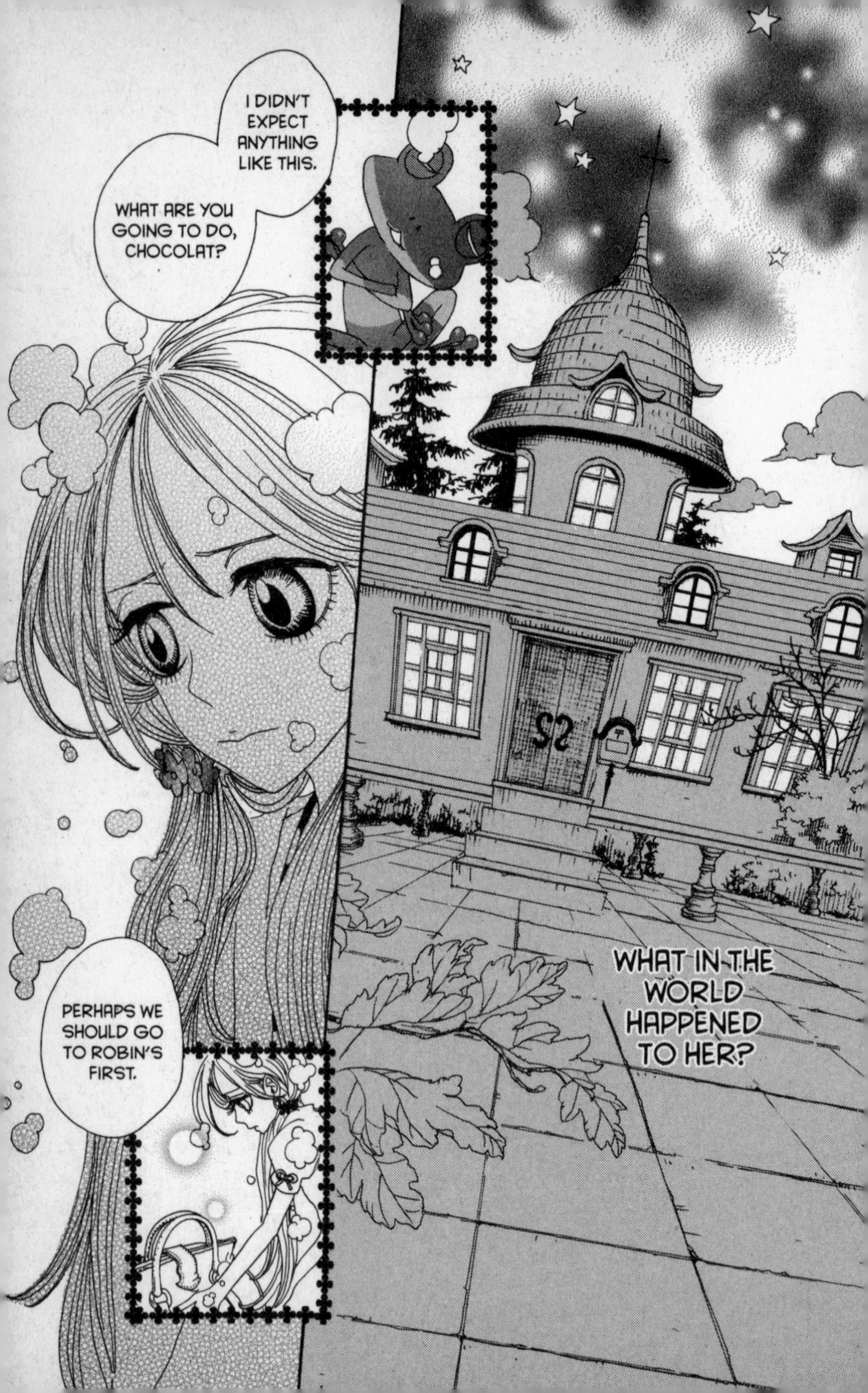
WHAT IN THE WORLD HAPPENED TO HER?
I DIDN'T EXPECT ANYTHING LIKE THIS.
WHAT ARE YOU GOING TO DO, CHOCOLAT?
PERHAPS WE SHOULD GO TO ROBIN'S FIRST.

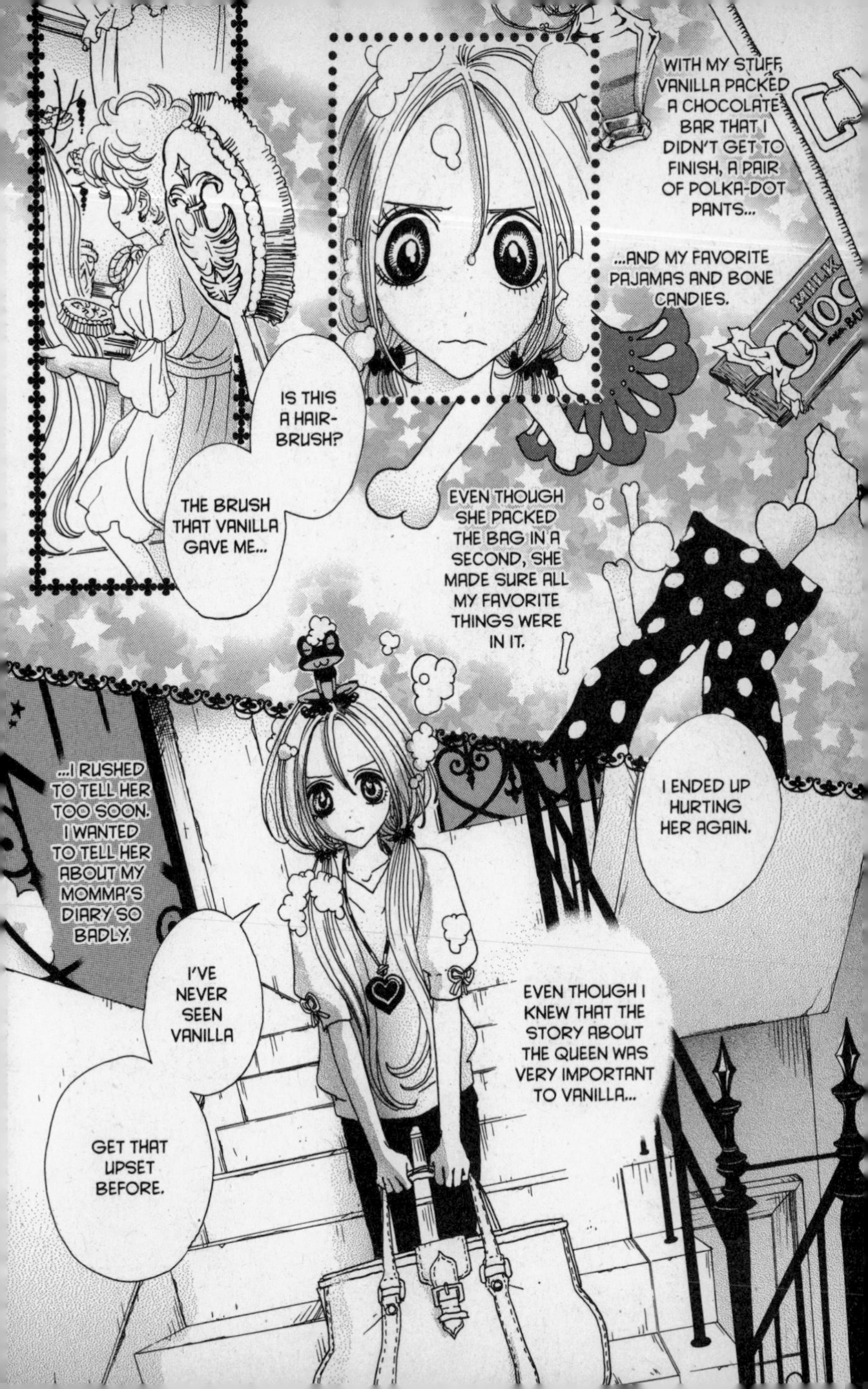
WITH MY STUFF, VANILLA PACKED A CHOCOLATE BAR THAT I DIDN'T GET TO FINISH, A PAIR OF POLKA-DOT PANTS...
...AND MY FAVORITE PAJAMAS AND BONE CANDIES.
EVEN THOUGH SHE PACKED THE BAG IN A SECOND, SHE MADE SURE ALL MY FAVORITE THINGS WERE IN IT.
IS THIS A HAIR-BRUSH?
THE BRUSH THAT VANILLA GAVE ME...
I ENDED UP HURTING HER AGAIN.
EVEN THOUGH I KNEW THAT THE STORY ABOUT THE QUEEN WAS VERY IMPORTANT TO VANILLA...
...I RUSHED TO TELL HER TOO SOON. I WANTED TO TELL HER ABOUT MY MOMMA'S DIARY SO BADLY.
I'VE NEVER SEEN VANILLA
GET THAT UPSET BEFORE.

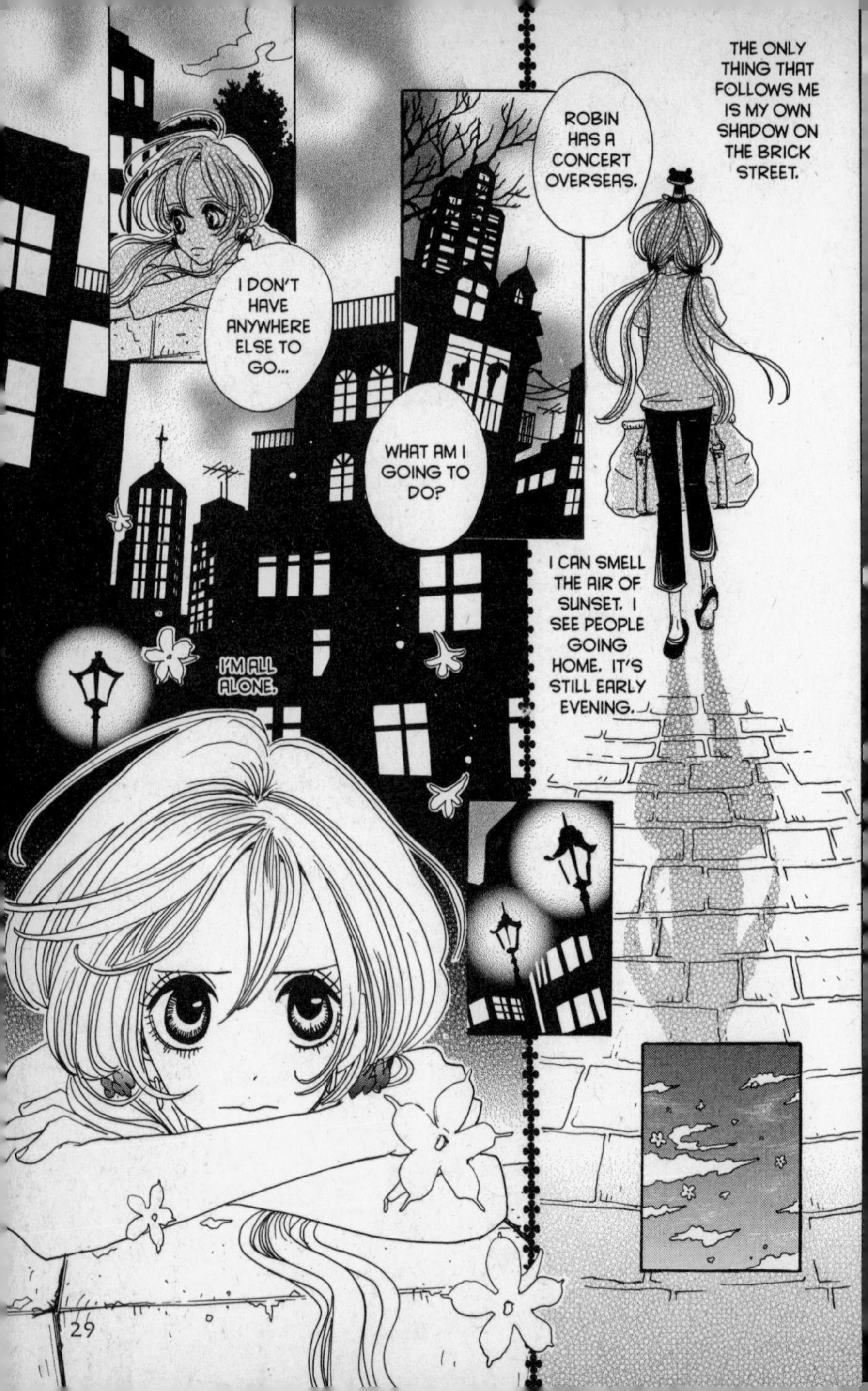

THE ONLY THING THAT FOLLOWS ME IS MY OWN SHADOW ON THE BRICK STREET.
ROBIN HAS A CONCERT OVERSEAS.
I CAN SMELL THE AIR OF SUNSET. I SEE PEOPLE GOING HOME. IT'S STILL EARLY EVENING.
I DON'T HAVE ANYWHERE ELSE TO GO...
WHAT AM I GOING TO DO?
I'M ALL ALONE.

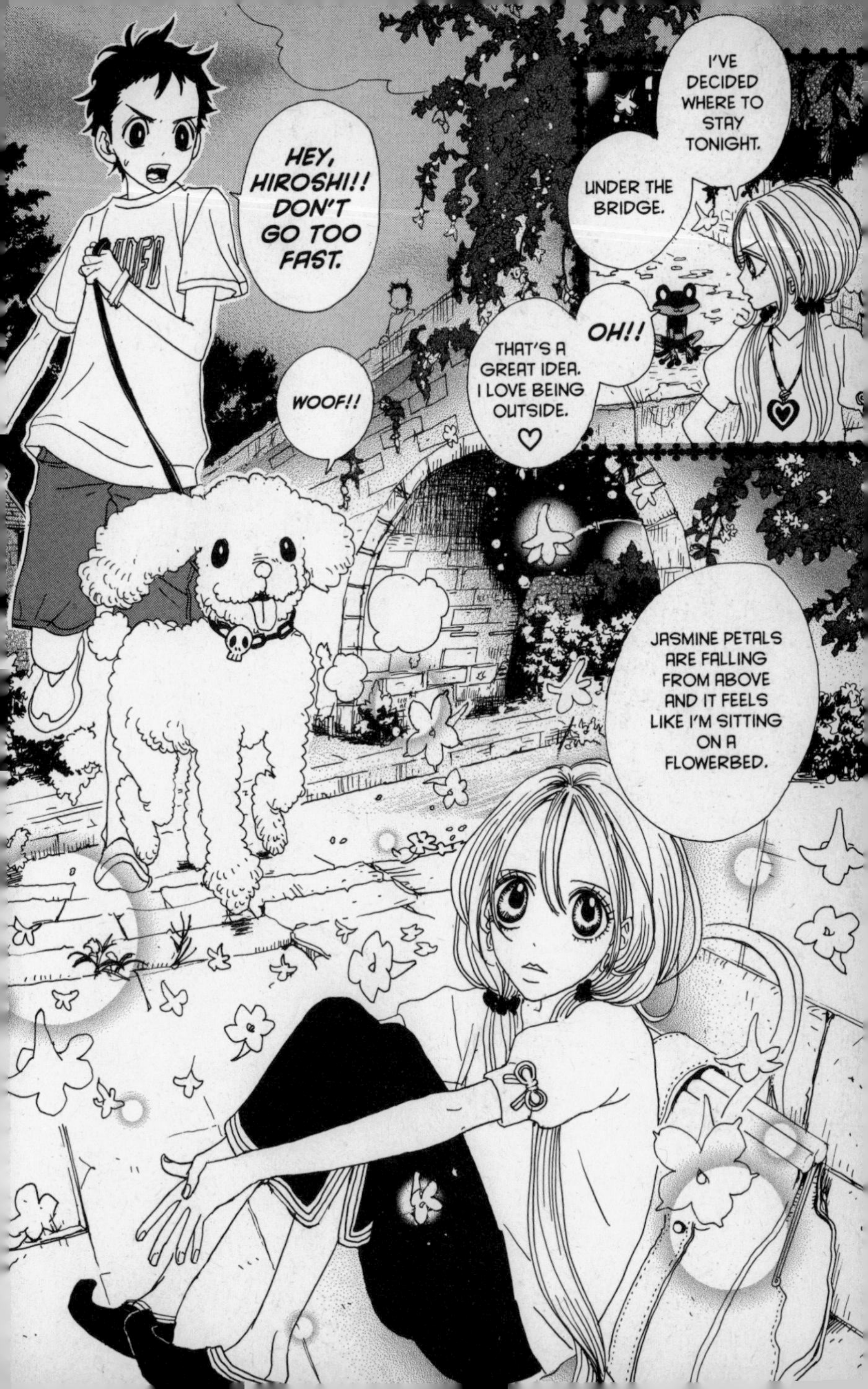
I'VE DECIDED WHERE TO STAY TONIGHT.
UNDER THE BRIDGE.
OH!!
THAT'S A GREAT IDEA. I LOVE BEING OUTSIDE. ♡
HEY, HIROSHI!! DON'T GO TOO FAST.
WOOF!!
JASMINE PETALS ARE FALLING FROM ABOVE AND IT FEELS LIKE I'M SITTING ON A FLOWERBED.

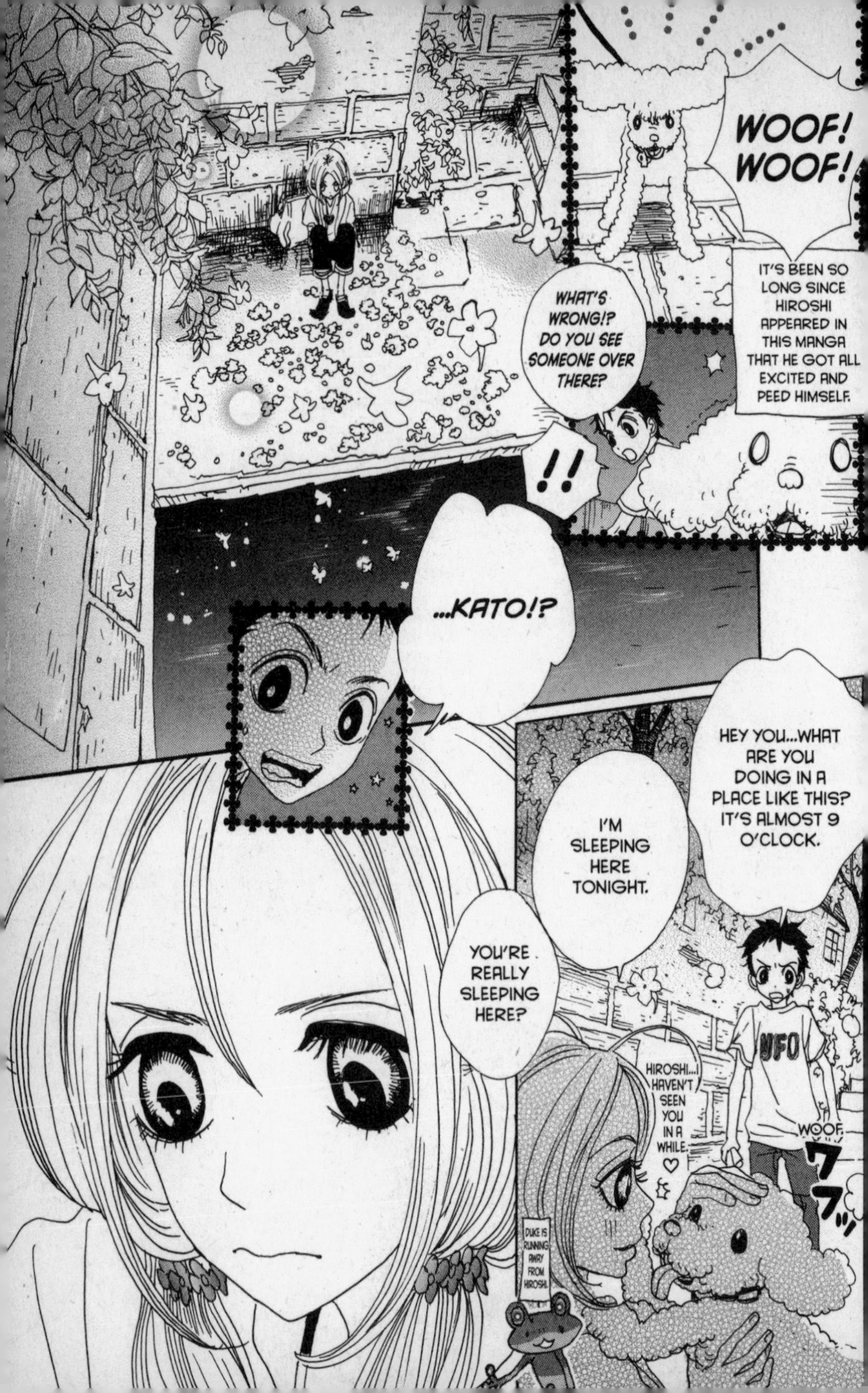
WOOF! WOOF!
IT'S BEEN SO LONG SINCE HIROSHI APPEARED IN THIS MANGA THAT HE GOT ALL EXCITED AND PEED HIMSELF.
WHAT'S WRONG!? DO YOU SEE SOMEONE OVER THERE?
!!
...KATO!?
HEY YOU...WHAT ARE YOU DOING IN A PLACE LIKE THIS? IT'S ALMOST 9 O'CLOCK.
I'M SLEEPING HERE TONIGHT.
YOU'RE REALLY SLEEPING HERE?
HIROSHI...I HAVEN'T SEEN YOU IN A WHILE.
WOOF.
ワフッ
DUKE IS RUNNING AWAY FROM HIROSHI.

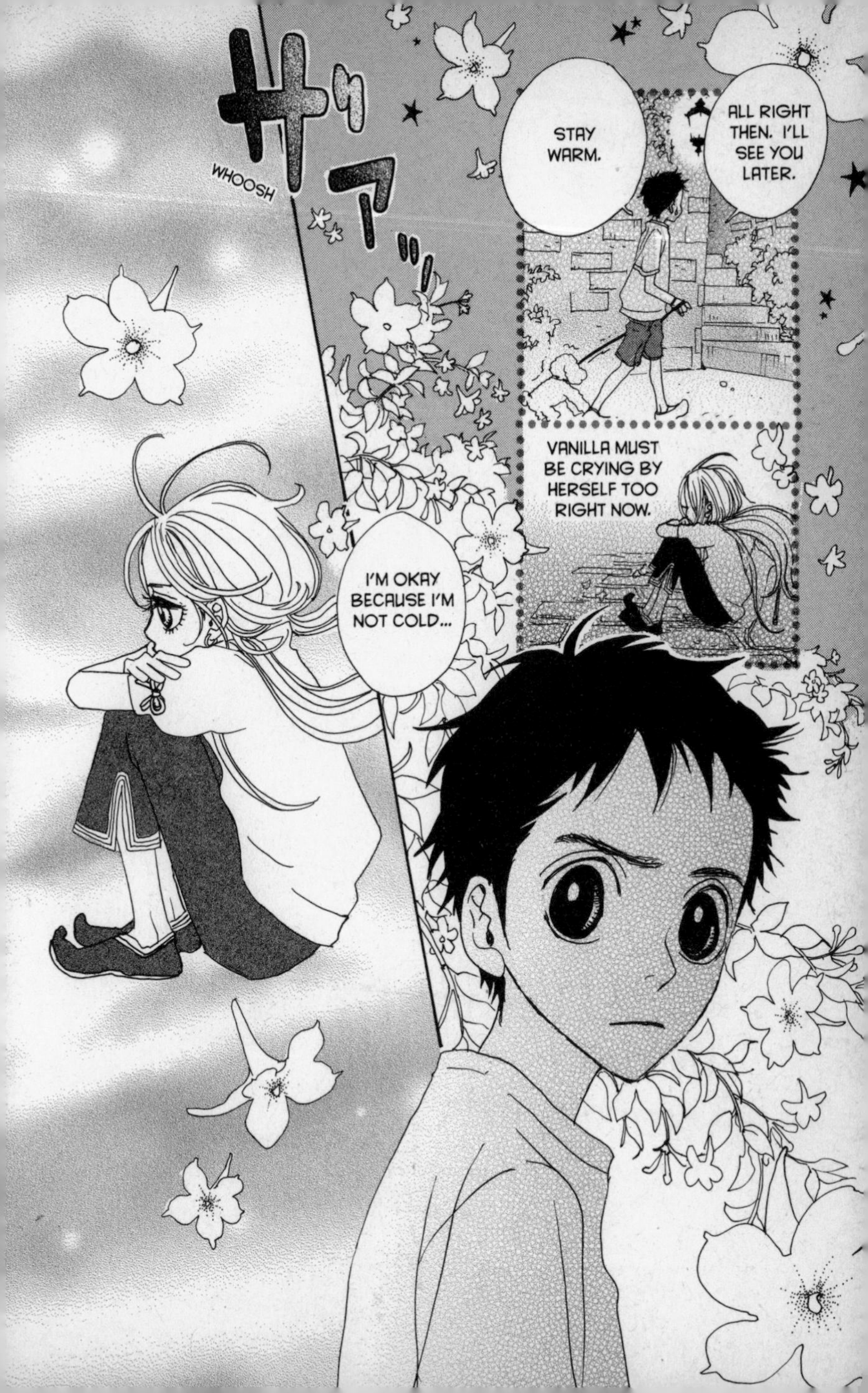
ALL RIGHT THEN. I'LL SEE YOU LATER.
STAY WARM.
VANILLA MUST BE CRYING BY HERSELF TOO RIGHT NOW.
I'M OKAY BECAUSE I'M NOT COLD...
WHOOSH

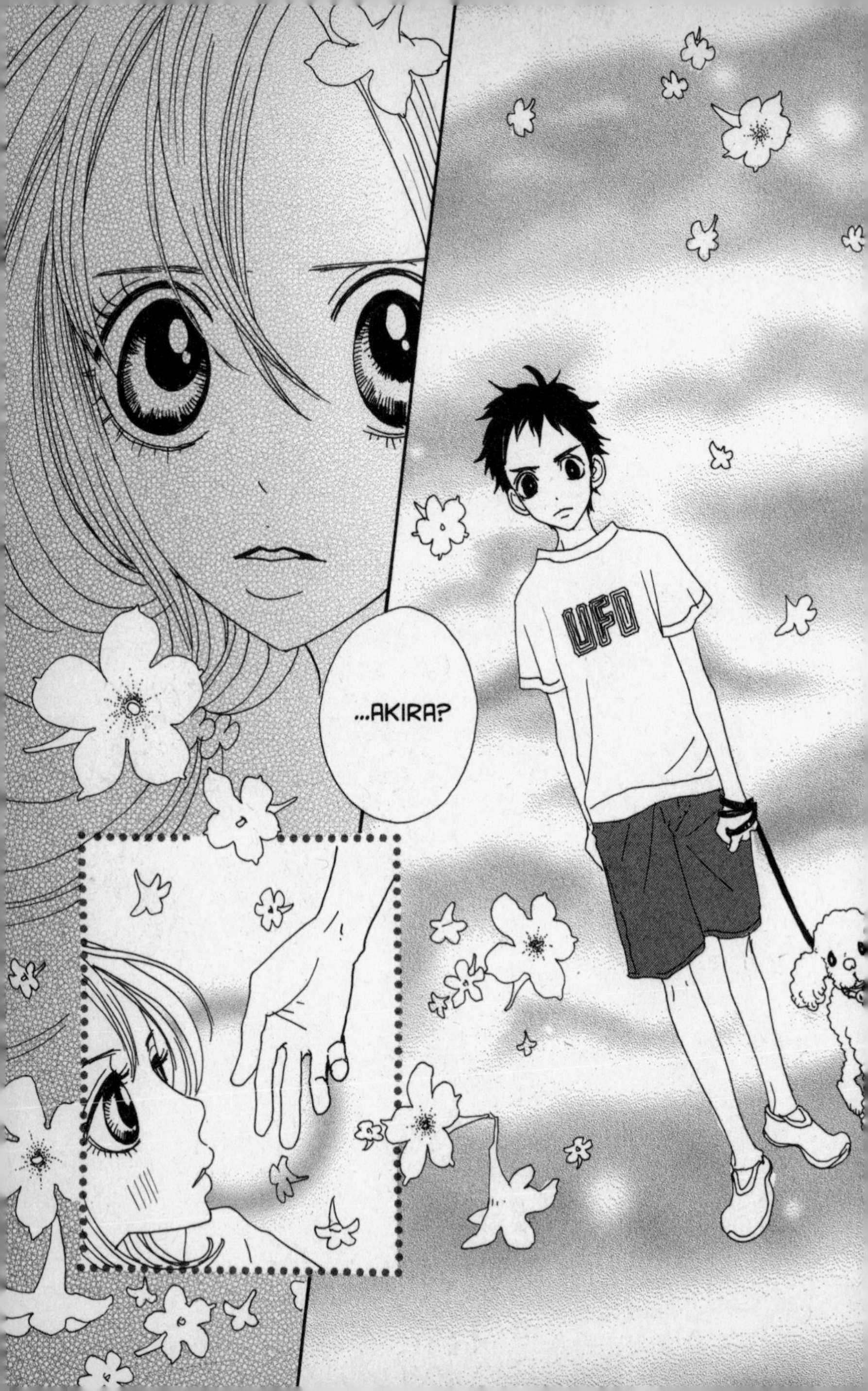
...AKIRA?

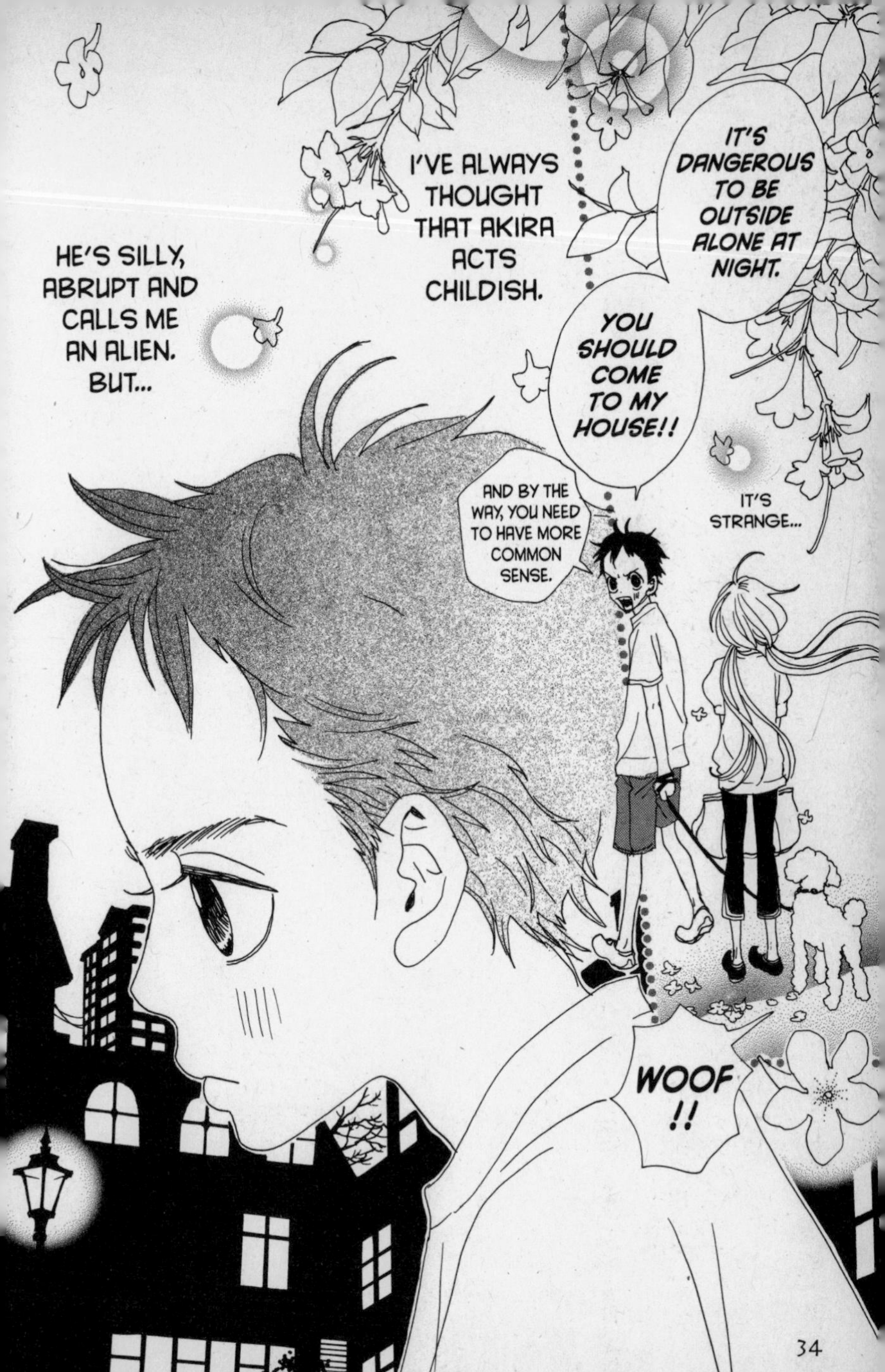
IT'S DANGEROUS TO BE OUTSIDE ALONE AT NIGHT.
YOU SHOULD COME TO MY HOUSE!!
I'VE ALWAYS THOUGHT THAT AKIRA ACTS CHILDISH.
HE'S SILLY, ABRUPT AND CALLS ME AN ALIEN. BUT...
IT'S STRANGE...
AND BY THE WAY, YOU NEED TO HAVE MORE COMMON SENSE.
WOOF !!

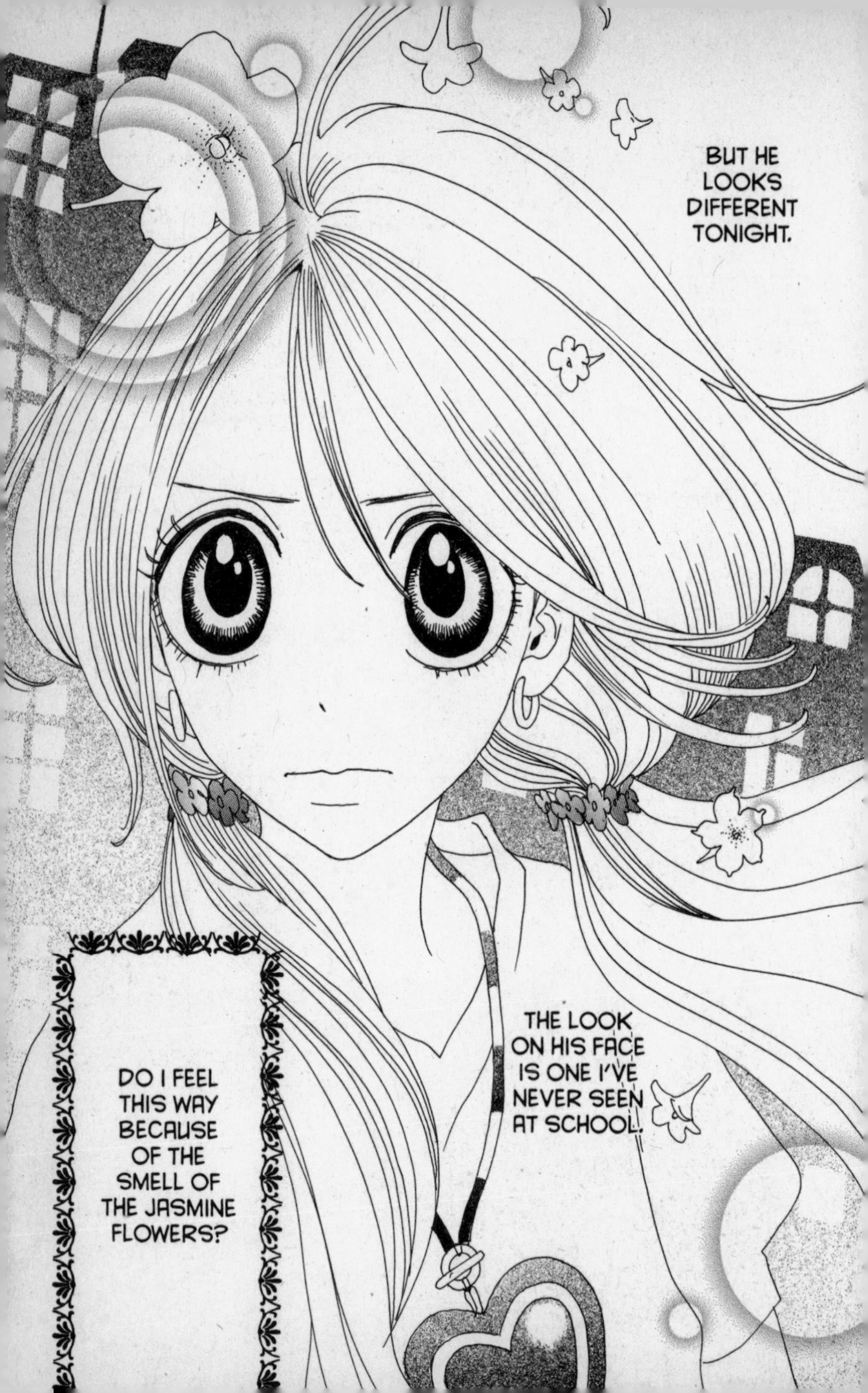
BUT HE LOOKS DIFFERENT TONIGHT.
THE LOOK ON HIS FACE IS ONE I'VE NEVER SEEN AT SCHOOL.
DO I FEEL THIS WAY BECAUSE OF THE SMELL OF THE JASMINE FLOWERS?

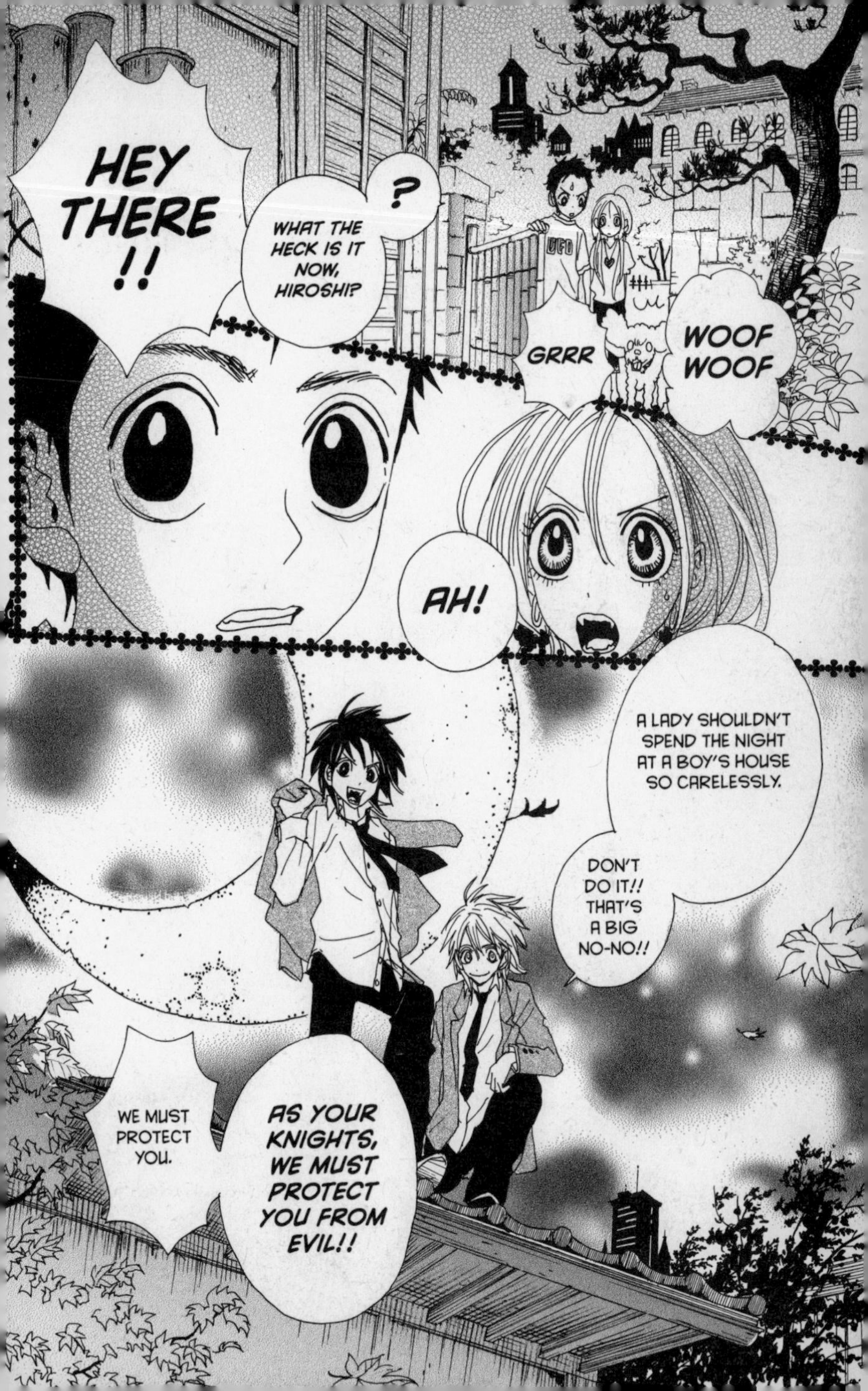
HEY THERE!!
?
WHAT THE HECK IS IT NOW, HIROSHI?
WOOF WOOF
GRRR
AH!
A LADY SHOULDN'T SPEND THE NIGHT AT A BOY'S HOUSE SO CARELESSLY.
DON'T DO IT!! THAT'S A BIG NO-NO!!
AS YOUR KNIGHTS, WE MUST PROTECT YOU FROM EVIL!!
WE MUST PROTECT YOU.

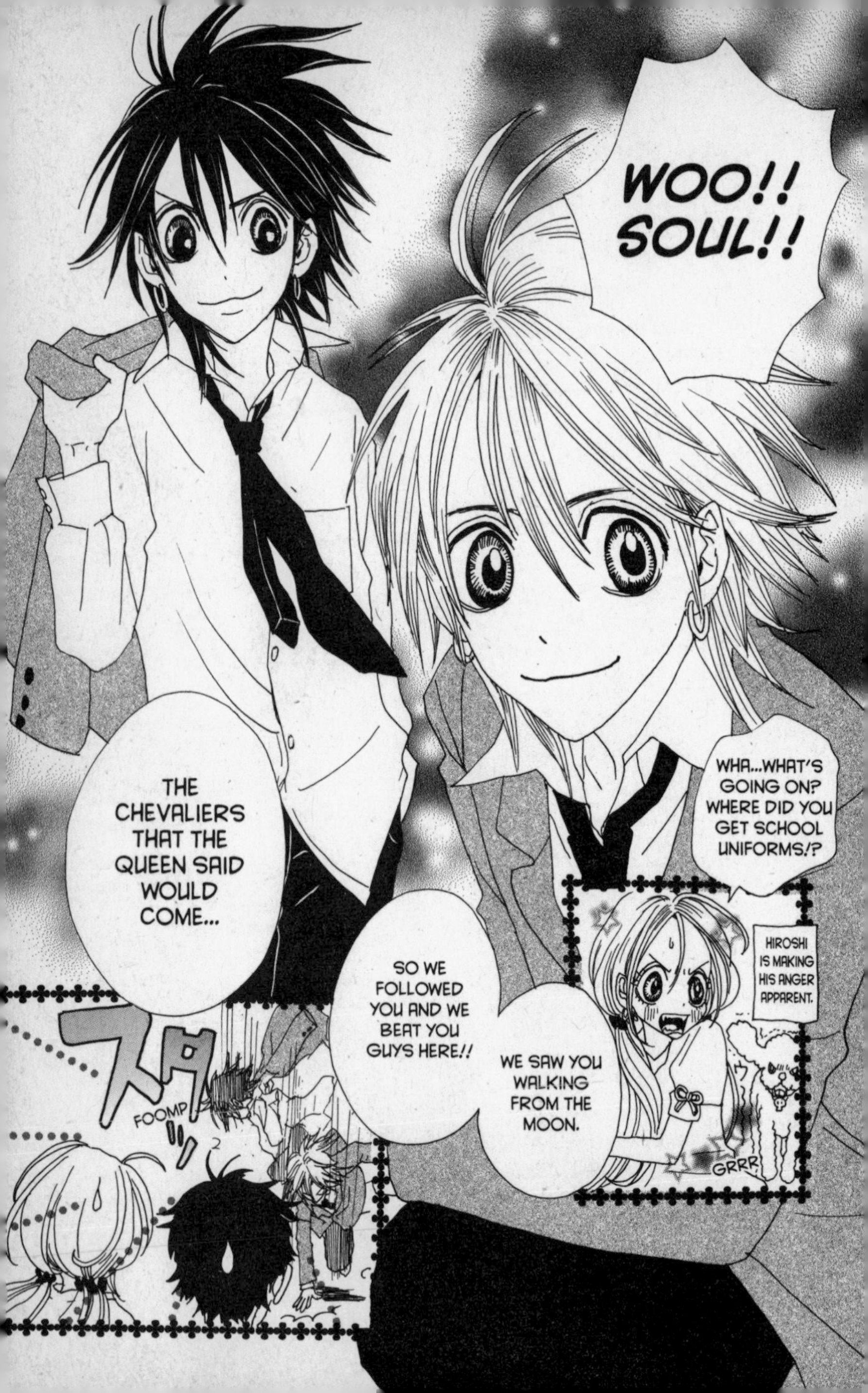
WOO!! SOUL!!
WHA...WHAT'S GOING ON? WHERE DID YOU GET SCHOOL UNIFORMS!?
HIROSHI IS MAKING HIS ANGER APPARENT.
GRRR
WE SAW YOU WALKING FROM THE MOON.
SO WE FOLLOWED YOU AND WE BEAT YOU GUYS HERE!!
THE CHEVALIERS THAT THE QUEEN SAID WOULD COME...
スタ
FOOMP

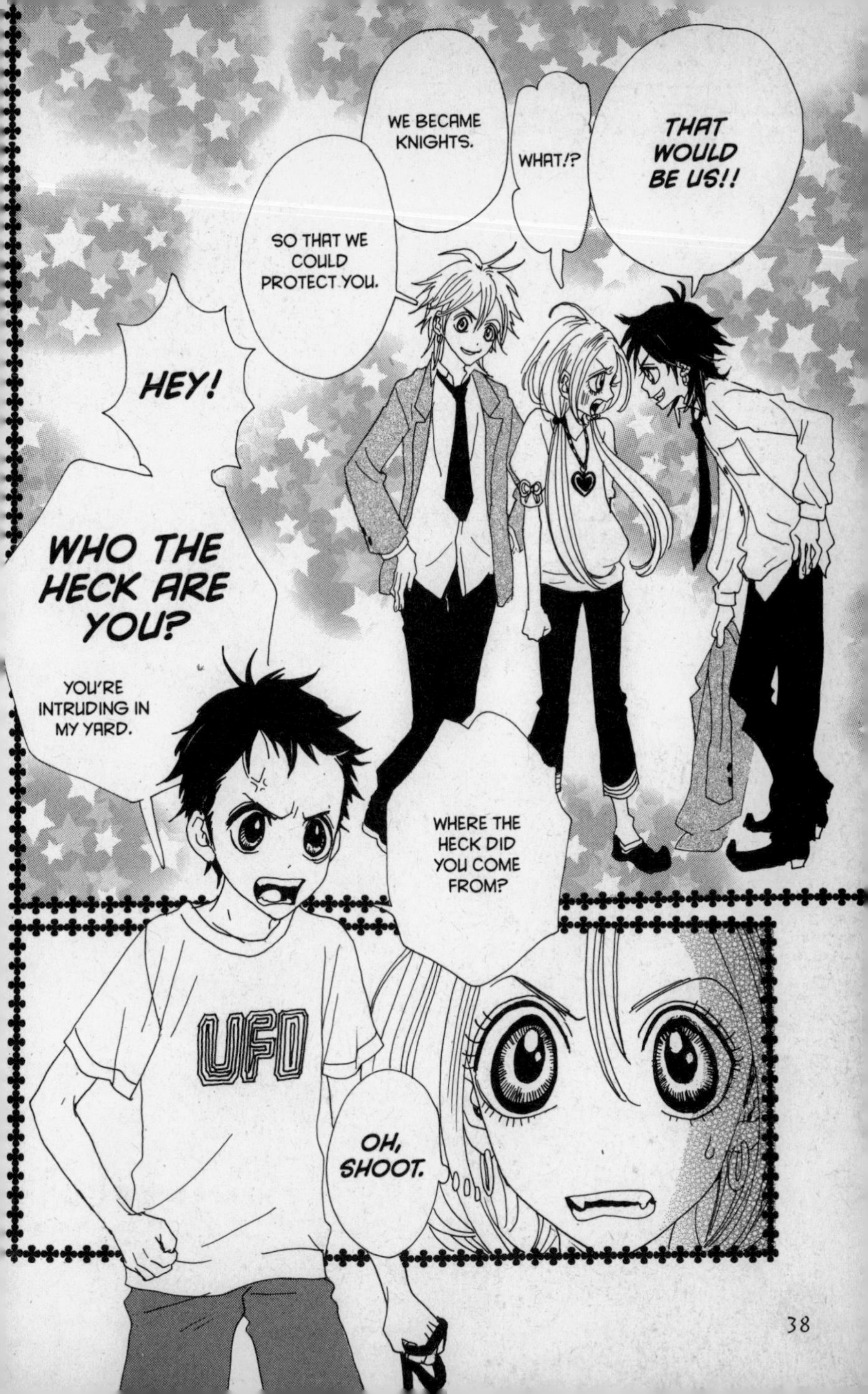
THAT WOULD BE US!!
WHAT!?
WE BECAME KNIGHTS.
SO THAT WE COULD PROTECT YOU.
HEY!
WHO THE HECK ARE YOU?
YOU'RE INTRUDING IN MY YARD.
WHERE THE HECK DID YOU COME FROM?
OH, SHOOT.

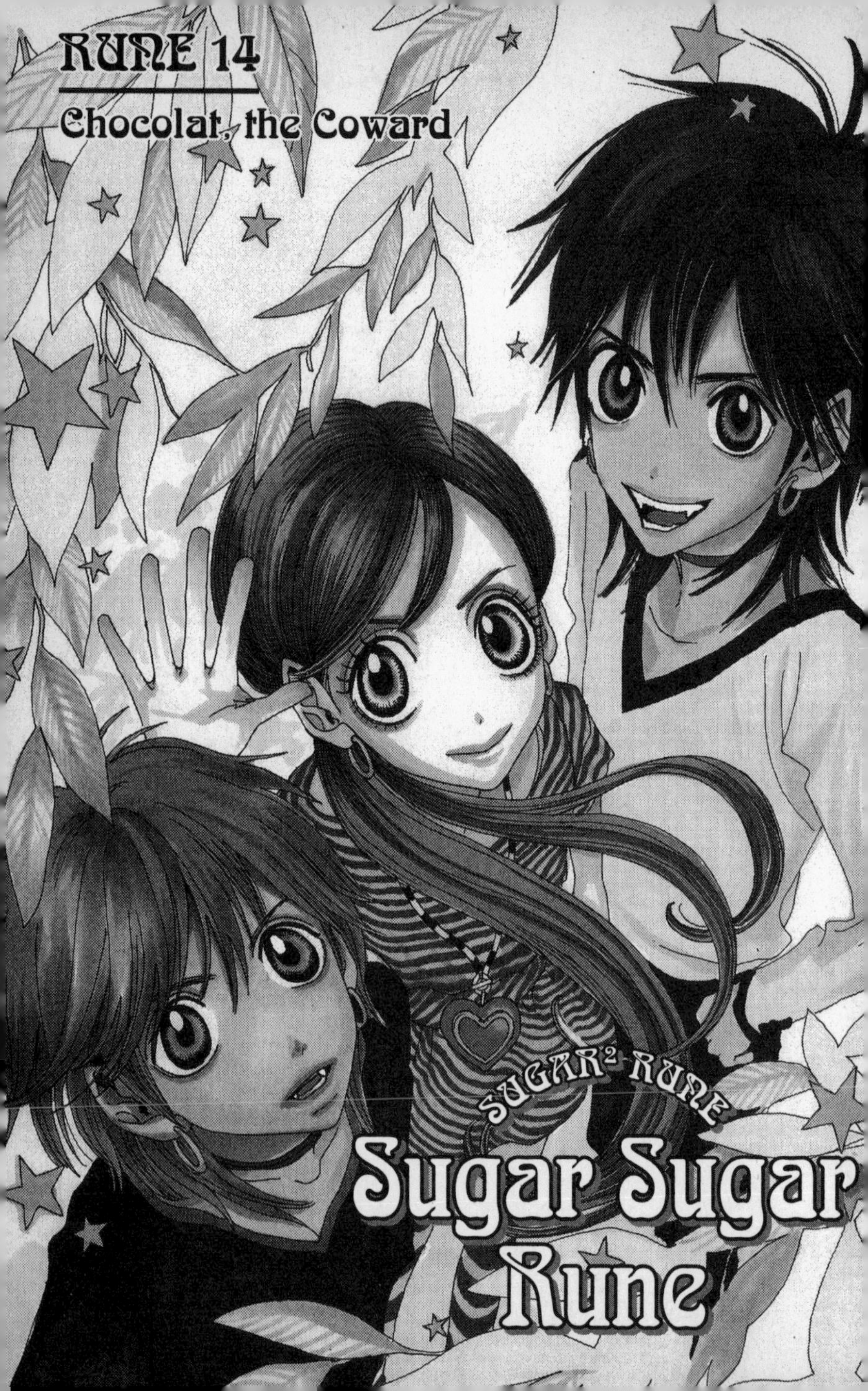
RUNE 14
Chocolat, the Coward
SUGAR² RUNE
Sugar Sugar Rune

THIS IS CHOCOLAT'S ROOM!

CHOCOLAT'S ROOM IS VERY CUTE. WE WOULD LOVE TO LIVE IN A HOUSE LIKE HERS!

▶ HERE'S THE SOFA AND THE COFFEE TABLE IN CHOCOLAT AND VANILLA'S LIVING ROOM. ON THE COFFEE TABLE THERE MANY OF THEIR FAVORITE SWEETS.

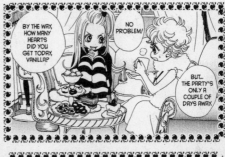

NO PROBLEM!
BY THE WAY, HOW MANY HEARTS DID YOU GET TODAY, VANILLA?
BUT... THE PARTY'S ONLY A COUPLE OF DAYS AWAY.

THE SPRING EXAM IS THE FIRST OFFICIAL EXAM GIVEN BY THE SENATE!
IF YOU PASS IT, YOU'LL BE GIVEN YOUR WITCH'S ROBE AND YOU WILL BE PROMOTED ONE GRADE.
BASICALLY, THIS WILL DECIDE YOUR FUTURE.

▲ THIS IS CHOCOLAT'S ROOM. THERE'S A HEART-SHAPED PILLOW ON HER SOFA. I WONDER IF THE BOOKS ON HER BOOKSHELF ARE TEXTBOOKS ABOUT SPELLS?

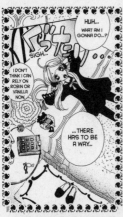

HUH... WHAT AM I GONNA DO...?
SIGH...
I DON'T THINK I CAN RELY ON ROBIN OR VANILLA NOW.
...THERE HAS TO BE A WAY...

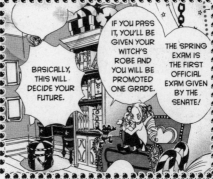

▲ THIS IS CHOCOLAT'S BED. YOU CAN ALSO SEE A HEAT PILLOW THERE. BELIEVE IT OR NOT, DUKE'S PILLOW IS A LEAF!

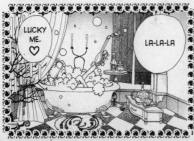

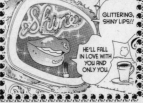

Shine
GLITTERING, SHINY LIPS!!
HE'LL FALL IN LOVE WITH YOU AND ONLY YOU.

▲ THE TV IN THEIR LIVING ROOM IS COVERED WITH SOFT FUR.

▼ AS YOU'VE SEEN, THIS IS CHOCOLAT'S BATHROOM. SHE HAS MANY TYPES OF BATH OILS.

LA-LA-LA
LUCKY ME. ♡

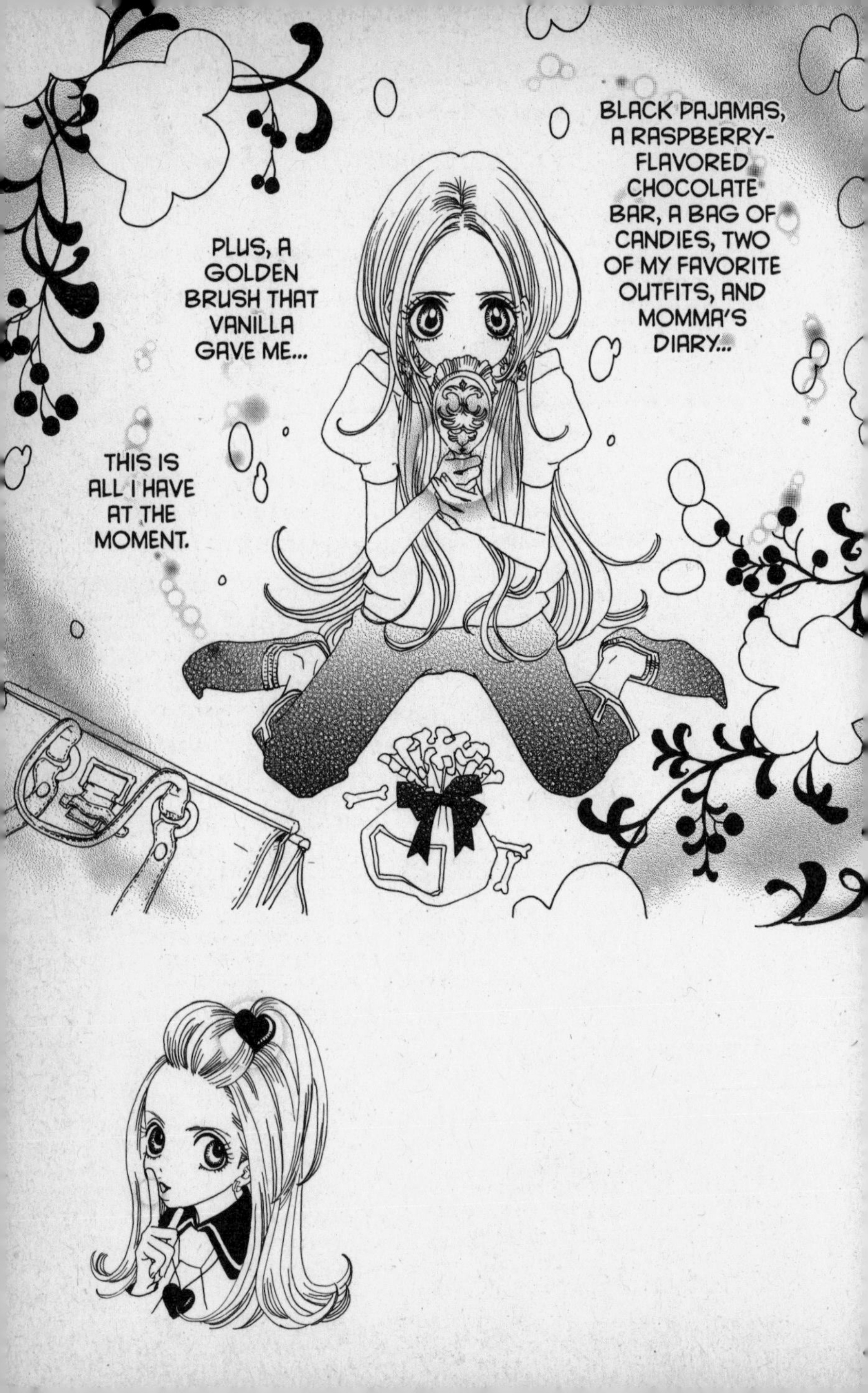
BLACK PAJAMAS, A RASPBERRY-FLAVORED CHOCOLATE BAR, A BAG OF CANDIES, TWO OF MY FAVORITE OUTFITS, AND MOMMA'S DIARY...
PLUS, A GOLDEN BRUSH THAT VANILLA GAVE ME...
THIS IS ALL I HAVE AT THE MOMENT.

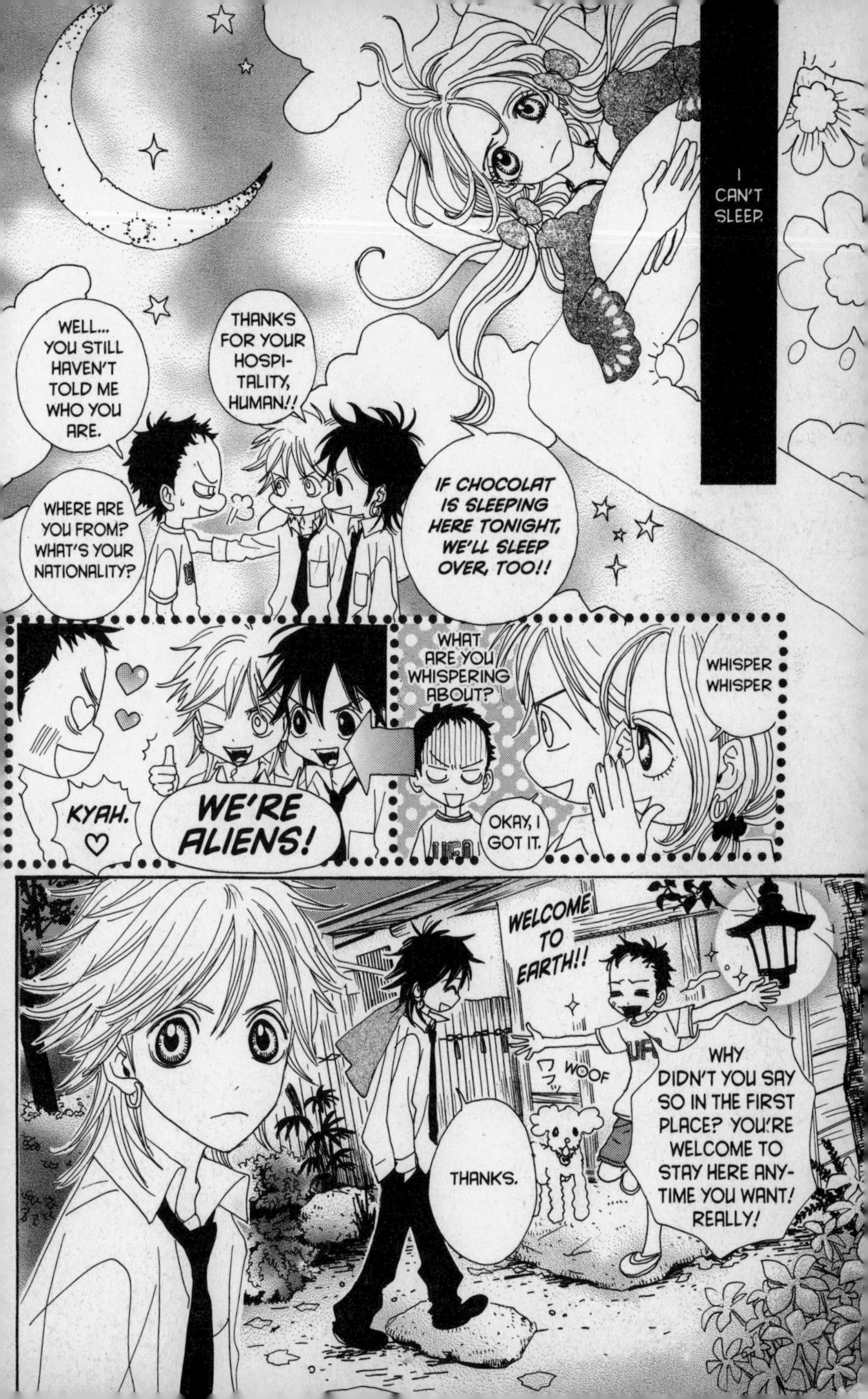
I CAN'T SLEEP.
IF CHOCOLAT IS SLEEPING HERE TONIGHT, WE'LL SLEEP OVER, TOO!!
THANKS FOR YOUR HOSPI-TALITY, HUMAN!!
WELL... YOU STILL HAVEN'T TOLD ME WHO YOU ARE.
WHERE ARE YOU FROM? WHAT'S YOUR NATIONALITY?
WHISPER WHISPER
WHAT ARE YOU WHISPERING ABOUT?
OKAY, I GOT IT.
WE'RE ALIENS!
KYAH. ♡
WELCOME TO EARTH!!
WHY DIDN'T YOU SAY SO IN THE FIRST PLACE? YOU'RE WELCOME TO STAY HERE ANY-TIME YOU WANT! REALLY!
WOOF
THANKS.

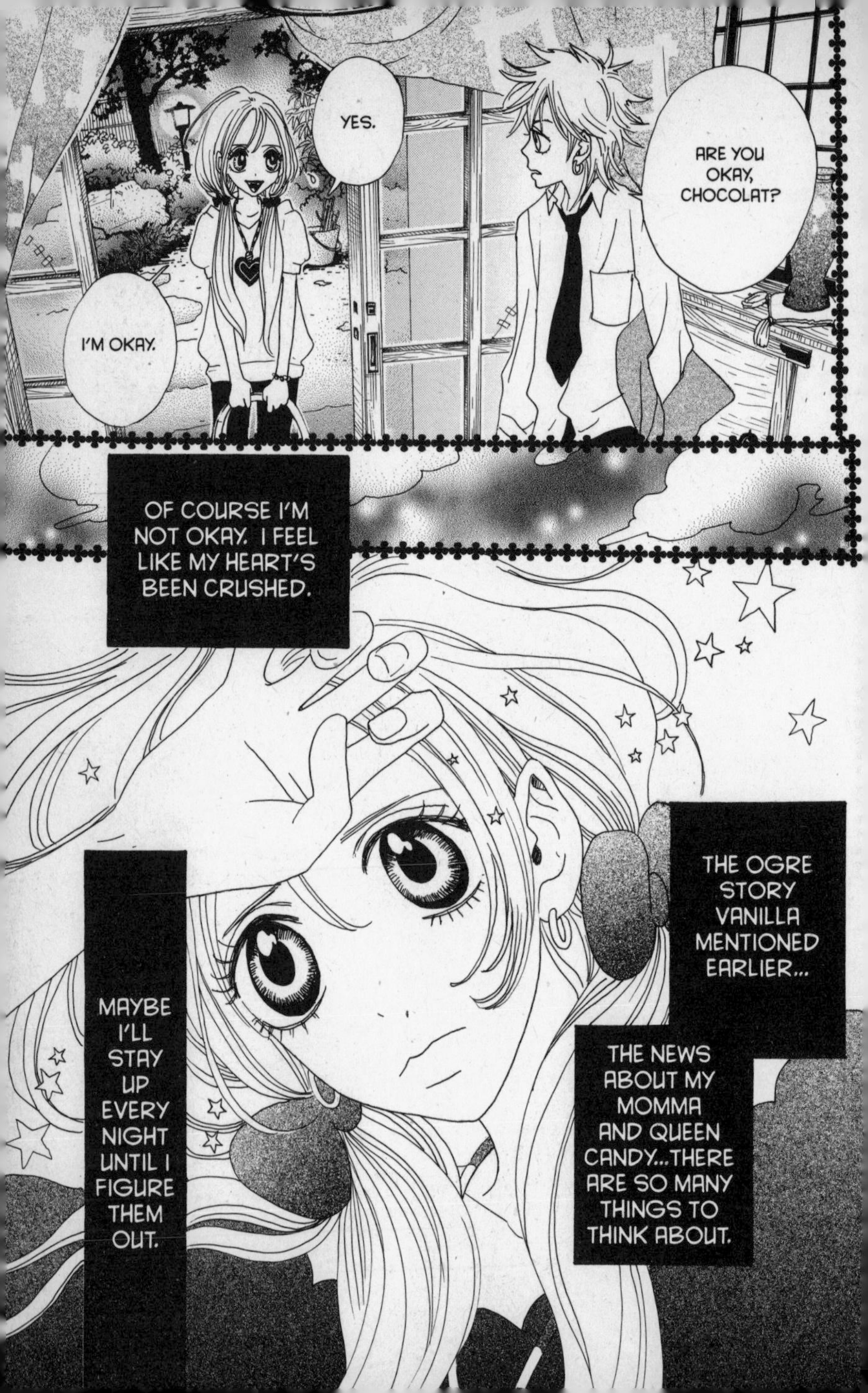
ARE YOU OKAY, CHOCOLAT?
YES.
I'M OKAY.
OF COURSE I'M NOT OKAY. I FEEL LIKE MY HEART'S BEEN CRUSHED.
THE OGRE STORY VANILLA MENTIONED EARLIER...
THE NEWS ABOUT MY MOMMA AND QUEEN CANDY...THERE ARE SO MANY THINGS TO THINK ABOUT.
MAYBE I'LL STAY UP EVERY NIGHT UNTIL I FIGURE THEM OUT.

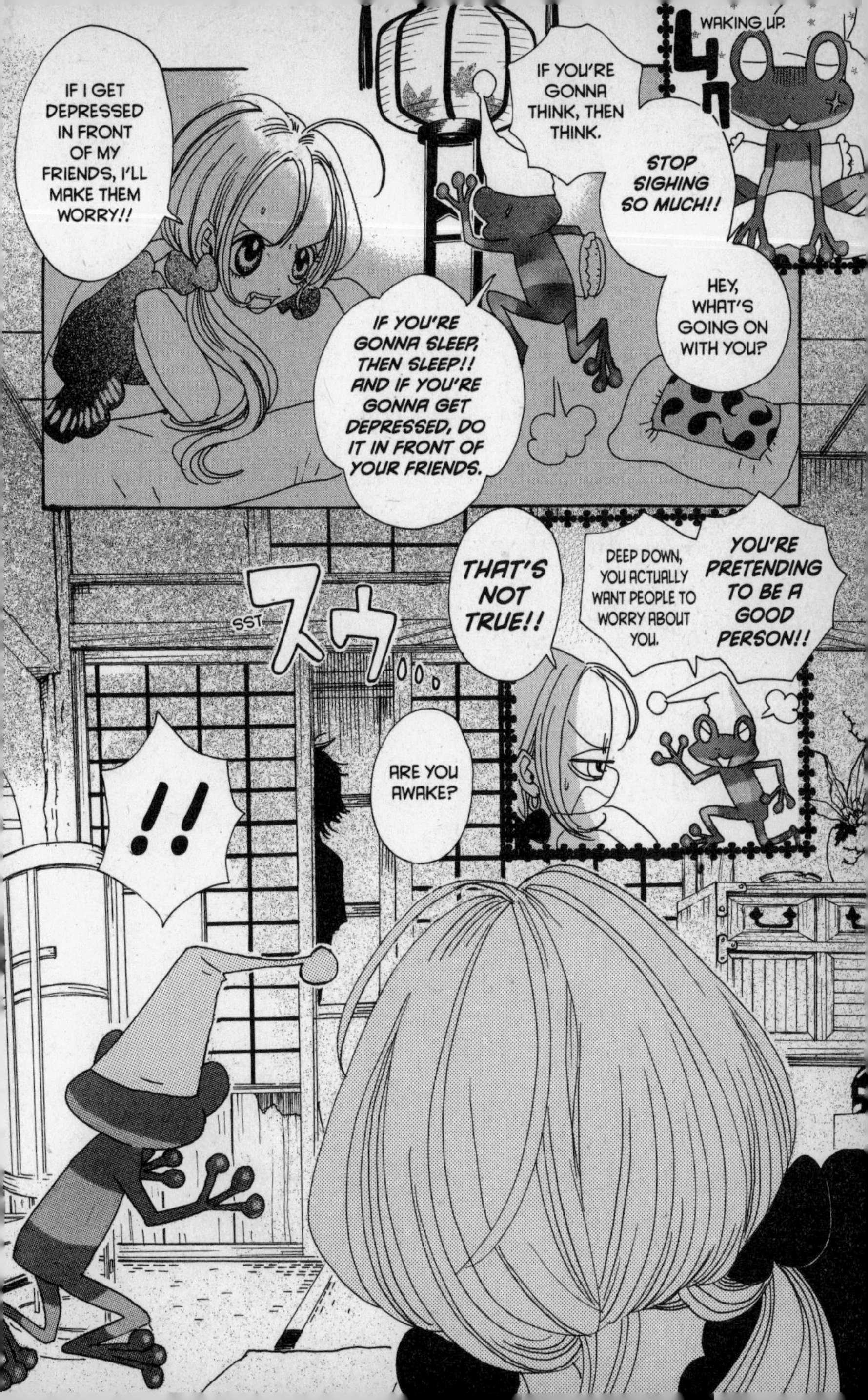
WAKING UP.
IF YOU'RE GONNA THINK, THEN THINK.
STOP SIGHING SO MUCH!!
HEY, WHAT'S GOING ON WITH YOU?
IF YOU'RE GONNA SLEEP, THEN SLEEP!! AND IF YOU'RE GONNA GET DEPRESSED, DO IT IN FRONT OF YOUR FRIENDS.
IF I GET DEPRESSED IN FRONT OF MY FRIENDS, I'LL MAKE THEM WORRY!!
YOU'RE PRETENDING TO BE A GOOD PERSON!!
DEEP DOWN, YOU ACTUALLY WANT PEOPLE TO WORRY ABOUT YOU.
THAT'S NOT TRUE!!
SST スウ
ARE YOU AWAKE?
!!

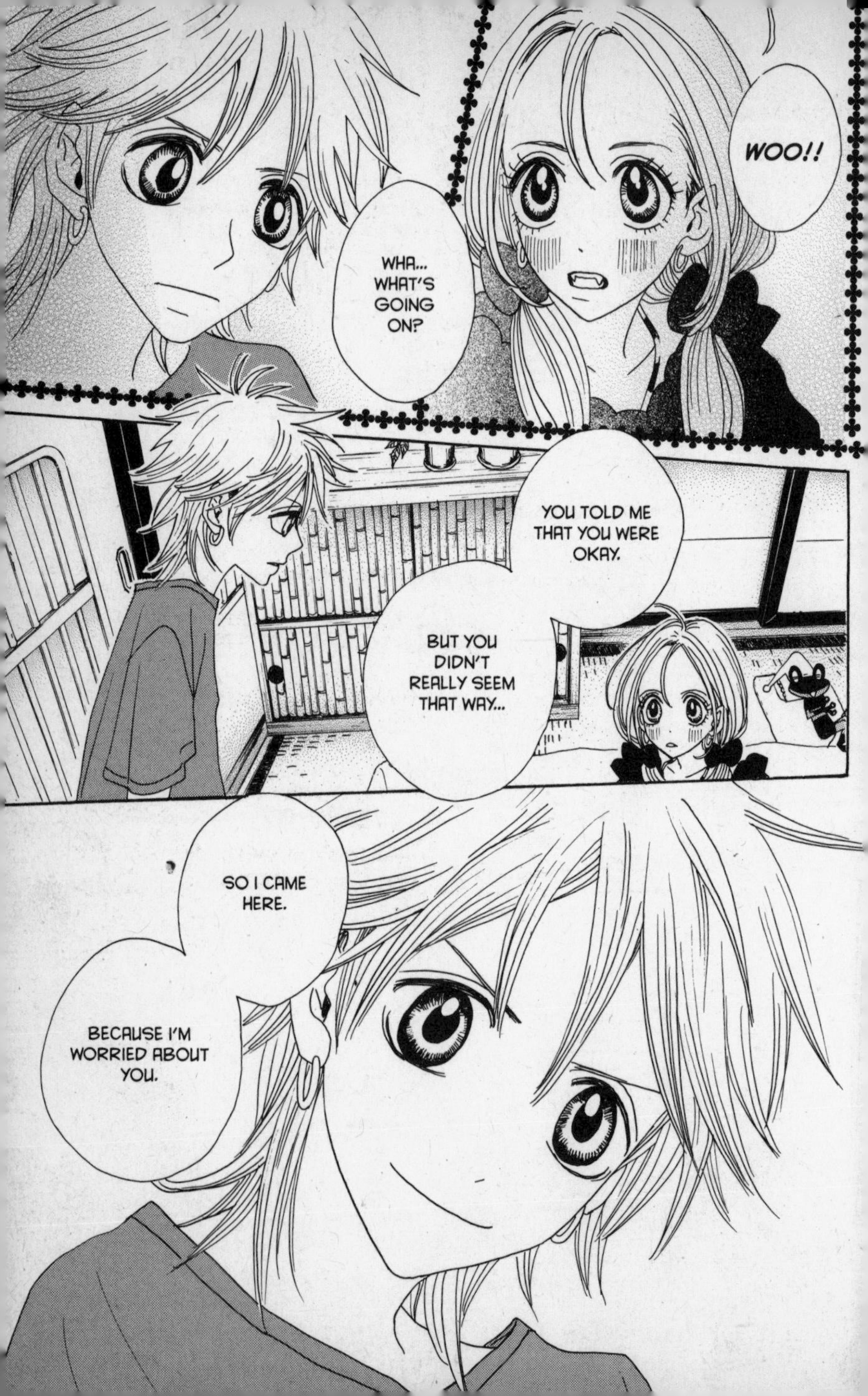
WOO!!
WHA... WHAT'S GOING ON?
YOU TOLD ME THAT YOU WERE OKAY.
BUT YOU DIDN'T REALLY SEEM THAT WAY...
SO I CAME HERE.
BECAUSE I'M WORRIED ABOUT YOU.

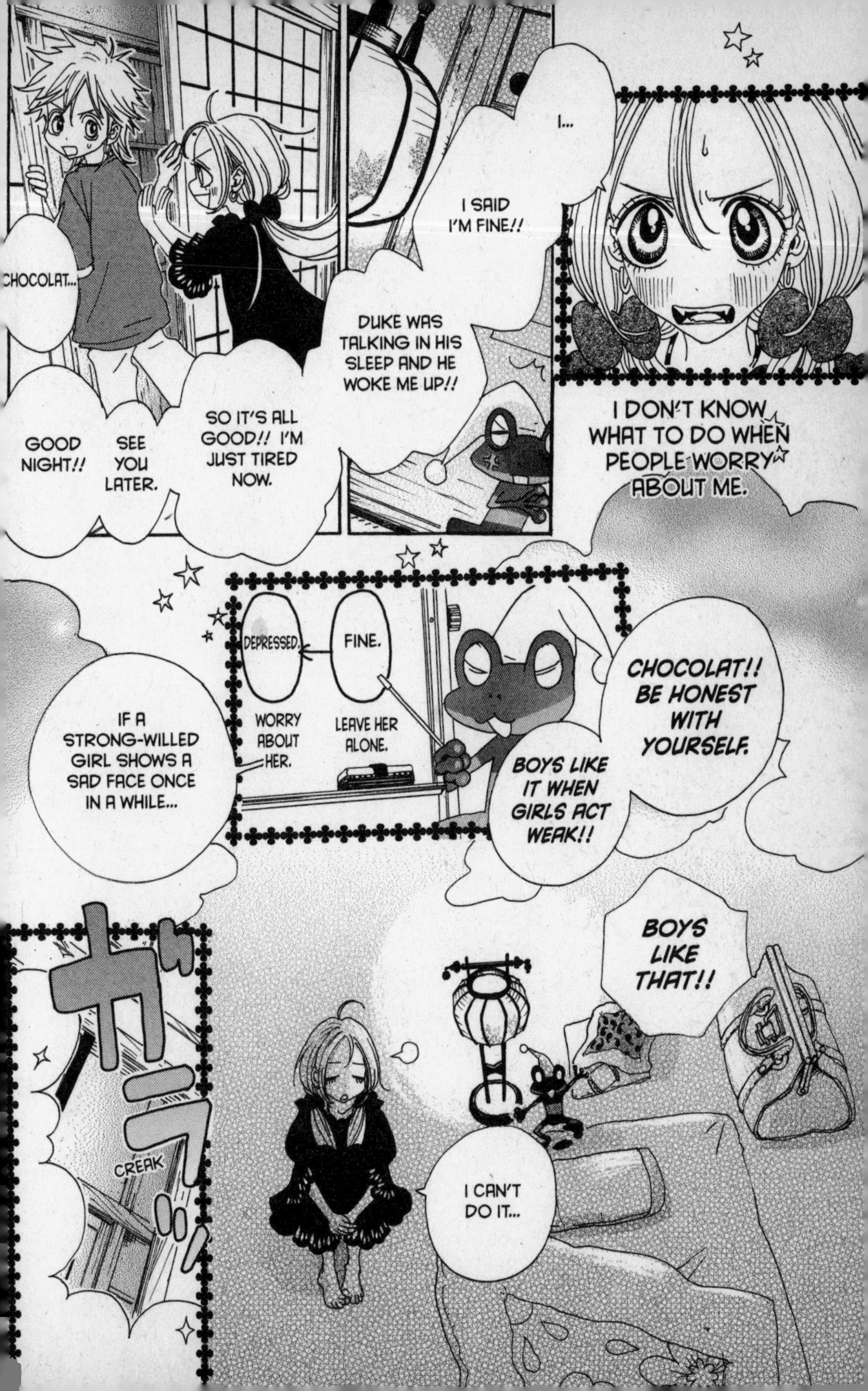
I...
I SAID I'M FINE!!
DUKE WAS TALKING IN HIS SLEEP AND HE WOKE ME UP!!
CHOCOLAT...
SO IT'S ALL GOOD!! I'M JUST TIRED NOW.
SEE YOU LATER.
GOOD NIGHT!!
I DON'T KNOW WHAT TO DO WHEN PEOPLE WORRY ABOUT ME.
CHOCOLAT!! BE HONEST WITH YOURSELF.
BOYS LIKE IT WHEN GIRLS ACT WEAK!!
FINE.
LEAVE HER ALONE.
DEPRESSED.
WORRY ABOUT HER.
IF A STRONG-WILLED GIRL SHOWS A SAD FACE ONCE IN A WHILE...
BOYS LIKE THAT!!
I CAN'T DO IT...
CREAK

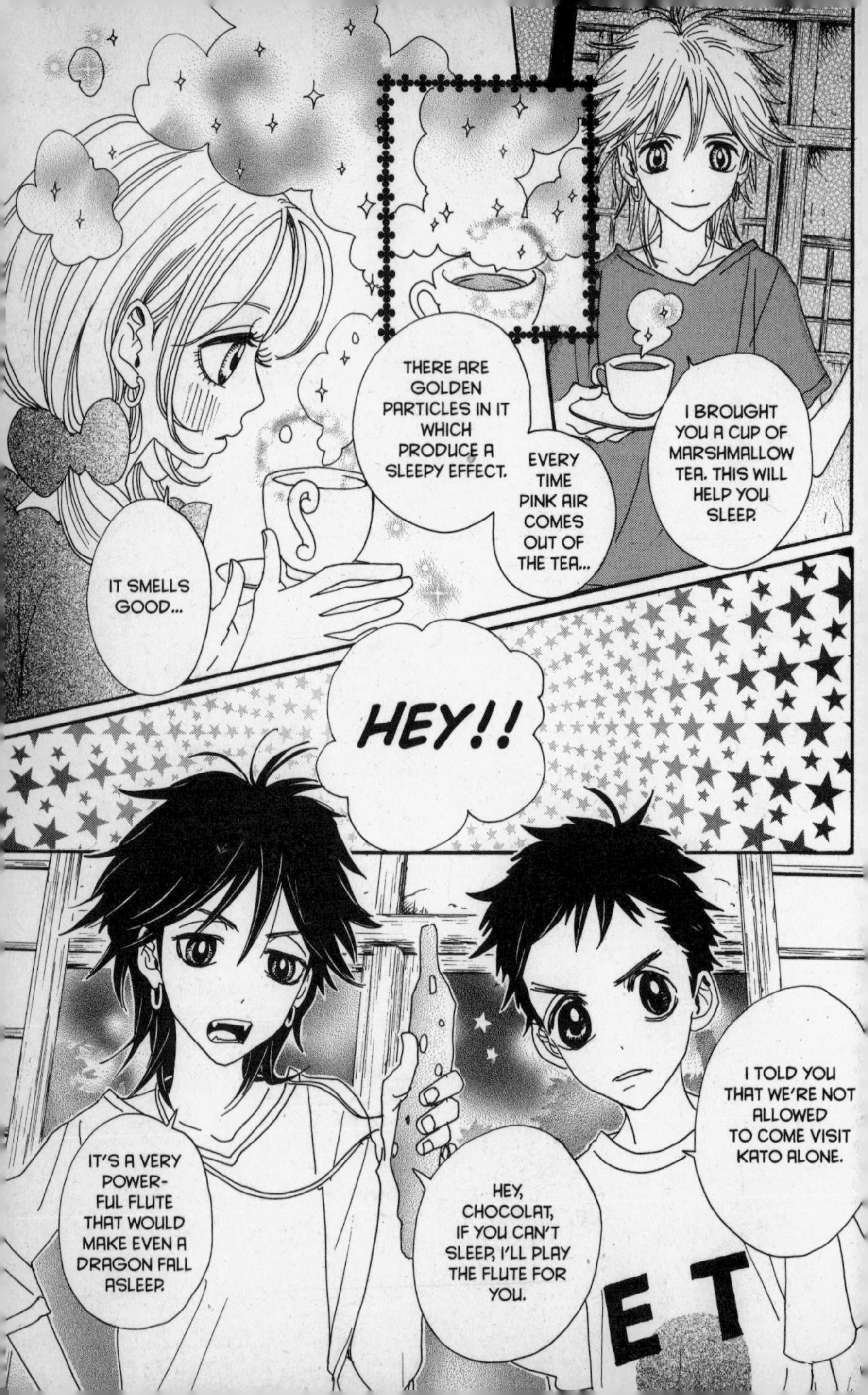
I BROUGHT YOU A CUP OF MARSHMALLOW TEA. THIS WILL HELP YOU SLEEP.
EVERY TIME PINK AIR COMES OUT OF THE TEA...
THERE ARE GOLDEN PARTICLES IN IT WHICH PRODUCE A SLEEPY EFFECT.
IT SMELLS GOOD...
HEY!!
I TOLD YOU THAT WE'RE NOT ALLOWED TO COME VISIT KATO ALONE.
HEY, CHOCOLAT, IF YOU CAN'T SLEEP, I'LL PLAY THE FLUTE FOR YOU.
IT'S A VERY POWER-FUL FLUTE THAT WOULD MAKE EVEN A DRAGON FALL ASLEEP.

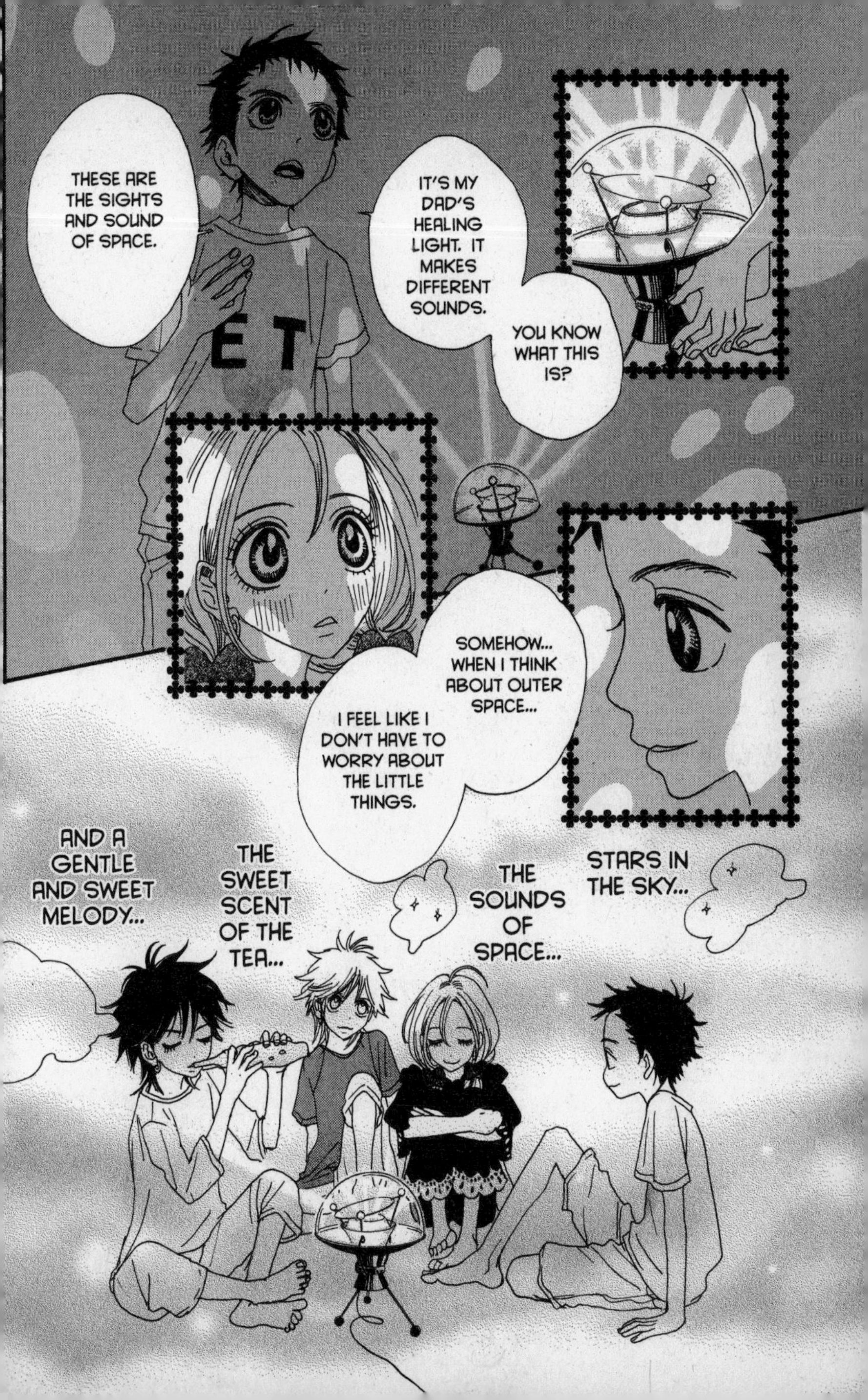
YOU KNOW WHAT THIS IS?
IT'S MY DAD'S HEALING LIGHT. IT MAKES DIFFERENT SOUNDS.
THESE ARE THE SIGHTS AND SOUND OF SPACE.
SOMEHOW... WHEN I THINK ABOUT OUTER SPACE...
I FEEL LIKE I DON'T HAVE TO WORRY ABOUT THE LITTLE THINGS.
STARS IN THE SKY...
THE SOUNDS OF SPACE...
THE SWEET SCENT OF THE TEA...
AND A GENTLE AND SWEET MELODY...

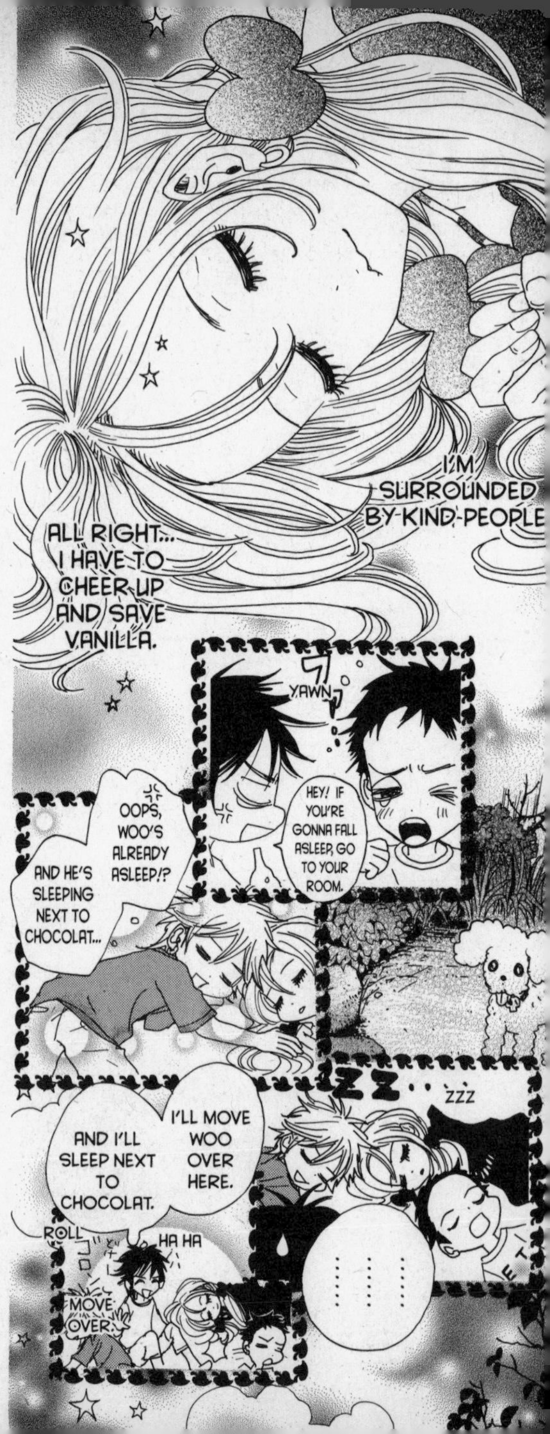
I'M SURROUNDED BY KIND PEOPLE
ALL RIGHT... I HAVE TO CHEER UP AND SAVE VANILLA.
YAWN
HEY! IF YOU'RE GONNA FALL ASLEEP, GO TO YOUR ROOM.
OOPS, WOO'S ALREADY ASLEEP!?
AND HE'S SLEEPING NEXT TO CHOCOLAT...
ZZ...
ZZZ
......
I'LL MOVE WOO OVER HERE.
AND I'LL SLEEP NEXT TO CHOCOLAT.
HA HA
ROLL
MOVE OVER

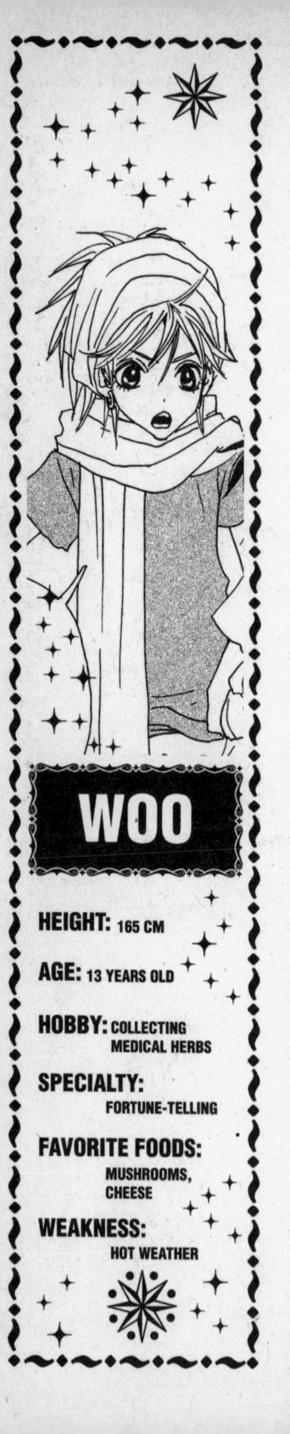

WOO

HEIGHT: 165 CM

AGE: 13 YEARS OLD

HOBBY: COLLECTING MEDICAL HERBS

SPECIALTY: FORTUNE-TELLING

FAVORITE FOODS: MUSHROOMS, CHEESE

WEAKNESS: HOT WEATHER

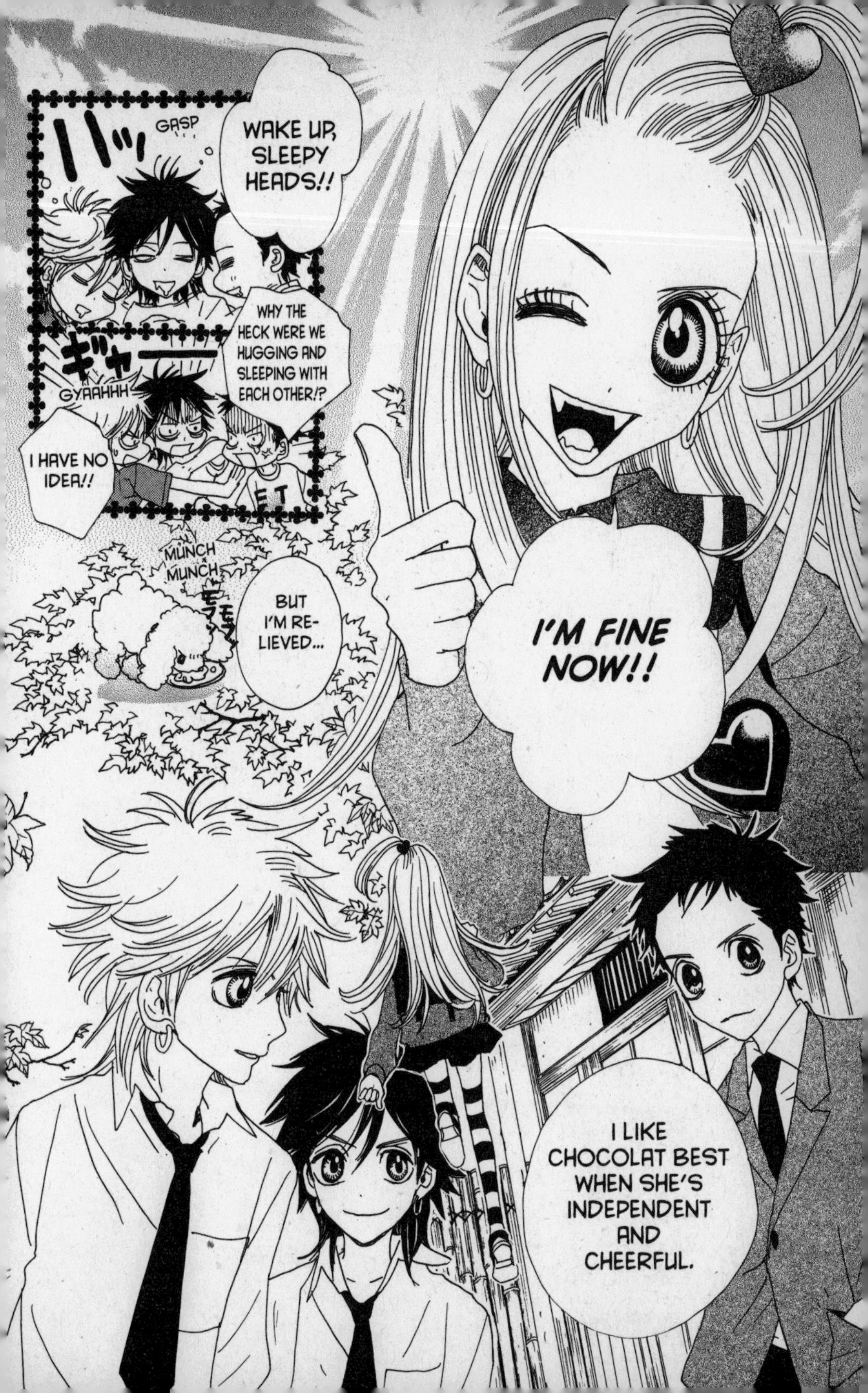
WAKE UP, SLEEPY HEADS!!
ハッ
GASP
WHY THE HECK WERE WE HUGGING AND SLEEPING WITH EACH OTHER!?
ギャー
GYAAHHH
I HAVE NO IDEA!!
MUNCH MUNCH
BUT I'M RE-LIEVED...
I'M FINE NOW!!
I LIKE CHOCOLAT BEST WHEN SHE'S INDEPENDENT AND CHEERFUL.

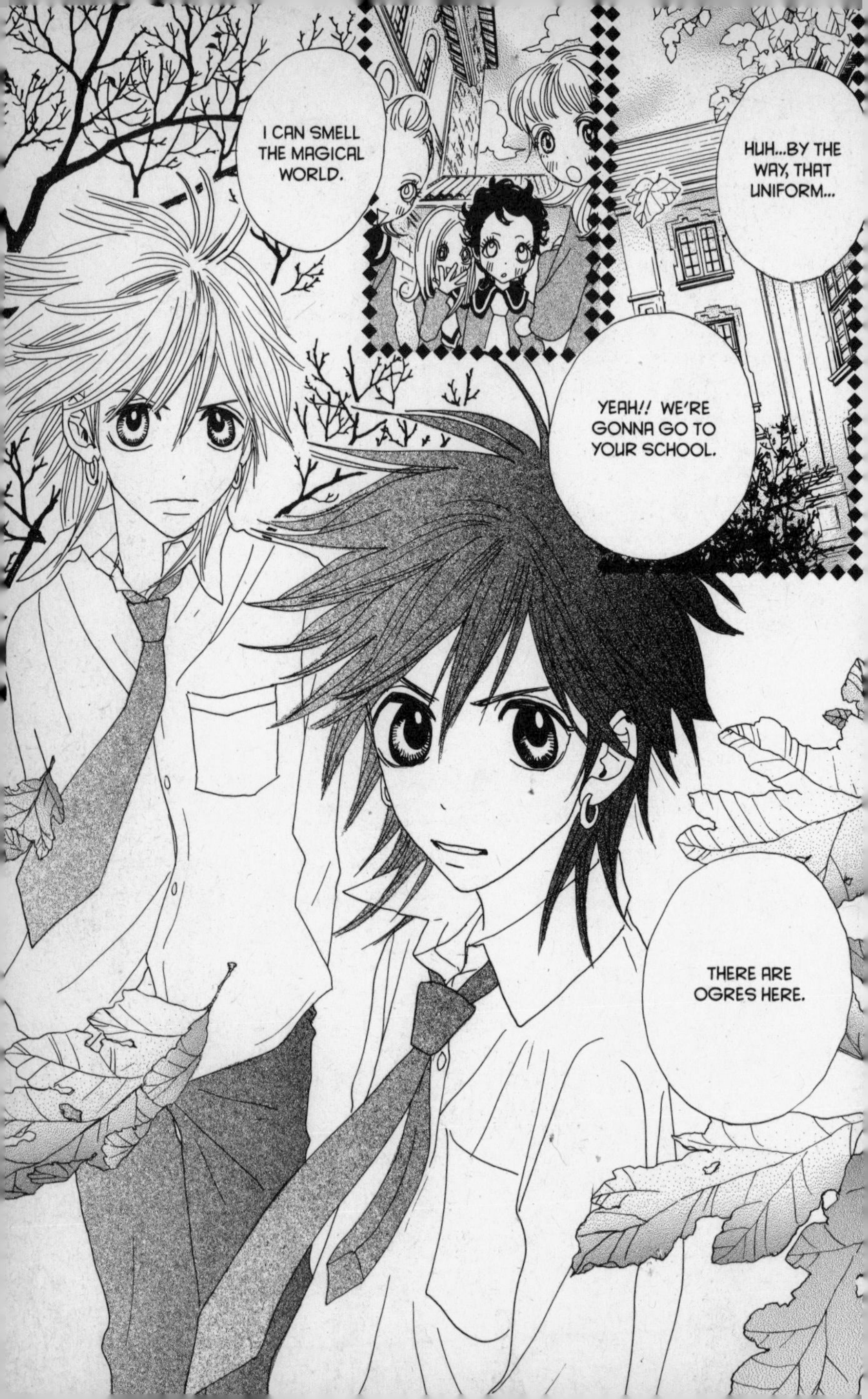
HUH...BY THE WAY, THAT UNIFORM...
I CAN SMELL THE MAGICAL WORLD.
YEAH!! WE'RE GONNA GO TO YOUR SCHOOL.
THERE ARE OGRES HERE.

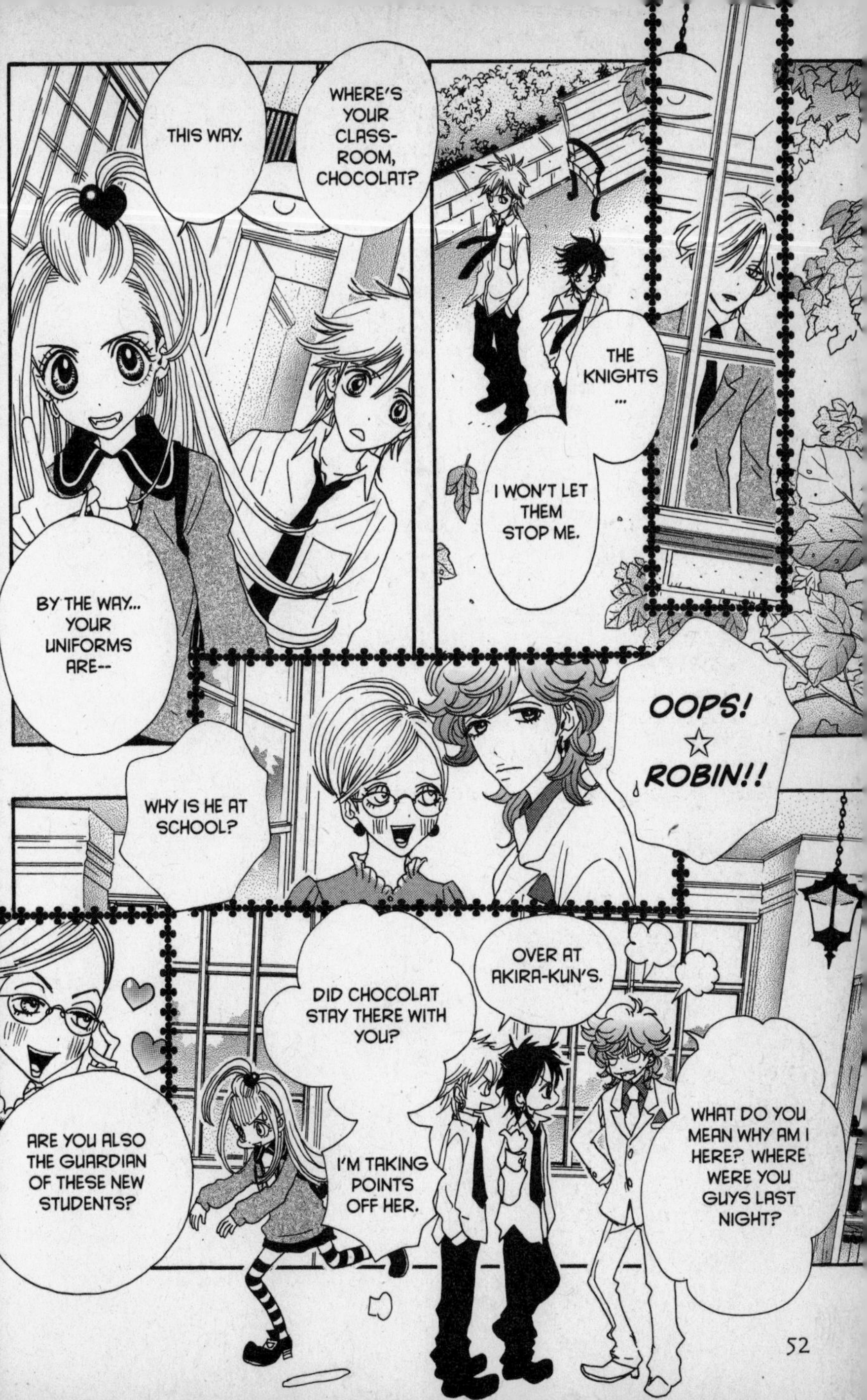
THE KNIGHTS...
I WON'T LET THEM STOP ME.
WHERE'S YOUR CLASS-ROOM, CHOCOLAT?
THIS WAY.
BY THE WAY... YOUR UNIFORMS ARE--
OOPS! ☆ ROBIN!!
WHY IS HE AT SCHOOL?
WHAT DO YOU MEAN WHY AM I HERE? WHERE WERE YOU GUYS LAST NIGHT?
OVER AT AKIRA-KUN'S.
DID CHOCOLAT STAY THERE WITH YOU?
I'M TAKING POINTS OFF HER.
ARE YOU ALSO THE GUARDIAN OF THESE NEW STUDENTS?

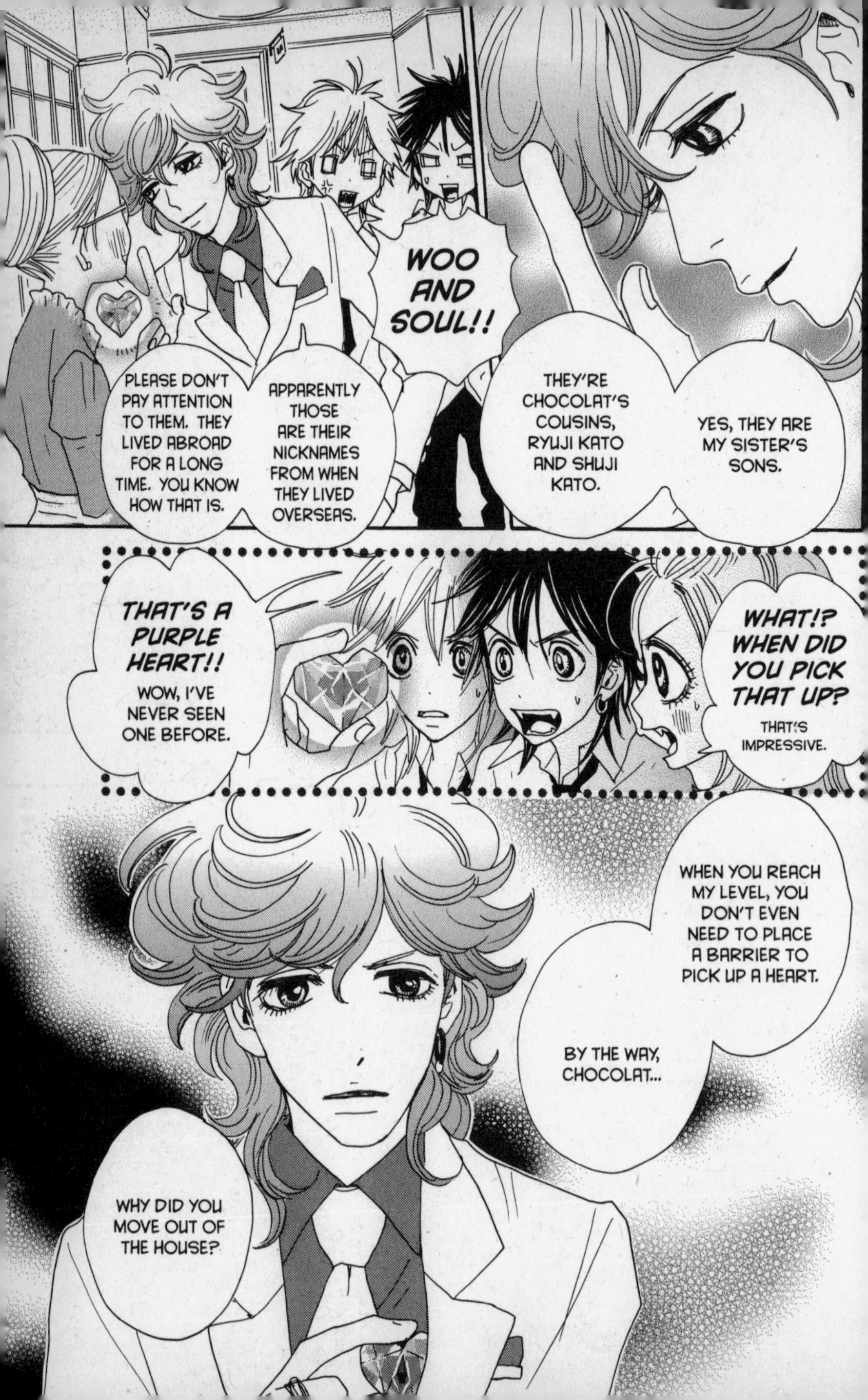
YES, THEY ARE MY SISTER'S SONS.
THEY'RE CHOCOLAT'S COUSINS, RYUJI KATO AND SHUJI KATO.
WOO AND SOUL!!
APPARENTLY THOSE ARE THEIR NICKNAMES FROM WHEN THEY LIVED OVERSEAS.
PLEASE DON'T PAY ATTENTION TO THEM. THEY LIVED ABROAD FOR A LONG TIME. YOU KNOW HOW THAT IS.
WHAT!? WHEN DID YOU PICK THAT UP?
THAT'S IMPRESSIVE.
THAT'S A PURPLE HEART!!
WOW, I'VE NEVER SEEN ONE BEFORE.
WHEN YOU REACH MY LEVEL, YOU DON'T EVEN NEED TO PLACE A BARRIER TO PICK UP A HEART.
BY THE WAY, CHOCOLAT...
WHY DID YOU MOVE OUT OF THE HOUSE?

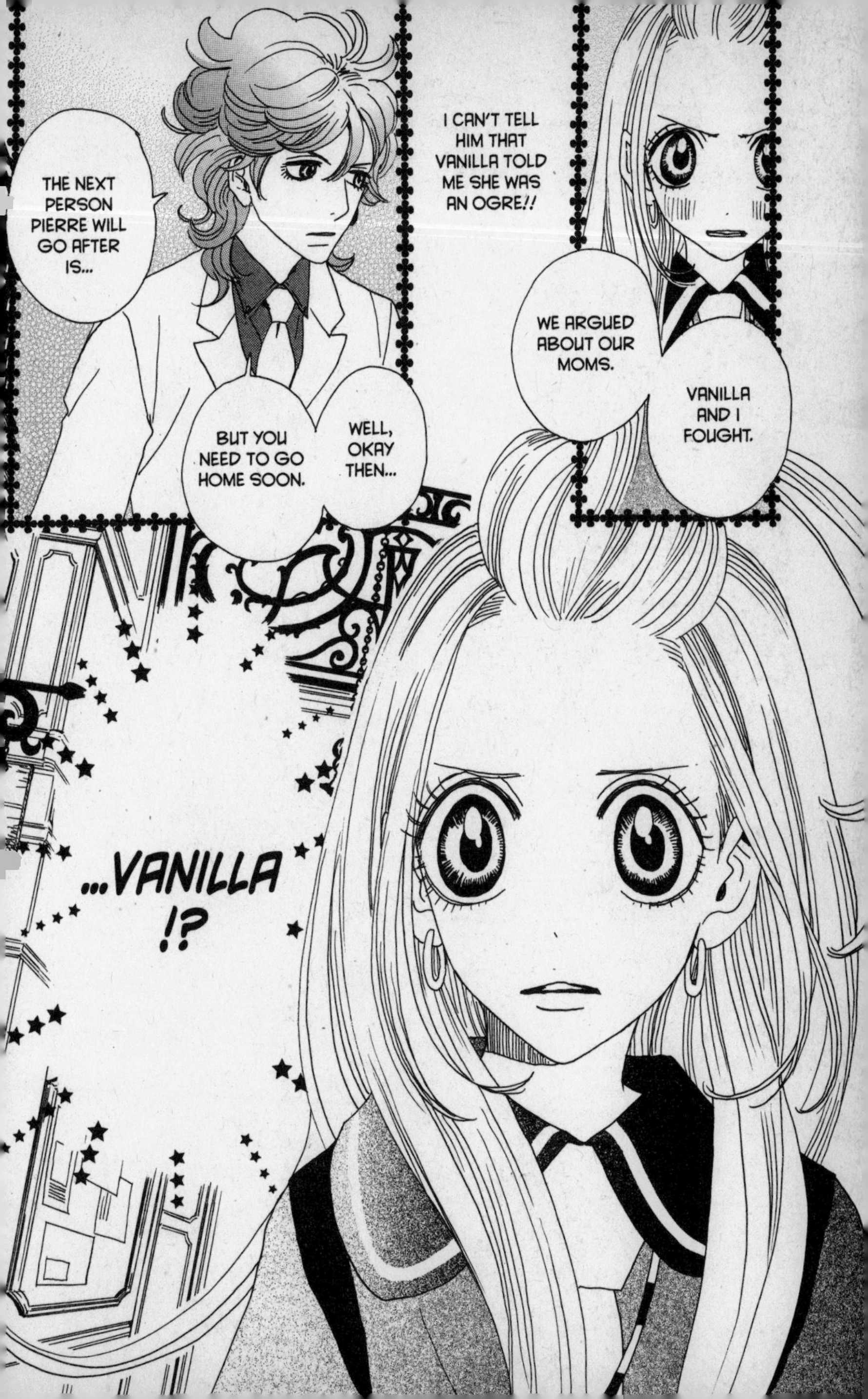
I CAN'T TELL HIM THAT VANILLA TOLD ME SHE WAS AN OGRE!!
VANILLA AND I FOUGHT.
WE ARGUED ABOUT OUR MOMS.
WELL, OKAY THEN...
BUT YOU NEED TO GO HOME SOON.
THE NEXT PERSON PIERRE WILL GO AFTER IS...
...VANILLA !?

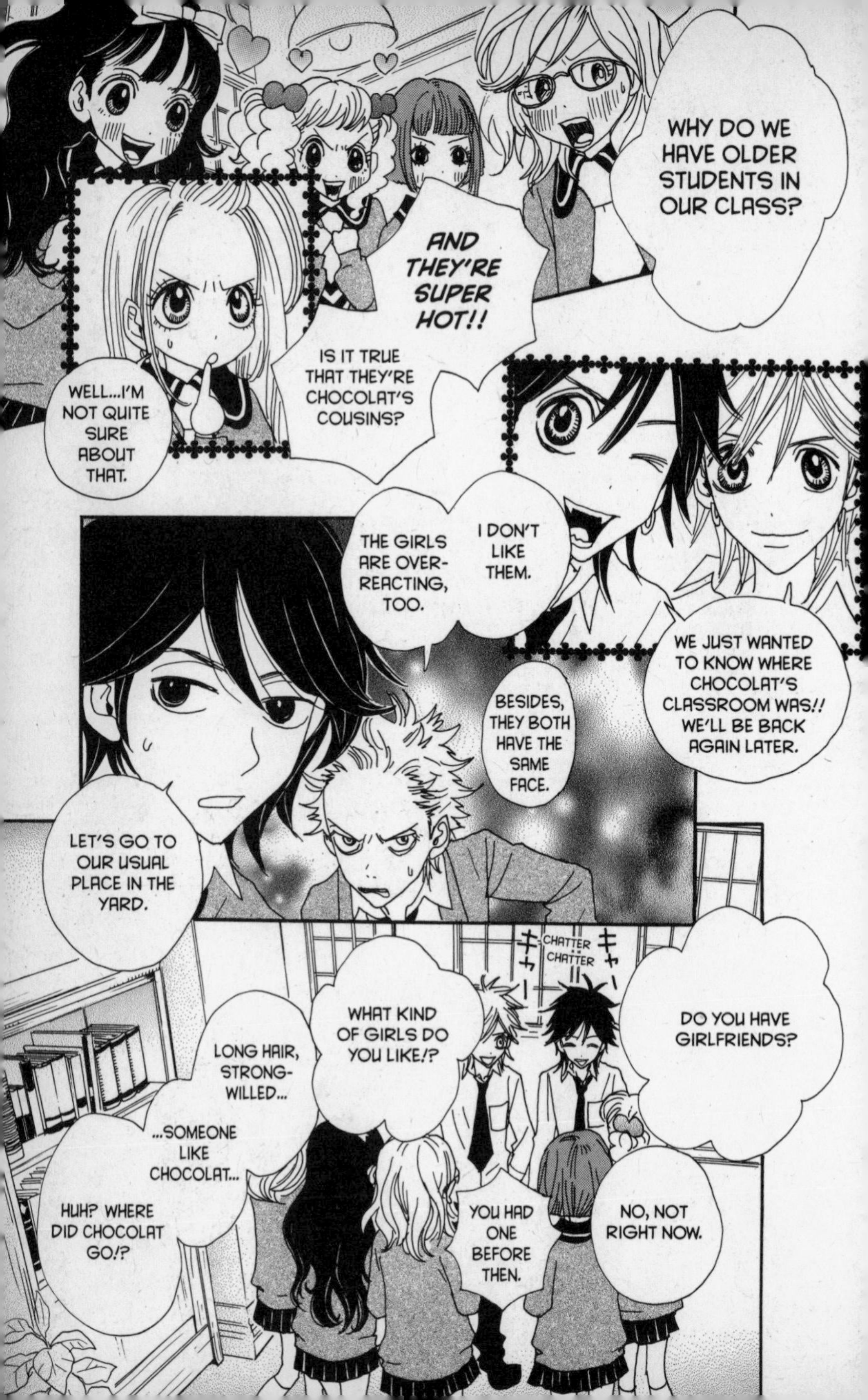
WHY DO WE HAVE OLDER STUDENTS IN OUR CLASS?
AND THEY'RE SUPER HOT!!
IS IT TRUE THAT THEY'RE CHOCOLAT'S COUSINS?
WELL...I'M NOT QUITE SURE ABOUT THAT.
WE JUST WANTED TO KNOW WHERE CHOCOLAT'S CLASSROOM WAS!! WE'LL BE BACK AGAIN LATER.
I DON'T LIKE THEM.
THE GIRLS ARE OVER-REACTING, TOO.
BESIDES, THEY BOTH HAVE THE SAME FACE.
LET'S GO TO OUR USUAL PLACE IN THE YARD.
キャー
CHATTER CHATTER
キャー
DO YOU HAVE GIRLFRIENDS?
WHAT KIND OF GIRLS DO YOU LIKE!?
NO, NOT RIGHT NOW.
YOU HAD ONE BEFORE THEN.
LONG HAIR, STRONG-WILLED...
...SOMEONE LIKE CHOCOLAT...
HUH? WHERE DID CHOCOLAT GO!?

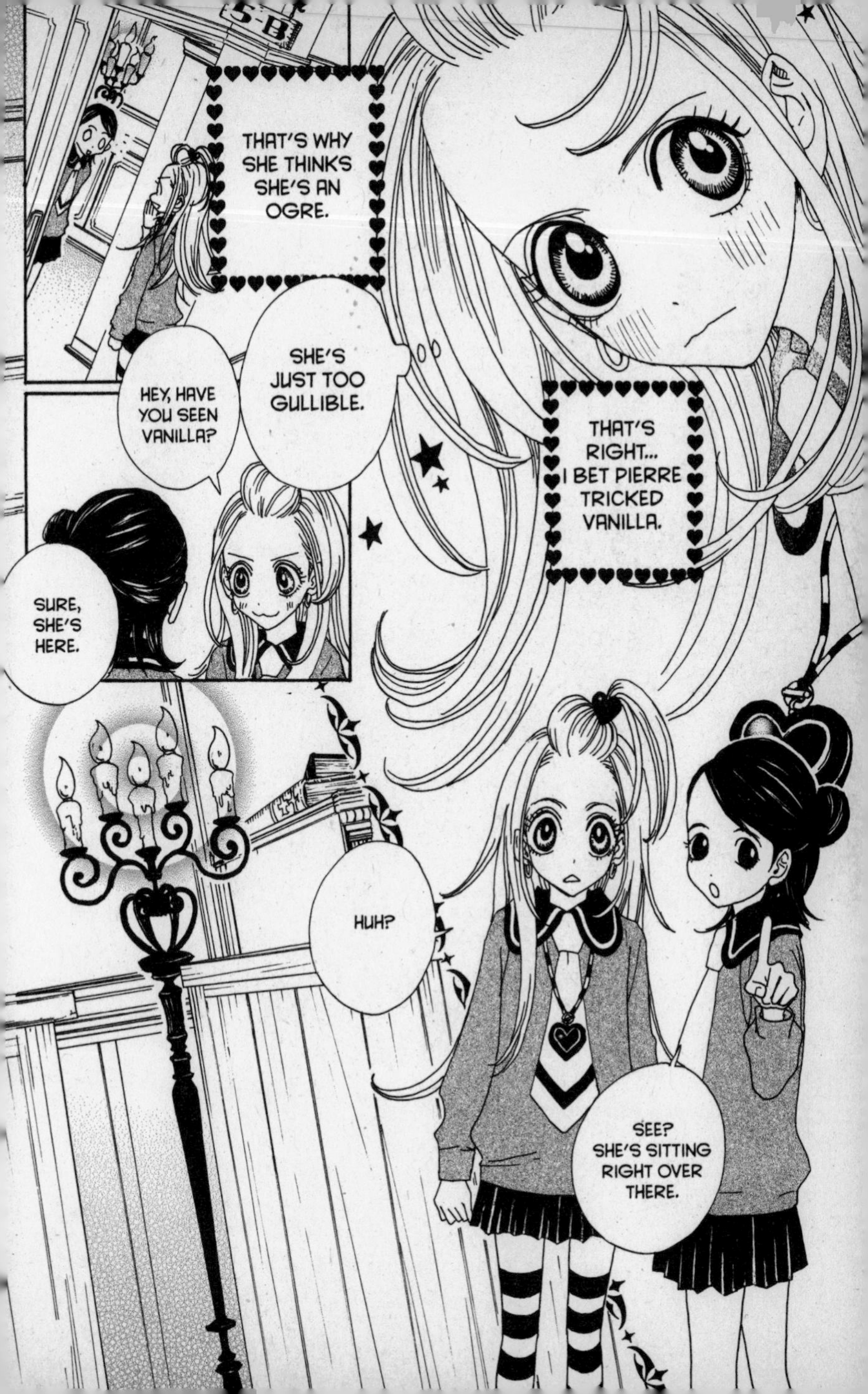
THAT'S RIGHT... I BET PIERRE TRICKED VANILLA.
THAT'S WHY SHE THINKS SHE'S AN OGRE.
SHE'S JUST TOO GULLIBLE.
HEY, HAVE YOU SEEN VANILLA?
SURE, SHE'S HERE.
HUH?
SEE? SHE'S SITTING RIGHT OVER THERE.

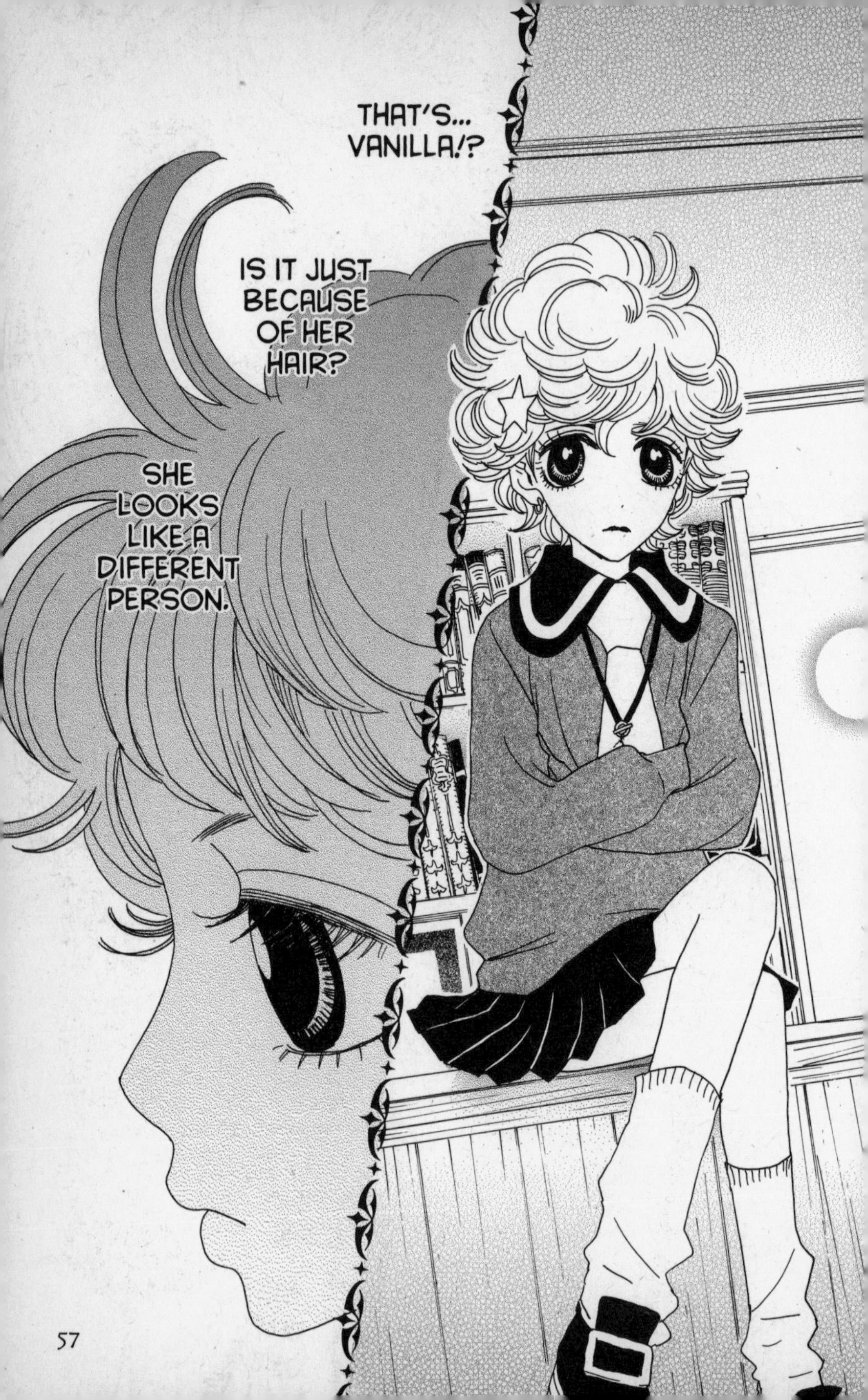
THAT'S... VANILLA!?
IS IT JUST BECAUSE OF HER HAIR?
SHE LOOKS LIKE A DIFFERENT PERSON.

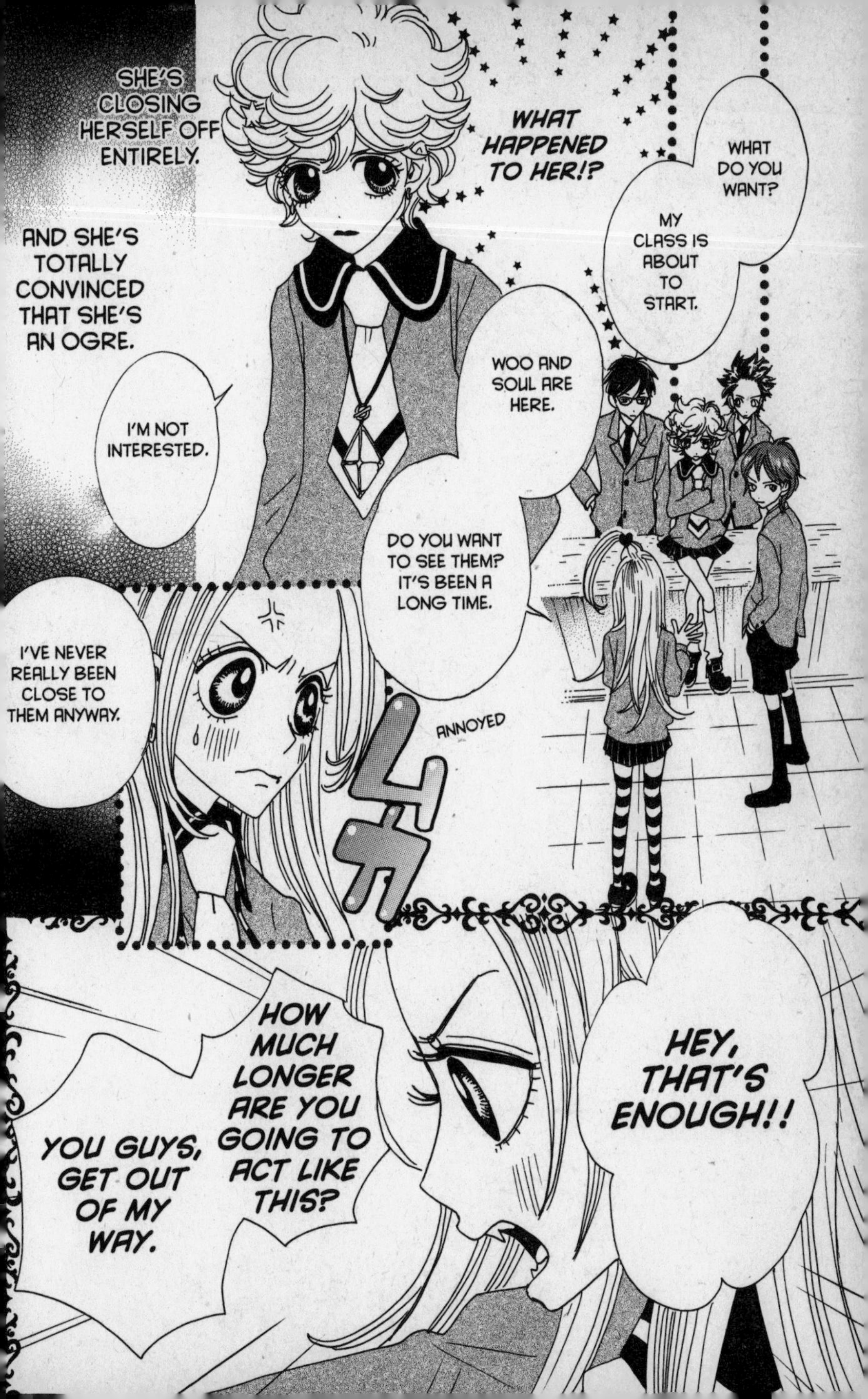
WHAT DO YOU WANT?
MY CLASS IS ABOUT TO START.
WHAT HAPPENED TO HER!?
WOO AND SOUL ARE HERE.
DO YOU WANT TO SEE THEM? IT'S BEEN A LONG TIME.
I'M NOT INTERESTED.
SHE'S CLOSING HERSELF OFF ENTIRELY.
AND SHE'S TOTALLY CONVINCED THAT SHE'S AN OGRE.
I'VE NEVER REALLY BEEN CLOSE TO THEM ANYWAY.
ANNOYED
HEY, THAT'S ENOUGH!!
HOW MUCH LONGER ARE YOU GOING TO ACT LIKE THIS?
YOU GUYS, GET OUT OF MY WAY.

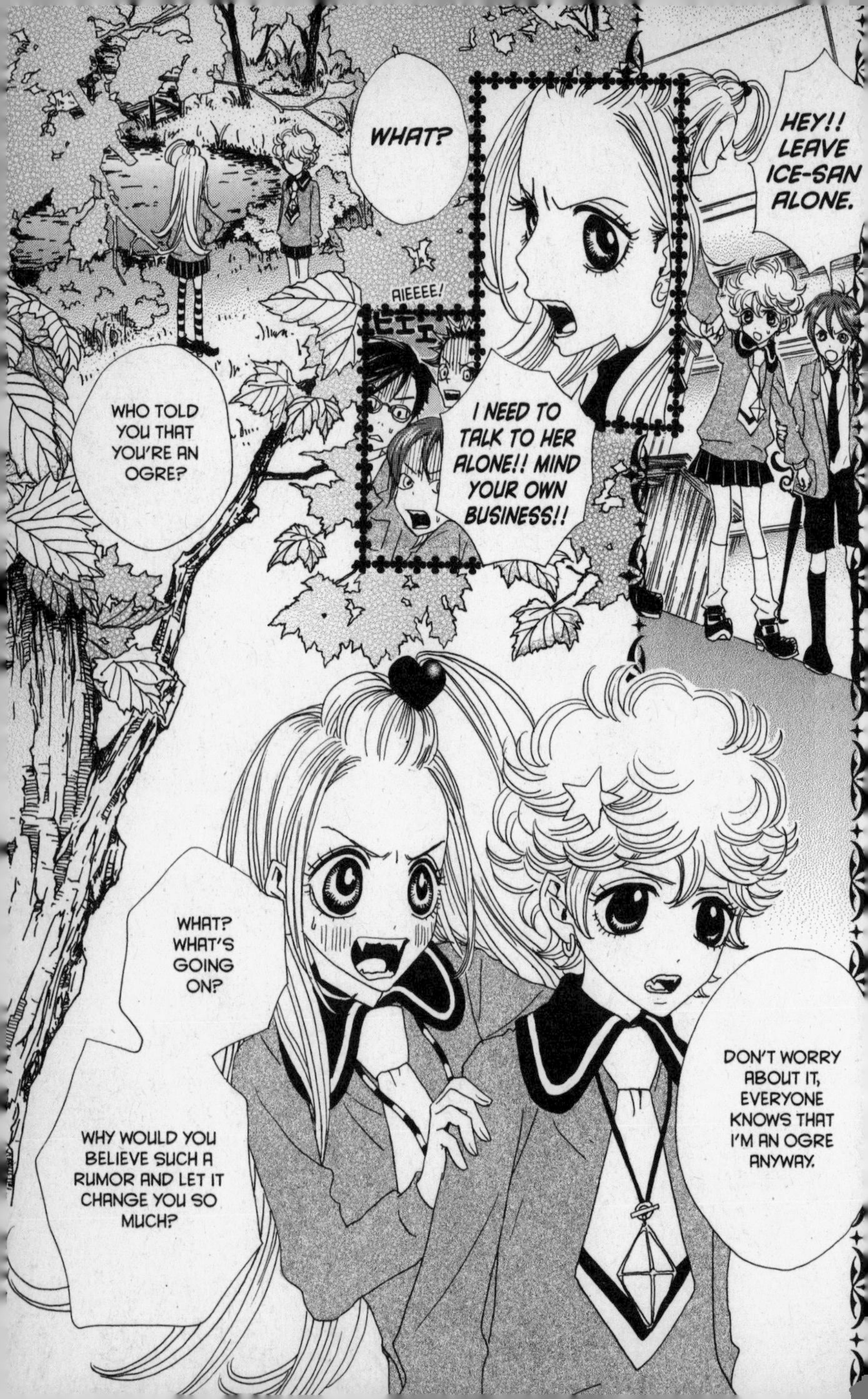
HEY!! LEAVE ICE-SAN ALONE.
WHAT?
I NEED TO TALK TO HER ALONE!! MIND YOUR OWN BUSINESS!!
AIEEEE!
WHO TOLD YOU THAT YOU'RE AN OGRE?
DON'T WORRY ABOUT IT, EVERYONE KNOWS THAT I'M AN OGRE ANYWAY.
WHAT? WHAT'S GOING ON?
WHY WOULD YOU BELIEVE SUCH A RUMOR AND LET IT CHANGE YOU SO MUCH?

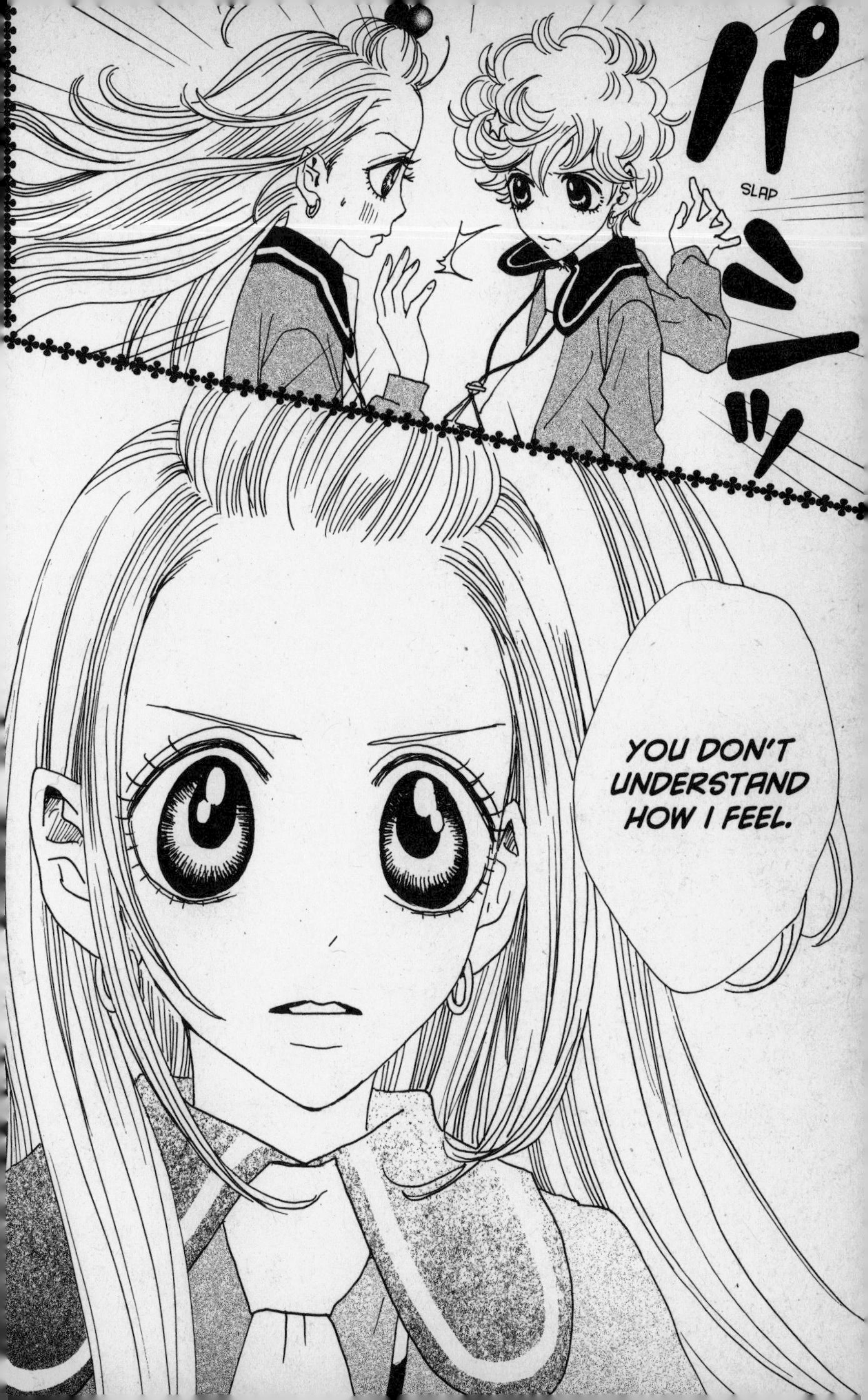
パシーッ
SLAP
YOU DON'T UNDERSTAND HOW I FEEL.

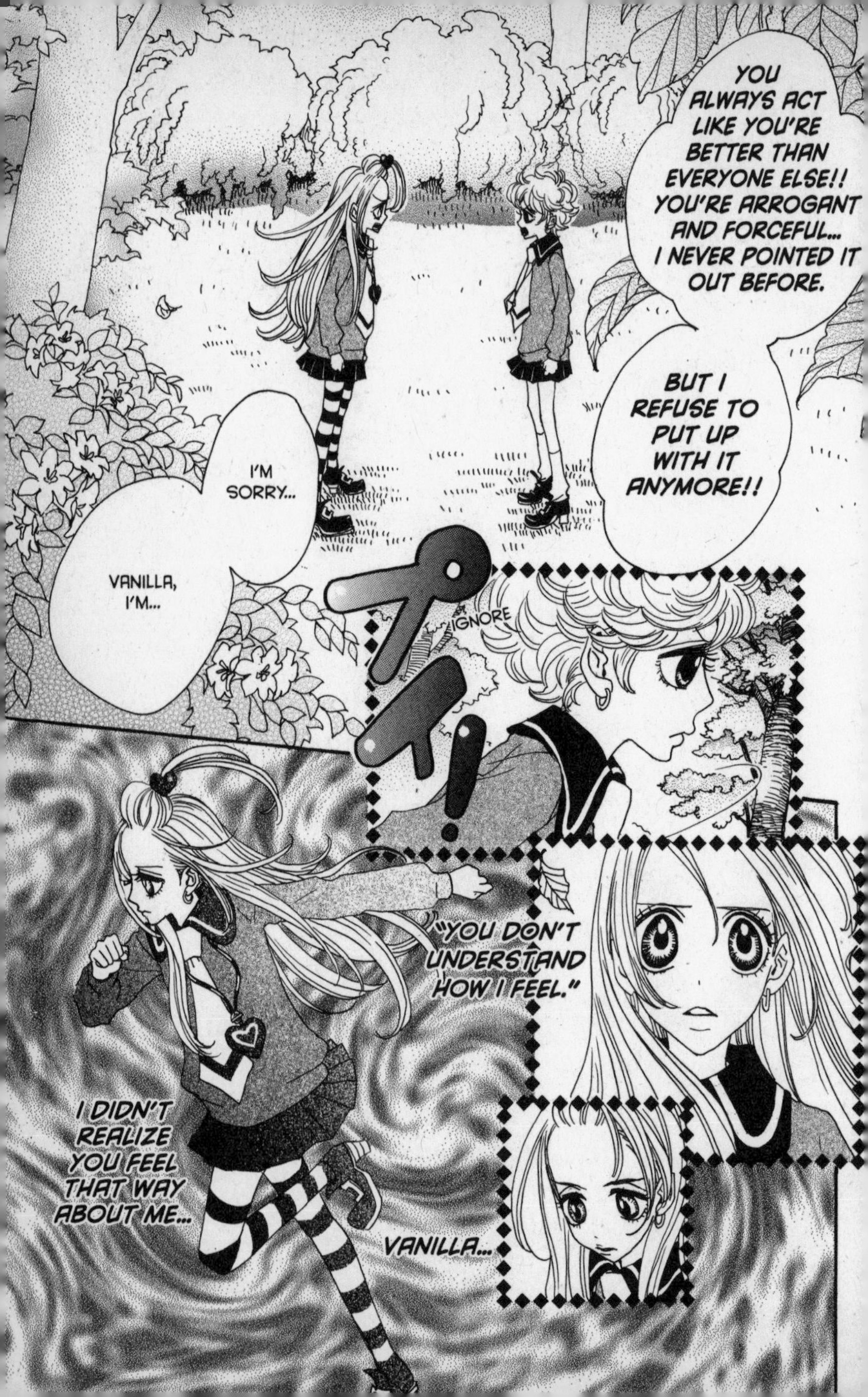
YOU ALWAYS ACT LIKE YOU'RE BETTER THAN EVERYONE ELSE!! YOU'RE ARROGANT AND FORCEFUL... I NEVER POINTED IT OUT BEFORE.
BUT I REFUSE TO PUT UP WITH IT ANYMORE!!
I'M SORRY...
VANILLA, I'M...
プイ!
IGNORE
"YOU DON'T UNDERSTAND HOW I FEEL."
VANILLA...
I DIDN'T REALIZE YOU FEEL THAT WAY ABOUT ME...

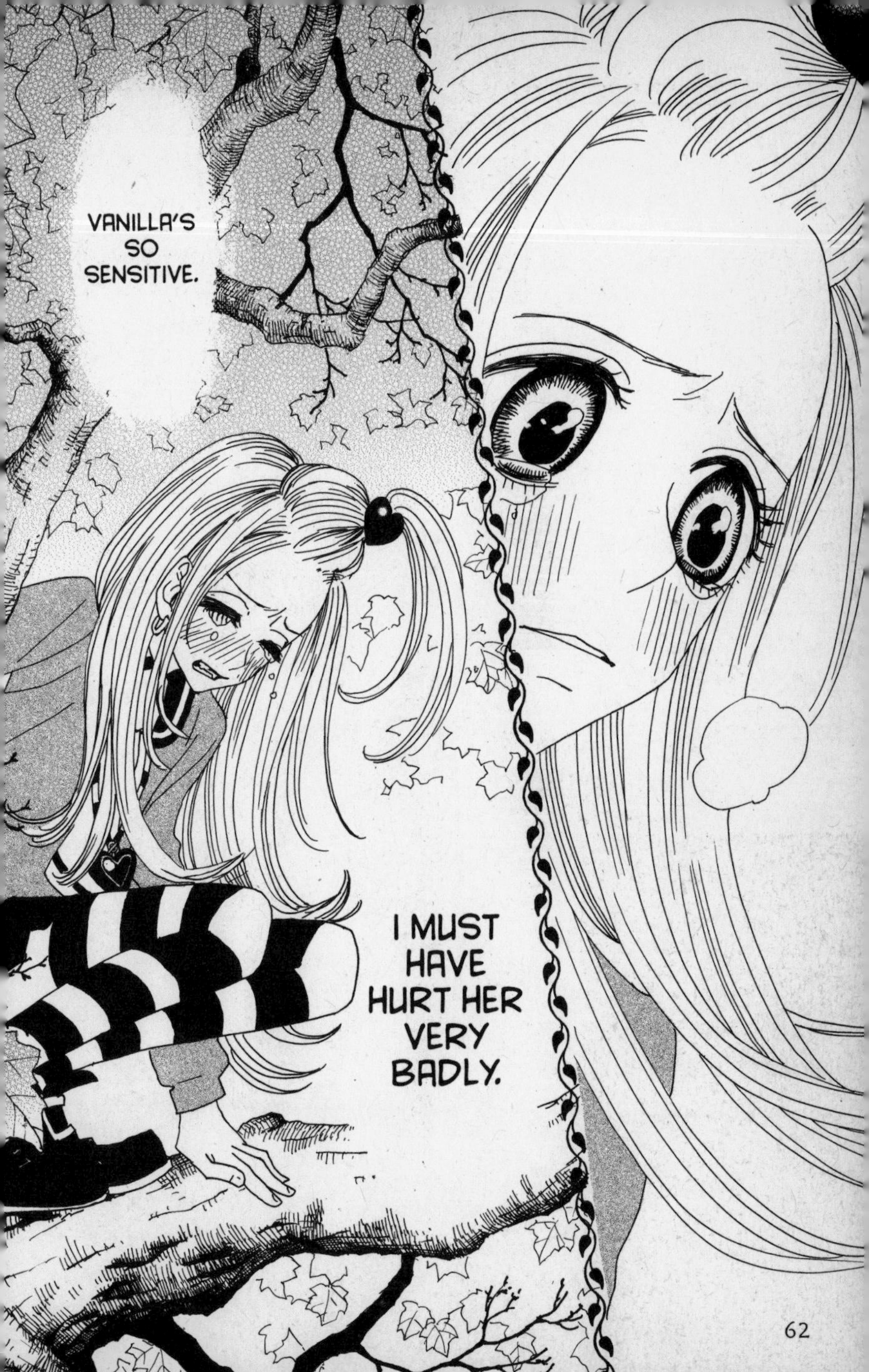
VANILLA'S SO SENSITIVE.
I MUST HAVE HURT HER VERY BADLY.

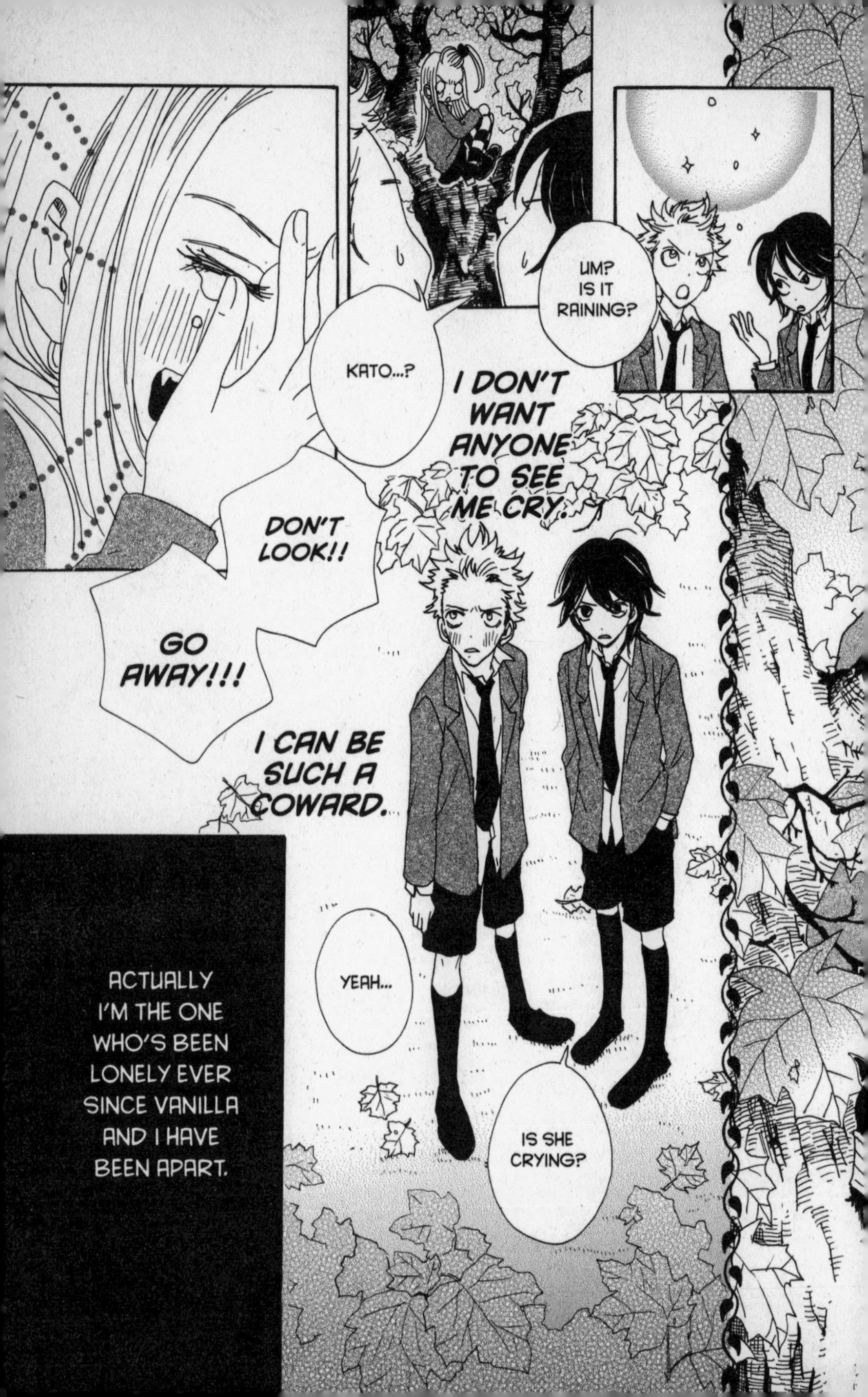
UM? IS IT RAINING?
KATO...?
I DON'T WANT ANYONE TO SEE ME CRY.
DON'T LOOK!!
GO AWAY!!!
I CAN BE SUCH A COWARD.
IS SHE CRYING?
YEAH...
ACTUALLY I'M THE ONE WHO'S BEEN LONELY EVER SINCE VANILLA AND I HAVE BEEN APART.

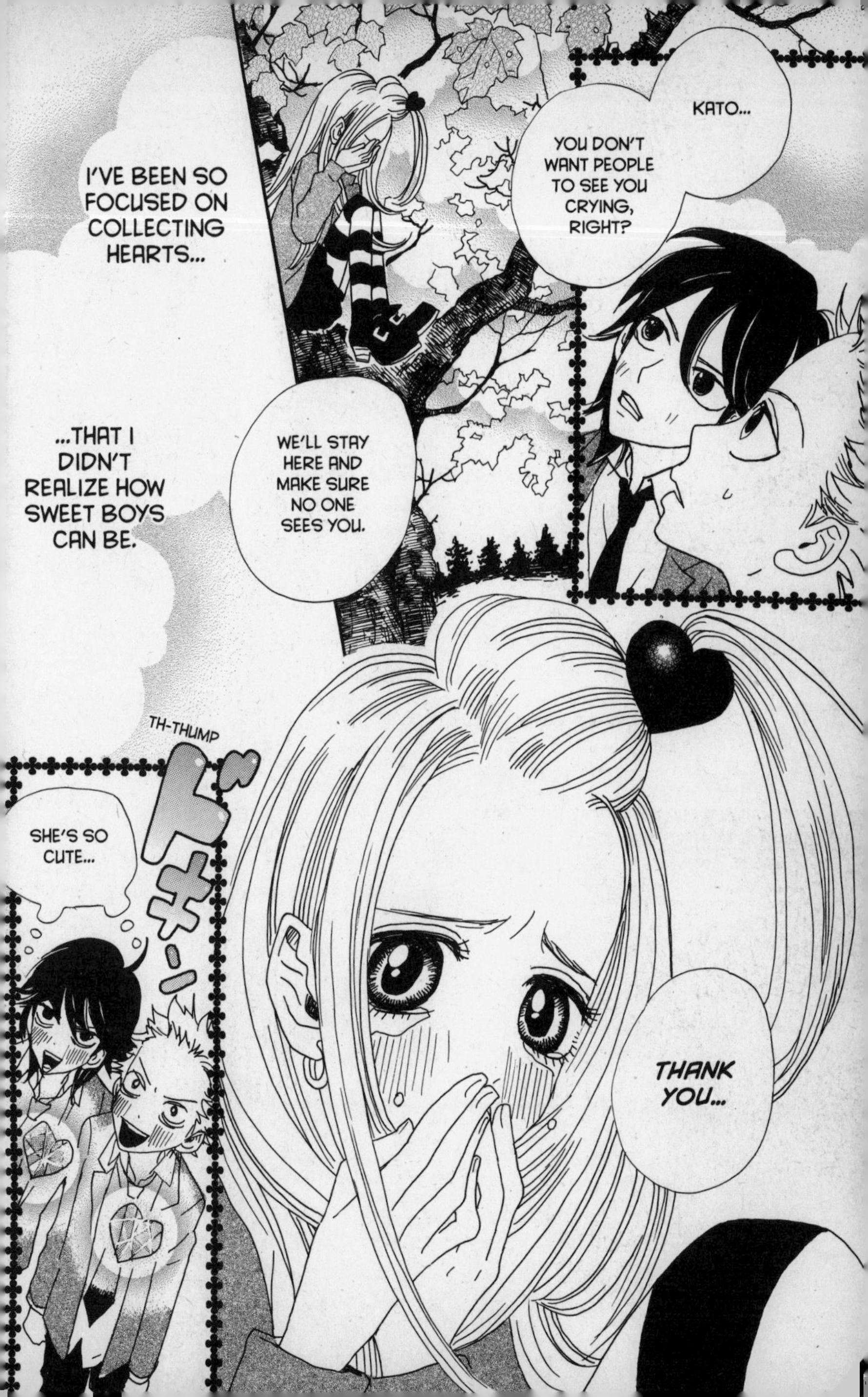
KATO...
YOU DON'T WANT PEOPLE TO SEE YOU CRYING, RIGHT?
WE'LL STAY HERE AND MAKE SURE NO ONE SEES YOU.
I'VE BEEN SO FOCUSED ON COLLECTING HEARTS...
...THAT I DIDN'T REALIZE HOW SWEET BOYS CAN BE.
THANK YOU...
TH-THUMP
ドキー
SHE'S SO CUTE...

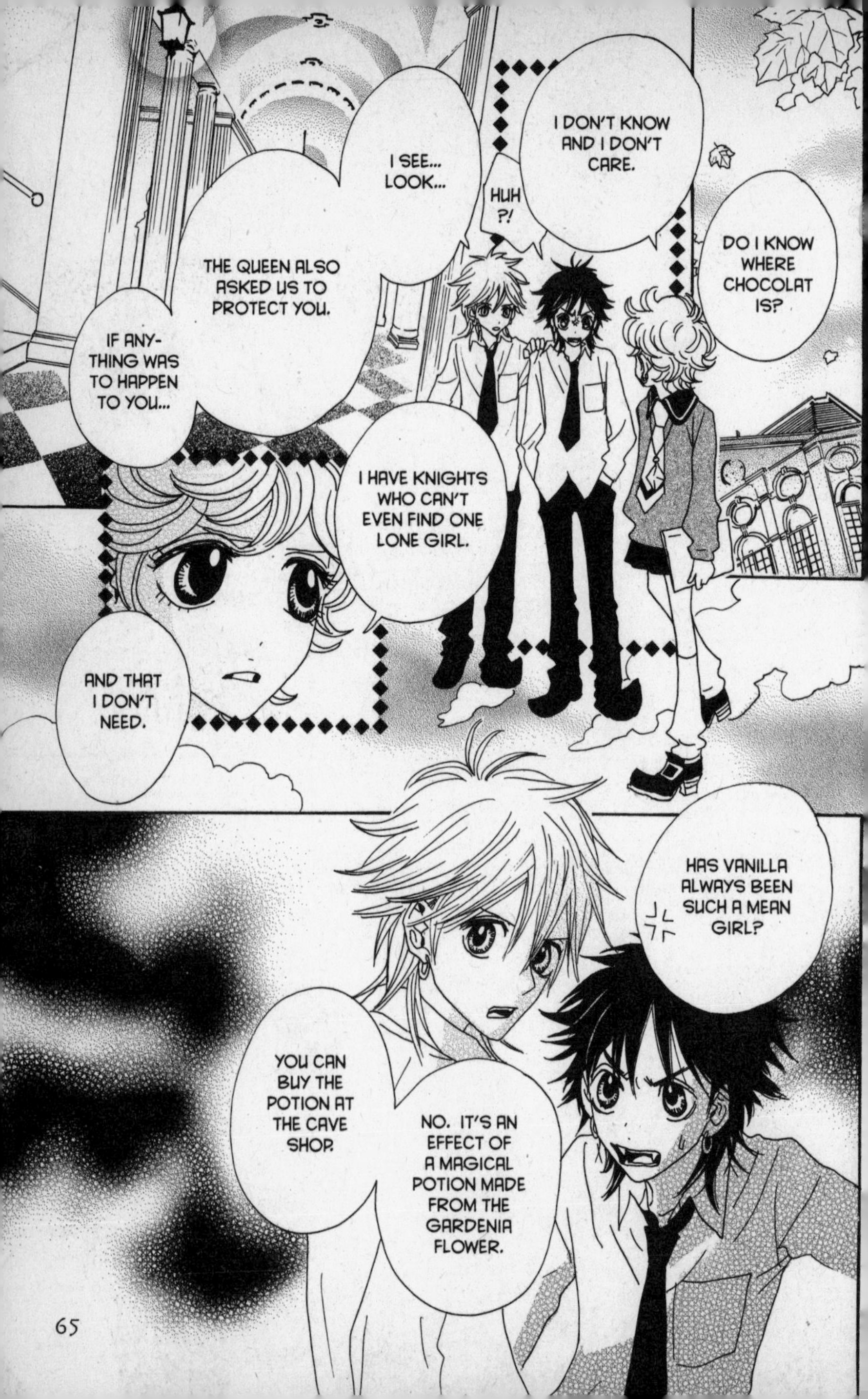
DO I KNOW WHERE CHOCOLAT IS?
I DON'T KNOW AND I DON'T CARE.
HUH ?!
I SEE... LOOK...
THE QUEEN ALSO ASKED US TO PROTECT YOU.
IF ANY-THING WAS TO HAPPEN TO YOU...
I HAVE KNIGHTS WHO CAN'T EVEN FIND ONE LONE GIRL.
AND THAT I DON'T NEED.
HAS VANILLA ALWAYS BEEN SUCH A MEAN GIRL?
NO. IT'S AN EFFECT OF A MAGICAL POTION MADE FROM THE GARDENIA FLOWER.
YOU CAN BUY THE POTION AT THE CAVE SHOP.

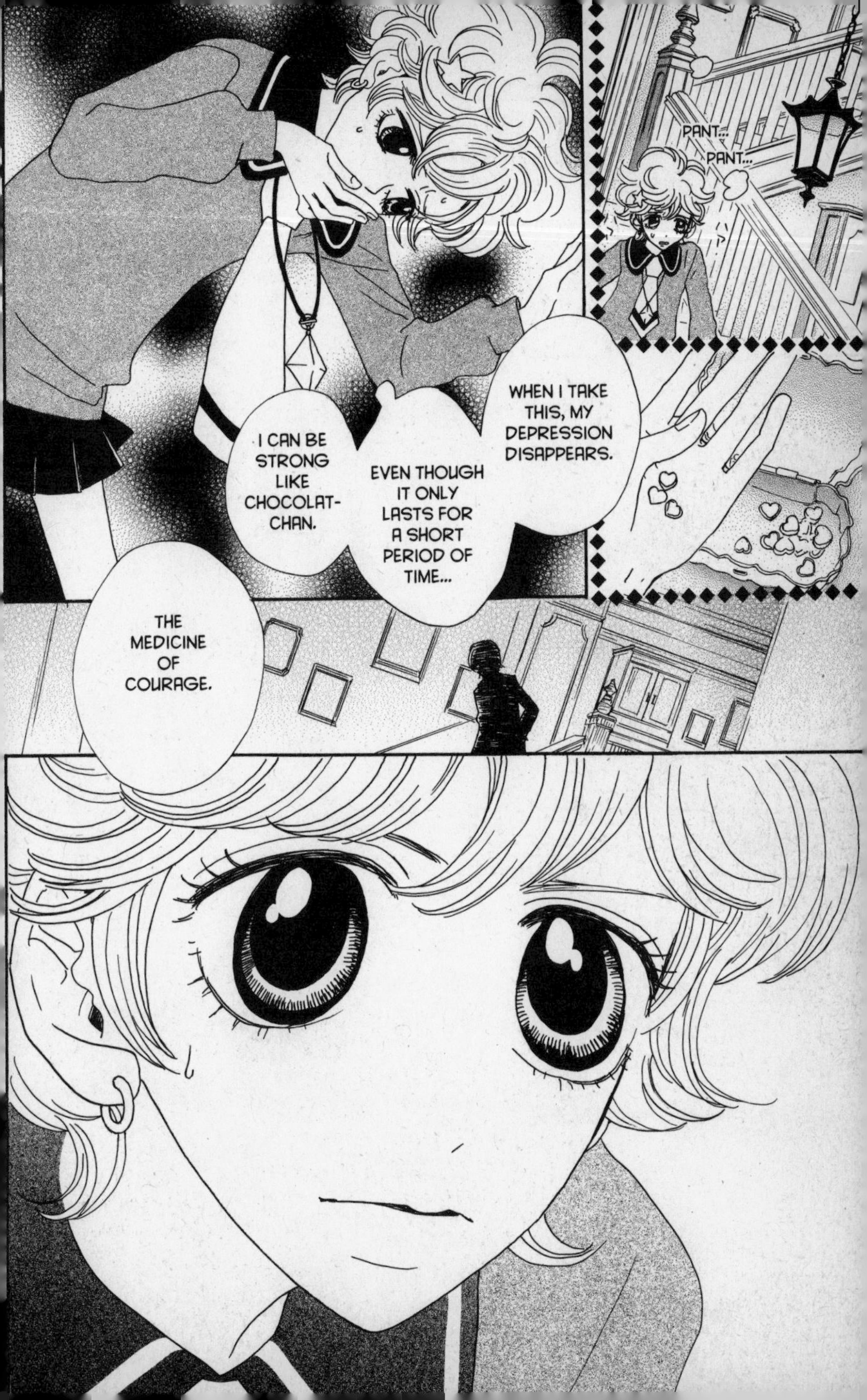
PANT... PANT...
WHEN I TAKE THIS, MY DEPRESSION DISAPPEARS.
EVEN THOUGH IT ONLY LASTS FOR A SHORT PERIOD OF TIME...
I CAN BE STRONG LIKE CHOCOLAT-CHAN.
THE MEDICINE OF COURAGE.

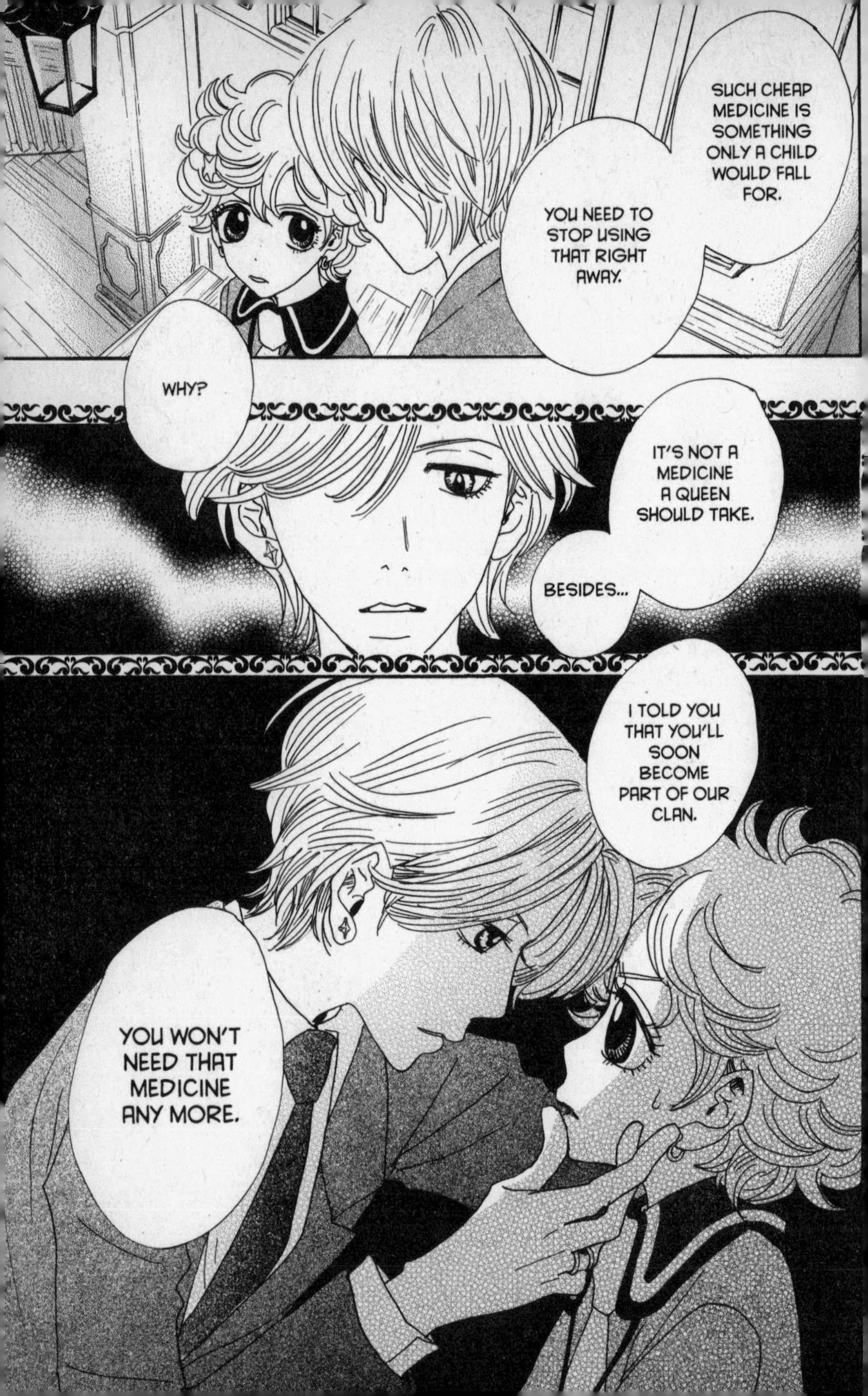
SUCH CHEAP MEDICINE IS SOMETHING ONLY A CHILD WOULD FALL FOR.
YOU NEED TO STOP USING THAT RIGHT AWAY.
WHY?
IT'S NOT A MEDICINE A QUEEN SHOULD TAKE.
BESIDES...
I TOLD YOU THAT YOU'LL SOON BECOME PART OF OUR CLAN.
YOU WON'T NEED THAT MEDICINE ANY MORE.

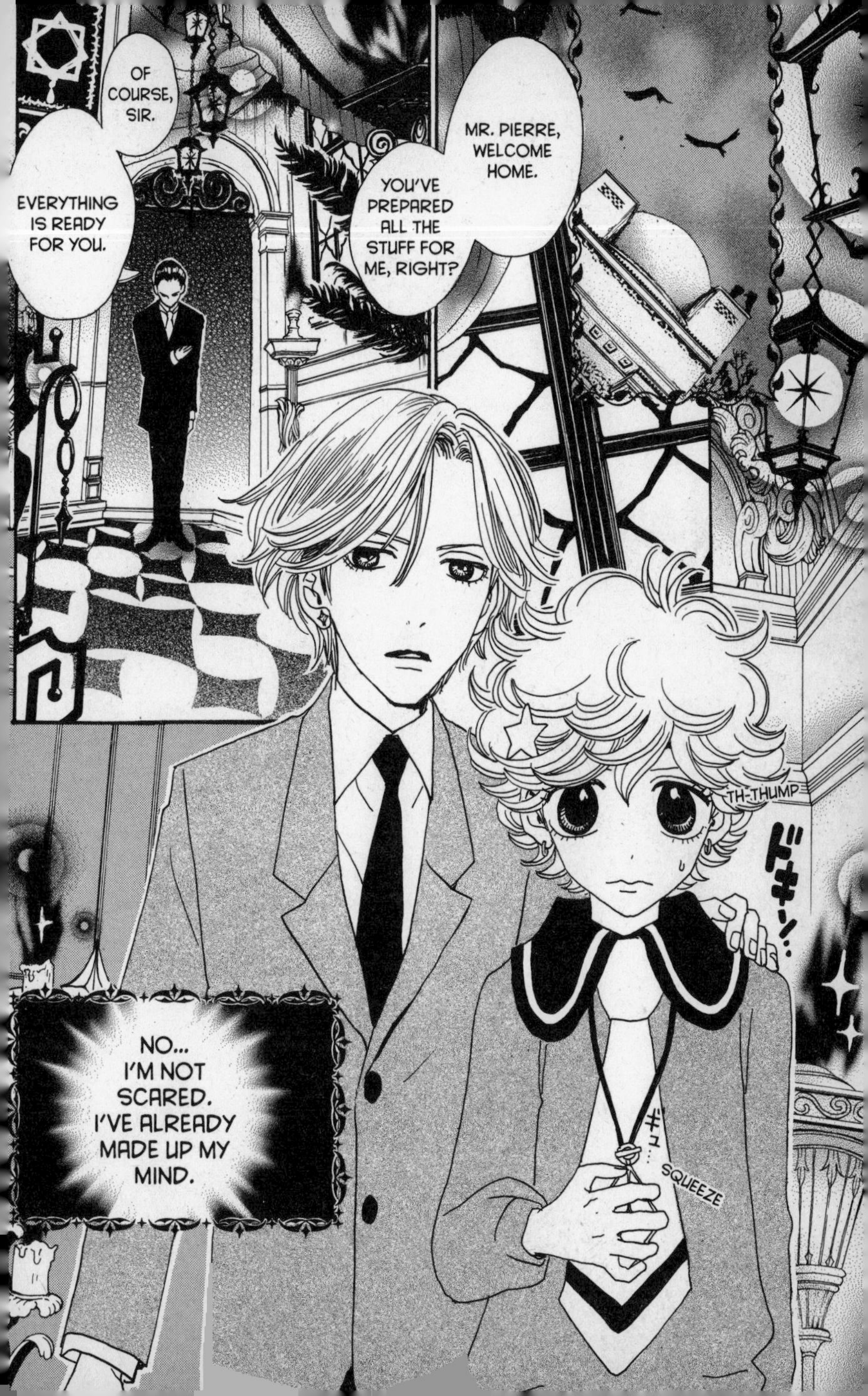

MR. PIERRE, WELCOME HOME.
YOU'VE PREPARED ALL THE STUFF FOR ME, RIGHT?
OF COURSE, SIR.
EVERYTHING IS READY FOR YOU.
TH-THUMP
ドキン…
NO... I'M NOT SCARED. I'VE ALREADY MADE UP MY MIND.
ギュ…
SQUEEZE

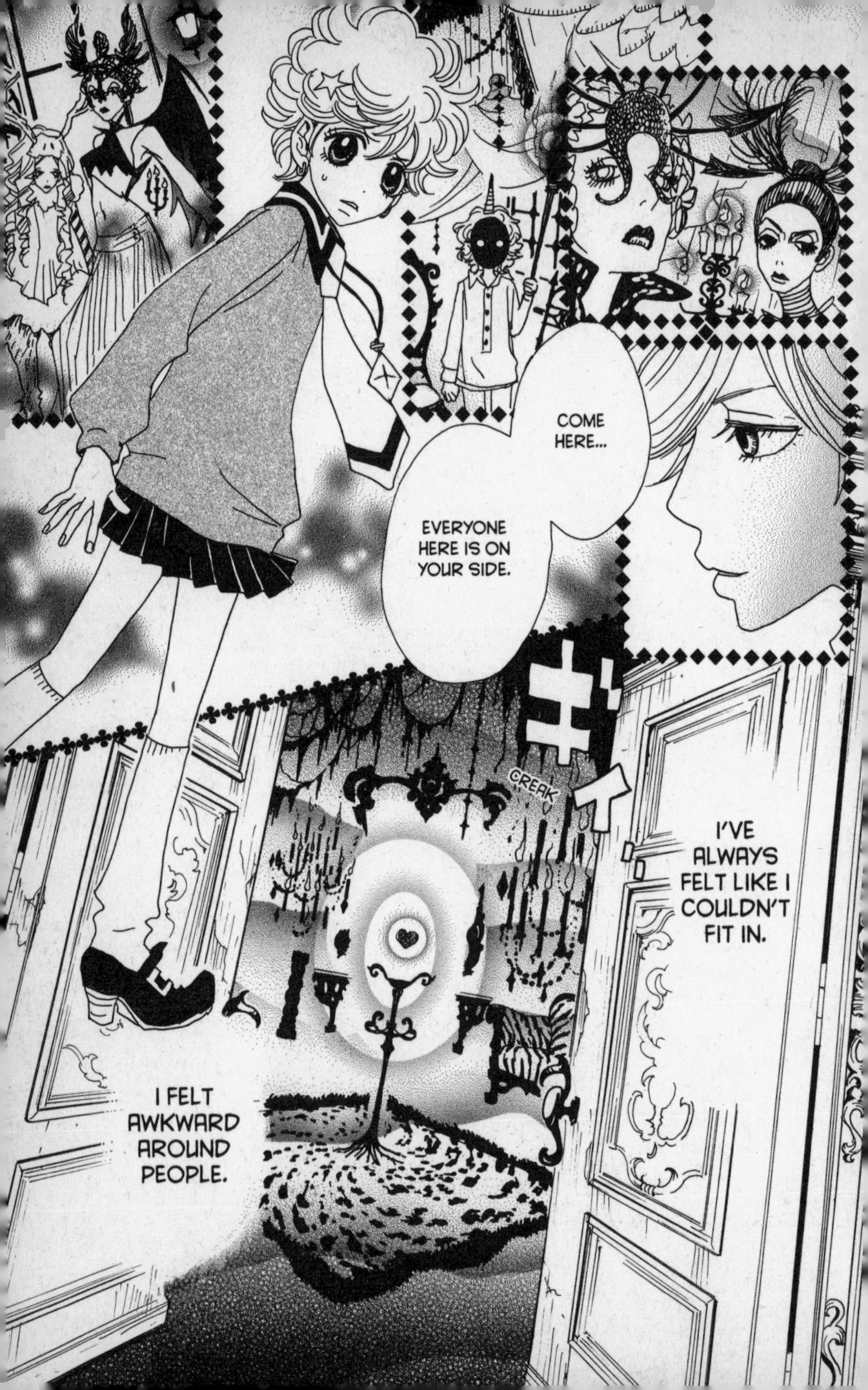
COME HERE...
EVERYONE HERE IS ON YOUR SIDE.
I'VE ALWAYS FELT LIKE I COULDN'T FIT IN.
CREAK
I FELT AWKWARD AROUND PEOPLE.

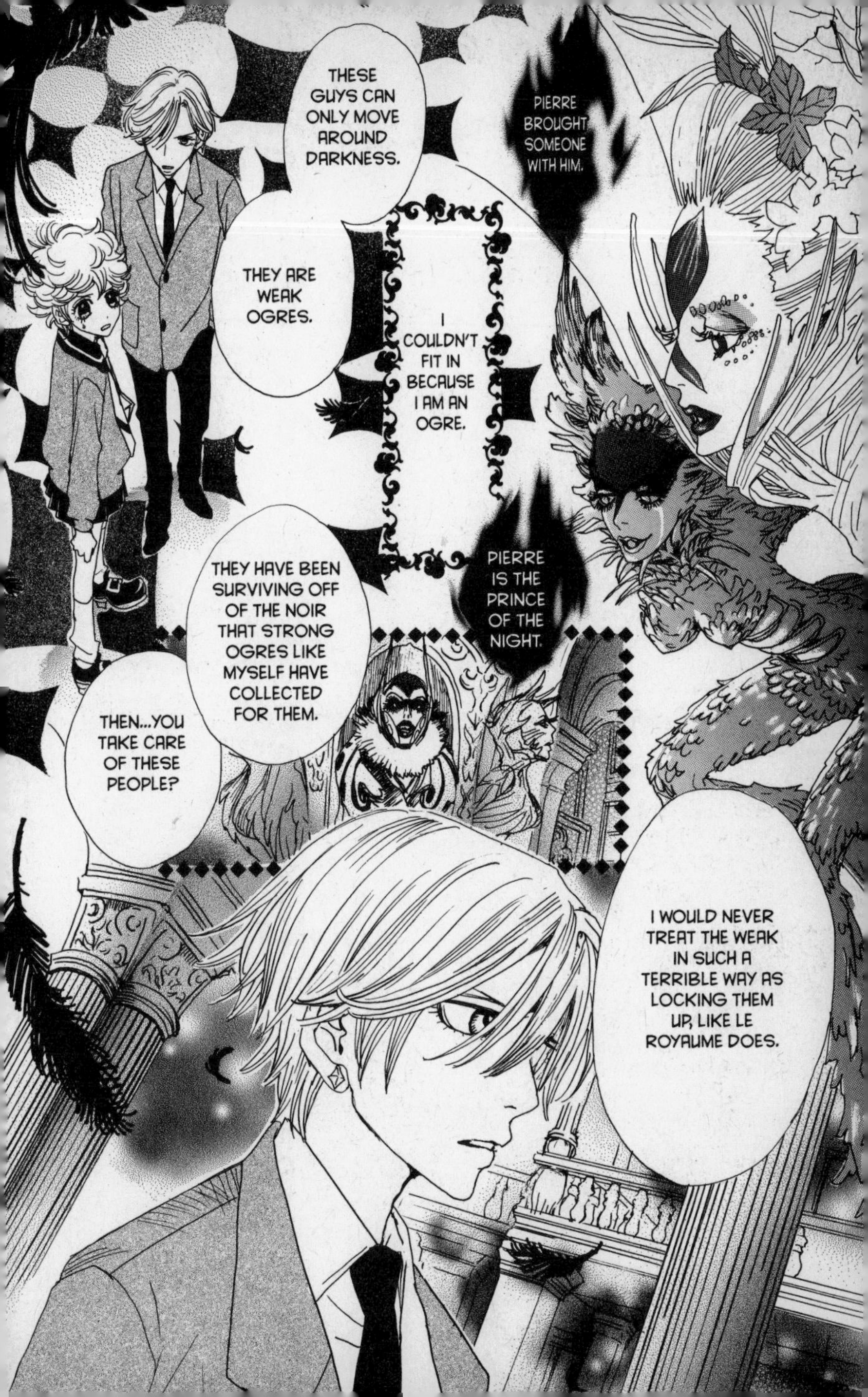
PIERRE BROUGHT SOMEONE WITH HIM.
THESE GUYS CAN ONLY MOVE AROUND DARKNESS.
THEY ARE WEAK OGRES.
I COULDN'T FIT IN BECAUSE I AM AN OGRE.
PIERRE IS THE PRINCE OF THE NIGHT.
THEY HAVE BEEN SURVIVING OFF OF THE NOIR THAT STRONG OGRES LIKE MYSELF HAVE COLLECTED FOR THEM.
THEN...YOU TAKE CARE OF THESE PEOPLE?
I WOULD NEVER TREAT THE WEAK IN SUCH A TERRIBLE WAY AS LOCKING THEM UP, LIKE LE ROYAUME DOES.

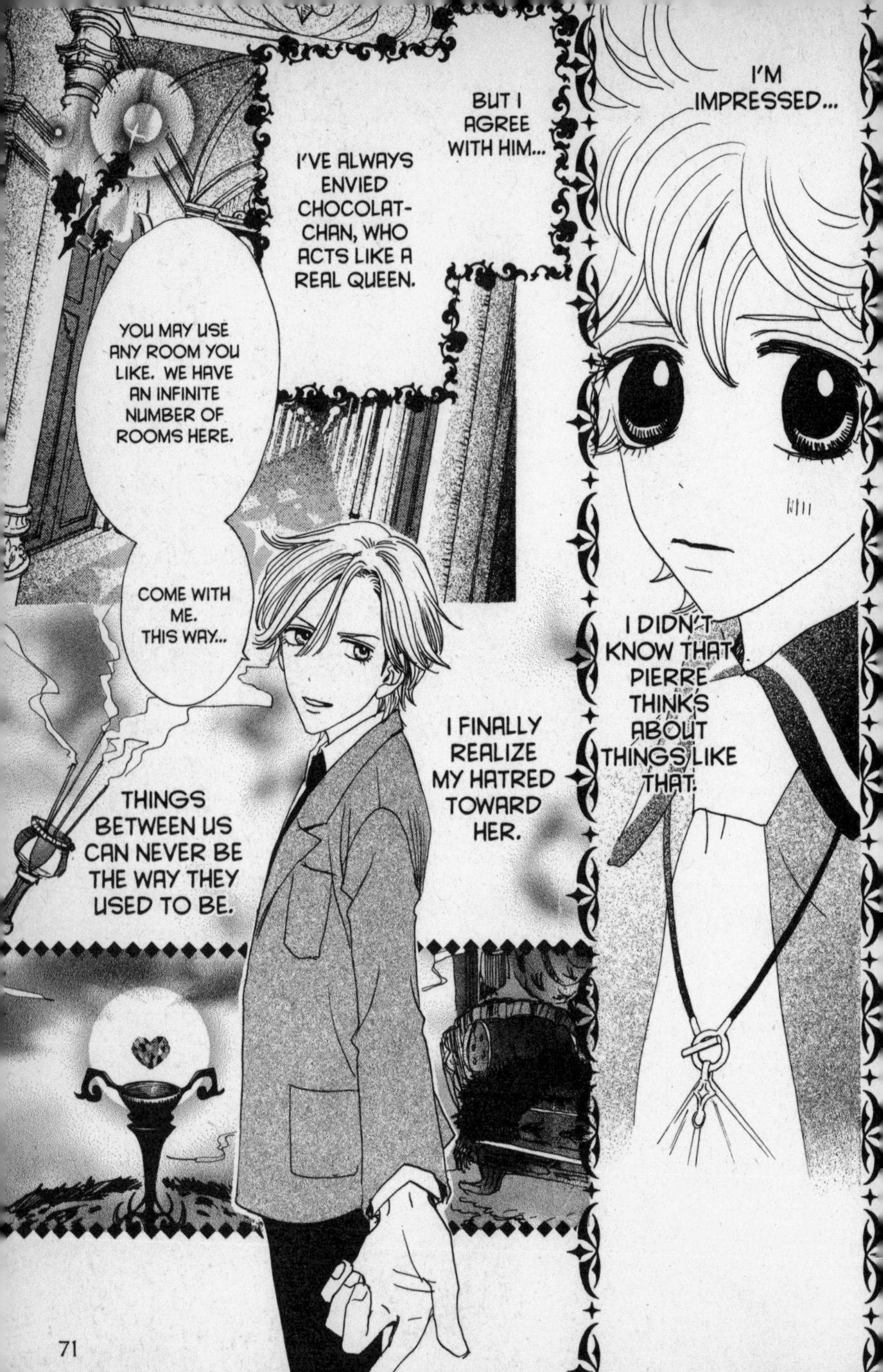
I'M IMPRESSED...
I DIDN'T KNOW THAT PIERRE THINKS ABOUT THINGS LIKE THAT.
BUT I AGREE WITH HIM...
I'VE ALWAYS ENVIED CHOCOLAT-CHAN, WHO ACTS LIKE A REAL QUEEN.
YOU MAY USE ANY ROOM YOU LIKE. WE HAVE AN INFINITE NUMBER OF ROOMS HERE.
COME WITH ME. THIS WAY...
I FINALLY REALIZE MY HATRED TOWARD HER.
THINGS BETWEEN US CAN NEVER BE THE WAY THEY USED TO BE.

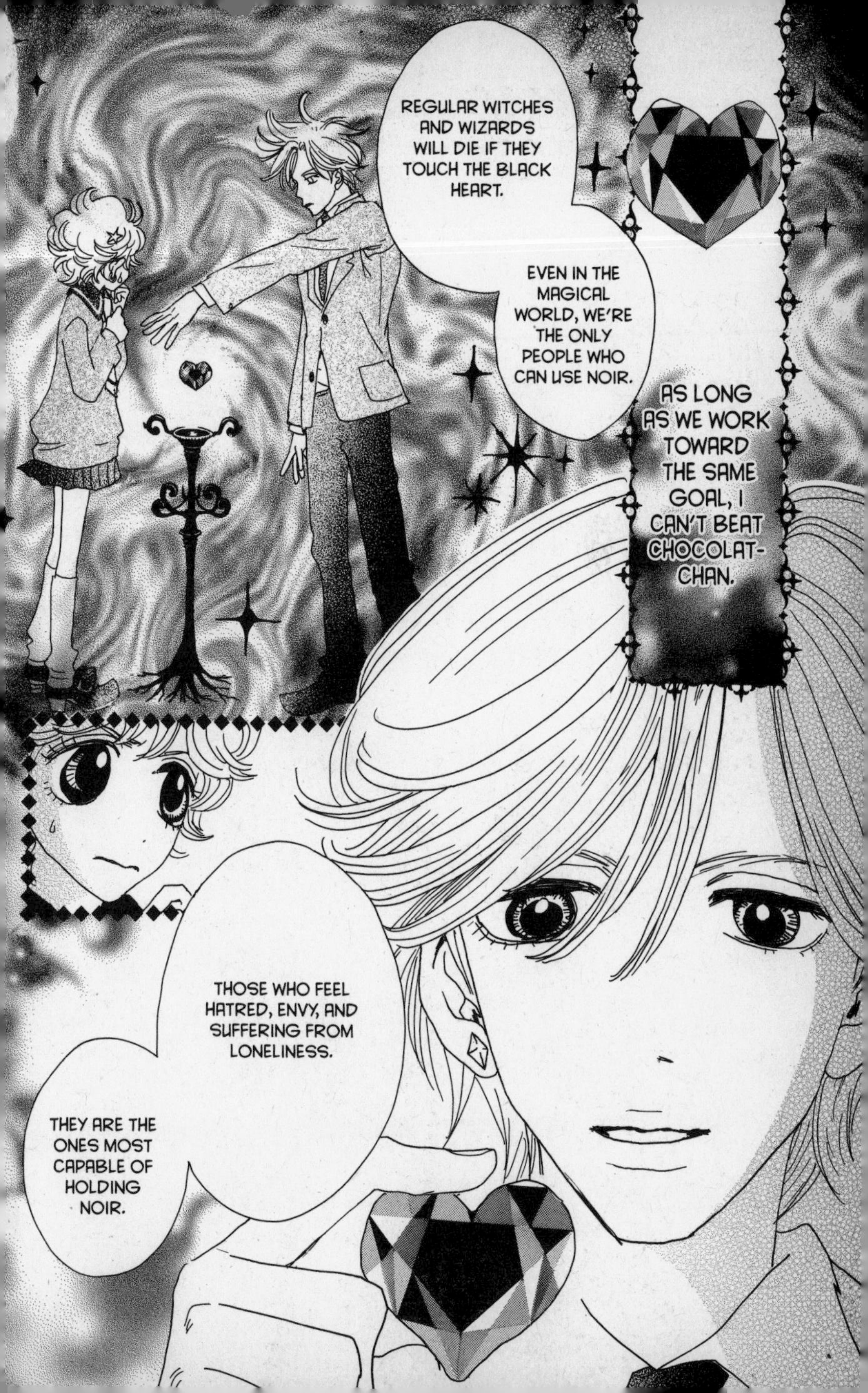
REGULAR WITCHES AND WIZARDS WILL DIE IF THEY TOUCH THE BLACK HEART.
EVEN IN THE MAGICAL WORLD, WE'RE THE ONLY PEOPLE WHO CAN USE NOIR.
AS LONG AS WE WORK TOWARD THE SAME GOAL, I CAN'T BEAT CHOCOLAT-CHAN.
THOSE WHO FEEL HATRED, ENVY, AND SUFFERING FROM LONELINESS.
THEY ARE THE ONES MOST CAPABLE OF HOLDING NOIR.

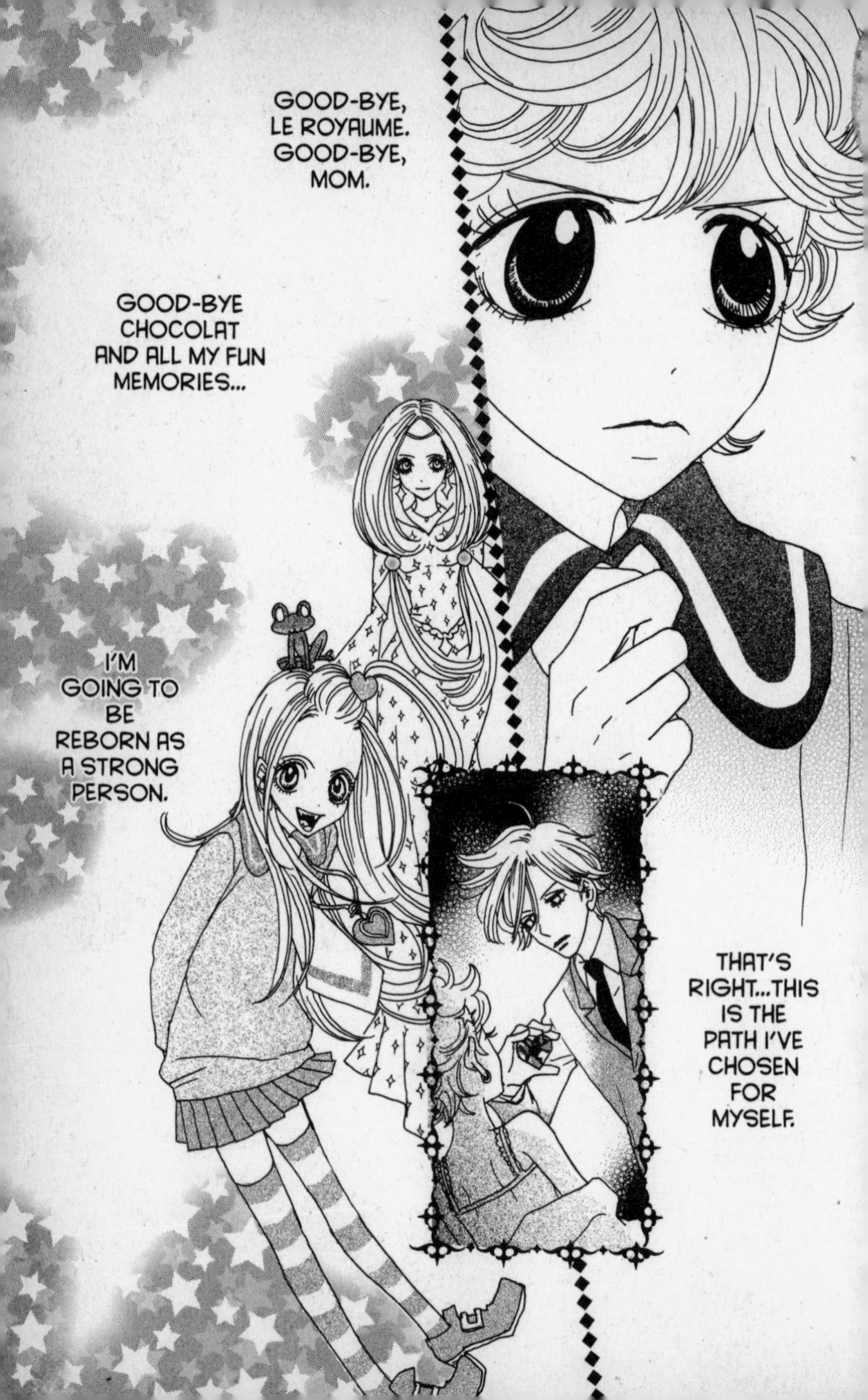
GOOD-BYE, LE ROYAUME. GOOD-BYE, MOM.
GOOD-BYE CHOCOLAT AND ALL MY FUN MEMORIES...
I'M GOING TO BE REBORN AS A STRONG PERSON.
THAT'S RIGHT...THIS IS THE PATH I'VE CHOSEN FOR MYSELF.

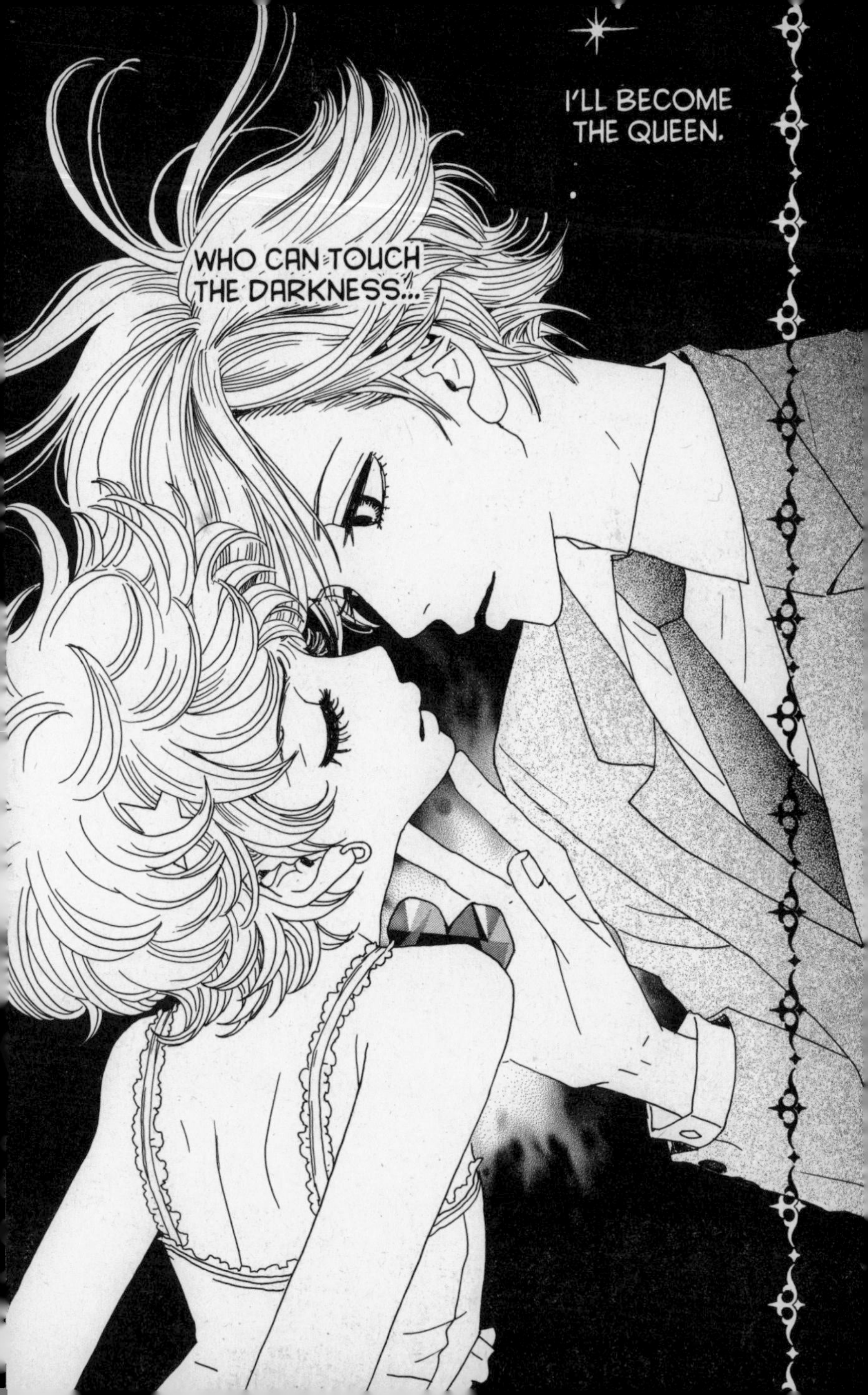
I'LL BECOME THE QUEEN.
WHO CAN TOUCH THE DARKNESS...

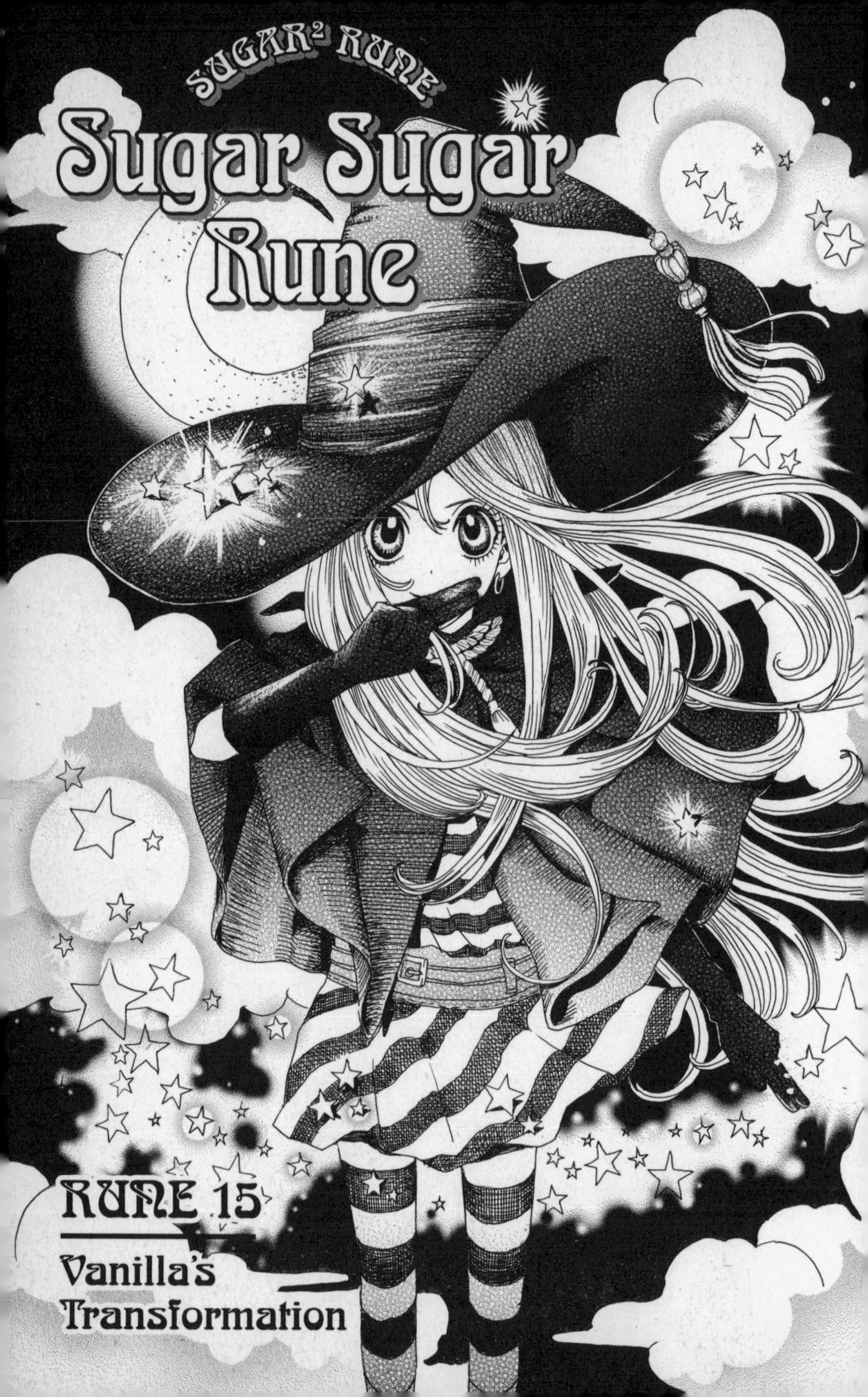
SUGAR² RUNE
Sugar Sugar Rune
RUNE 15
Vanilla's Transformation

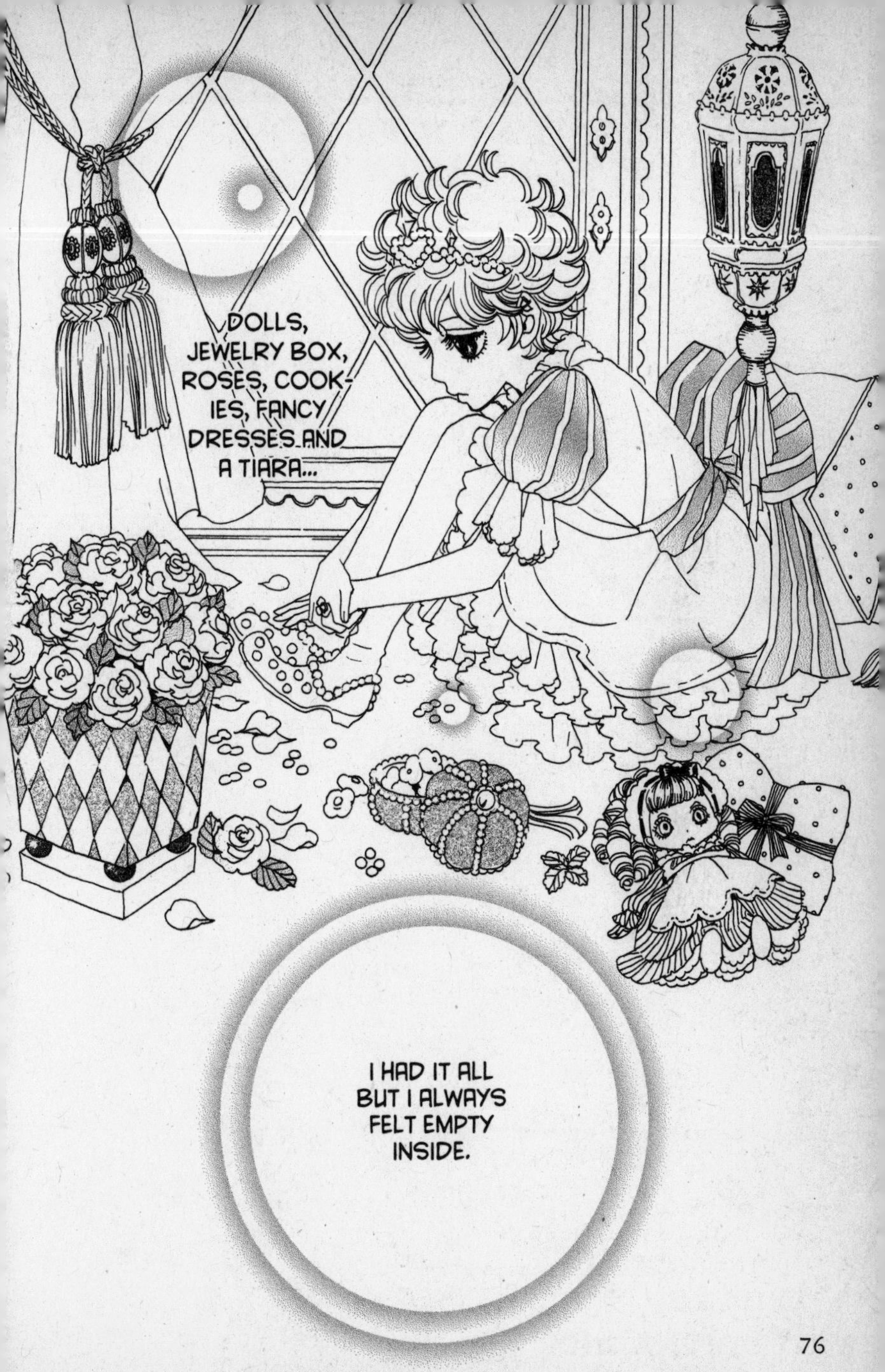
DOLLS, JEWELRY BOX, ROSES, COOK-IES, FANCY DRESSES AND A TIARA...
I HAD IT ALL BUT I ALWAYS FELT EMPTY INSIDE.

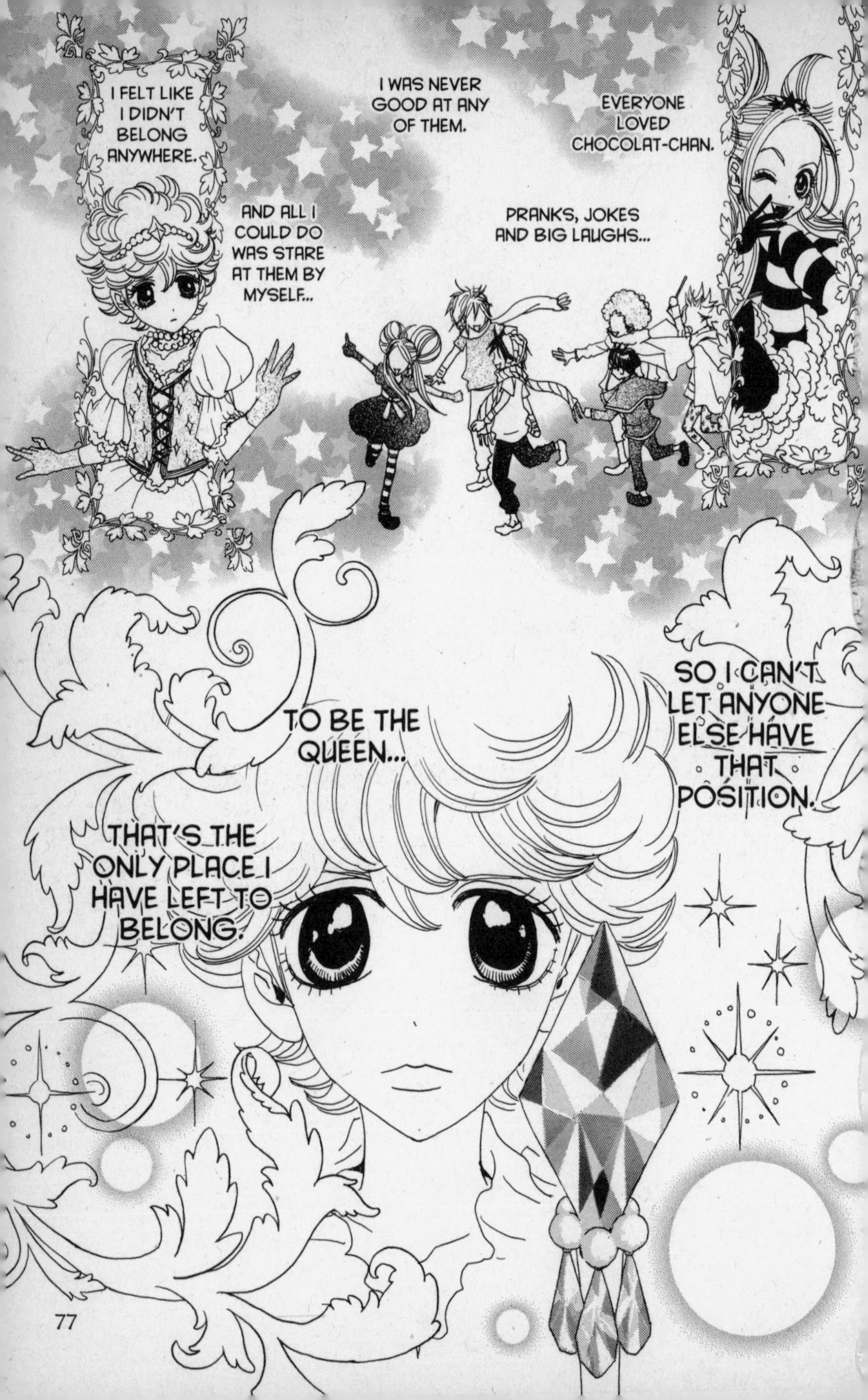
EVERYONE LOVED CHOCOLAT-CHAN.
PRANKS, JOKES AND BIG LAUGHS...
I WAS NEVER GOOD AT ANY OF THEM.
I FELT LIKE I DIDN'T BELONG ANYWHERE.
AND ALL I COULD DO WAS STARE AT THEM BY MYSELF...
SO I CAN'T LET ANYONE ELSE HAVE THAT POSITION.
TO BE THE QUEEN...
THAT'S THE ONLY PLACE I HAVE LEFT TO BELONG.

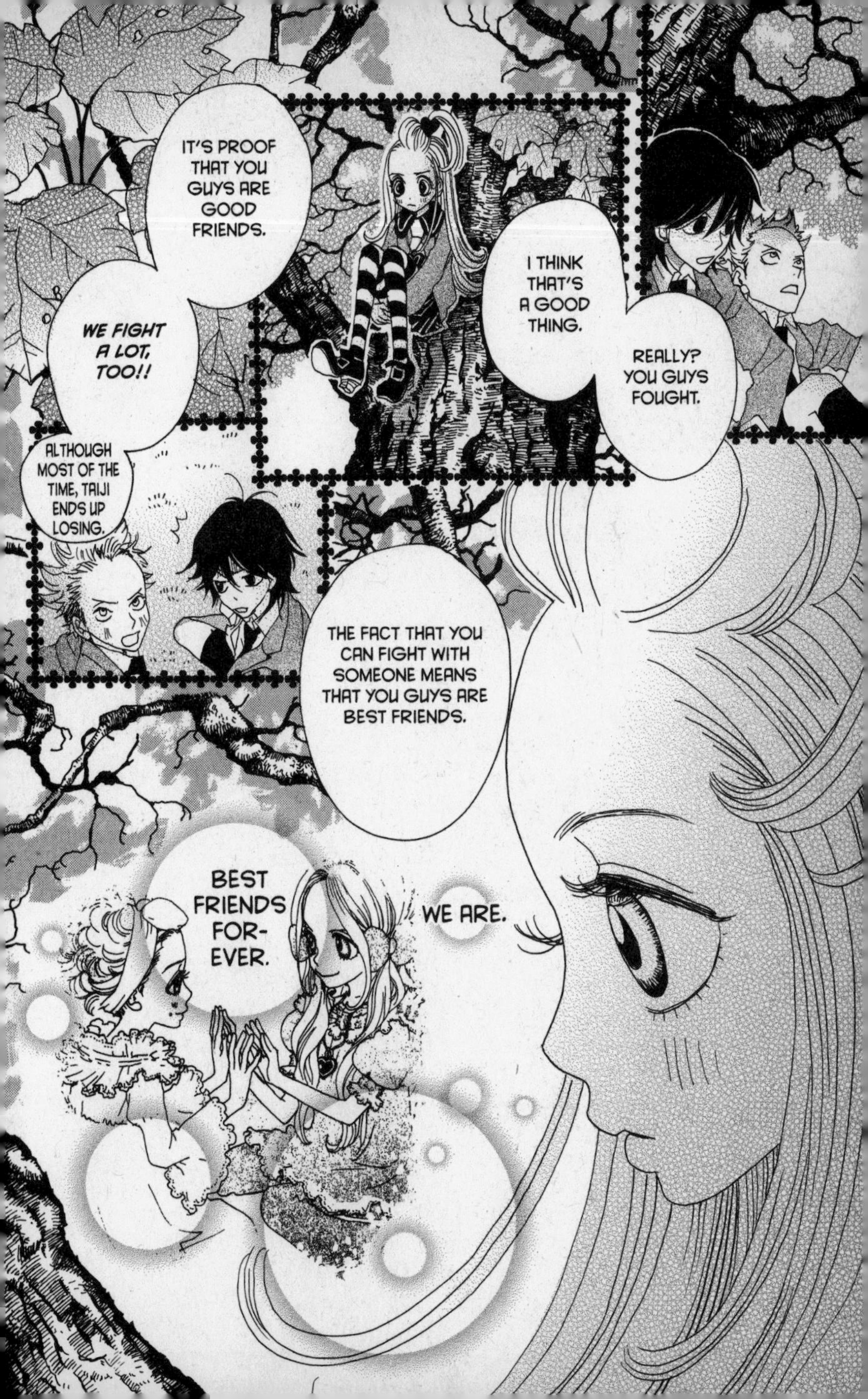
REALLY? YOU GUYS FOUGHT.
WE FIGHT A LOT, TOO!!
ALTHOUGH MOST OF THE TIME, TAIJI ENDS UP LOSING.
IT'S PROOF THAT YOU GUYS ARE GOOD FRIENDS.
I THINK THAT'S A GOOD THING.
THE FACT THAT YOU CAN FIGHT WITH SOMEONE MEANS THAT YOU GUYS ARE BEST FRIENDS.
WE ARE.
BEST FRIENDS FOR-EVER.

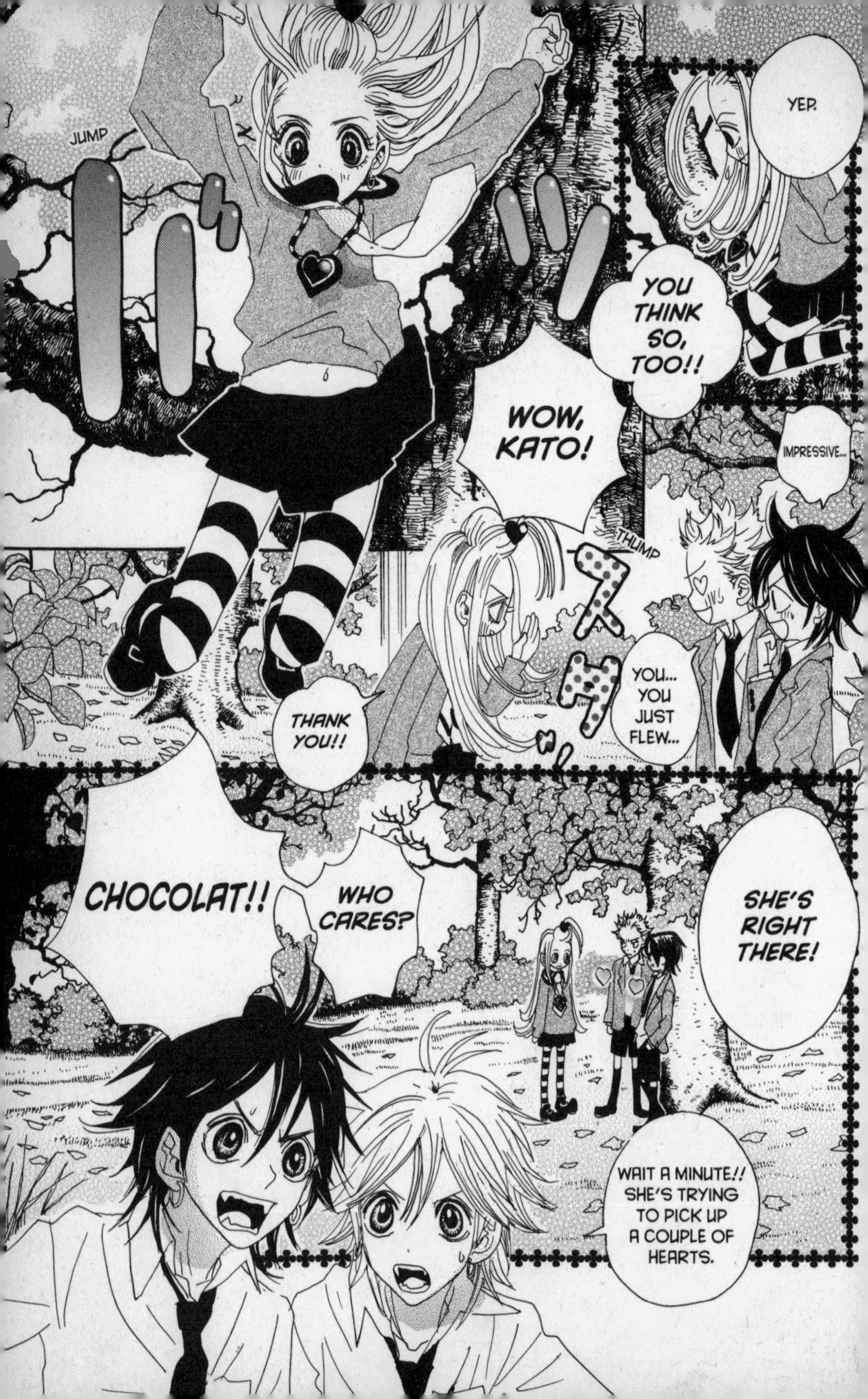
YEP.
YOU THINK SO, TOO!!
JUMP
WOW, KATO!
THANK YOU!!
IMPRESSIVE...
THUMP
YOU... YOU JUST FLEW...
SHE'S RIGHT THERE!
WAIT A MINUTE!! SHE'S TRYING TO PICK UP A COUPLE OF HEARTS.
WHO CARES?
CHOCOLAT!!

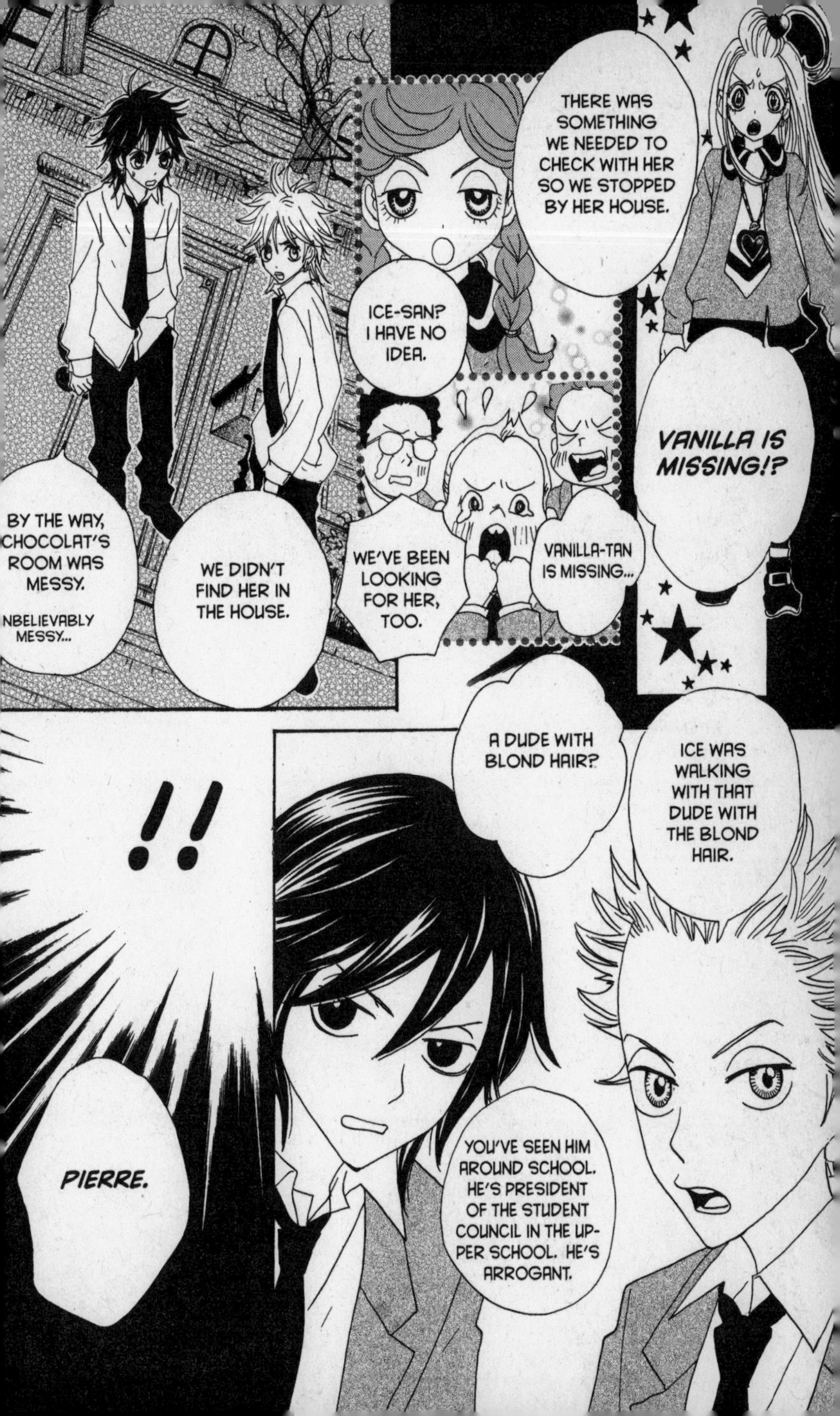
THERE WAS SOMETHING WE NEEDED TO CHECK WITH HER SO WE STOPPED BY HER HOUSE.
VANILLA IS MISSING!?
ICE-SAN? I HAVE NO IDEA.
VANILLA-TAN IS MISSING...
WE'VE BEEN LOOKING FOR HER, TOO.
WE DIDN'T FIND HER IN THE HOUSE.
BY THE WAY, CHOCOLAT'S ROOM WAS MESSY.
NBELIEVABLY MESSY...
ICE WAS WALKING WITH THAT DUDE WITH THE BLOND HAIR.
A DUDE WITH BLOND HAIR?
YOU'VE SEEN HIM AROUND SCHOOL. HE'S PRESIDENT OF THE STUDENT COUNCIL IN THE UP-PER SCHOOL. HE'S ARROGANT.
!!
PIERRE.

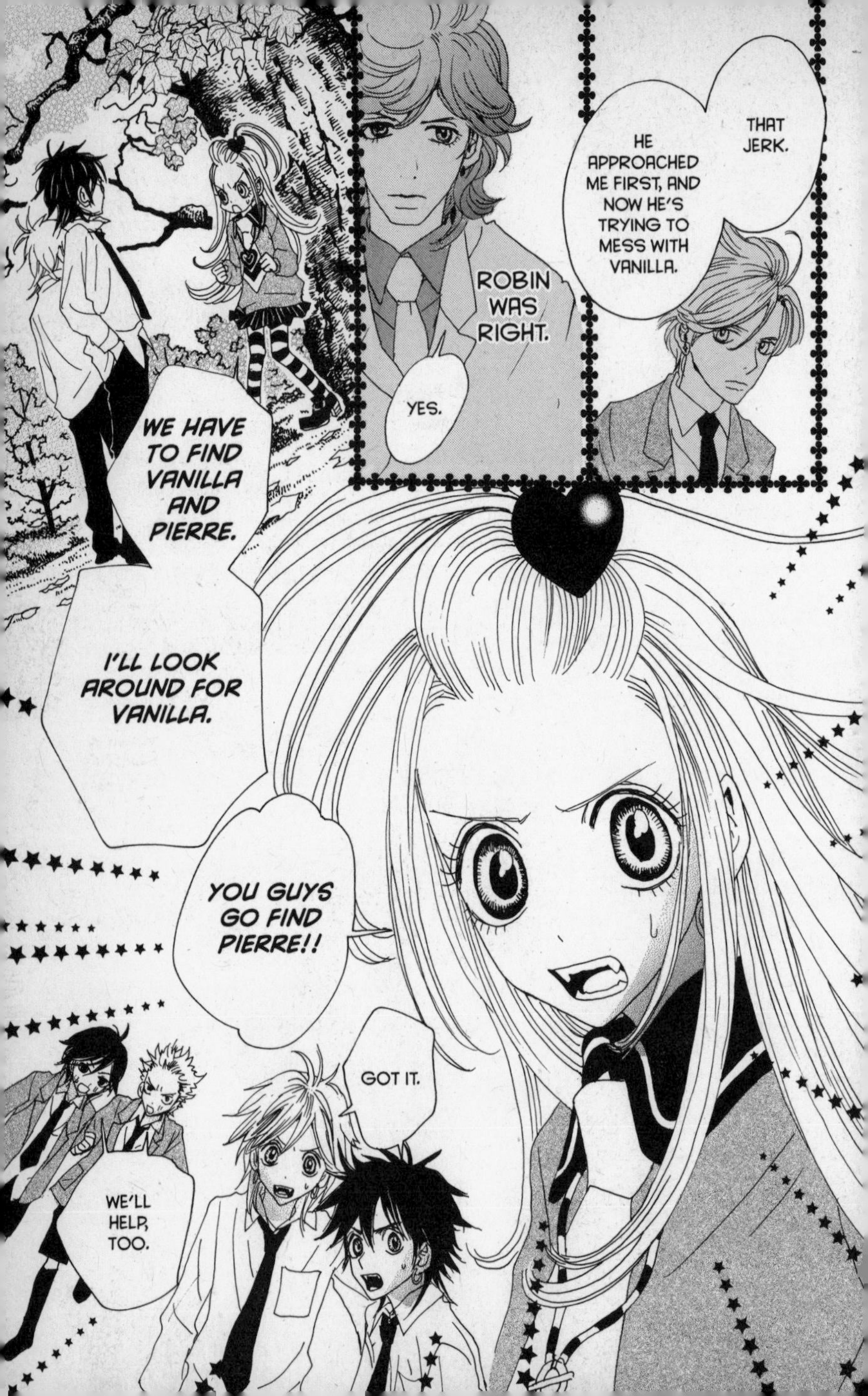
THAT JERK.
HE APPROACHED ME FIRST, AND NOW HE'S TRYING TO MESS WITH VANILLA.
ROBIN WAS RIGHT.
YES.
WE HAVE TO FIND VANILLA AND PIERRE.
I'LL LOOK AROUND FOR VANILLA.
YOU GUYS GO FIND PIERRE!!
GOT IT.
WE'LL HELP, TOO.

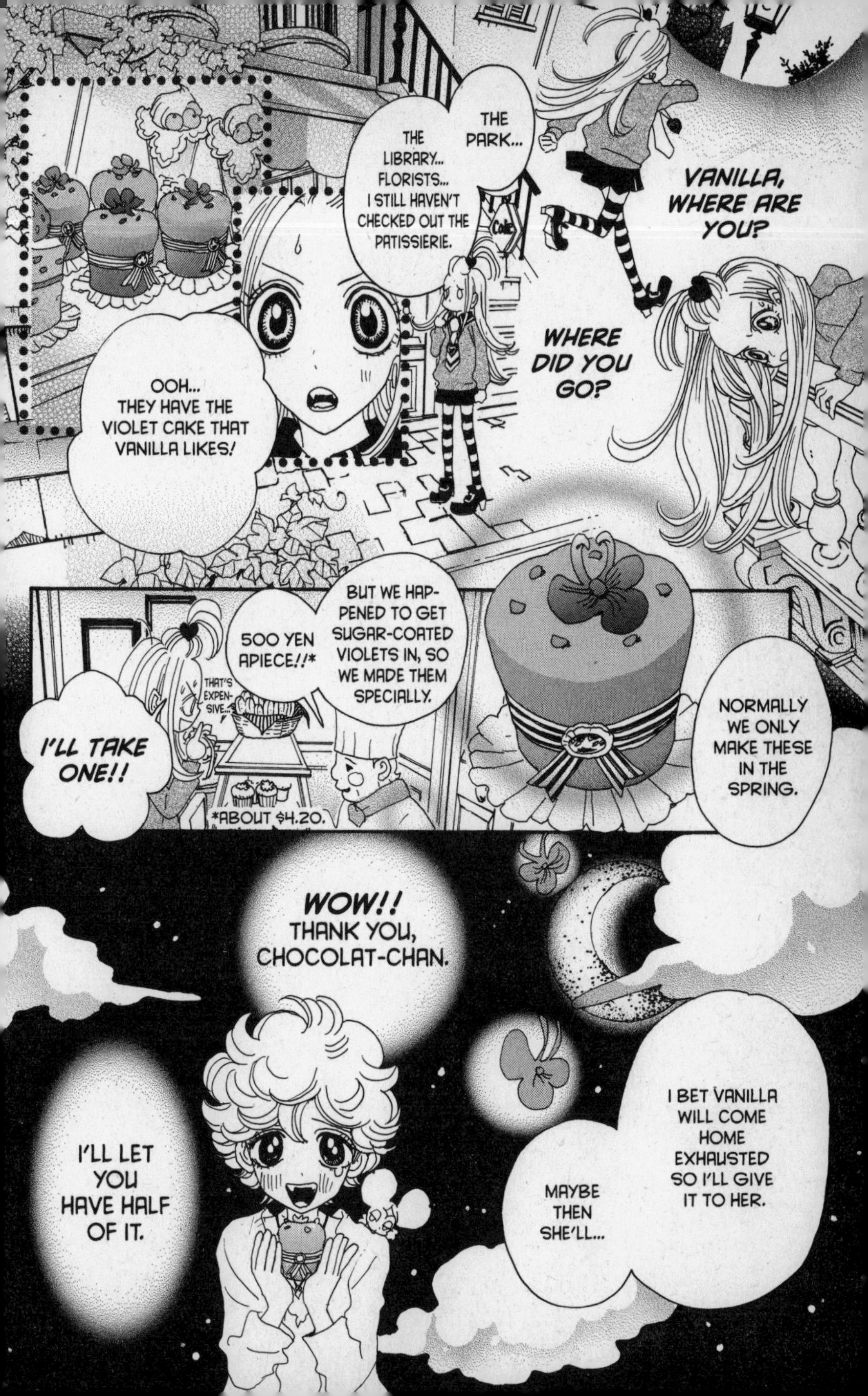
VANILLA, WHERE ARE YOU?
WHERE DID YOU GO?
THE PARK...
THE LIBRARY... FLORISTS... I STILL HAVEN'T CHECKED OUT THE PATISSIERIE.
OOH... THEY HAVE THE VIOLET CAKE THAT VANILLA LIKES!
NORMALLY WE ONLY MAKE THESE IN THE SPRING.
BUT WE HAPPENED TO GET SUGAR-COATED VIOLETS IN, SO WE MADE THEM SPECIALLY.
500 YEN APIECE!!*
THAT'S EXPENSIVE...
I'LL TAKE ONE!!
*ABOUT $4.20.
I BET VANILLA WILL COME HOME EXHAUSTED SO I'LL GIVE IT TO HER.
MAYBE THEN SHE'LL...
WOW!! THANK YOU, CHOCOLAT-CHAN.
I'LL LET YOU HAVE HALF OF IT.

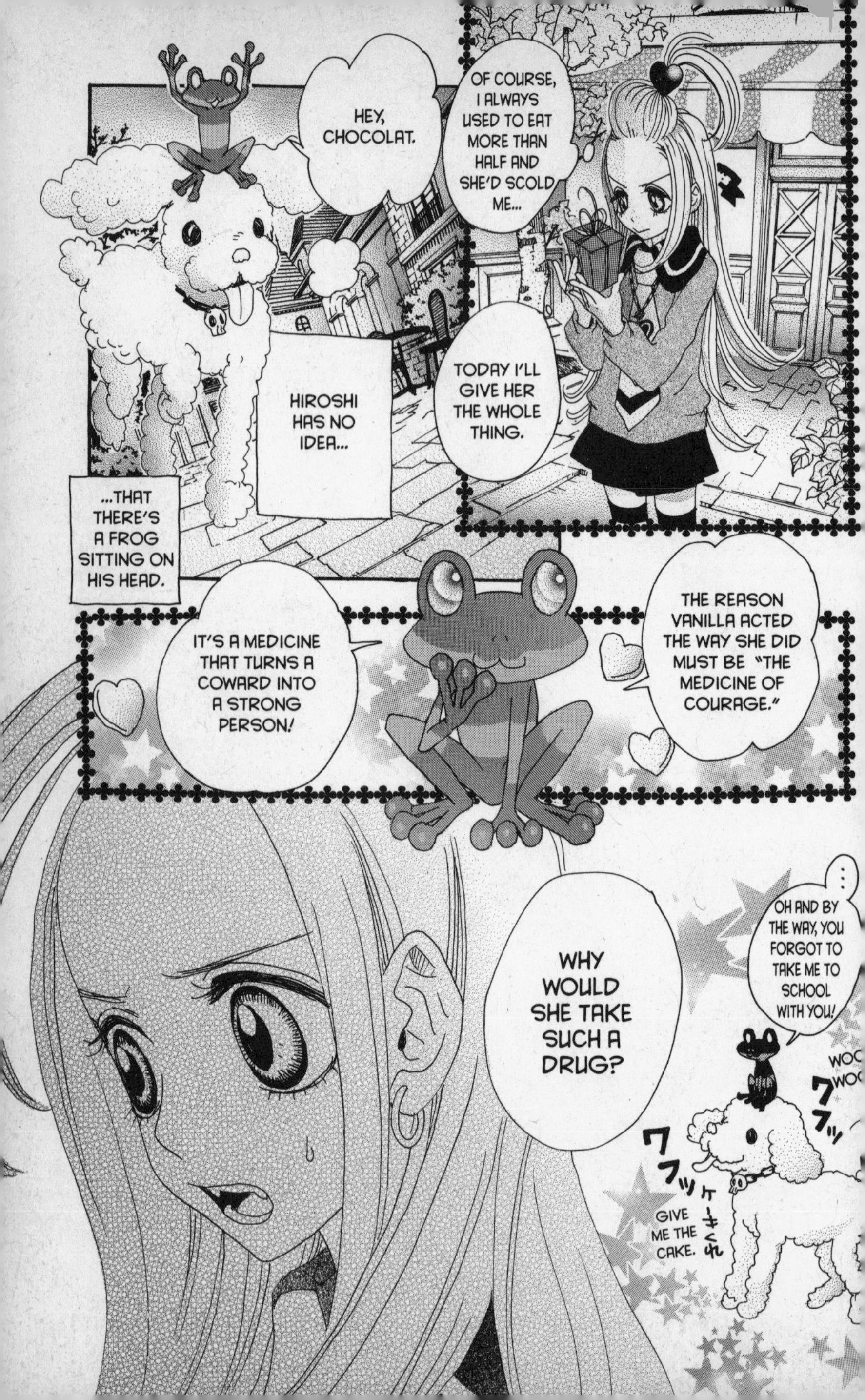

OF COURSE, I ALWAYS USED TO EAT MORE THAN HALF AND SHE'D SCOLD ME...
TODAY I'LL GIVE HER THE WHOLE THING.
HEY, CHOCOLAT.
HIROSHI HAS NO IDEA...
...THAT THERE'S A FROG SITTING ON HIS HEAD.
THE REASON VANILLA ACTED THE WAY SHE DID MUST BE "THE MEDICINE OF COURAGE."
IT'S A MEDICINE THAT TURNS A COWARD INTO A STRONG PERSON!
...
OH AND BY THE WAY, YOU FORGOT TO TAKE ME TO SCHOOL WITH YOU!
ワフッ
ワフッ
ケーキくれ
GIVE ME THE CAKE.
WHY WOULD SHE TAKE SUCH A DRUG?

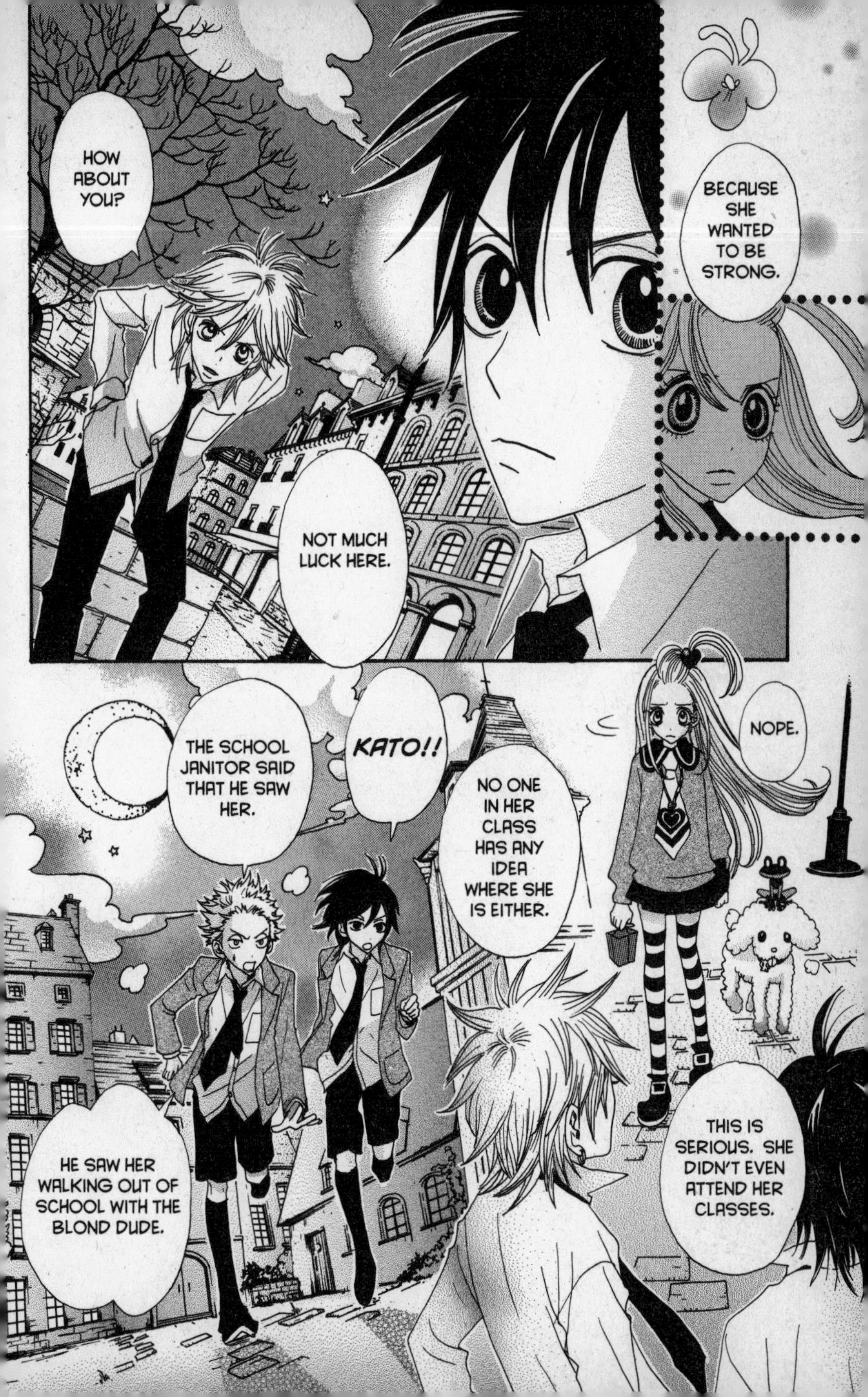
BECAUSE SHE WANTED TO BE STRONG.
HOW ABOUT YOU?
NOT MUCH LUCK HERE.
NOPE.
NO ONE IN HER CLASS HAS ANY IDEA WHERE SHE IS EITHER.
THIS IS SERIOUS. SHE DIDN'T EVEN ATTEND HER CLASSES.
KATO!!
THE SCHOOL JANITOR SAID THAT HE SAW HER.
HE SAW HER WALKING OUT OF SCHOOL WITH THE BLOND DUDE.

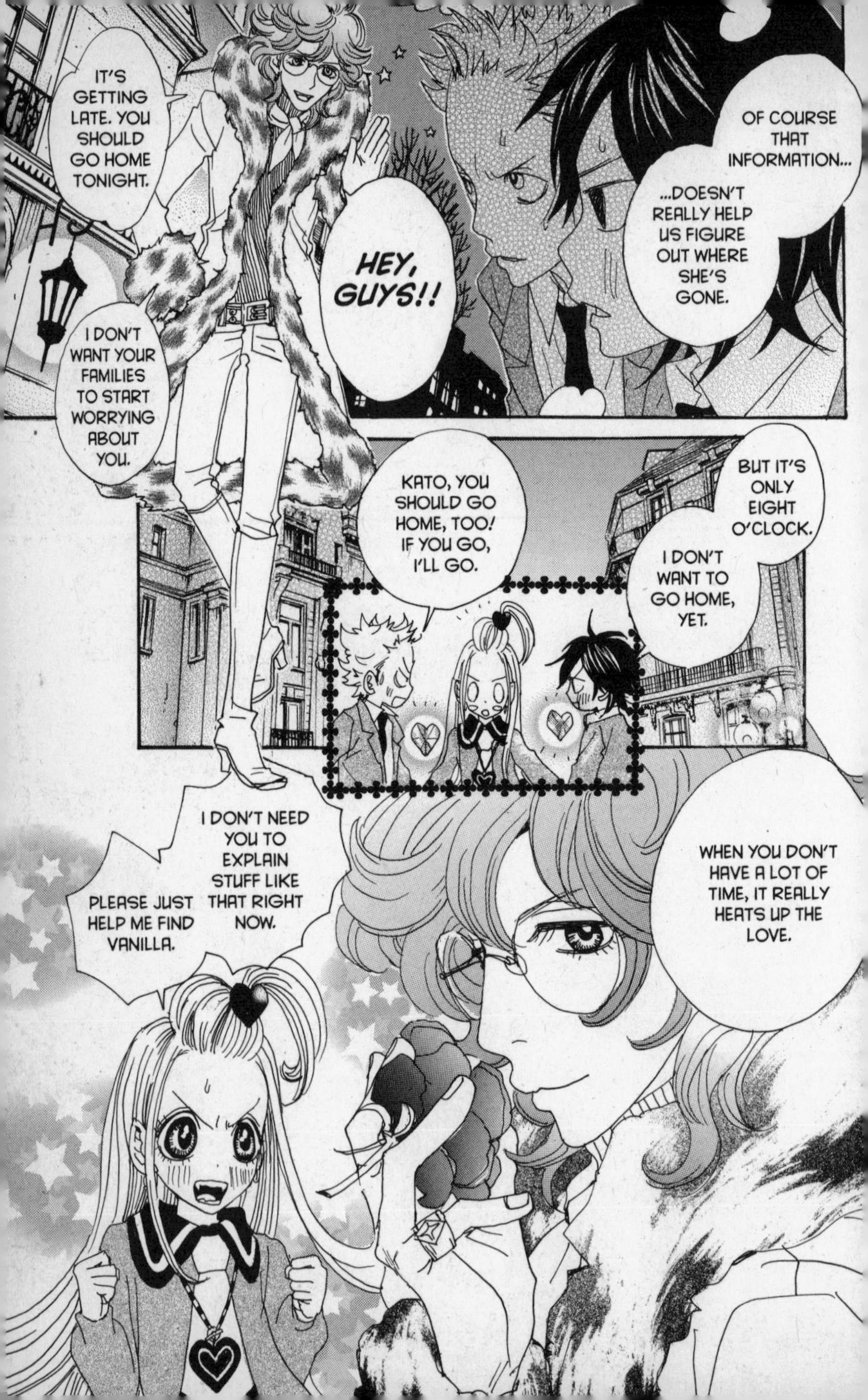
OF COURSE THAT INFORMATION...
...DOESN'T REALLY HELP US FIGURE OUT WHERE SHE'S GONE.
HEY, GUYS!!
IT'S GETTING LATE. YOU SHOULD GO HOME TONIGHT.
I DON'T WANT YOUR FAMILIES TO START WORRYING ABOUT YOU.
BUT IT'S ONLY EIGHT O'CLOCK.
I DON'T WANT TO GO HOME, YET.
KATO, YOU SHOULD GO HOME, TOO! IF YOU GO, I'LL GO.
WHEN YOU DON'T HAVE A LOT OF TIME, IT REALLY HEATS UP THE LOVE.
I DON'T NEED YOU TO EXPLAIN STUFF LIKE THAT RIGHT NOW.
PLEASE JUST HELP ME FIND VANILLA.

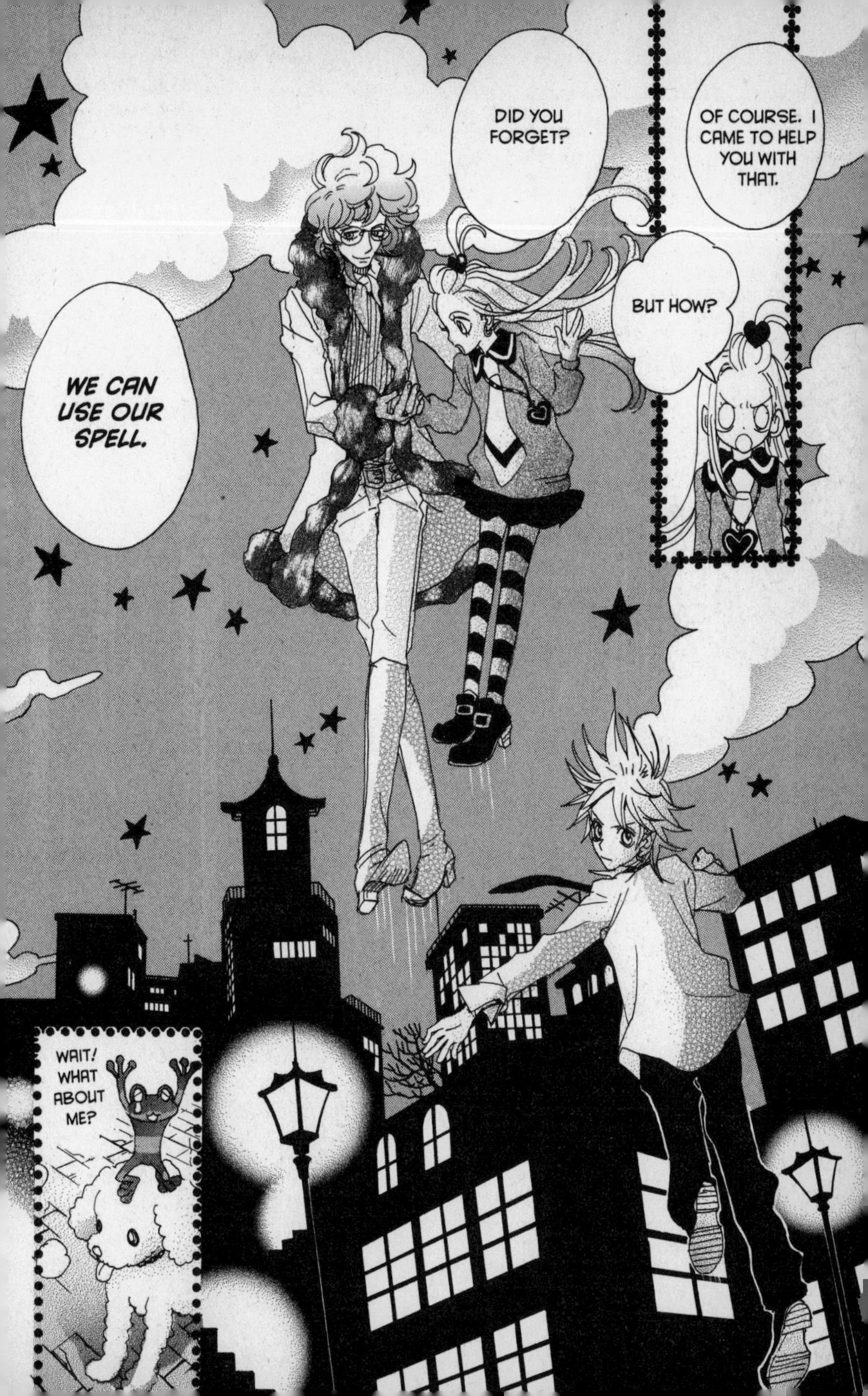
OF COURSE. I CAME TO HELP YOU WITH THAT.
DID YOU FORGET?
BUT HOW?
WE CAN USE OUR SPELL.
WAIT! WHAT ABOUT ME?

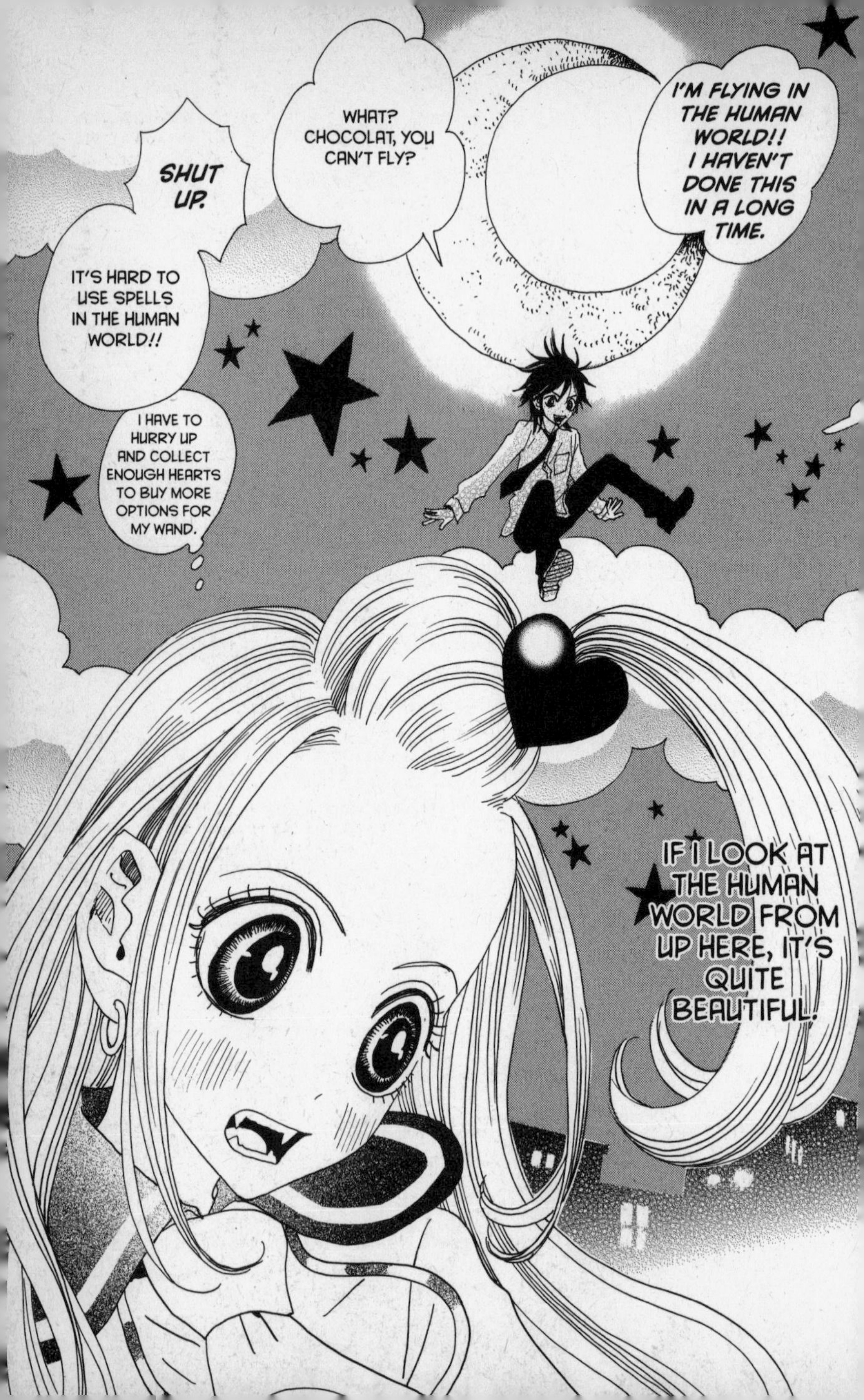
I'M FLYING IN THE HUMAN WORLD!! I HAVEN'T DONE THIS IN A LONG TIME.
WHAT? CHOCOLAT, YOU CAN'T FLY?
SHUT UP.
IT'S HARD TO USE SPELLS IN THE HUMAN WORLD!!
I HAVE TO HURRY UP AND COLLECT ENOUGH HEARTS TO BUY MORE OPTIONS FOR MY WAND.
IF I LOOK AT THE HUMAN WORLD FROM UP HERE, IT'S QUITE BEAUTIFUL.

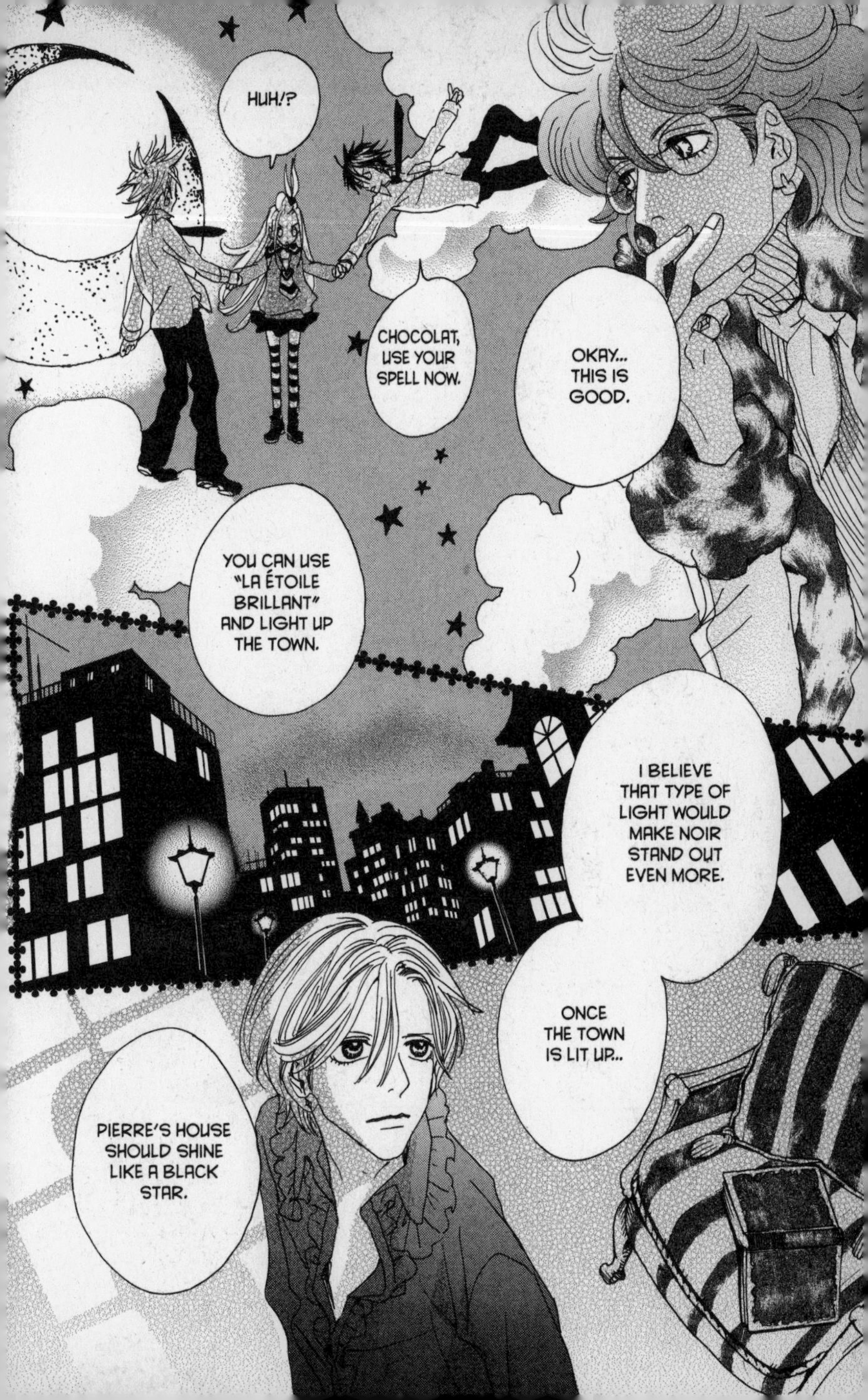
CHOCOLAT, USE YOUR SPELL NOW.
HUH!?
YOU CAN USE "LA ÉTOILE BRILLANT" AND LIGHT UP THE TOWN.
OKAY... THIS IS GOOD.
I BELIEVE THAT TYPE OF LIGHT WOULD MAKE NOIR STAND OUT EVEN MORE.
ONCE THE TOWN IS LIT UP...
PIERRE'S HOUSE SHOULD SHINE LIKE A BLACK STAR.

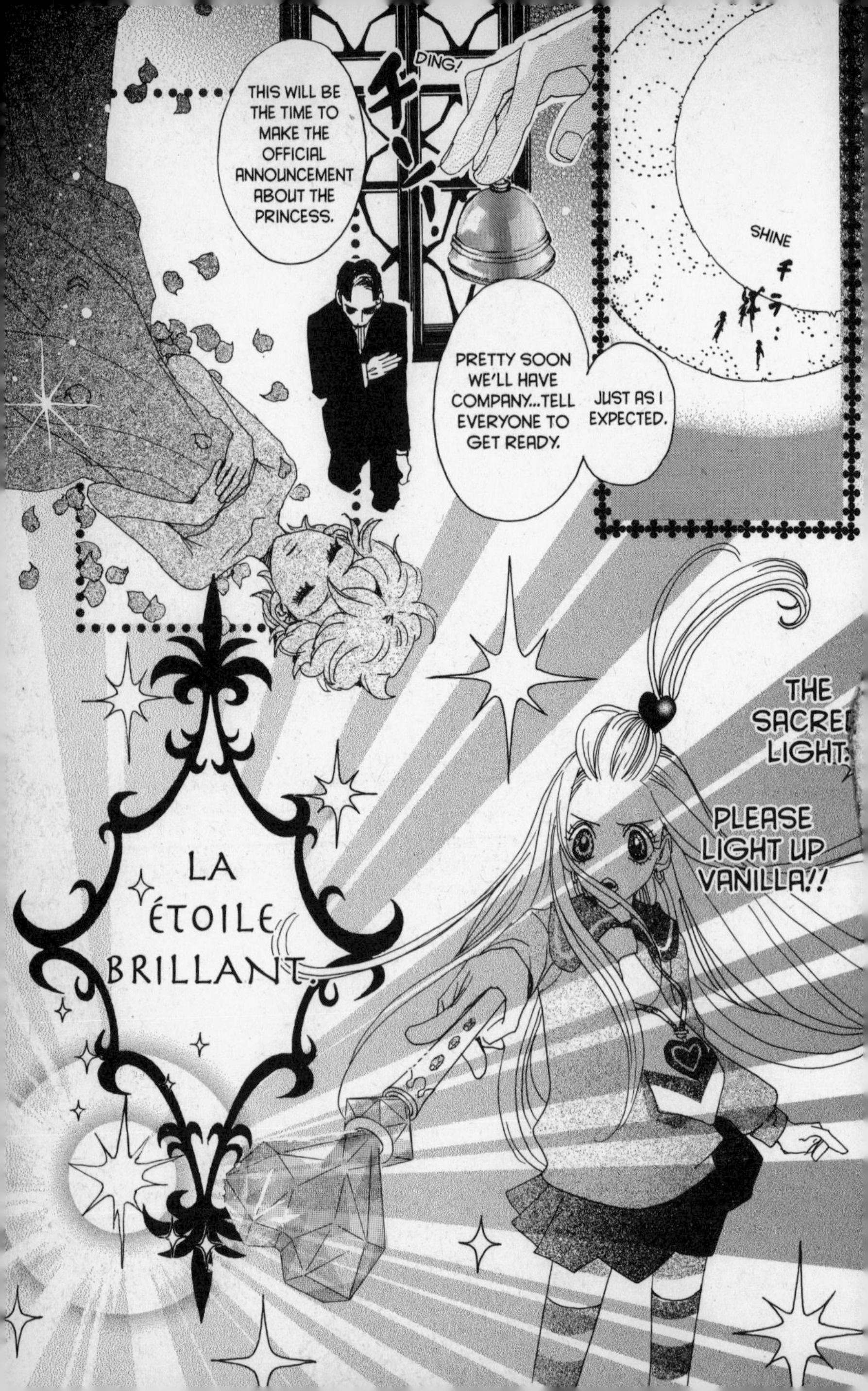
SHINE
JUST AS I EXPECTED.
DING!
THIS WILL BE THE TIME TO MAKE THE OFFICIAL ANNOUNCEMENT ABOUT THE PRINCESS.
PRETTY SOON WE'LL HAVE COMPANY...TELL EVERYONE TO GET READY.
THE SACRED LIGHT.
PLEASE LIGHT UP VANILLA!!
LA ÉTOILE BRILLANT.

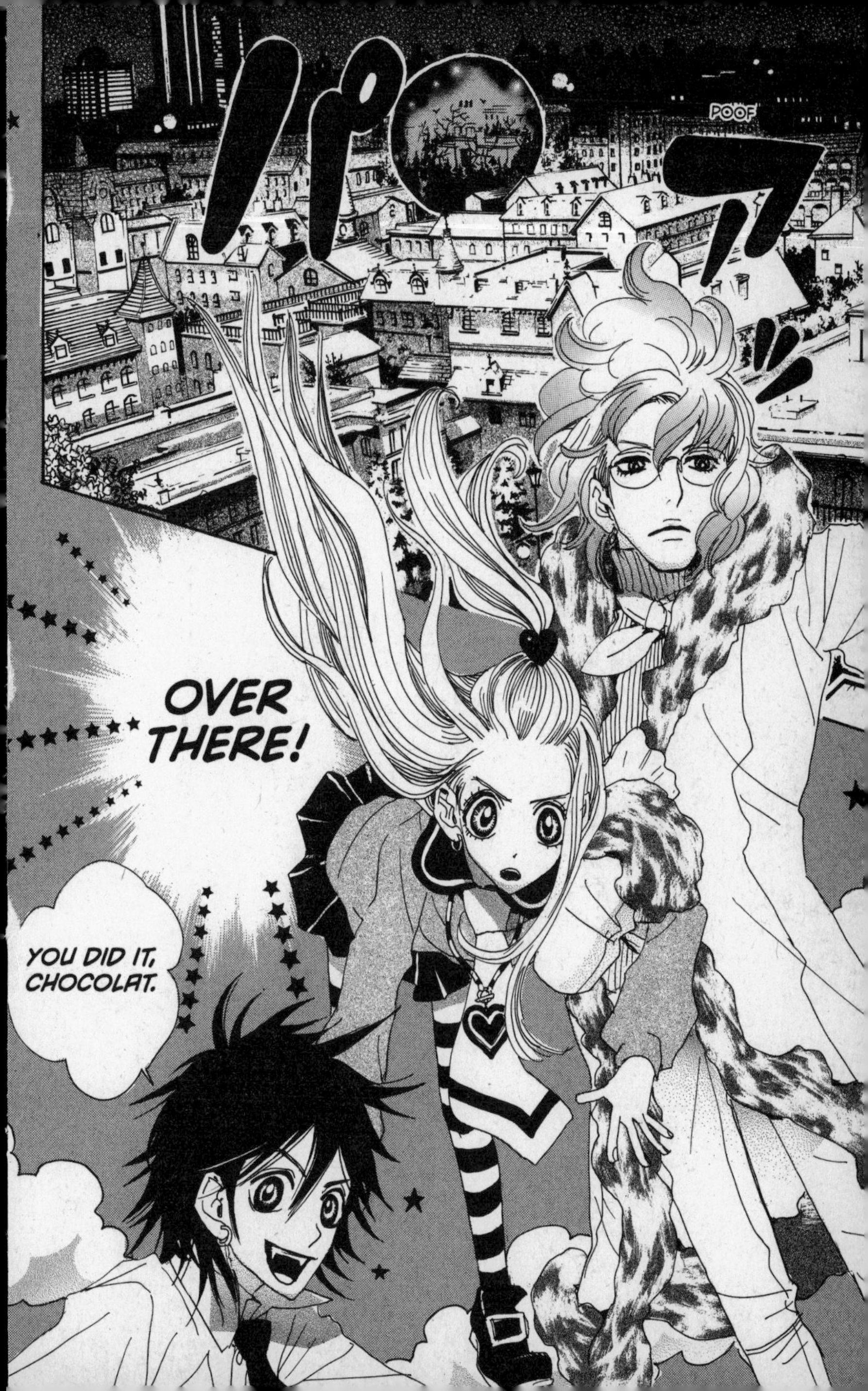
パフ
POOF
OVER THERE!
YOU DID IT, CHOCOLAT.

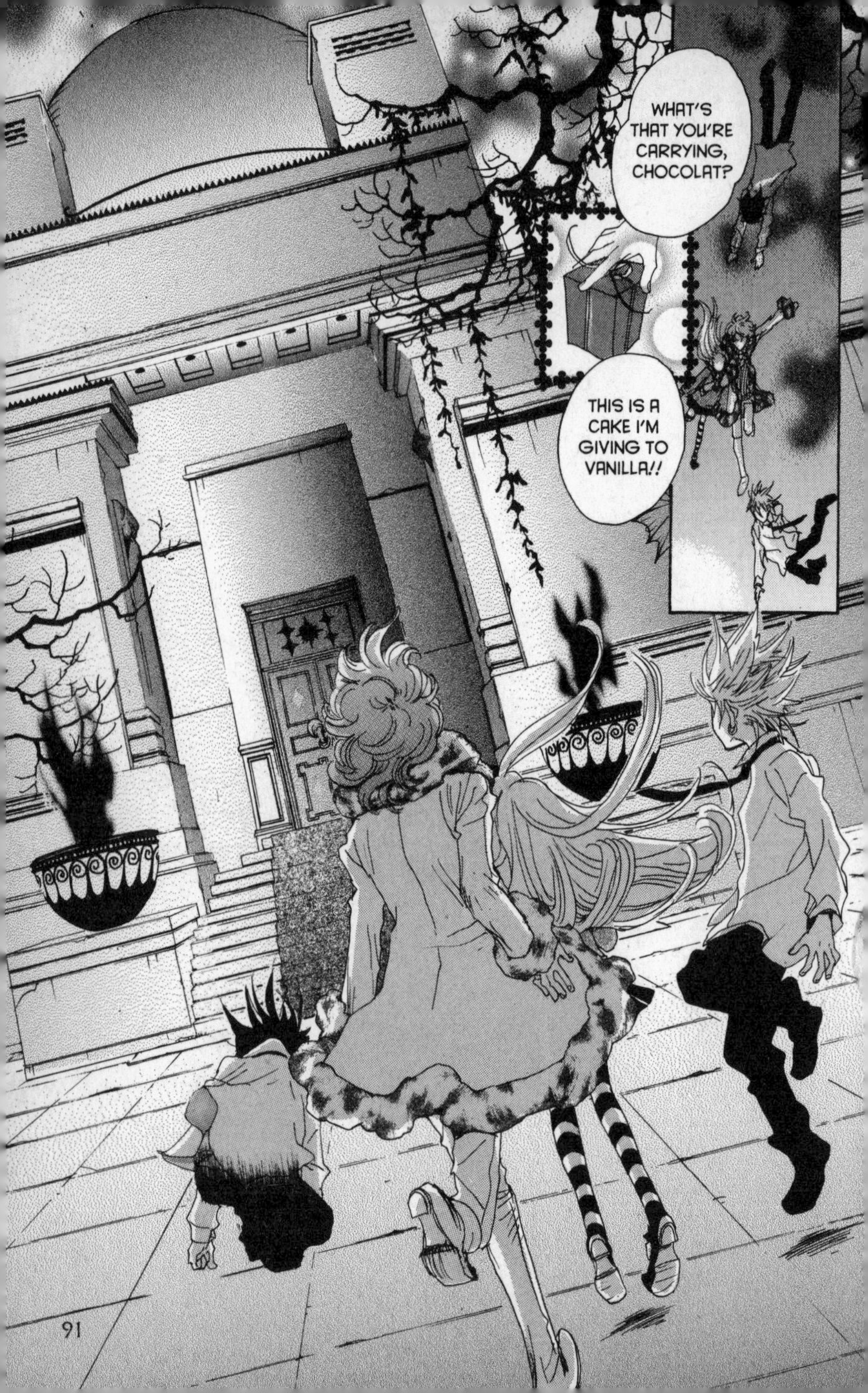
WHAT'S THAT YOU'RE CARRYING, CHOCOLAT?
THIS IS A CAKE I'M GIVING TO VANILLA!!

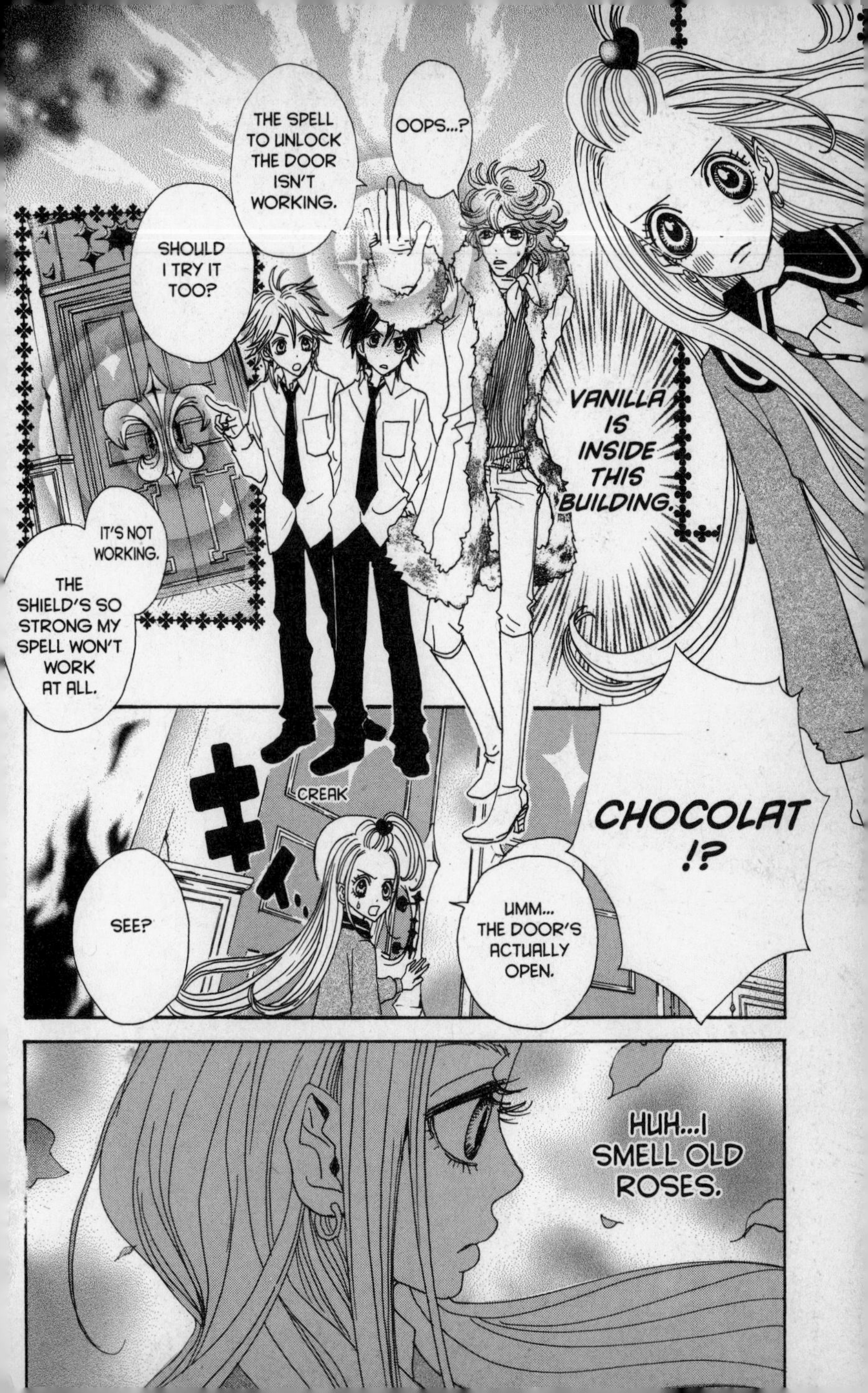
VANILLA IS INSIDE THIS BUILDING.
OOPS...?
THE SPELL TO UNLOCK THE DOOR ISN'T WORKING.
SHOULD I TRY IT TOO?
IT'S NOT WORKING.
THE SHIELD'S SO STRONG MY SPELL WON'T WORK AT ALL.
CHOCOLAT !?
UMM... THE DOOR'S ACTUALLY OPEN.
CREAK
SEE?
HUH...I SMELL OLD ROSES.

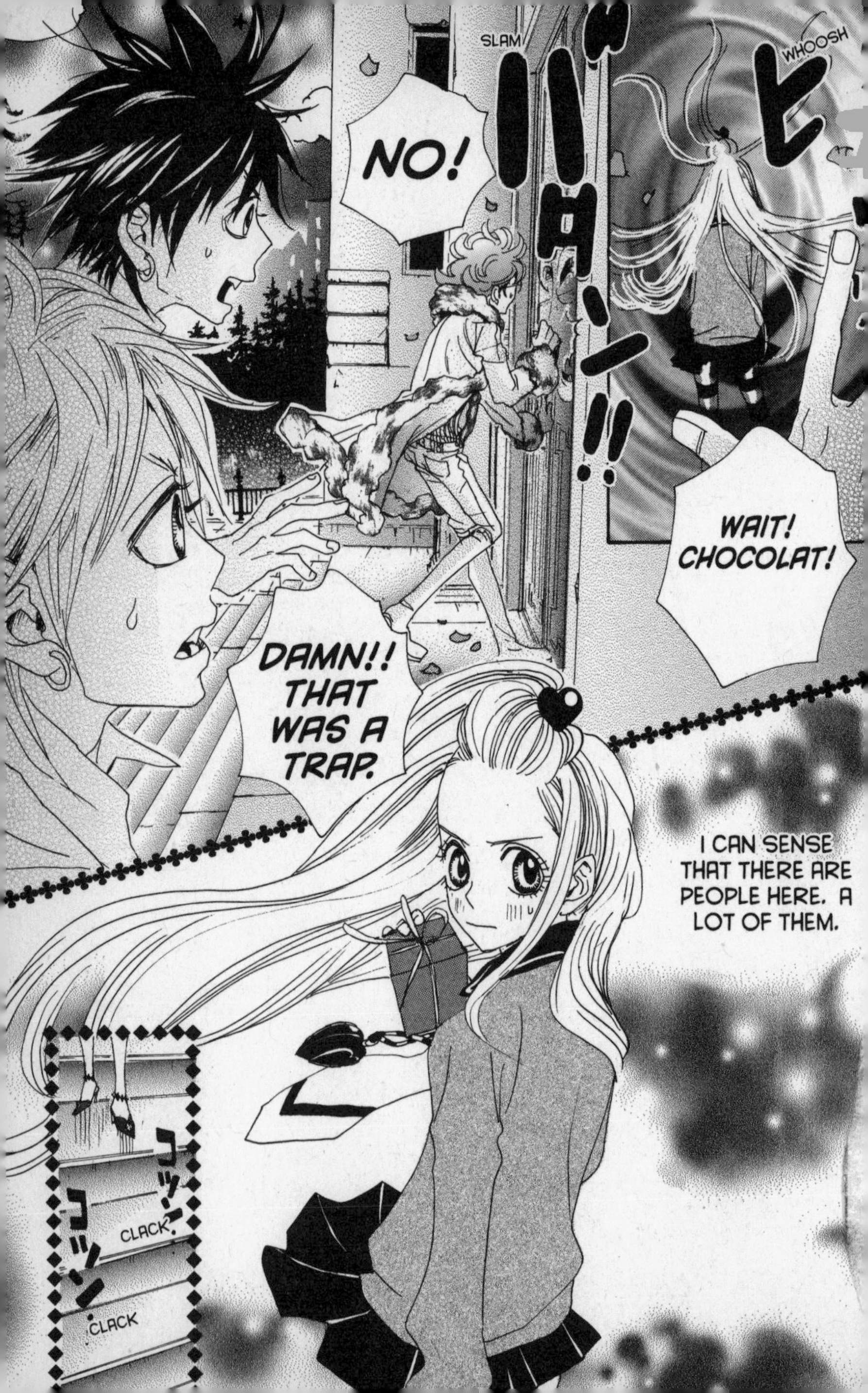
WHOOSH
SLAM
NO!
WAIT! CHOCOLAT!
DAMN!! THAT WAS A TRAP.
I CAN SENSE THAT THERE ARE PEOPLE HERE. A LOT OF THEM.
CLACK
CLACK

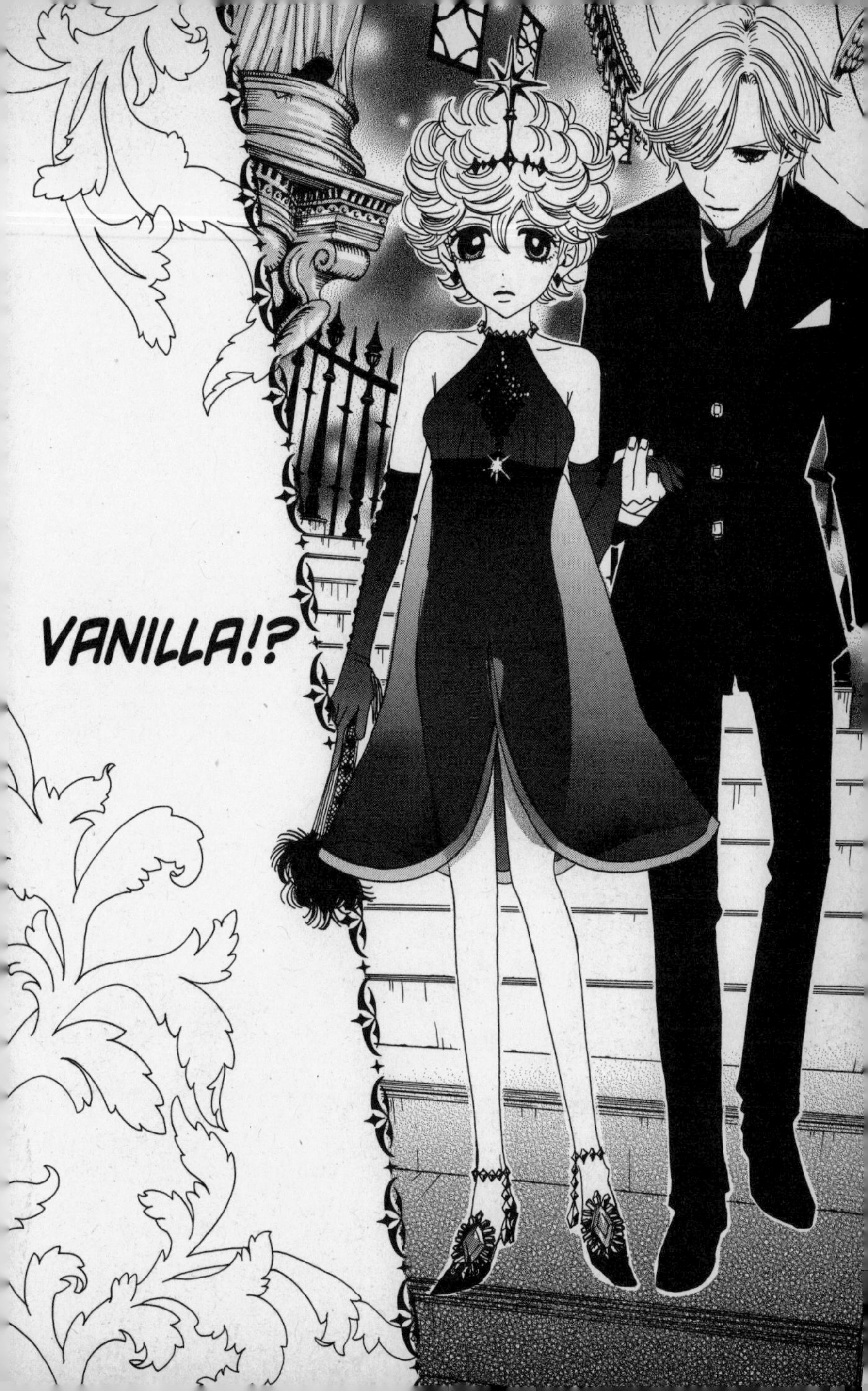
VANILLA!?

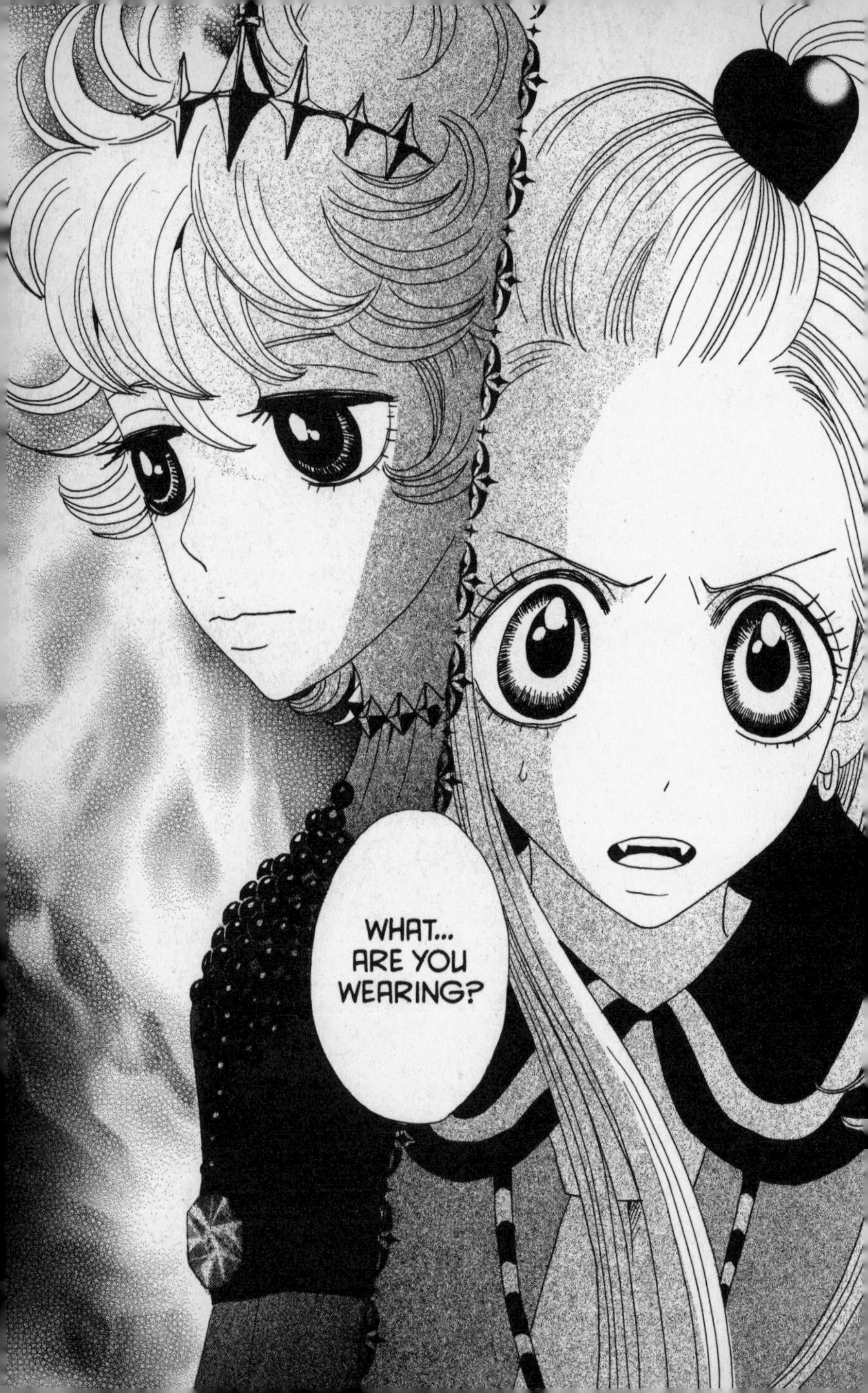
WHAT... ARE YOU WEARING?

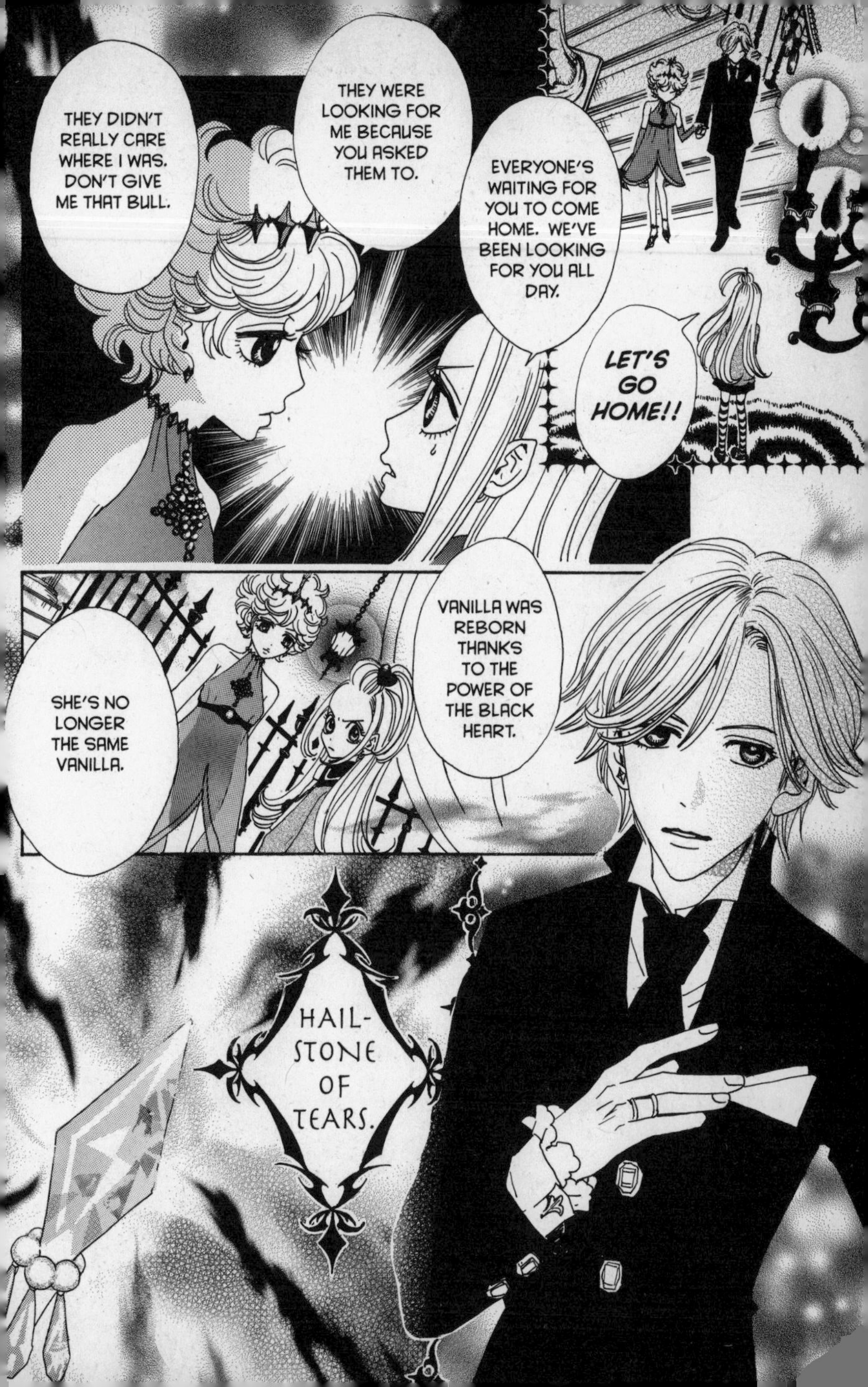
LET'S GO HOME!!
EVERYONE'S WAITING FOR YOU TO COME HOME. WE'VE BEEN LOOKING FOR YOU ALL DAY.
THEY WERE LOOKING FOR ME BECAUSE YOU ASKED THEM TO.
THEY DIDN'T REALLY CARE WHERE I WAS. DON'T GIVE ME THAT BULL.
VANILLA WAS REBORN THANKS TO THE POWER OF THE BLACK HEART.
SHE'S NO LONGER THE SAME VANILLA.
HAIL-STONE OF TEARS.

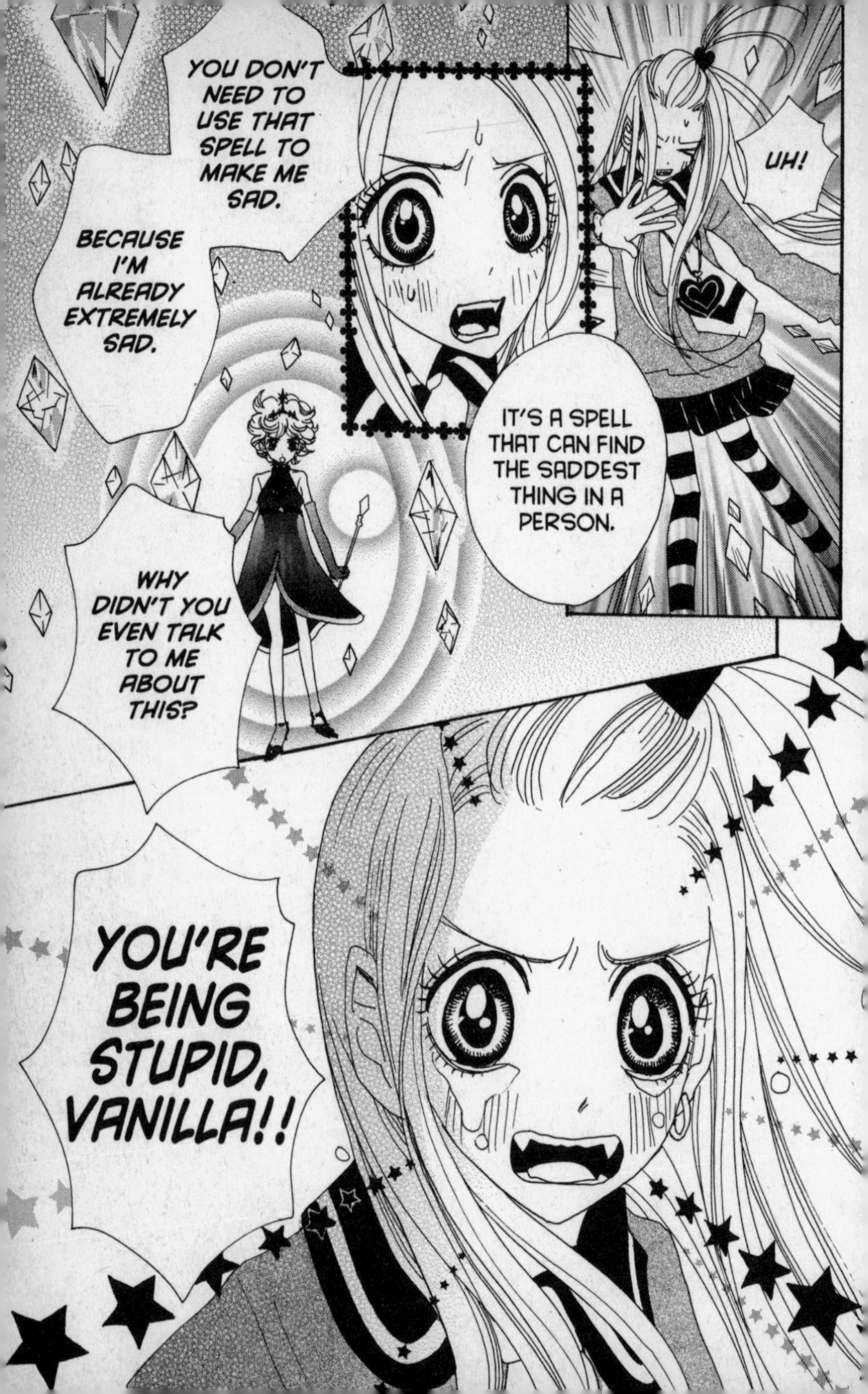
UH!
IT'S A SPELL THAT CAN FIND THE SADDEST THING IN A PERSON.
YOU DON'T NEED TO USE THAT SPELL TO MAKE ME SAD.
BECAUSE I'M ALREADY EXTREMELY SAD.
WHY DIDN'T YOU EVEN TALK TO ME ABOUT THIS?
YOU'RE BEING STUPID, VANILLA!!

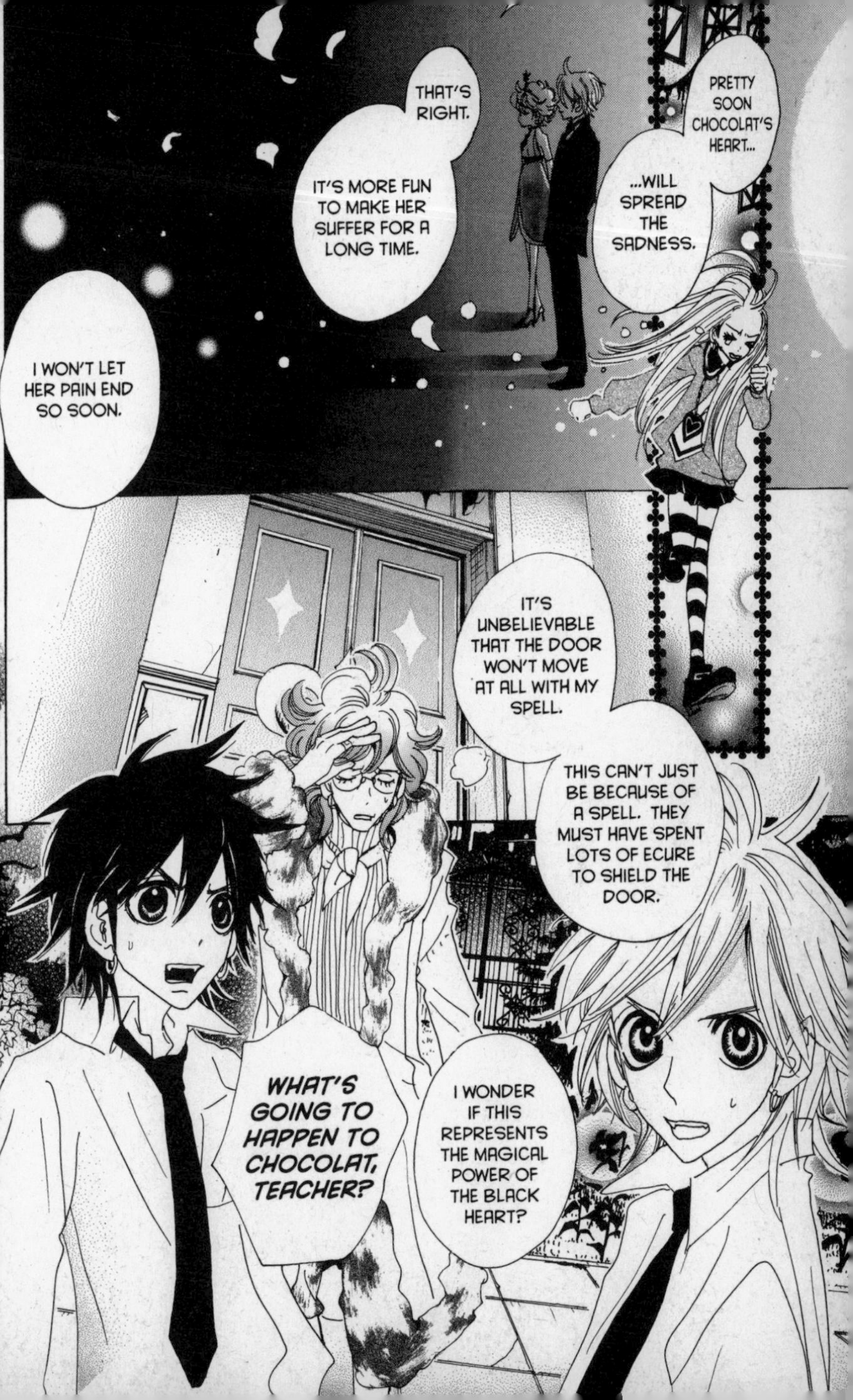
PRETTY SOON CHOCOLAT'S HEART...
...WILL SPREAD THE SADNESS.
THAT'S RIGHT.
IT'S MORE FUN TO MAKE HER SUFFER FOR A LONG TIME.
I WON'T LET HER PAIN END SO SOON.
IT'S UNBELIEVABLE THAT THE DOOR WON'T MOVE AT ALL WITH MY SPELL.
THIS CAN'T JUST BE BECAUSE OF A SPELL. THEY MUST HAVE SPENT LOTS OF ECURE TO SHIELD THE DOOR.
I WONDER IF THIS REPRESENTS THE MAGICAL POWER OF THE BLACK HEART?
WHAT'S GOING TO HAPPEN TO CHOCOLAT, TEACHER?

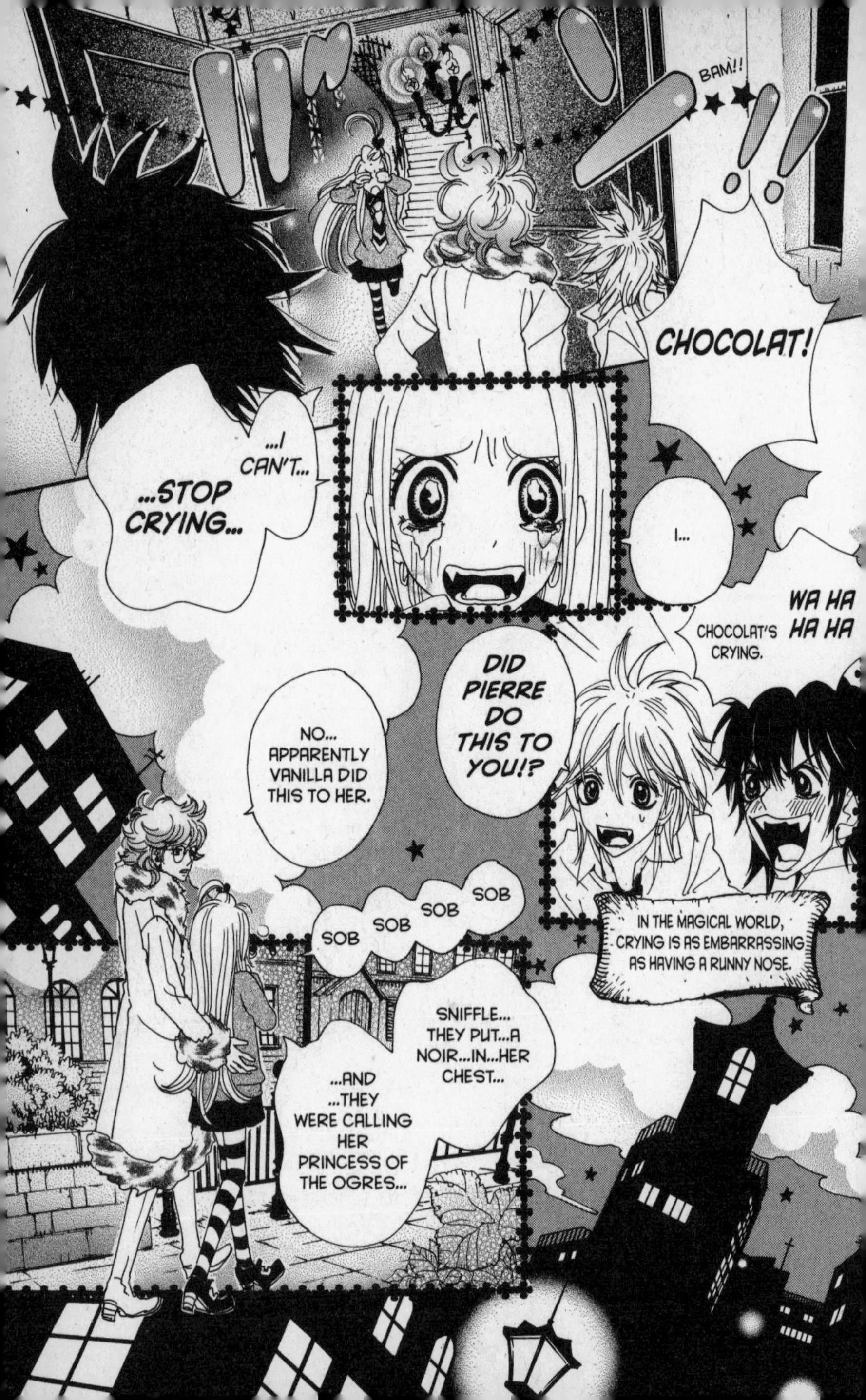

BAM!!
CHOCOLAT!
I...
...I CAN'T...
...STOP CRYING...
WA HA HA HA
CHOCOLAT'S CRYING.
DID PIERRE DO THIS TO YOU!?
IN THE MAGICAL WORLD, CRYING IS AS EMBARRASSING AS HAVING A RUNNY NOSE.
NO... APPARENTLY VANILLA DID THIS TO HER.
SOB SOB SOB SOB
SNIFFLE... THEY PUT...A NOIR...IN...HER CHEST...
...AND ...THEY WERE CALLING HER PRINCESS OF THE OGRES...

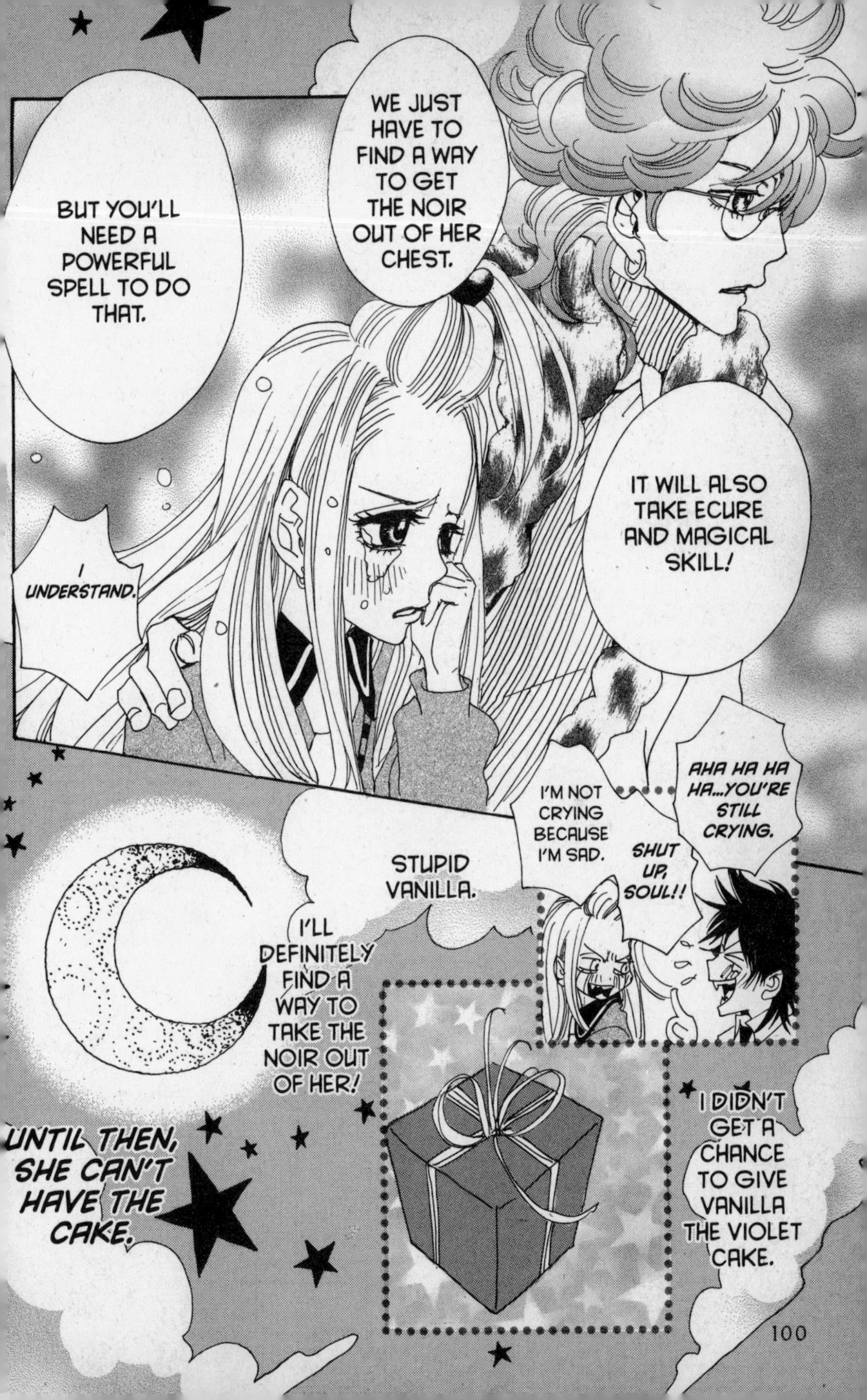
WE JUST HAVE TO FIND A WAY TO GET THE NOIR OUT OF HER CHEST.
BUT YOU'LL NEED A POWERFUL SPELL TO DO THAT.
IT WILL ALSO TAKE ECURE AND MAGICAL SKILL!
I UNDERSTAND.
AHA HA HA HA...YOU'RE STILL CRYING.
I'M NOT CRYING BECAUSE I'M SAD.
SHUT UP, SOUL!!
STUPID VANILLA.
I'LL DEFINITELY FIND A WAY TO TAKE THE NOIR OUT OF HER!
I DIDN'T GET A CHANCE TO GIVE VANILLA THE VIOLET CAKE.
UNTIL THEN, SHE CAN'T HAVE THE CAKE.

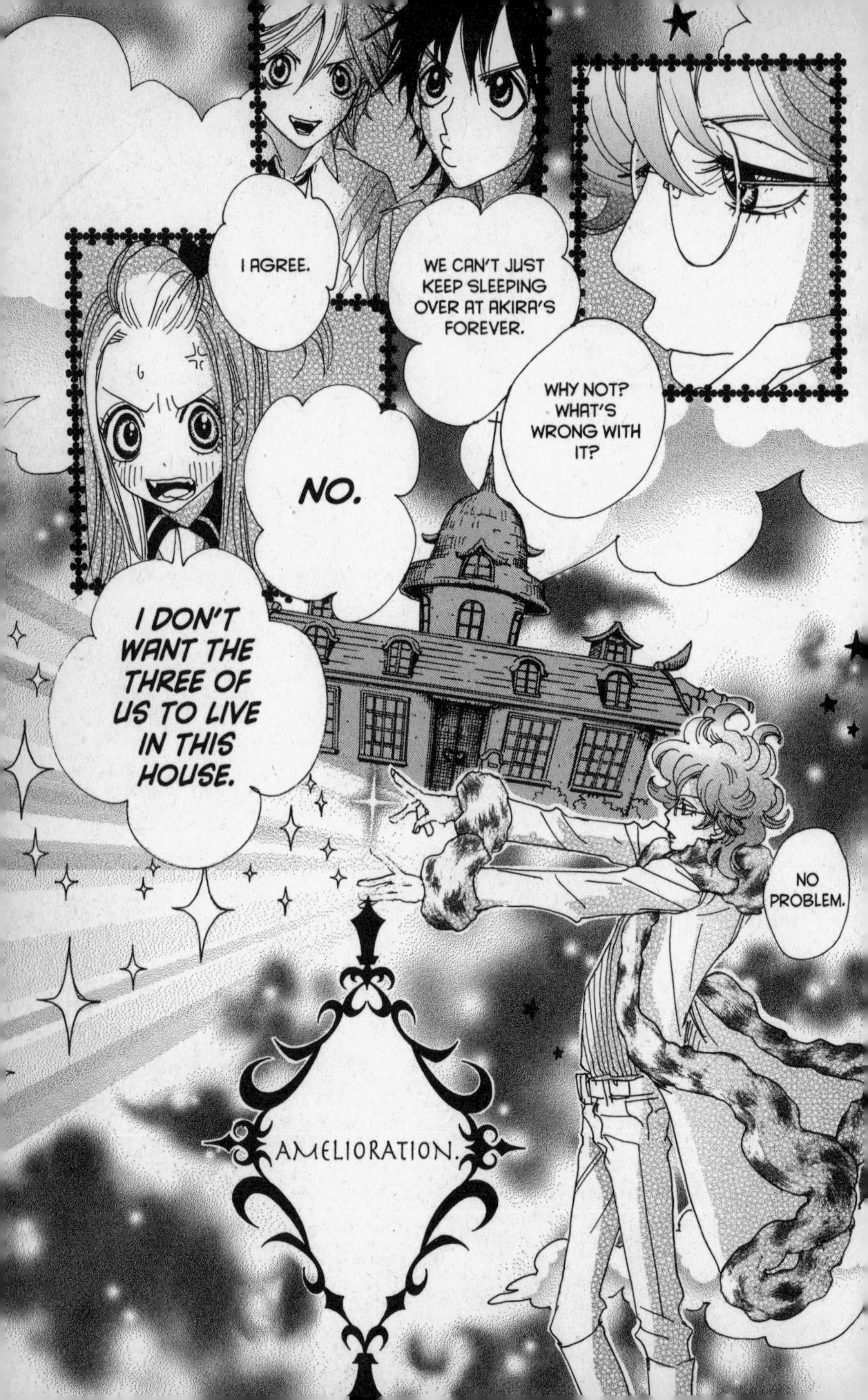
WE CAN'T JUST KEEP SLEEPING OVER AT AKIRA'S FOREVER.
I AGREE.
WHY NOT? WHAT'S WRONG WITH IT?
NO.
I DON'T WANT THE THREE OF US TO LIVE IN THIS HOUSE.
NO PROBLEM.
AMELIORATION.

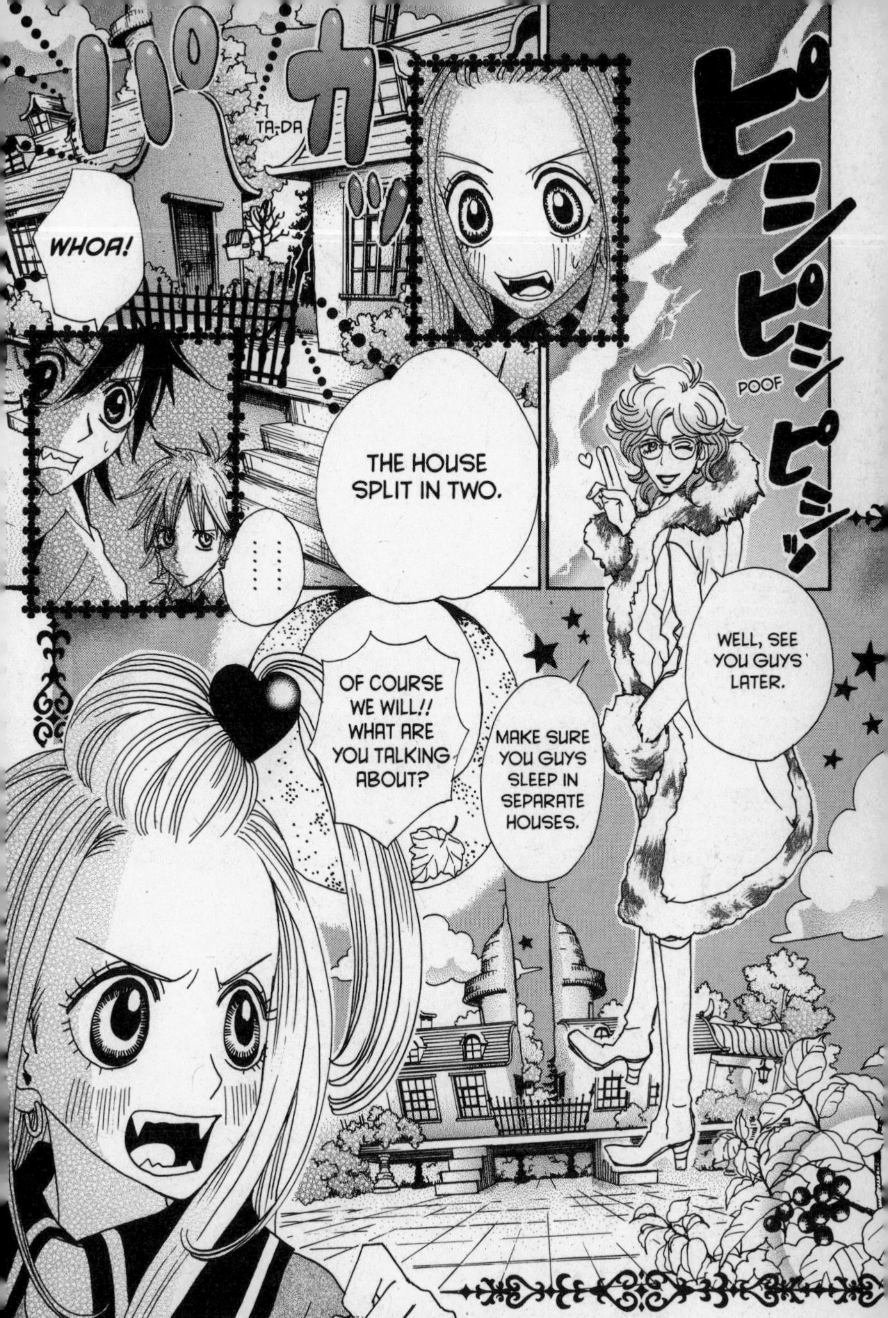
POOF
TA-DA
WHOA!
THE HOUSE SPLIT IN TWO.
......
WELL, SEE YOU GUYS LATER.
MAKE SURE YOU GUYS SLEEP IN SEPARATE HOUSES.
OF COURSE WE WILL!! WHAT ARE YOU TALKING ABOUT?

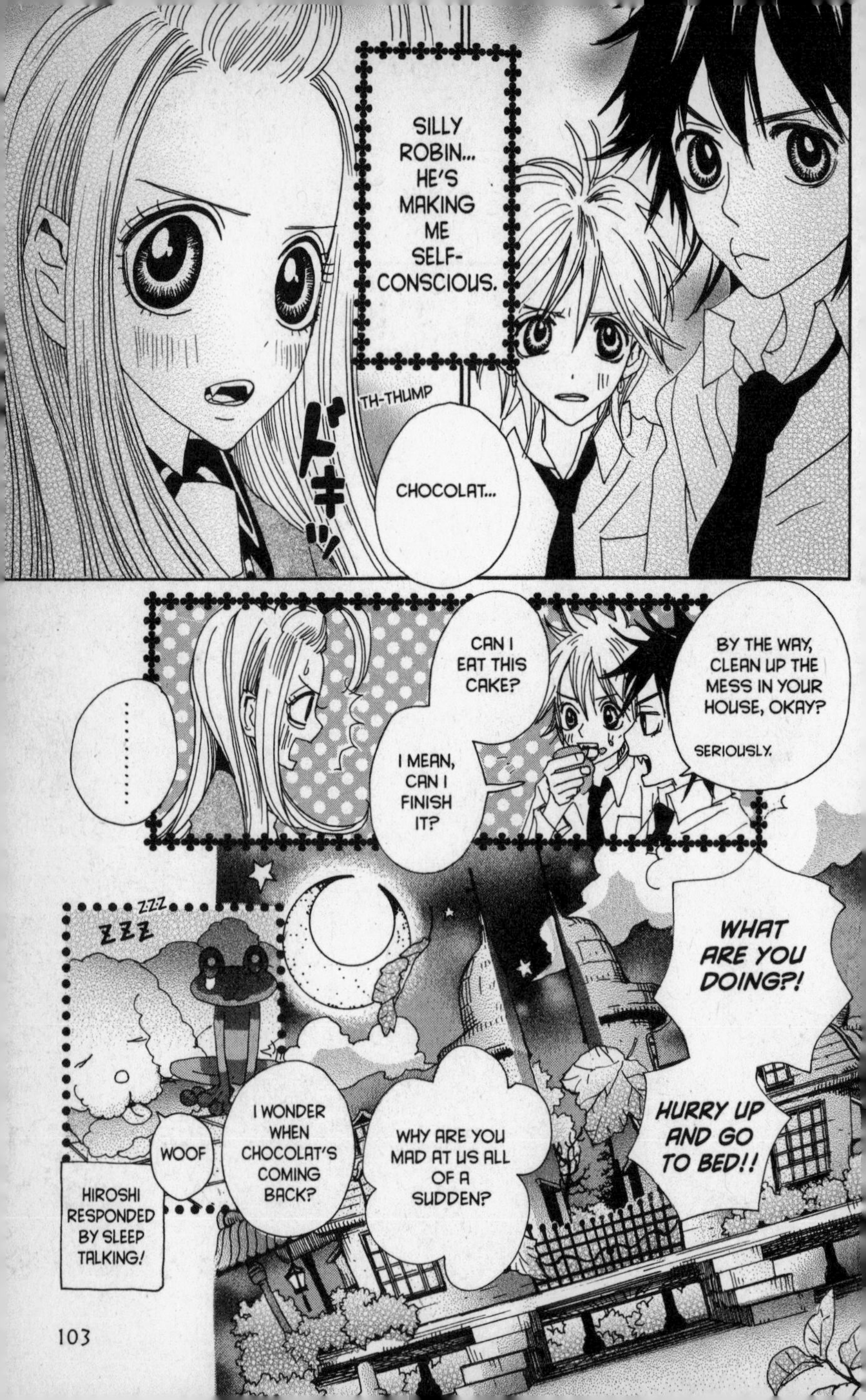
CHOCOLAT...
TH-THUMP
SILLY ROBIN... HE'S MAKING ME SELF-CONSCIOUS.
BY THE WAY, CLEAN UP THE MESS IN YOUR HOUSE, OKAY?
SERIOUSLY.
CAN I EAT THIS CAKE?
I MEAN, CAN I FINISH IT?
....
WHAT ARE YOU DOING?!
HURRY UP AND GO TO BED!!
WHY ARE YOU MAD AT US ALL OF A SUDDEN?
I WONDER WHEN CHOCOLAT'S COMING BACK?
Z-Z-Z
ZZZ
WOOF
HIROSHI RESPONDED BY SLEEP TALKING!

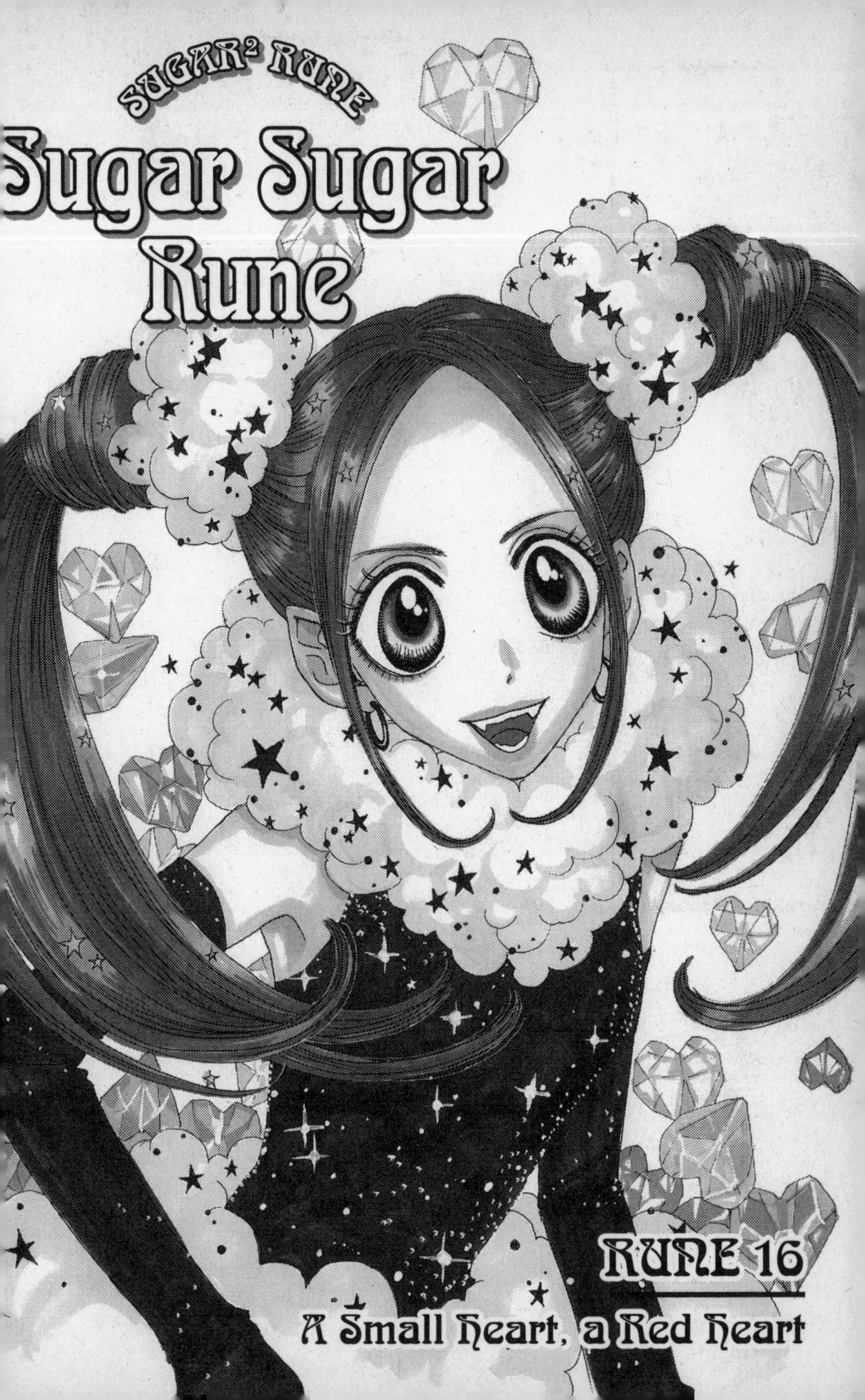
SUGAR² RUNE
Sugar Sugar Rune
RUNE 16
A Small Heart, a Red Heart

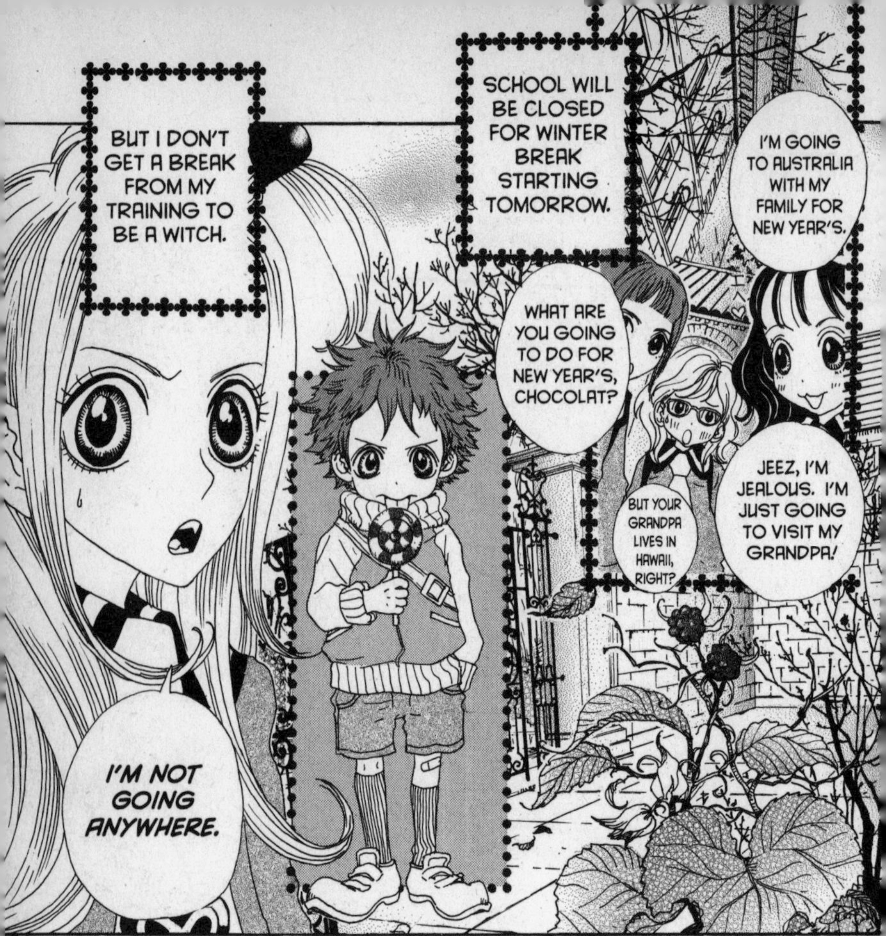
SCHOOL WILL BE CLOSED FOR WINTER BREAK STARTING TOMORROW.
I'M GOING TO AUSTRALIA WITH MY FAMILY FOR NEW YEAR'S.
JEEZ, I'M JEALOUS. I'M JUST GOING TO VISIT MY GRANDPA!
BUT YOUR GRANDPA LIVES IN HAWAII, RIGHT?
WHAT ARE YOU GOING TO DO FOR NEW YEAR'S, CHOCOLAT?
I'M NOT GOING ANYWHERE.
BUT I DON'T GET A BREAK FROM MY TRAINING TO BE A WITCH.

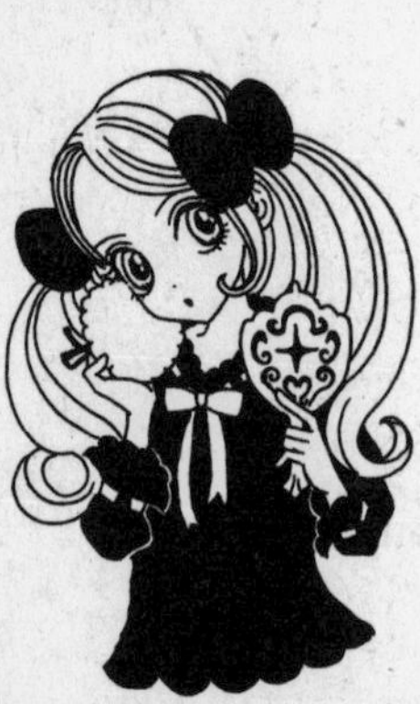

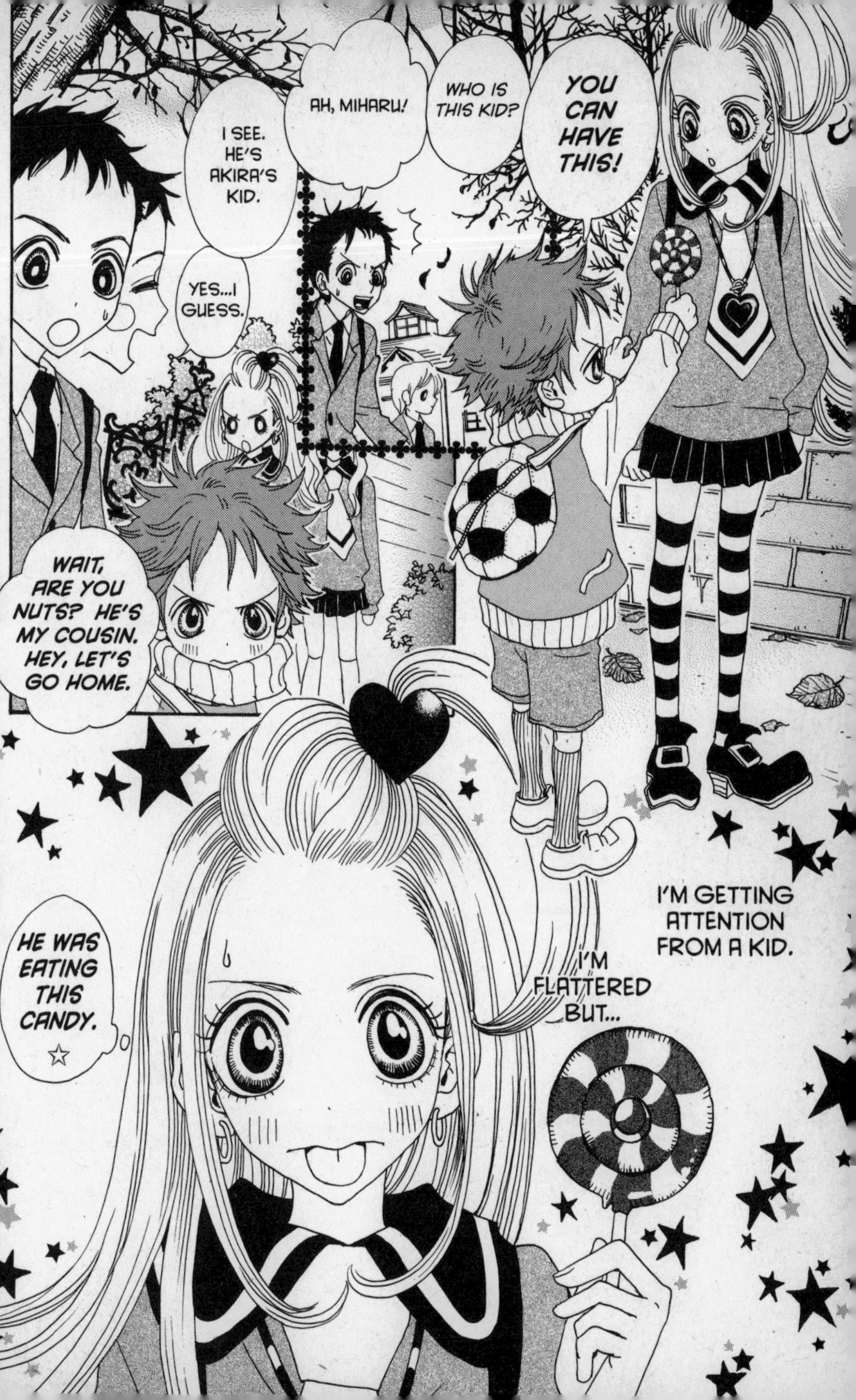
YOU CAN HAVE THIS!
WHO IS THIS KID?
AH, MIHARU!
I SEE. HE'S AKIRA'S KID.
YES...I GUESS.
WAIT, ARE YOU NUTS? HE'S MY COUSIN. HEY, LET'S GO HOME.
I'M GETTING ATTENTION FROM A KID.
I'M FLATTERED BUT...
HE WAS EATING THIS CANDY. ☆

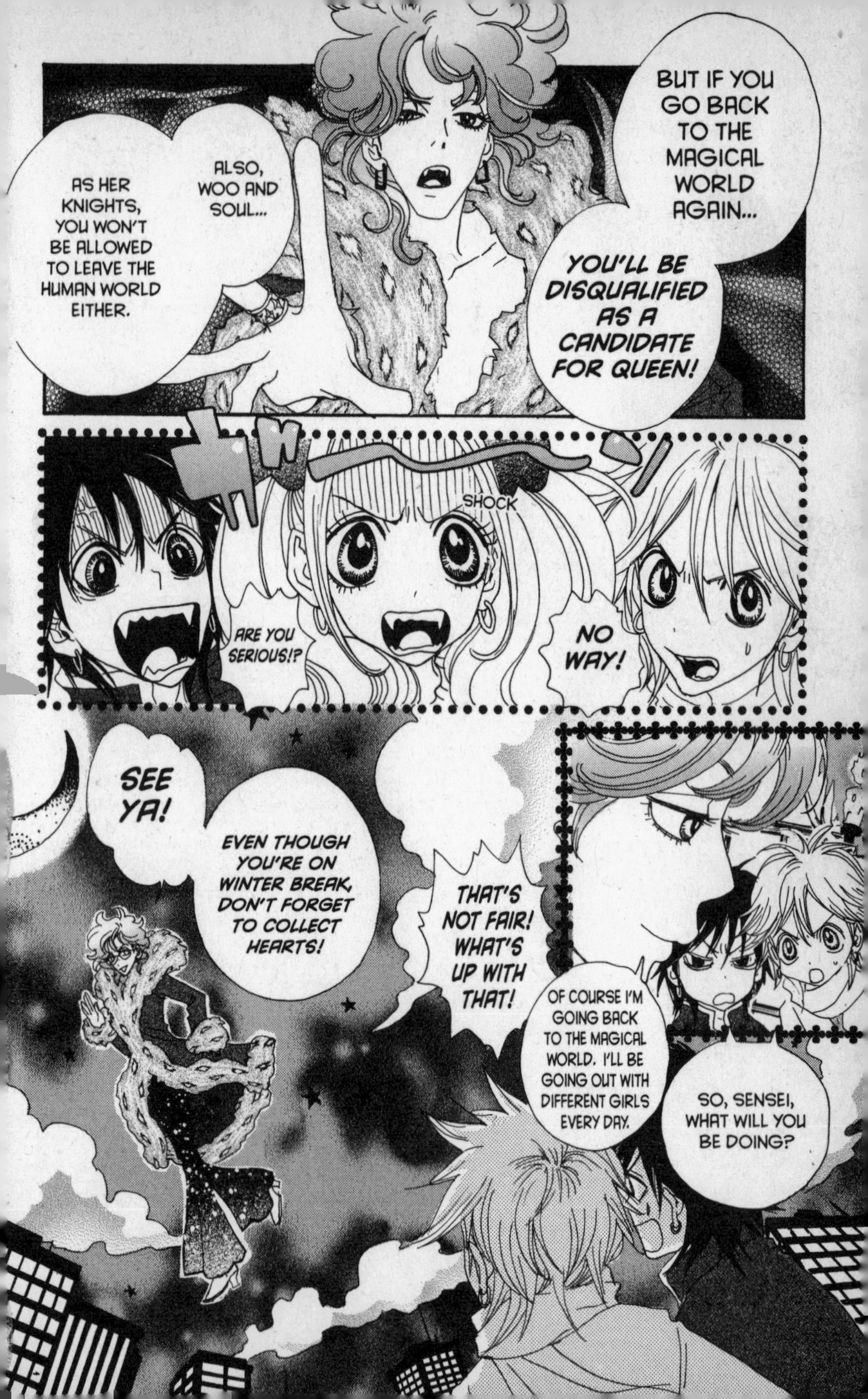
BUT IF YOU GO BACK TO THE MAGICAL WORLD AGAIN...
YOU'LL BE DISQUALIFIED AS A CANDIDATE FOR QUEEN!
ALSO, WOO AND SOUL...
AS HER KNIGHTS, YOU WON'T BE ALLOWED TO LEAVE THE HUMAN WORLD EITHER.
SHOCK
NO WAY!
ARE YOU SERIOUS!?
SEE YA!
EVEN THOUGH YOU'RE ON WINTER BREAK, DON'T FORGET TO COLLECT HEARTS!
THAT'S NOT FAIR! WHAT'S UP WITH THAT!
SO, SENSEI, WHAT WILL YOU BE DOING?
OF COURSE I'M GOING BACK TO THE MAGICAL WORLD. I'LL BE GOING OUT WITH DIFFERENT GIRLS EVERY DAY.

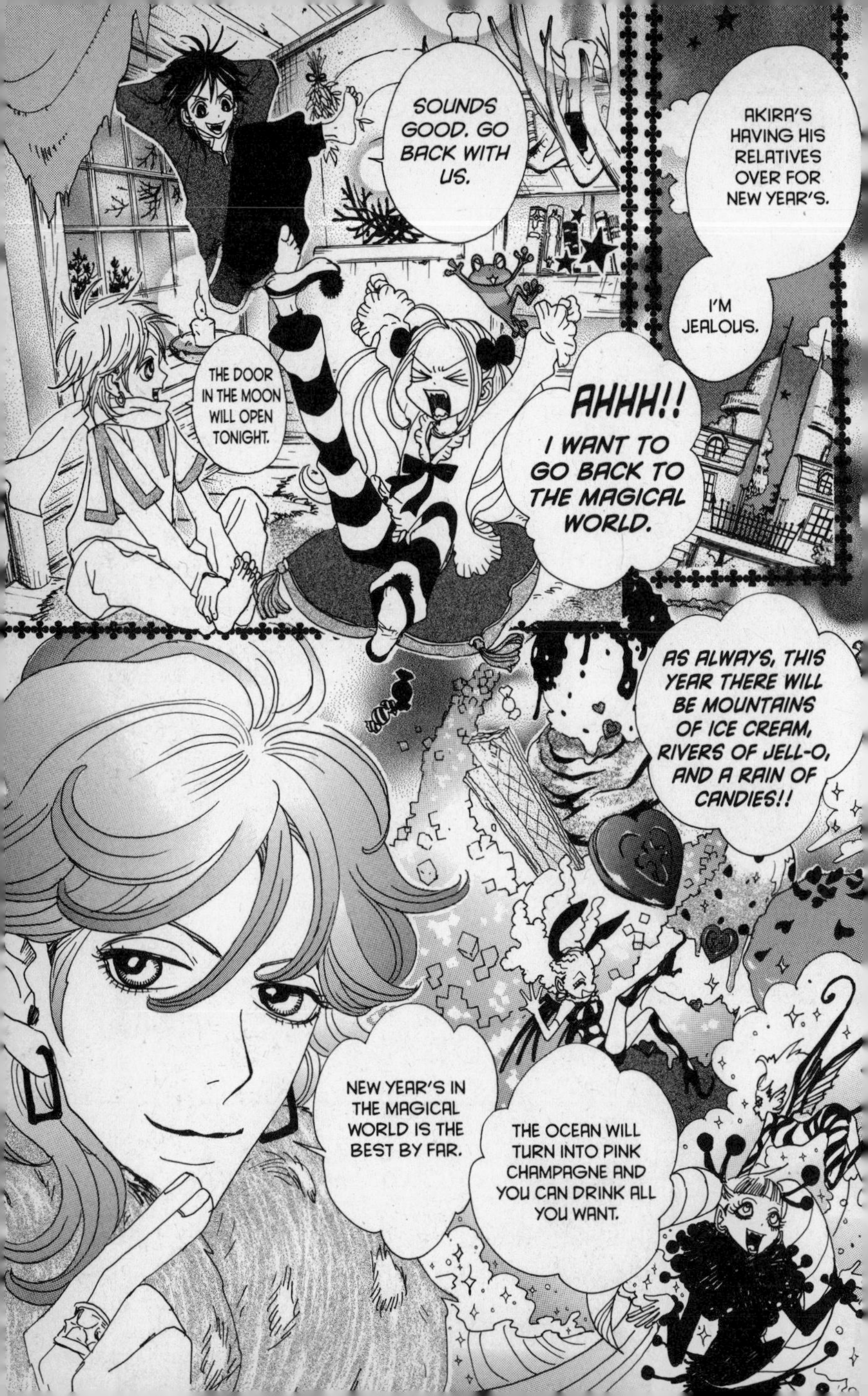
AKIRA'S HAVING HIS RELATIVES OVER FOR NEW YEAR'S.
I'M JEALOUS.
AHHH!! I WANT TO GO BACK TO THE MAGICAL WORLD.
THE DOOR IN THE MOON WILL OPEN TONIGHT.
SOUNDS GOOD. GO BACK WITH US.
AS ALWAYS, THIS YEAR THERE WILL BE MOUNTAINS OF ICE CREAM, RIVERS OF JELL-O, AND A RAIN OF CANDIES!!
THE OCEAN WILL TURN INTO PINK CHAMPAGNE AND YOU CAN DRINK ALL YOU WANT.
NEW YEAR'S IN THE MAGICAL WORLD IS THE BEST BY FAR.

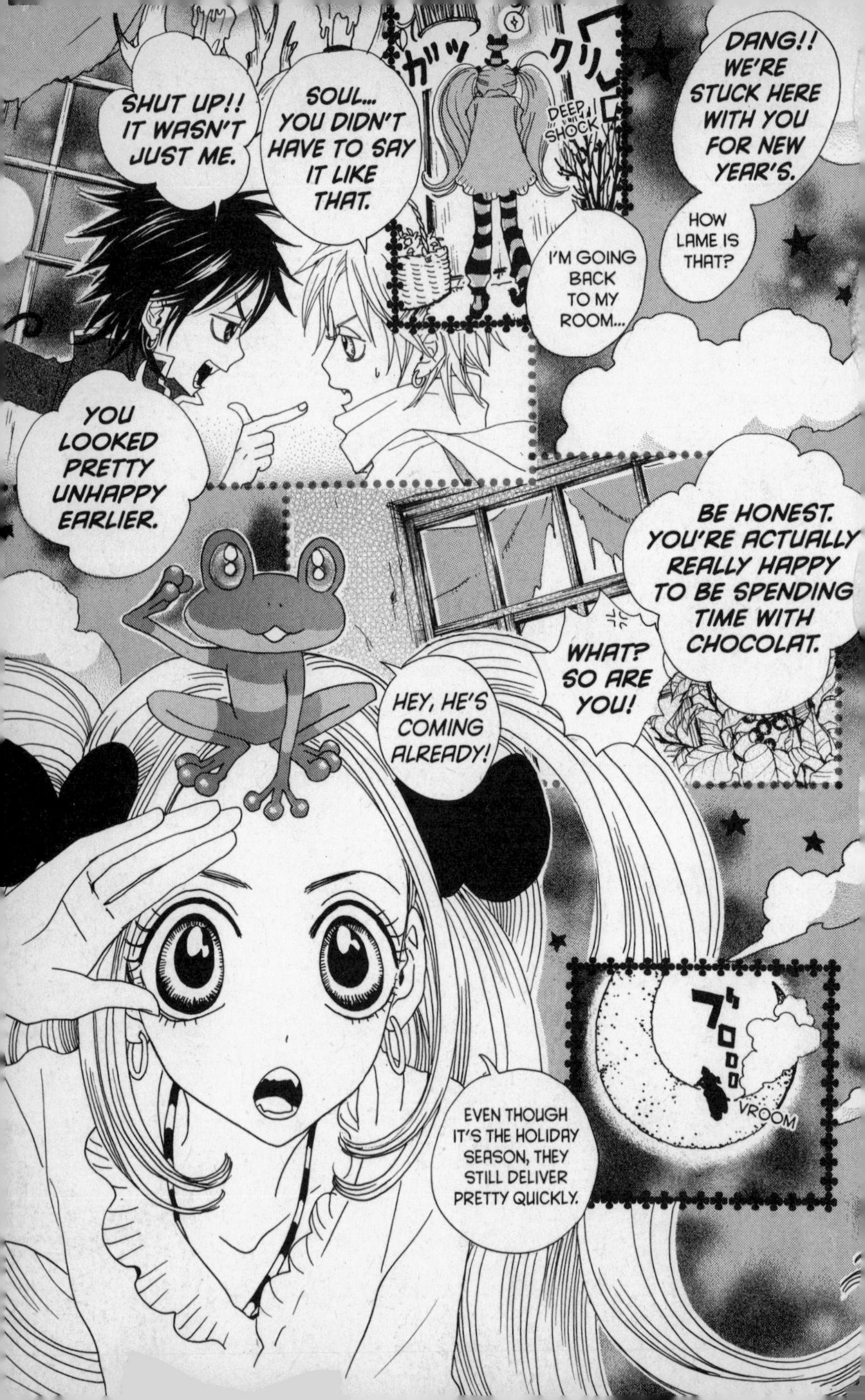
DANG!! WE'RE STUCK HERE WITH YOU FOR NEW YEAR'S.
HOW LAME IS THAT?
I'M GOING BACK TO MY ROOM...
ガッ クリ
DEEP SHOCK
SOUL... YOU DIDN'T HAVE TO SAY IT LIKE THAT.
SHUT UP!! IT WASN'T JUST ME.
YOU LOOKED PRETTY UNHAPPY EARLIER.
BE HONEST. YOU'RE ACTUALLY REALLY HAPPY TO BE SPENDING TIME WITH CHOCOLAT.
WHAT? SO ARE YOU!
ブロロロ
VROOM
HEY, HE'S COMING ALREADY!
EVEN THOUGH IT'S THE HOLIDAY SEASON, THEY STILL DELIVER PRETTY QUICKLY.

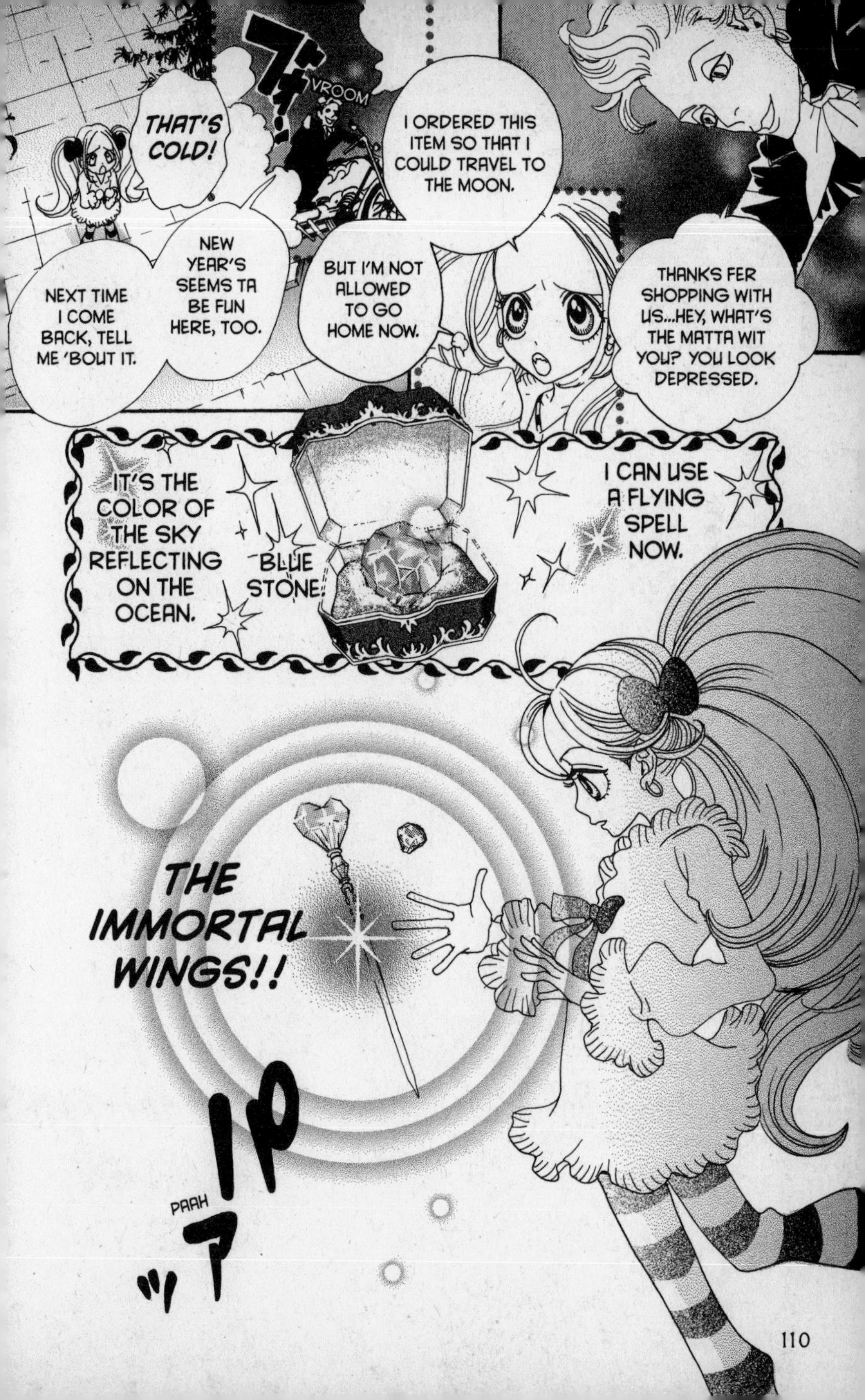
THANKS FER SHOPPING WITH US...HEY, WHAT'S THE MATTA WIT YOU? YOU LOOK DEPRESSED.
I ORDERED THIS ITEM SO THAT I COULD TRAVEL TO THE MOON.
BUT I'M NOT ALLOWED TO GO HOME NOW.
VROOM
NEW YEAR'S SEEMS TA BE FUN HERE, TOO.
NEXT TIME I COME BACK, TELL ME 'BOUT IT.
THAT'S COLD!
I CAN USE A FLYING SPELL NOW.
BLUE STONE
IT'S THE COLOR OF THE SKY REFLECTING ON THE OCEAN.
THE IMMORTAL WINGS!!
PAAH

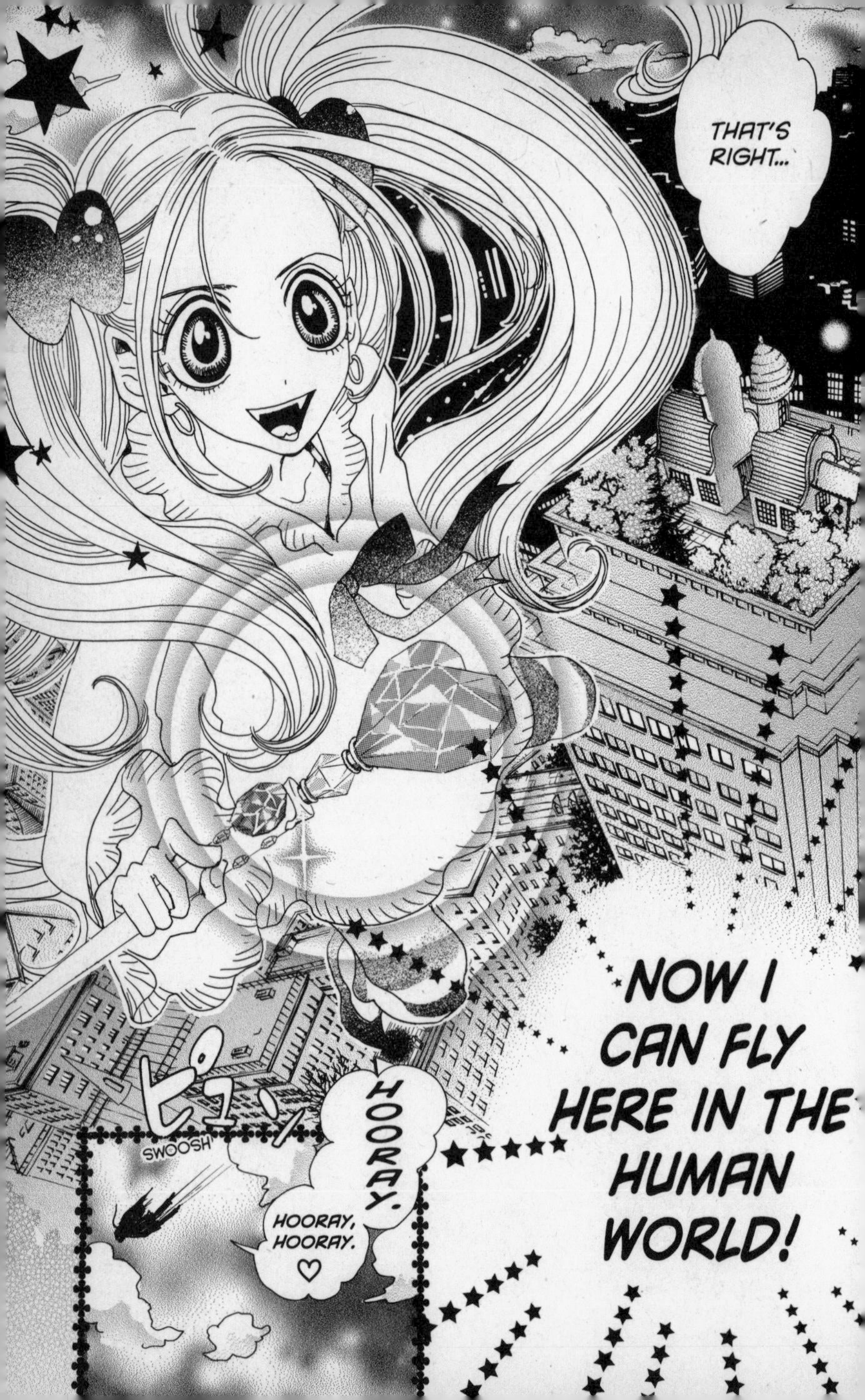
THAT'S RIGHT...
NOW I CAN FLY HERE IN THE HUMAN WORLD!
HOORAY.
HOORAY, HOORAY. ♡
ピュ〜
SWOOSH

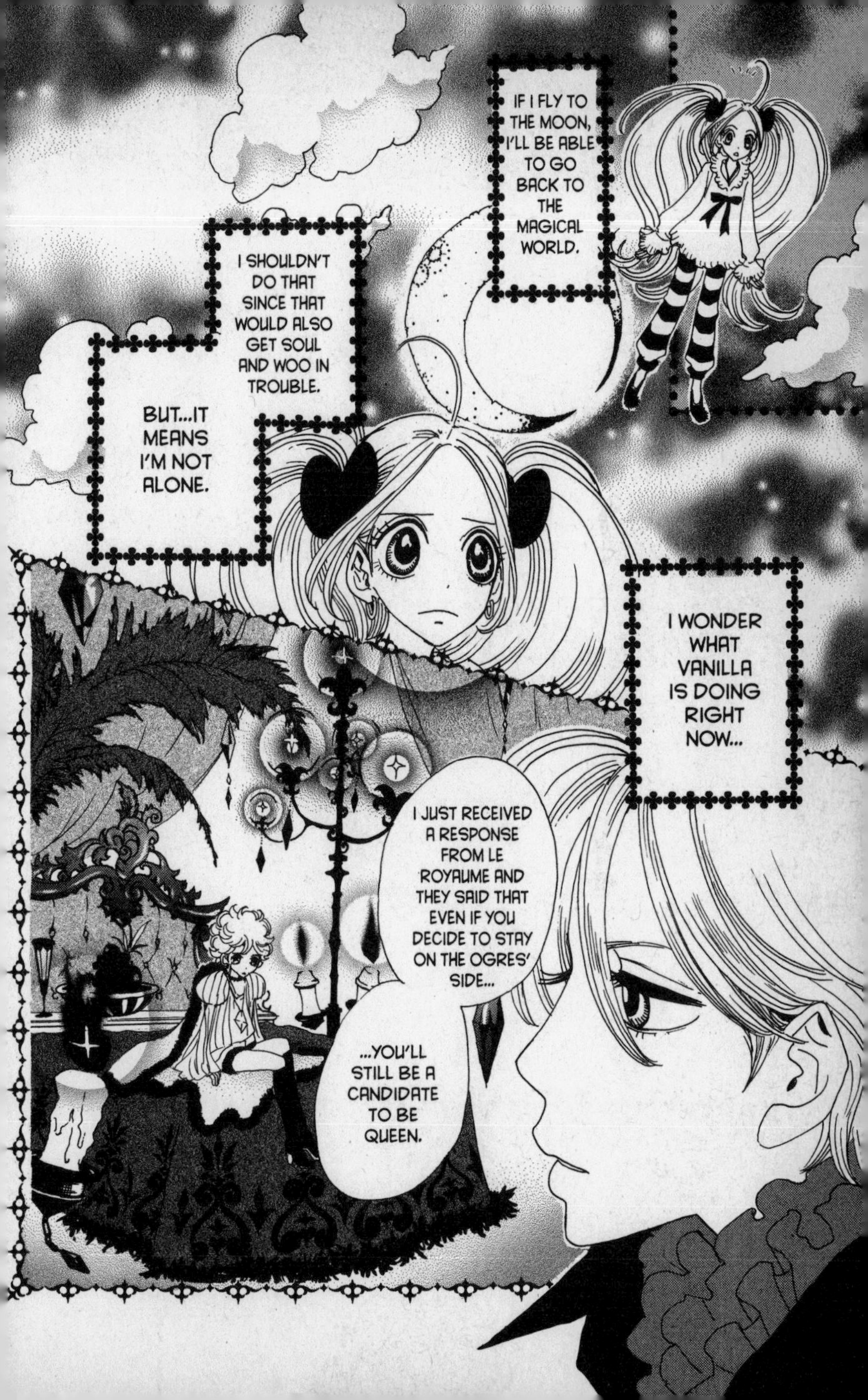
IF I FLY TO THE MOON, I'LL BE ABLE TO GO BACK TO THE MAGICAL WORLD.
I SHOULDN'T DO THAT SINCE THAT WOULD ALSO GET SOUL AND WOO IN TROUBLE.
BUT...IT MEANS I'M NOT ALONE.
I WONDER WHAT VANILLA IS DOING RIGHT NOW...
I JUST RECEIVED A RESPONSE FROM LE ROYAUME AND THEY SAID THAT EVEN IF YOU DECIDE TO STAY ON THE OGRES' SIDE...
...YOU'LL STILL BE A CANDIDATE TO BE QUEEN.

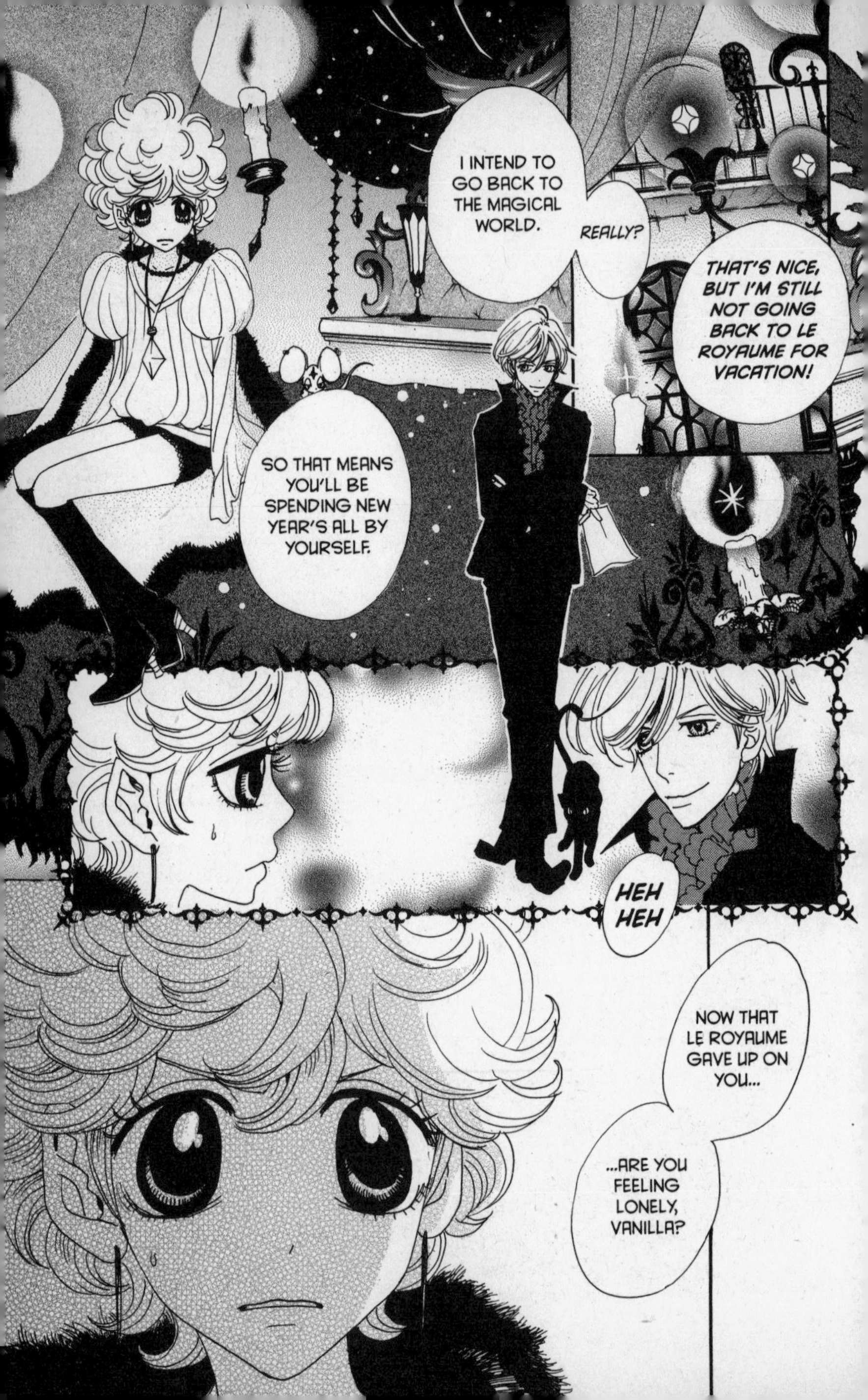
I INTEND TO GO BACK TO THE MAGICAL WORLD.
REALLY?
THAT'S NICE, BUT I'M STILL NOT GOING BACK TO LE ROYAUME FOR VACATION!
SO THAT MEANS YOU'LL BE SPENDING NEW YEAR'S ALL BY YOURSELF.
HEH HEH
NOW THAT LE ROYAUME GAVE UP ON YOU...
...ARE YOU FEELING LONELY, VANILLA?

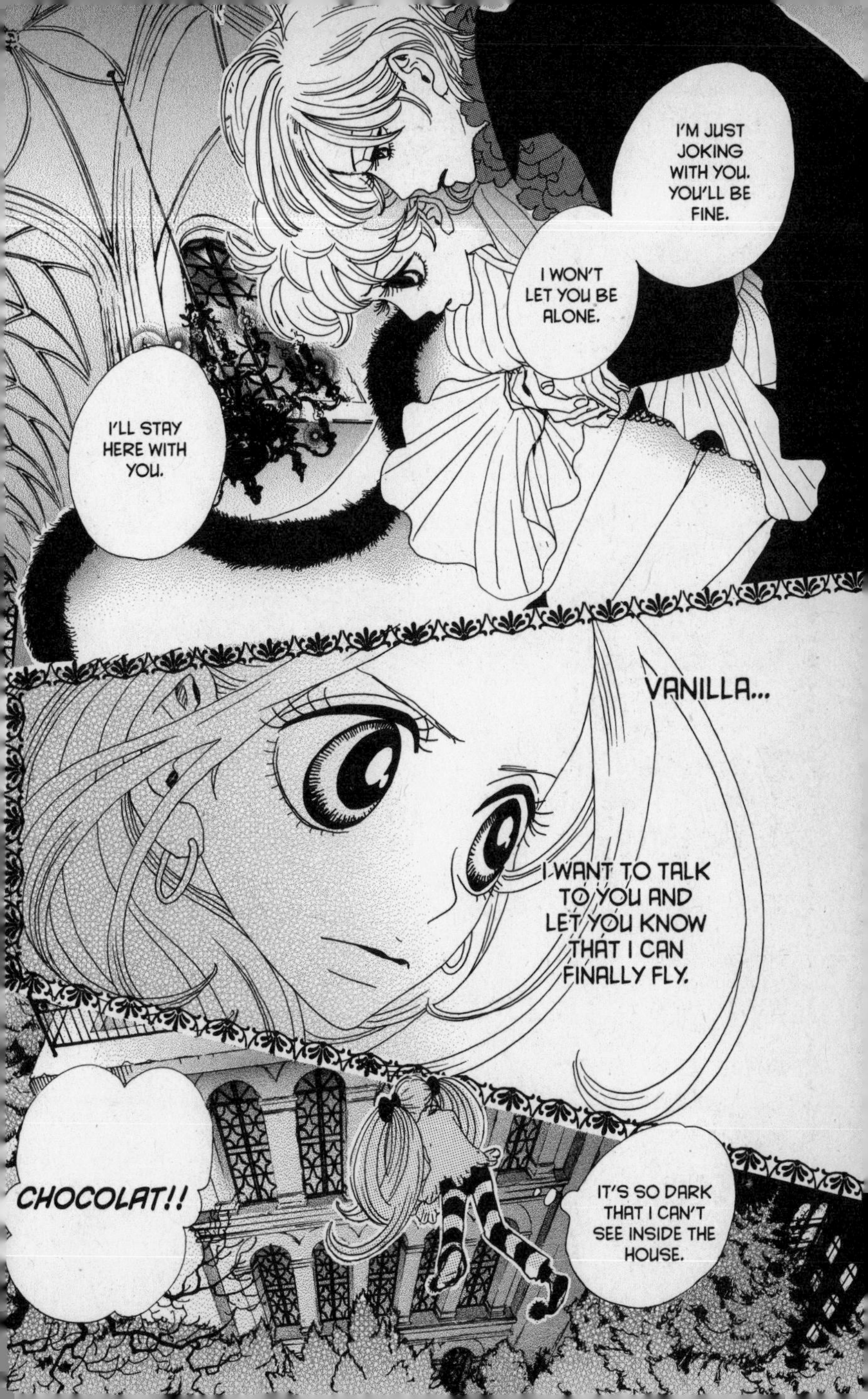
I'M JUST JOKING WITH YOU. YOU'LL BE FINE.
I WON'T LET YOU BE ALONE.
I'LL STAY HERE WITH YOU.
VANILLA...
I WANT TO TALK TO YOU AND LET YOU KNOW THAT I CAN FINALLY FLY.
IT'S SO DARK THAT I CAN'T SEE INSIDE THE HOUSE.
CHOCOLAT!!

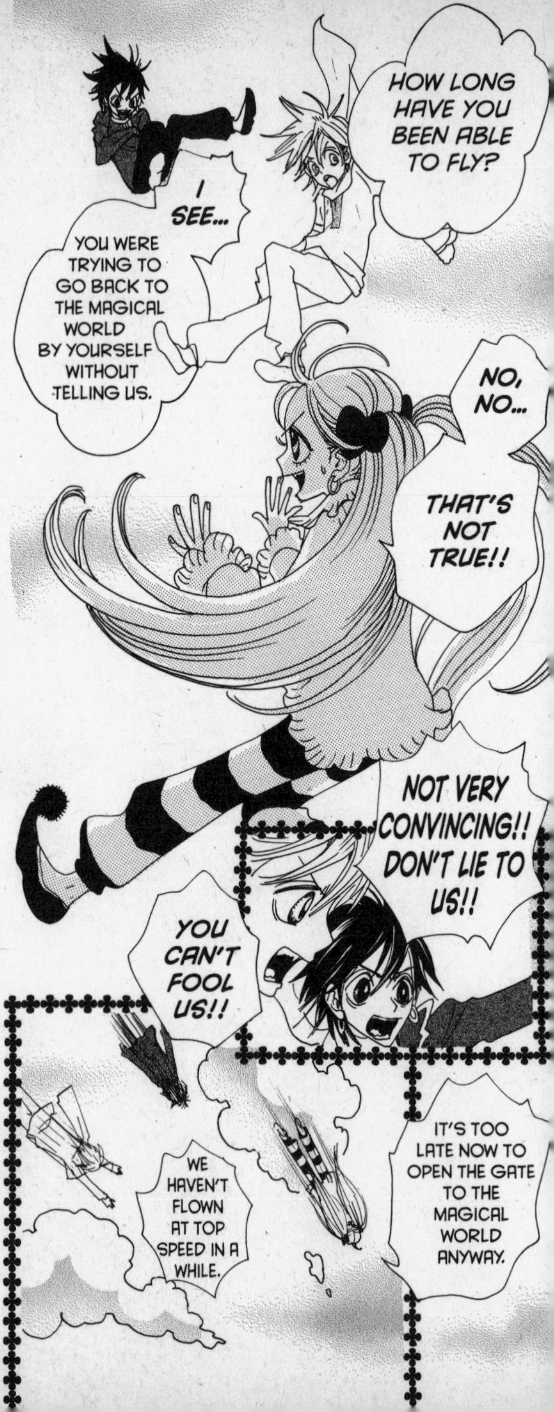
HOW LONG HAVE YOU BEEN ABLE TO FLY?
I SEE...
YOU WERE TRYING TO GO BACK TO THE MAGICAL WORLD BY YOURSELF WITHOUT TELLING US.
NO, NO...
THAT'S NOT TRUE!!
NOT VERY CONVINCING!! DON'T LIE TO US!!
YOU CAN'T FOOL US!!
IT'S TOO LATE NOW TO OPEN THE GATE TO THE MAGICAL WORLD ANYWAY.
WE HAVEN'T FLOWN AT TOP SPEED IN A WHILE.

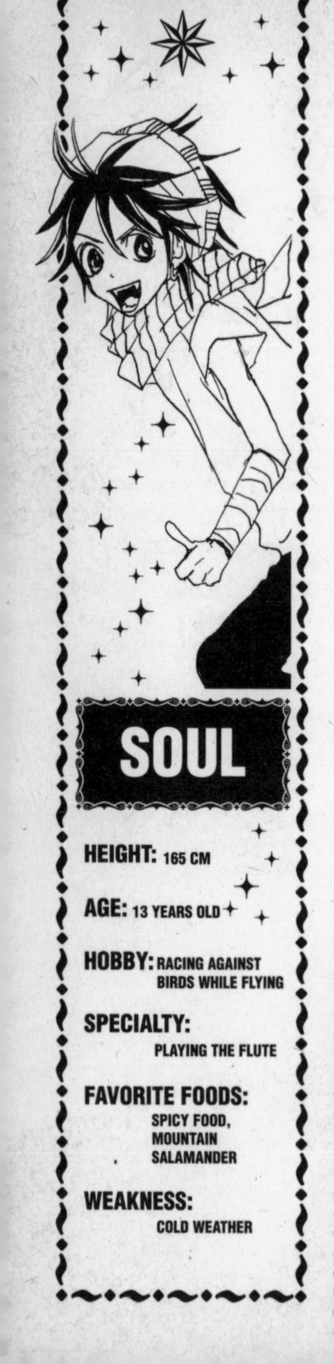

SOUL

HEIGHT: 165 CM

AGE: 13 YEARS OLD

HOBBY: RACING AGAINST BIRDS WHILE FLYING

SPECIALTY: PLAYING THE FLUTE

FAVORITE FOODS: SPICY FOOD, MOUNTAIN SALAMANDER

WEAKNESS: COLD WEATHER

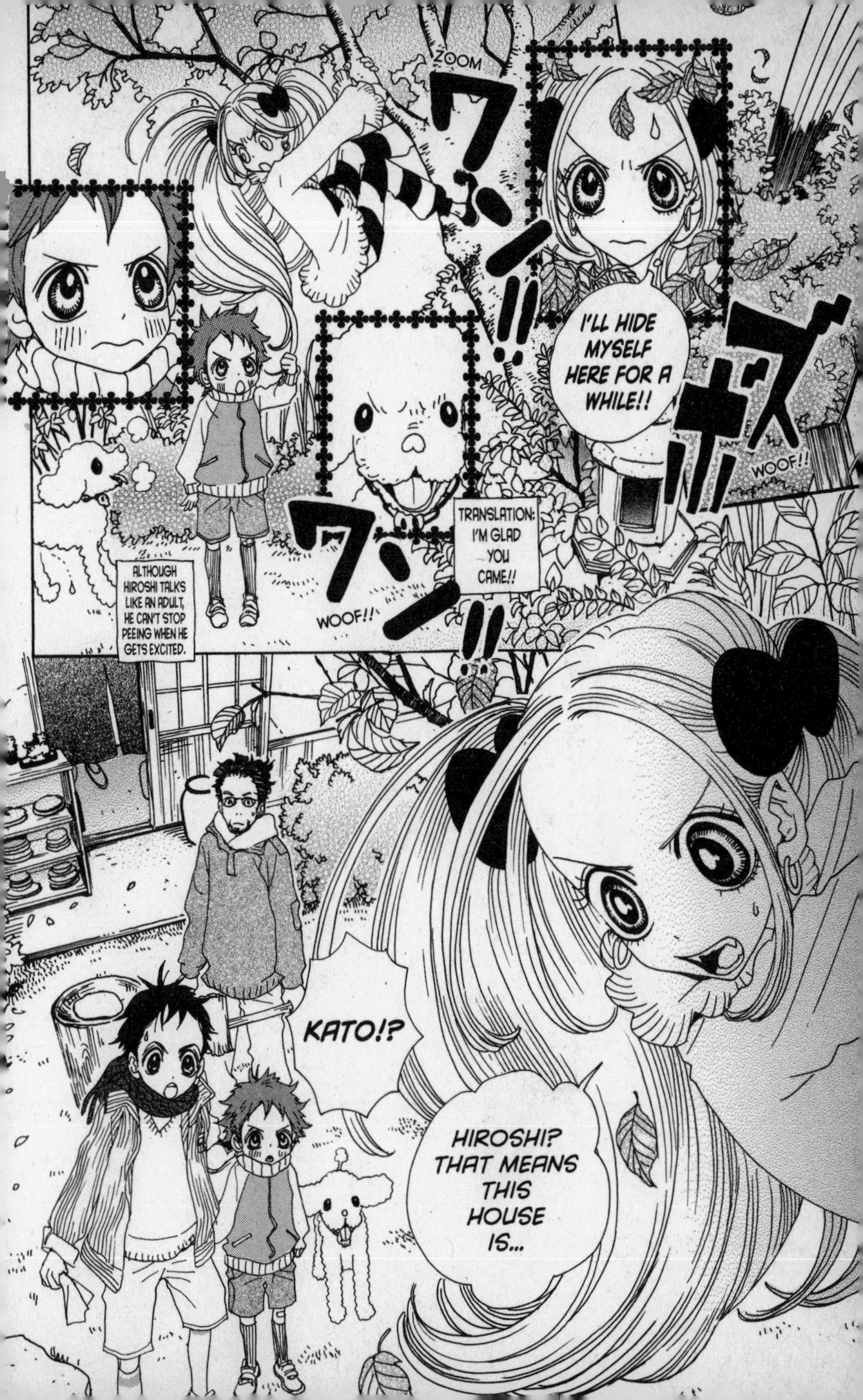
I'LL HIDE MYSELF HERE FOR A WHILE!!
WOOF!!
ZOOM
WOOF!!
TRANSLATION: I'M GLAD YOU CAME!!
ALTHOUGH HIROSHI TALKS LIKE AN ADULT, HE CAN'T STOP PEEING WHEN HE GETS EXCITED.
HIROSHI? THAT MEANS THIS HOUSE IS...
KATO!?

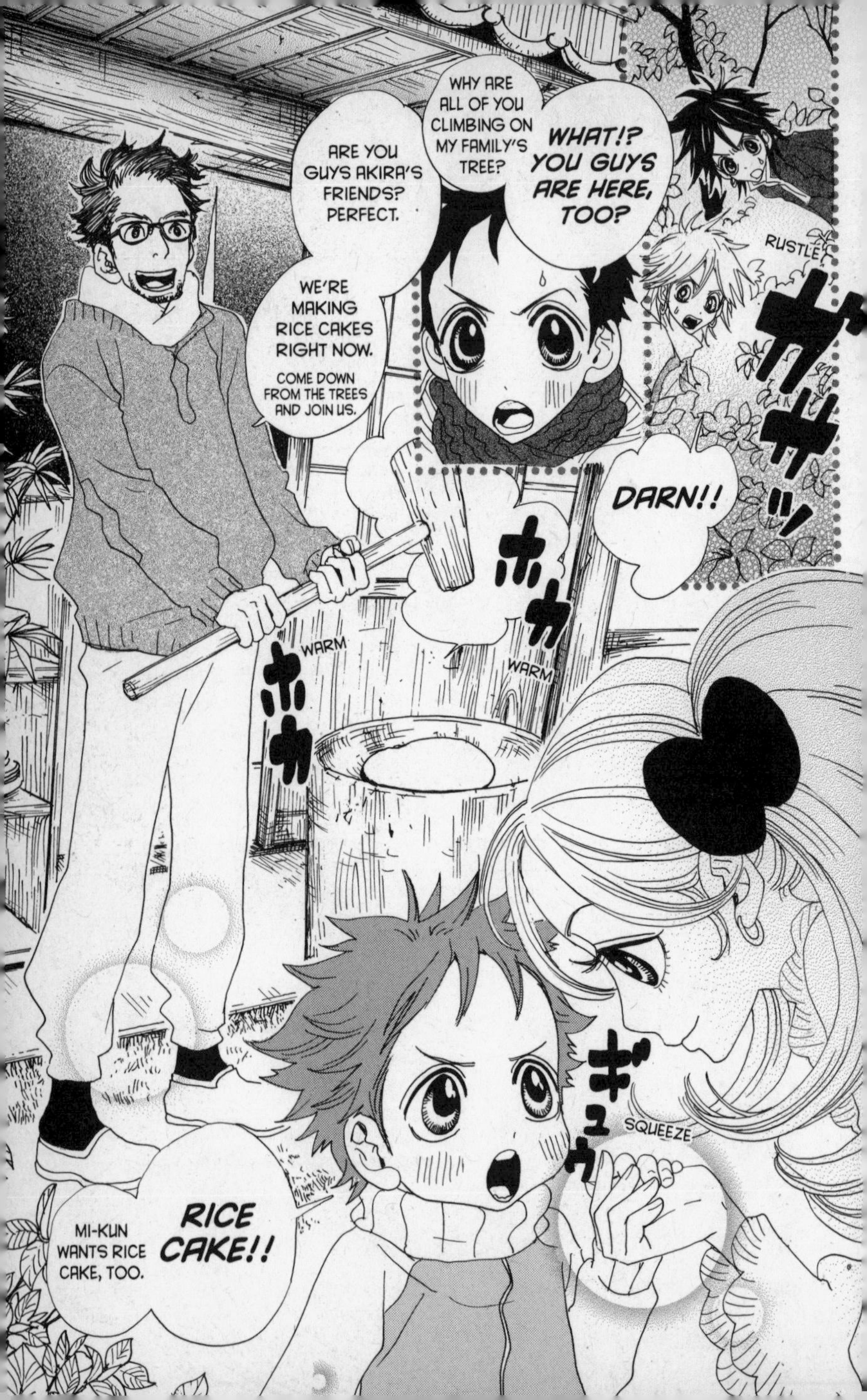
RUSTLE
DARN!!
WHAT!? YOU GUYS ARE HERE, TOO?
WHY ARE ALL OF YOU CLIMBING ON MY FAMILY'S TREE?
ARE YOU GUYS AKIRA'S FRIENDS? PERFECT.
WE'RE MAKING RICE CAKES RIGHT NOW.
COME DOWN FROM THE TREES AND JOIN US.
WARM
WARM
SQUEEZE
RICE CAKE!!
MI-KUN WANTS RICE CAKE, TOO.

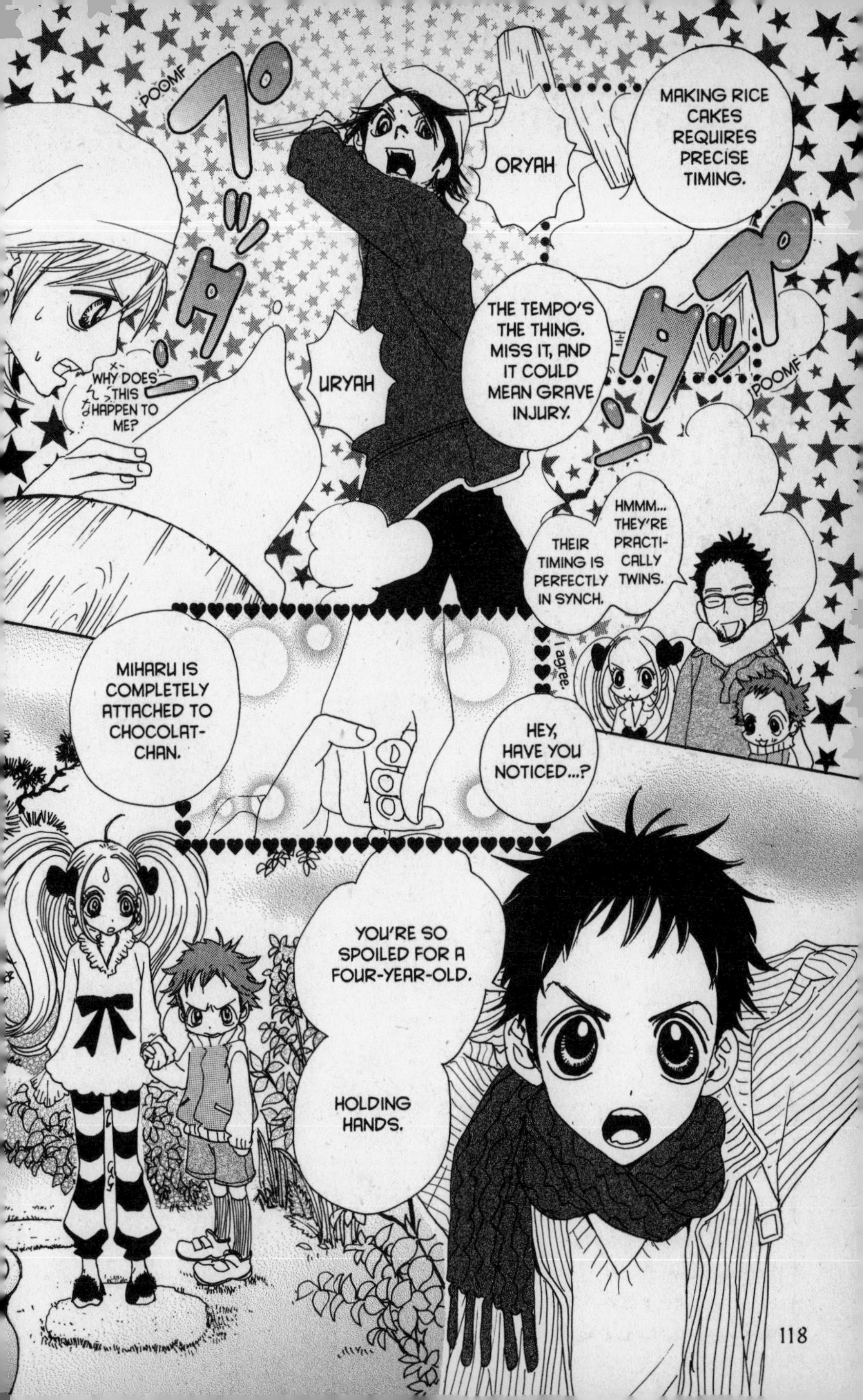
MAKING RICE CAKES REQUIRES PRECISE TIMING.
ORYAH
POOMF
THE TEMPO'S THE THING. MISS IT, AND IT COULD MEAN GRAVE INJURY.
POOMF
URYAH
WHY DOES THIS HAPPEN TO ME?
HMMM... THEY'RE PRACTI-CALLY TWINS.
THEIR TIMING IS PERFECTLY IN SYNCH.
I agree.
HEY, HAVE YOU NOTICED...?
MIHARU IS COMPLETELY ATTACHED TO CHOCOLAT-CHAN.
YOU'RE SO SPOILED FOR A FOUR-YEAR-OLD.
HOLDING HANDS.

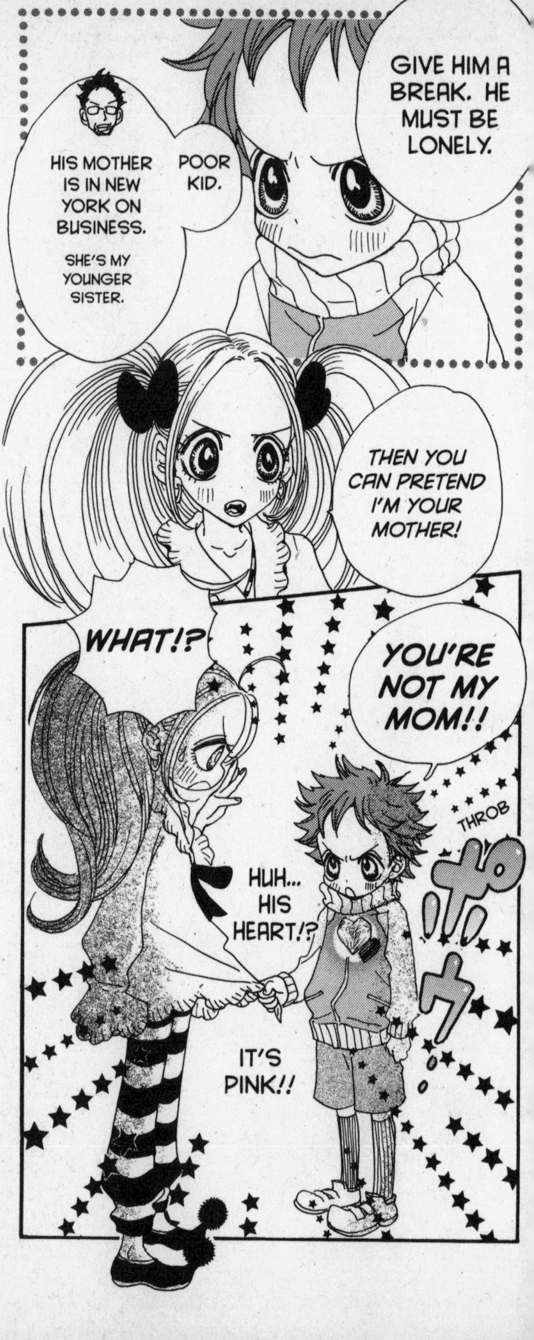
GIVE HIM A BREAK. HE MUST BE LONELY.
POOR KID.
HIS MOTHER IS IN NEW YORK ON BUSINESS.
SHE'S MY YOUNGER SISTER.
THEN YOU CAN PRETEND I'M YOUR MOTHER!
YOU'RE NOT MY MOM!!
WHAT!?
THROB
HUH... HIS HEART!?
IT'S PINK!!

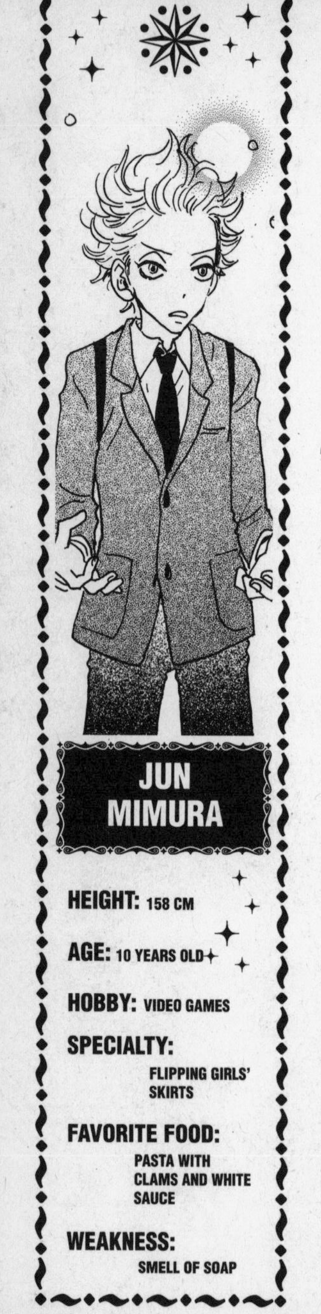

JUN MIMURA

HEIGHT: 158 CM

AGE: 10 YEARS OLD

HOBBY: VIDEO GAMES

SPECIALTY:
FLIPPING GIRLS' SKIRTS

FAVORITE FOOD:
PASTA WITH CLAMS AND WHITE SAUCE

WEAKNESS:
SMELL OF SOAP

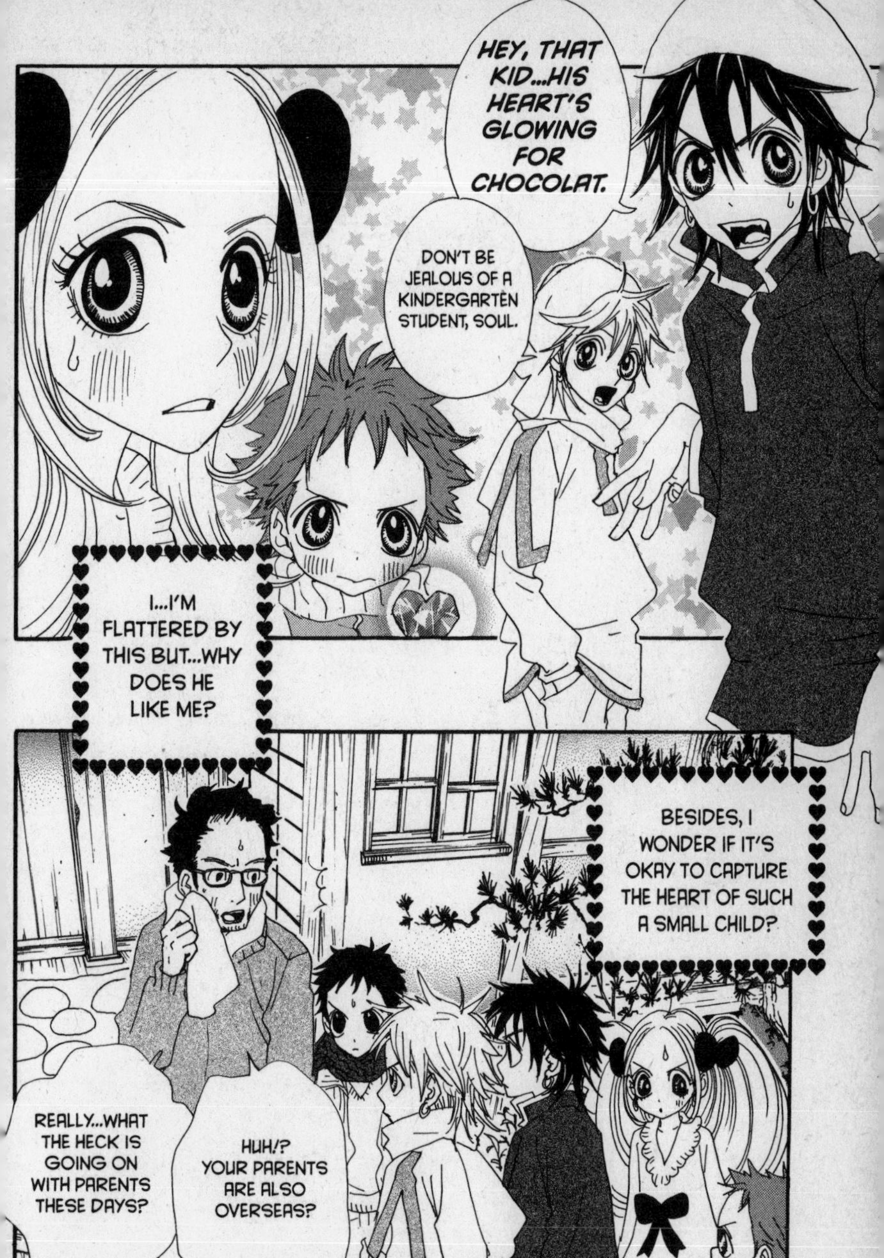
HEY, THAT KID...HIS HEART'S GLOWING FOR CHOCOLAT.
DON'T BE JEALOUS OF A KINDERGARTEN STUDENT, SOUL.
I...I'M FLATTERED BY THIS BUT...WHY DOES HE LIKE ME?
BESIDES, I WONDER IF IT'S OKAY TO CAPTURE THE HEART OF SUCH A SMALL CHILD?
HUH!? YOUR PARENTS ARE ALSO OVERSEAS?
REALLY...WHAT THE HECK IS GOING ON WITH PARENTS THESE DAYS?

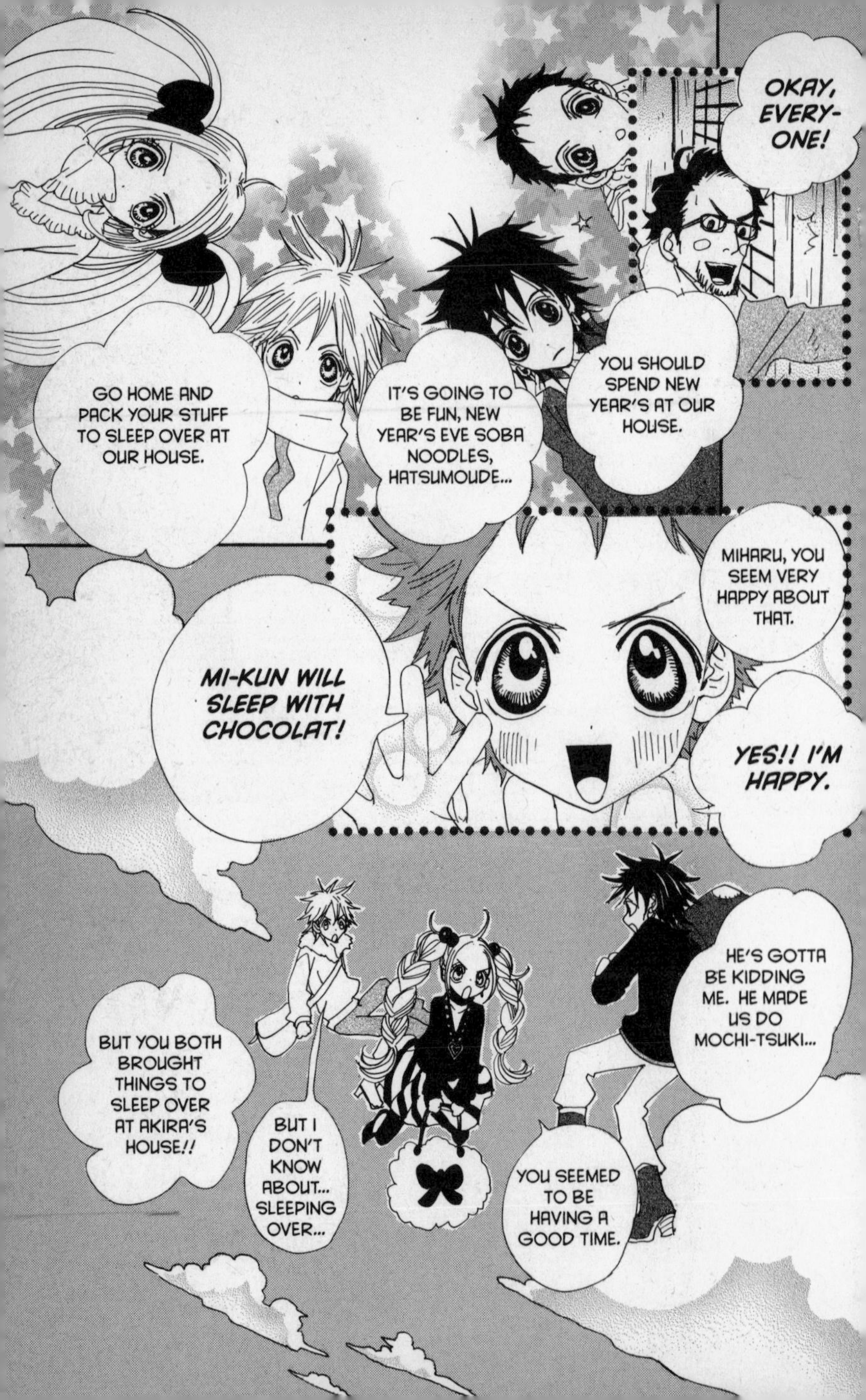
OKAY, EVERYONE!
YOU SHOULD SPEND NEW YEAR'S AT OUR HOUSE.
IT'S GOING TO BE FUN, NEW YEAR'S EVE SOBA NOODLES, HATSUMOUDE...
GO HOME AND PACK YOUR STUFF TO SLEEP OVER AT OUR HOUSE.
MIHARU, YOU SEEM VERY HAPPY ABOUT THAT.
YES!! I'M HAPPY.
MI-KUN WILL SLEEP WITH CHOCOLAT!
HE'S GOTTA BE KIDDING ME. HE MADE US DO MOCHI-TSUKI...
YOU SEEMED TO BE HAVING A GOOD TIME.
BUT I DON'T KNOW ABOUT... SLEEPING OVER...
BUT YOU BOTH BROUGHT THINGS TO SLEEP OVER AT AKIRA'S HOUSE!!

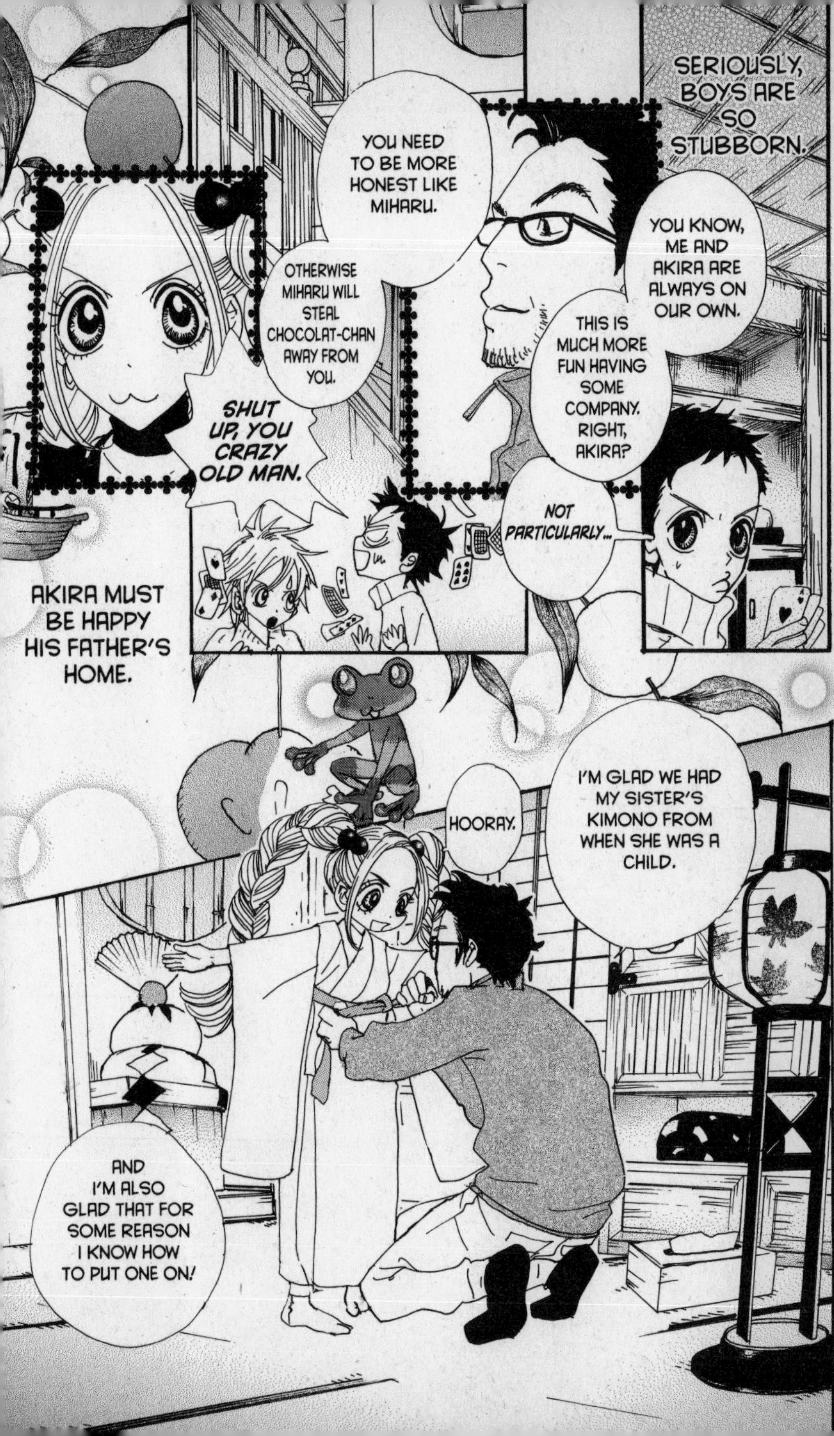
SERIOUSLY, BOYS ARE SO STUBBORN.
YOU KNOW, ME AND AKIRA ARE ALWAYS ON OUR OWN.
THIS IS MUCH MORE FUN HAVING SOME COMPANY. RIGHT, AKIRA?
NOT PARTICULARLY...
YOU NEED TO BE MORE HONEST LIKE MIHARU.
OTHERWISE MIHARU WILL STEAL CHOCOLAT-CHAN AWAY FROM YOU.
SHUT UP, YOU CRAZY OLD MAN.
AKIRA MUST BE HAPPY HIS FATHER'S HOME.
I'M GLAD WE HAD MY SISTER'S KIMONO FROM WHEN SHE WAS A CHILD.
HOORAY.
AND I'M ALSO GLAD THAT FOR SOME REASON I KNOW HOW TO PUT ONE ON!

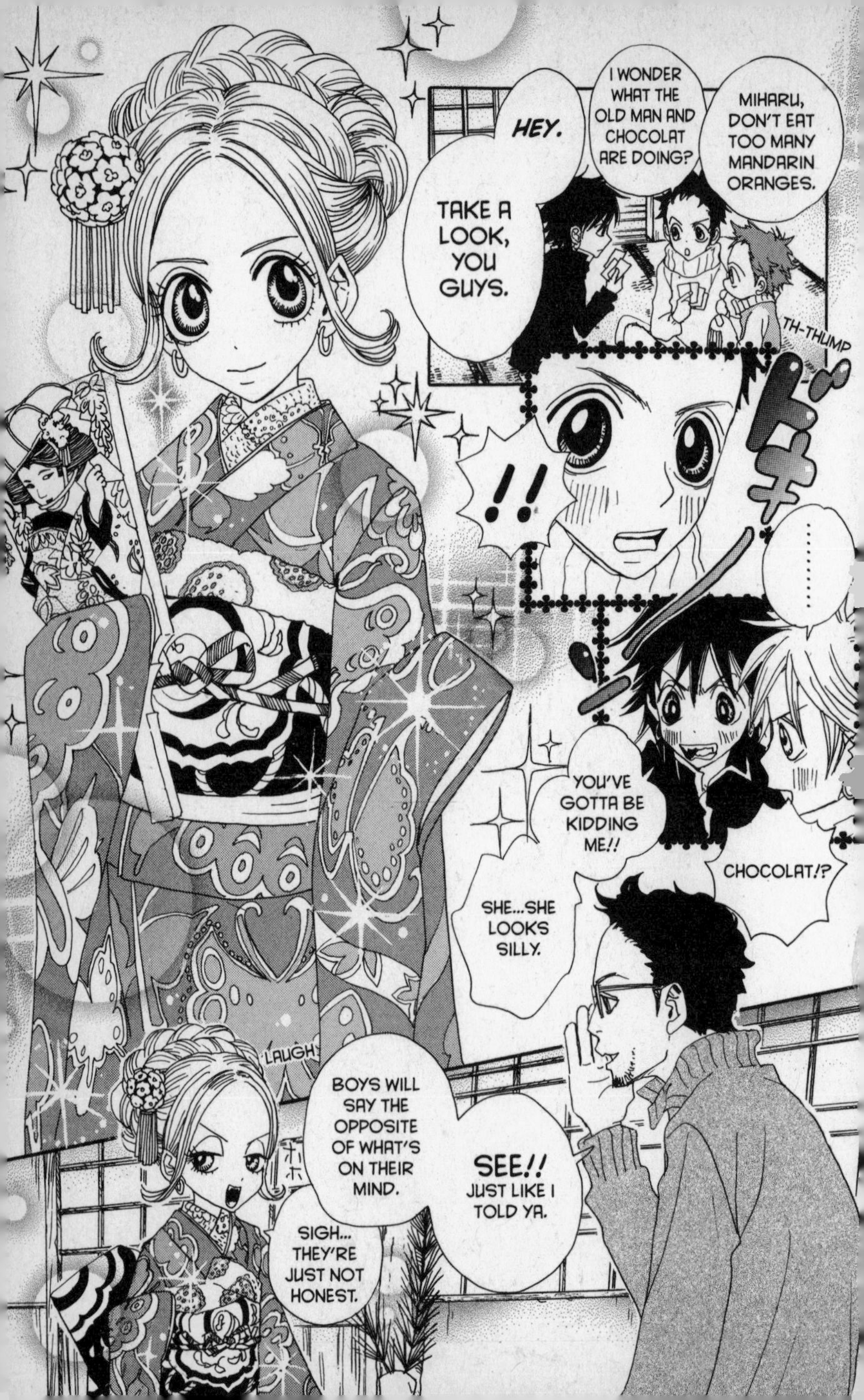
MIHARU, DON'T EAT TOO MANY MANDARIN ORANGES.
I WONDER WHAT THE OLD MAN AND CHOCOLAT ARE DOING?
HEY.
TAKE A LOOK, YOU GUYS.
TH-THUMP
ドキ
!!
......
CHOCOLAT!?
YOU'VE GOTTA BE KIDDING ME!!
SHE...SHE LOOKS SILLY.
SEE!! JUST LIKE I TOLD YA.
BOYS WILL SAY THE OPPOSITE OF WHAT'S ON THEIR MIND.
LAUGH
SIGH... THEY'RE JUST NOT HONEST.

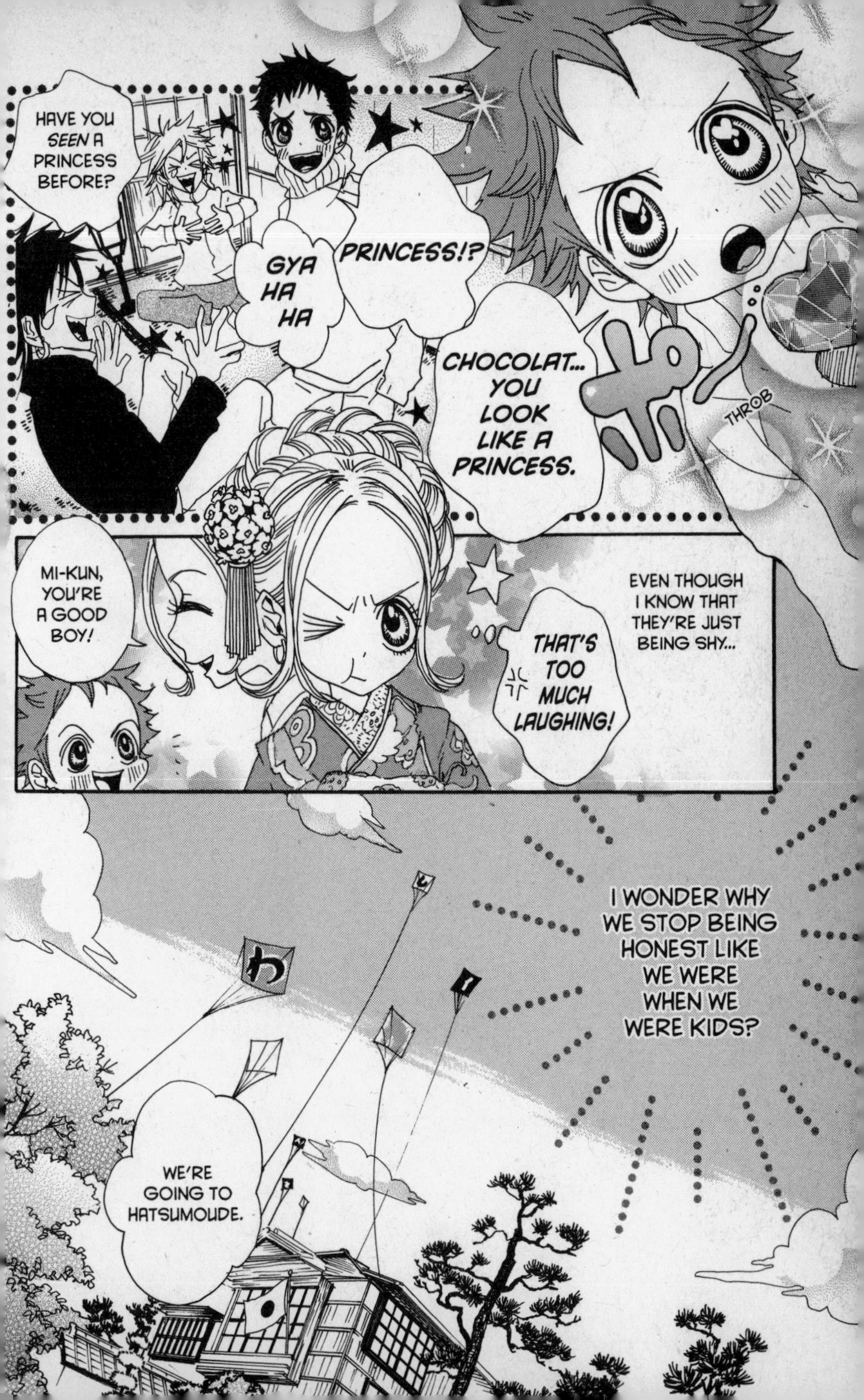
CHOCOLAT... YOU LOOK LIKE A PRINCESS.
THROB
PRINCESS!?
GYA HA HA
HAVE YOU SEEN A PRINCESS BEFORE?
EVEN THOUGH I KNOW THAT THEY'RE JUST BEING SHY...
THAT'S TOO MUCH LAUGHING!
MI-KUN, YOU'RE A GOOD BOY!
I WONDER WHY WE STOP BEING HONEST LIKE WE WERE WHEN WE WERE KIDS?
WE'RE GOING TO HATSUMOUDE.

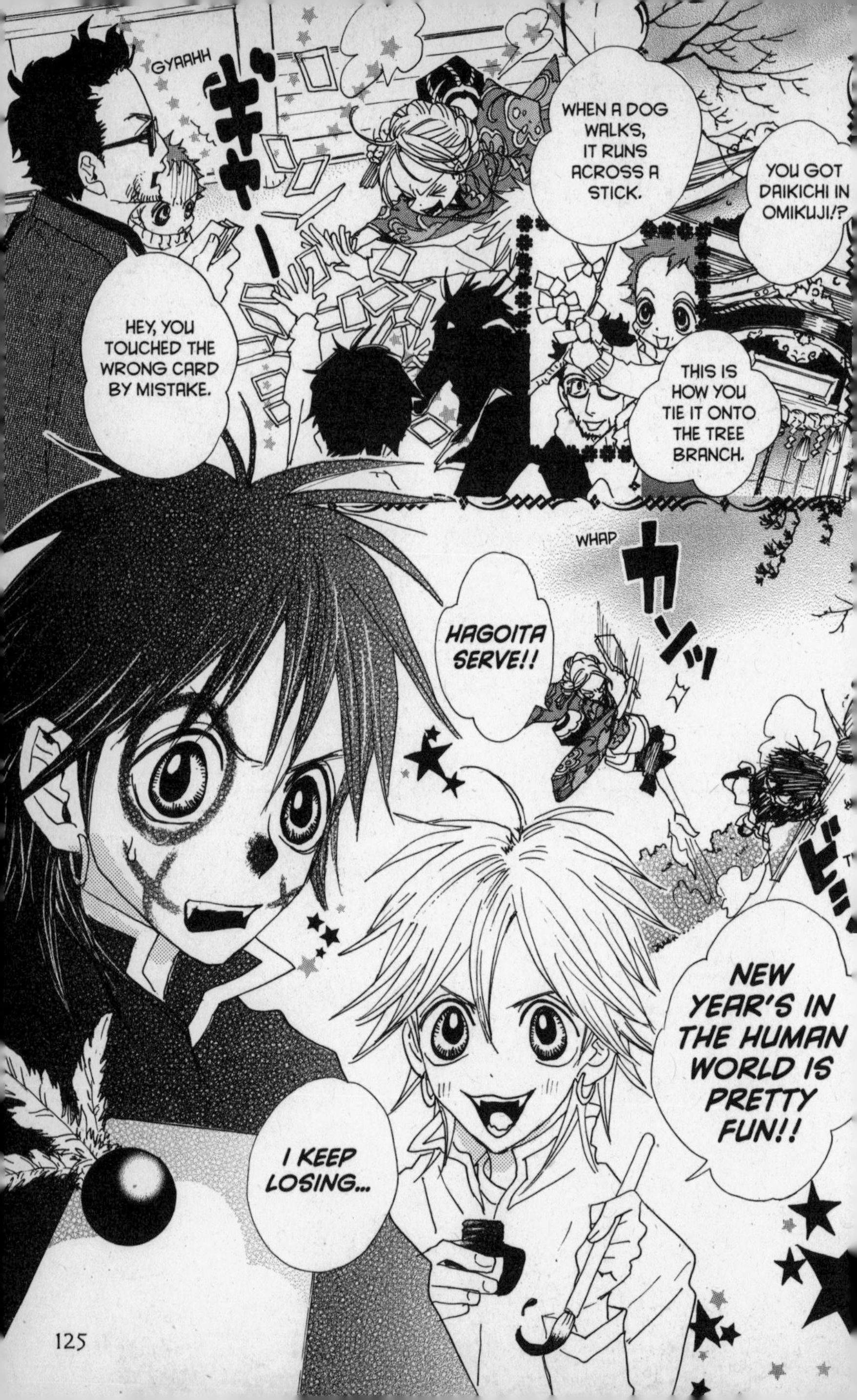
YOU GOT DAIKICHI IN OMIKUJI!?
THIS IS HOW YOU TIE IT ONTO THE TREE BRANCH.
WHEN A DOG WALKS, IT RUNS ACROSS A STICK.
GYAAHH
HEY, YOU TOUCHED THE WRONG CARD BY MISTAKE.
WHAP
HAGOITA SERVE!!
NEW YEAR'S IN THE HUMAN WORLD IS PRETTY FUN!!
I KEEP LOSING...

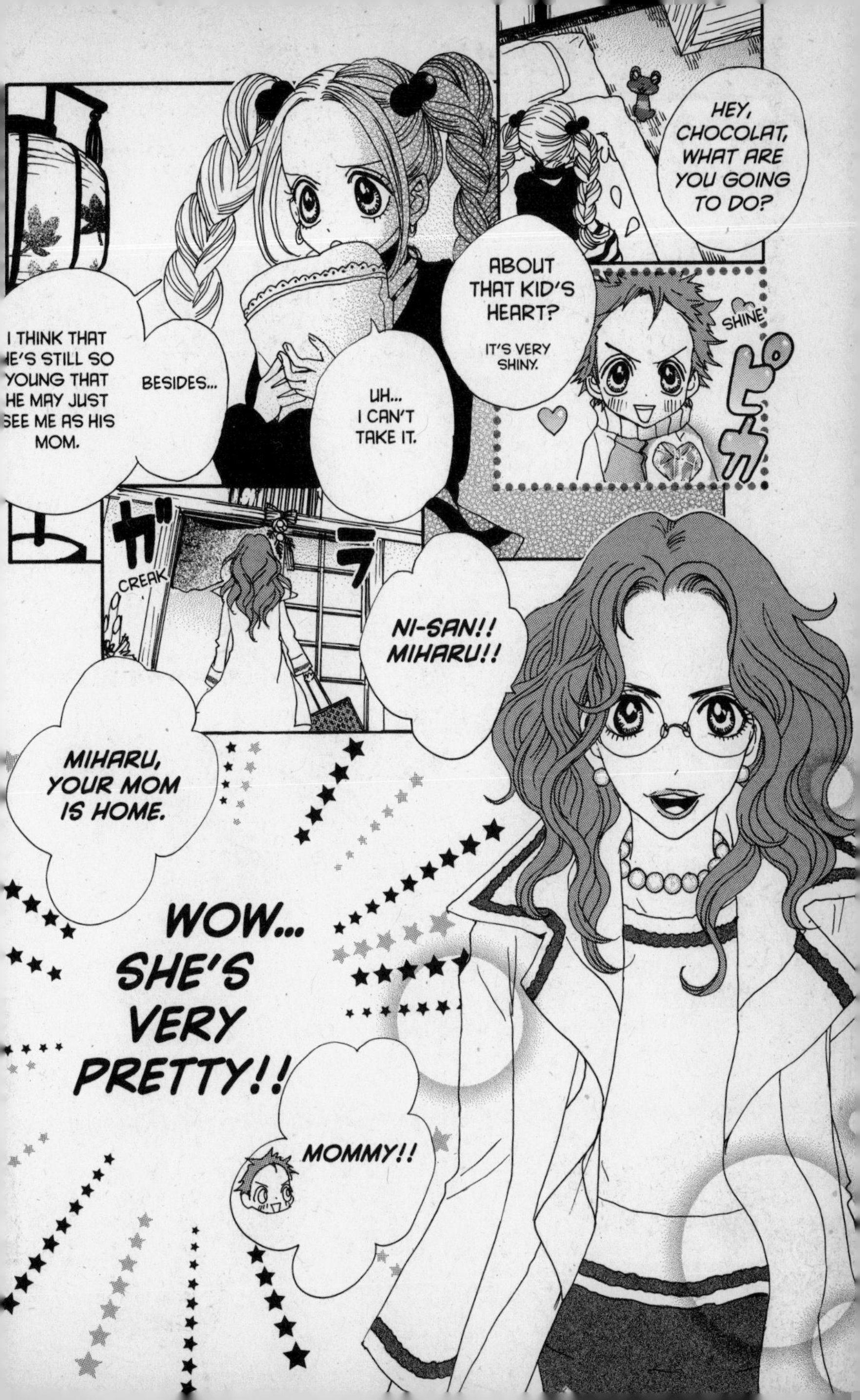
HEY, CHOCOLAT, WHAT ARE YOU GOING TO DO?
ABOUT THAT KID'S HEART?
IT'S VERY SHINY.
SHINE
UH... I CAN'T TAKE IT.
BESIDES...
I THINK THAT HE'S STILL SO YOUNG THAT HE MAY JUST SEE ME AS HIS MOM.
CREAK
NI-SAN!! MIHARU!!
MIHARU, YOUR MOM IS HOME.
WOW... SHE'S VERY PRETTY!!
MOMMY!!

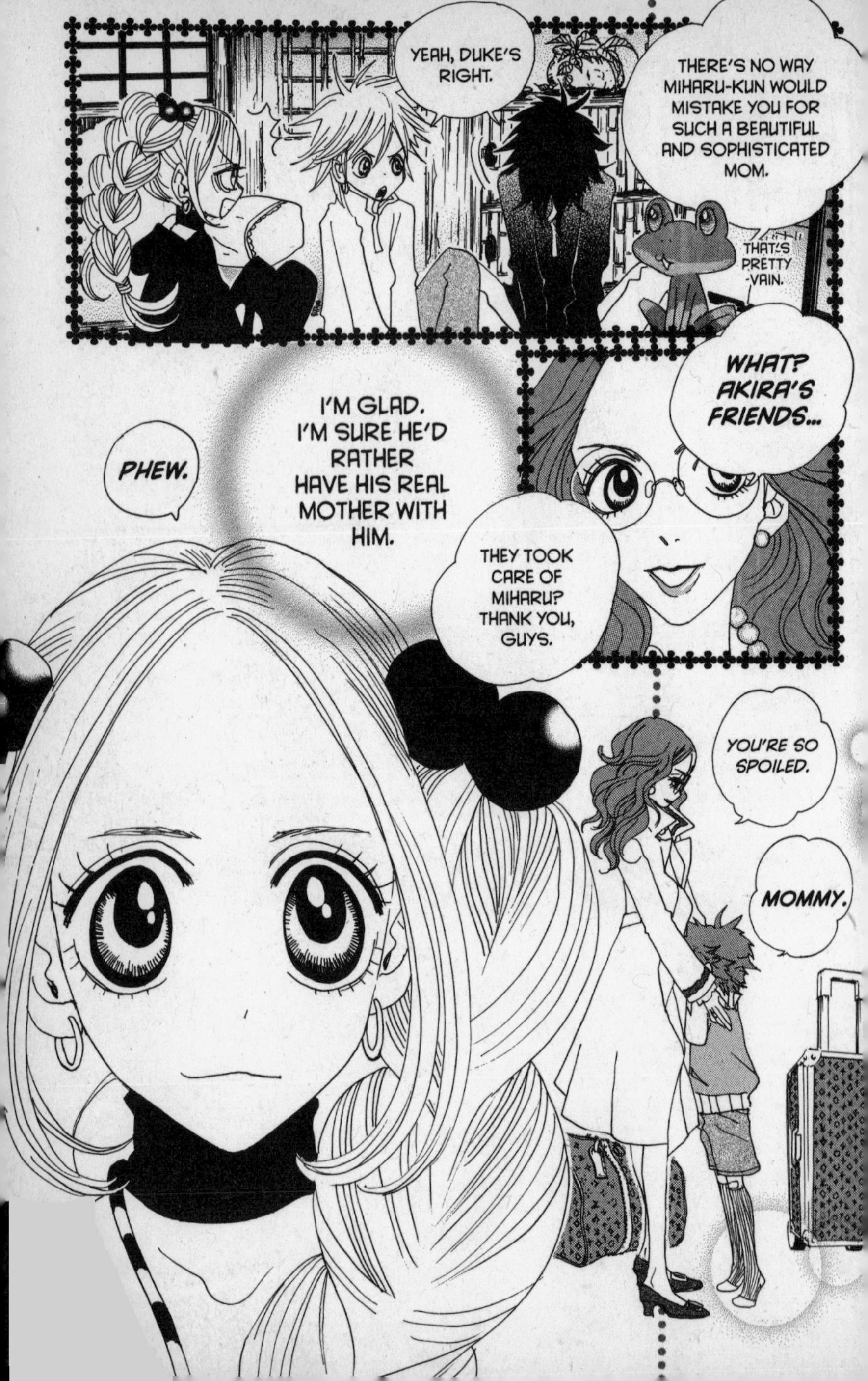
THERE'S NO WAY MIHARU-KUN WOULD MISTAKE YOU FOR SUCH A BEAUTIFUL AND SOPHISTICATED MOM.
THAT'S PRETTY VAIN.
YEAH, DUKE'S RIGHT.
WHAT? AKIRA'S FRIENDS...
THEY TOOK CARE OF MIHARU? THANK YOU, GUYS.
YOU'RE SO SPOILED.
MOMMY.
I'M GLAD. I'M SURE HE'D RATHER HAVE HIS REAL MOTHER WITH HIM.
PHEW.

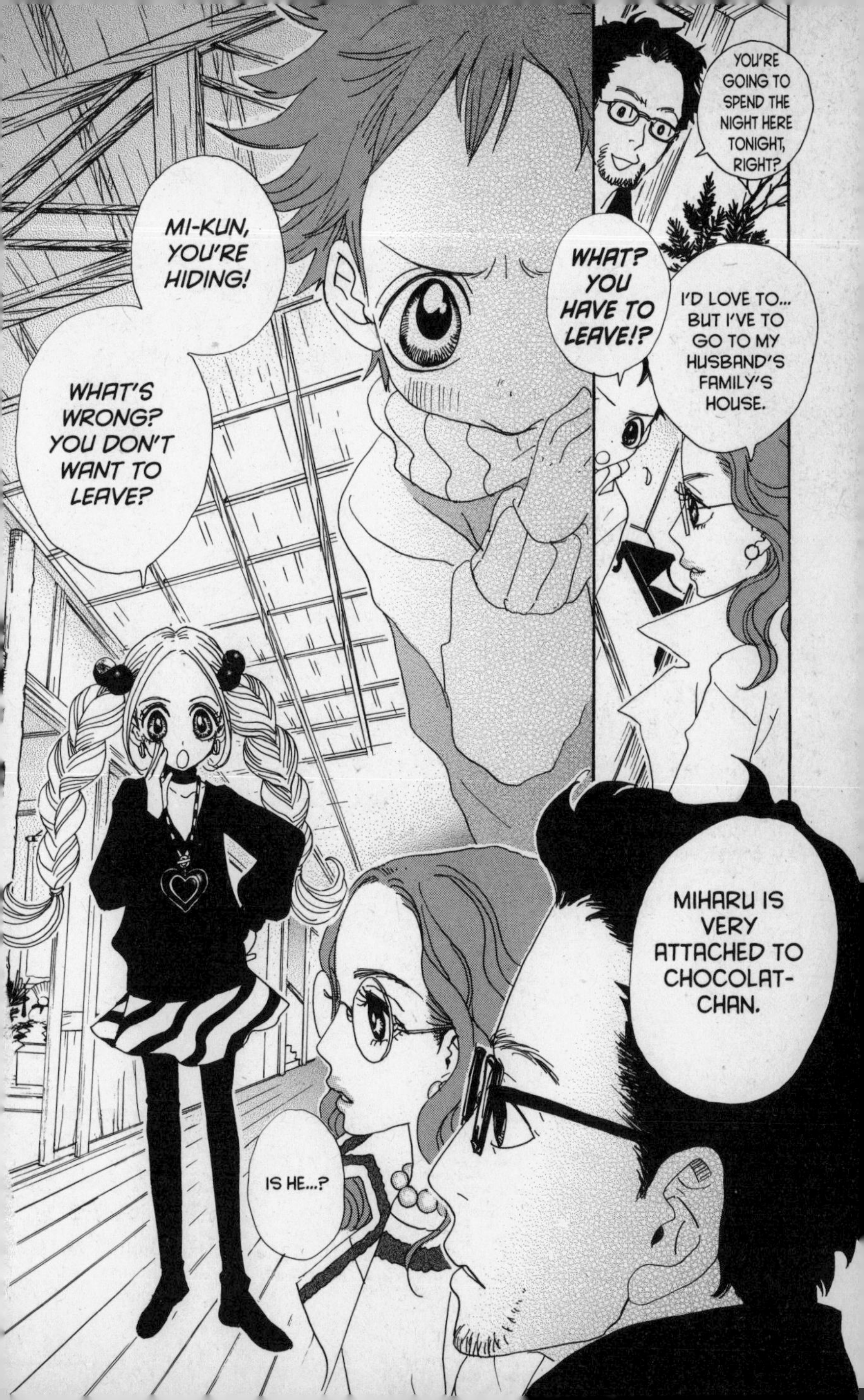
YOU'RE GOING TO SPEND THE NIGHT HERE TONIGHT, RIGHT?
I'D LOVE TO... BUT I'VE TO GO TO MY HUSBAND'S FAMILY'S HOUSE.
WHAT? YOU HAVE TO LEAVE!?
MI-KUN, YOU'RE HIDING!
WHAT'S WRONG? YOU DON'T WANT TO LEAVE?
MIHARU IS VERY ATTACHED TO CHOCOLAT-CHAN.
IS HE...?

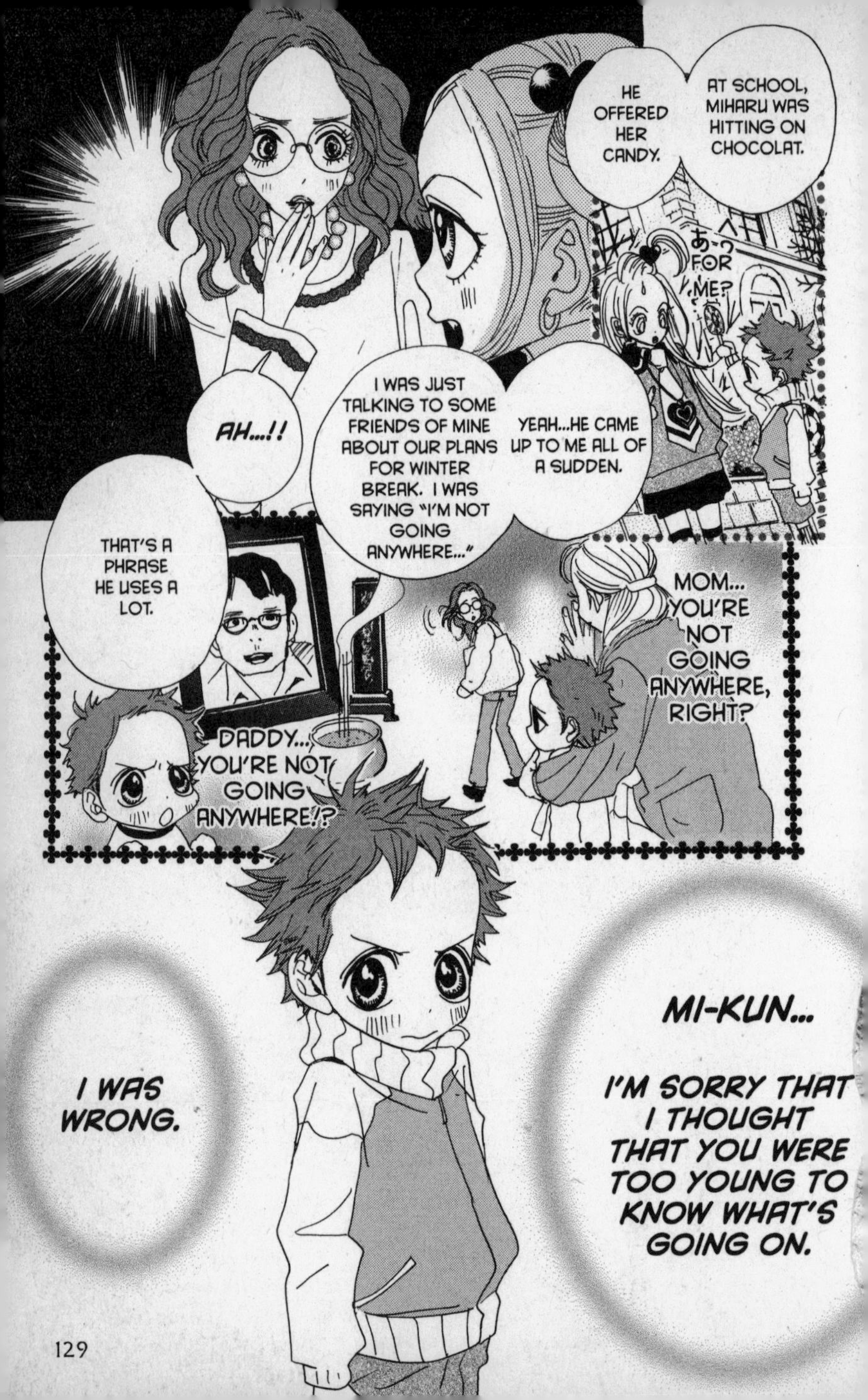

AT SCHOOL, MIHARU WAS HITTING ON CHOCOLAT.
HE OFFERED HER CANDY.
あーっ FOR ME?
YEAH...HE CAME UP TO ME ALL OF A SUDDEN.
I WAS JUST TALKING TO SOME FRIENDS OF MINE ABOUT OUR PLANS FOR WINTER BREAK. I WAS SAYING "I'M NOT GOING ANYWHERE..."
AH...!!
THAT'S A PHRASE HE USES A LOT.
MOM... YOU'RE NOT GOING ANYWHERE, RIGHT?
DADDY... YOU'RE NOT GOING ANYWHERE!?
MI-KUN...
I'M SORRY THAT I THOUGHT THAT YOU WERE TOO YOUNG TO KNOW WHAT'S GOING ON.
I WAS WRONG.

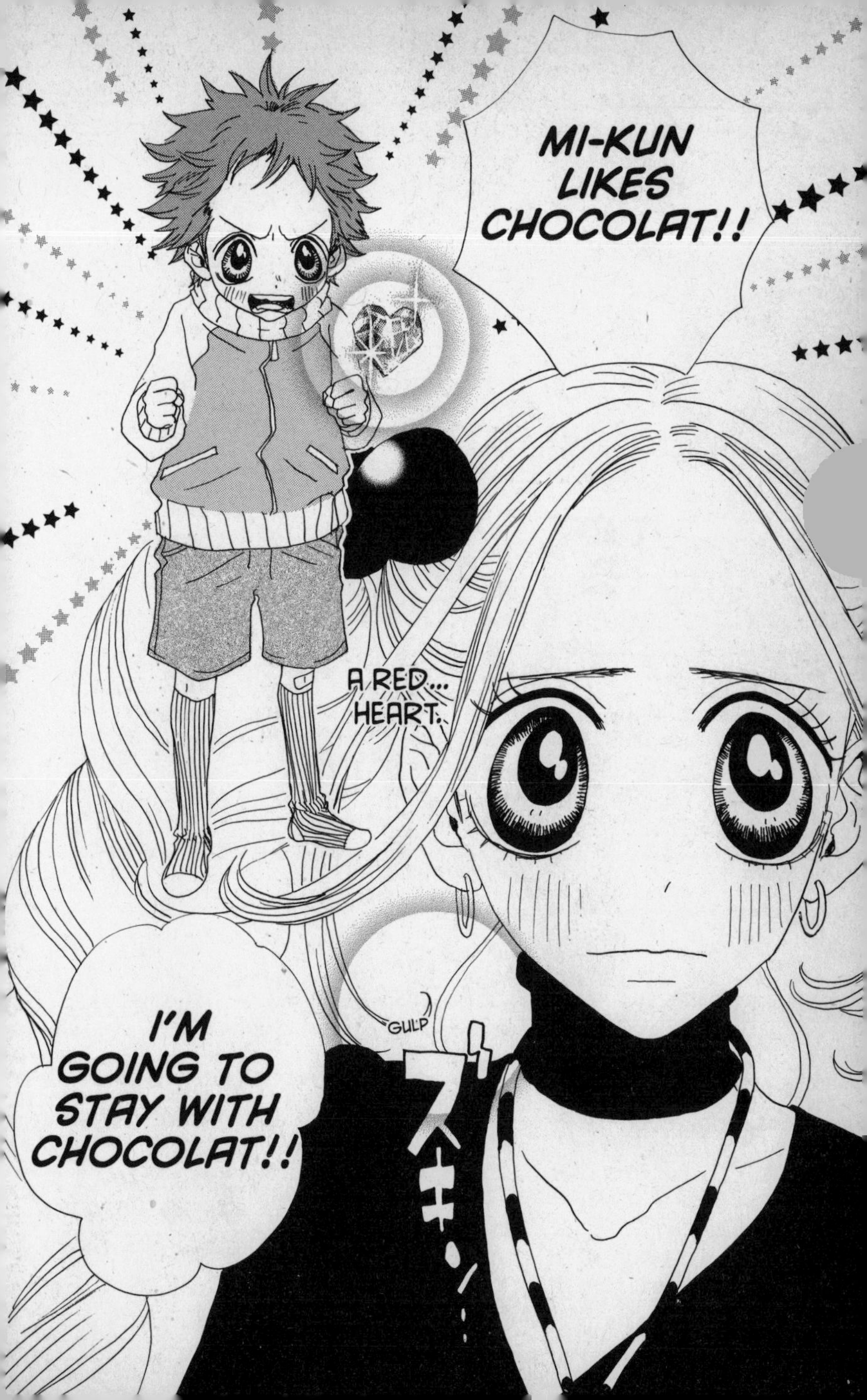
MI-KUN LIKES CHOCOLAT!!
A RED... HEART.
I'M GOING TO STAY WITH CHOCOLAT!!
GULP

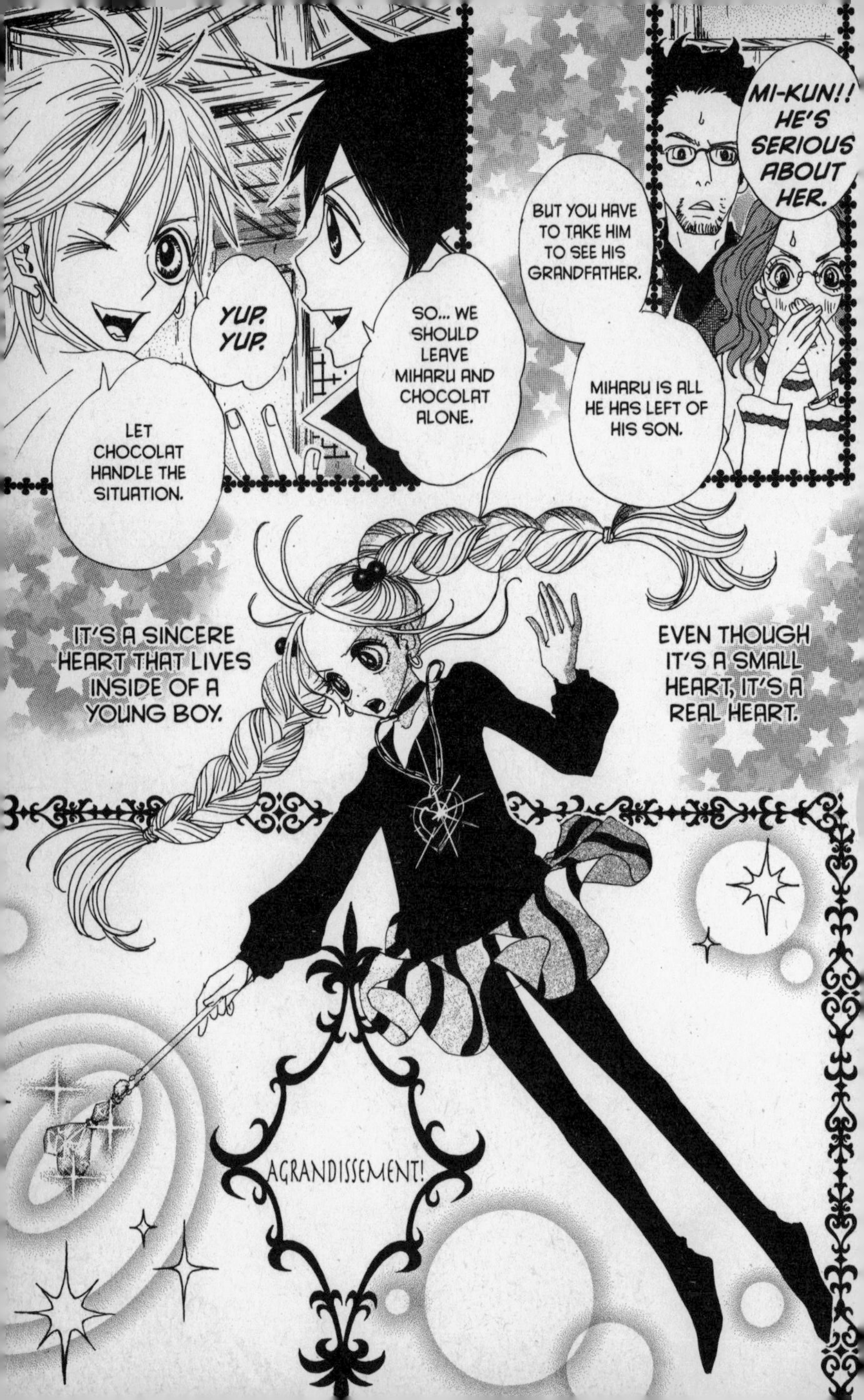
MI-KUN!! HE'S SERIOUS ABOUT HER.
BUT YOU HAVE TO TAKE HIM TO SEE HIS GRANDFATHER.
MIHARU IS ALL HE HAS LEFT OF HIS SON.
SO... WE SHOULD LEAVE MIHARU AND CHOCOLAT ALONE.
YUP. YUP.
LET CHOCOLAT HANDLE THE SITUATION.
EVEN THOUGH IT'S A SMALL HEART, IT'S A REAL HEART.
IT'S A SINCERE HEART THAT LIVES INSIDE OF A YOUNG BOY.
AGRANDISSEMENT!

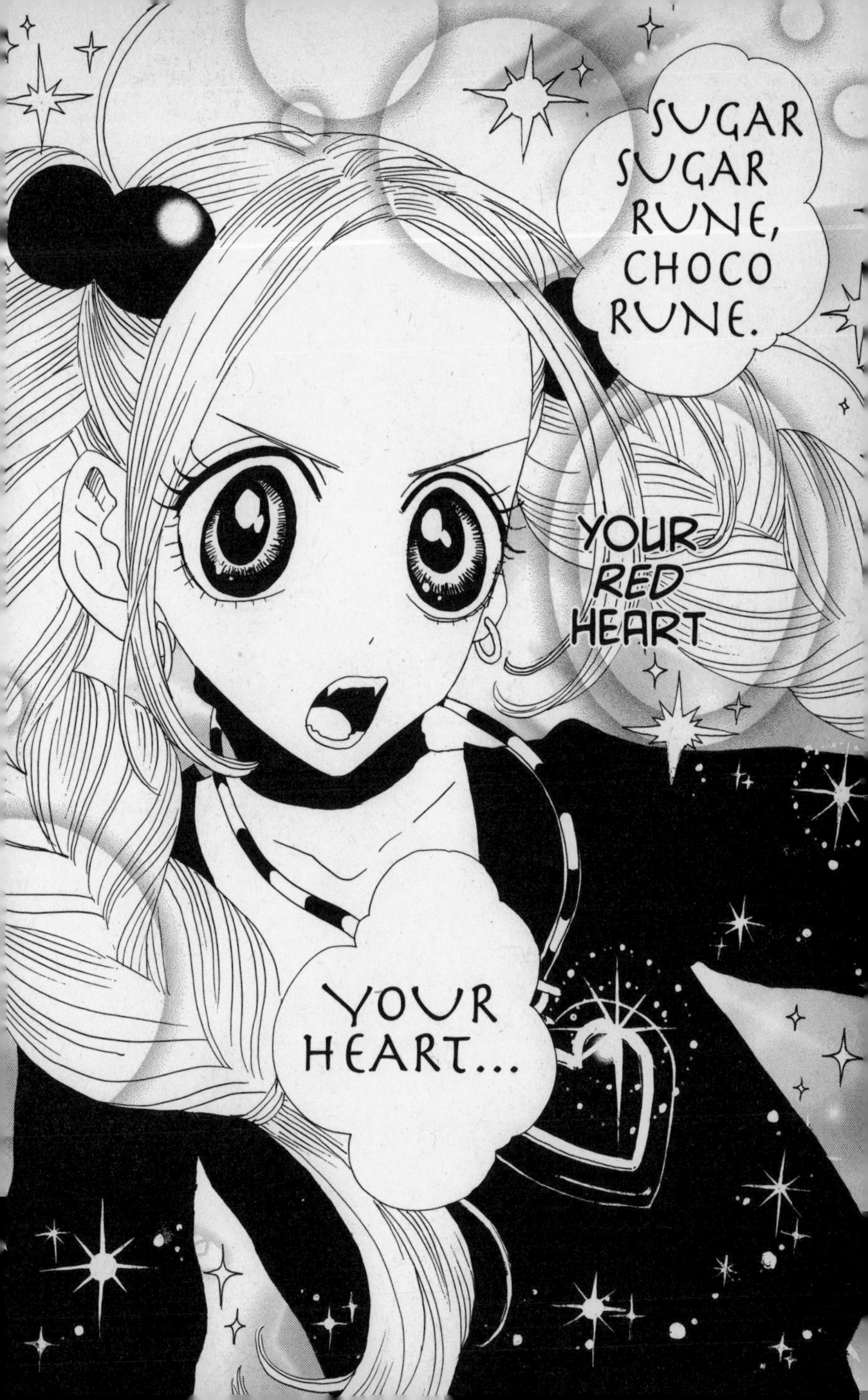
SUGAR SUGAR RUNE, CHOCO RUNE.
YOUR RED HEART
YOUR HEART...

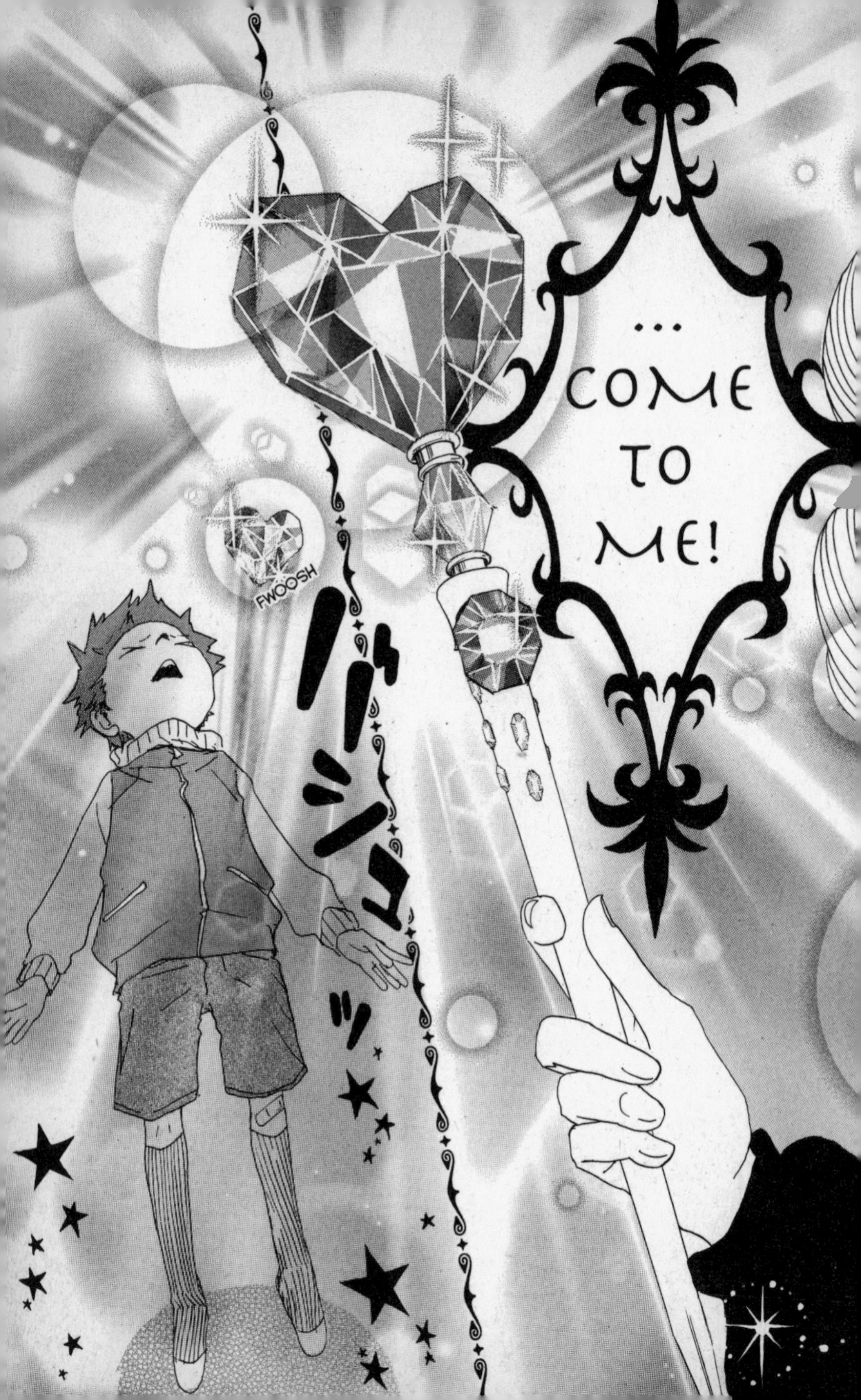
...COME TO ME!
FWOOSH

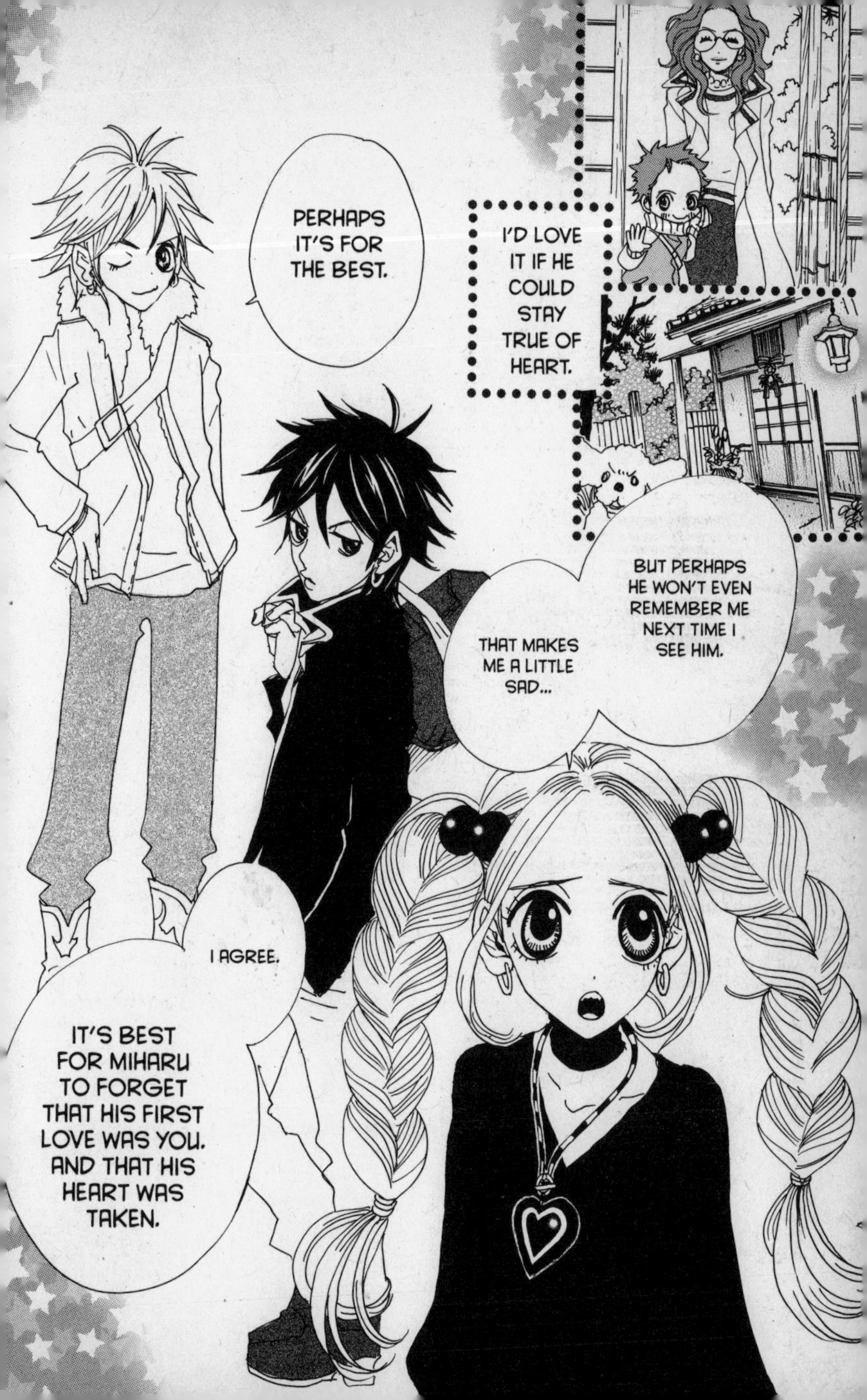
I'D LOVE IT IF HE COULD STAY TRUE OF HEART.
BUT PERHAPS HE WON'T EVEN REMEMBER ME NEXT TIME I SEE HIM.
THAT MAKES ME A LITTLE SAD...
PERHAPS IT'S FOR THE BEST.
I AGREE.
IT'S BEST FOR MIHARU TO FORGET THAT HIS FIRST LOVE WAS YOU. AND THAT HIS HEART WAS TAKEN.

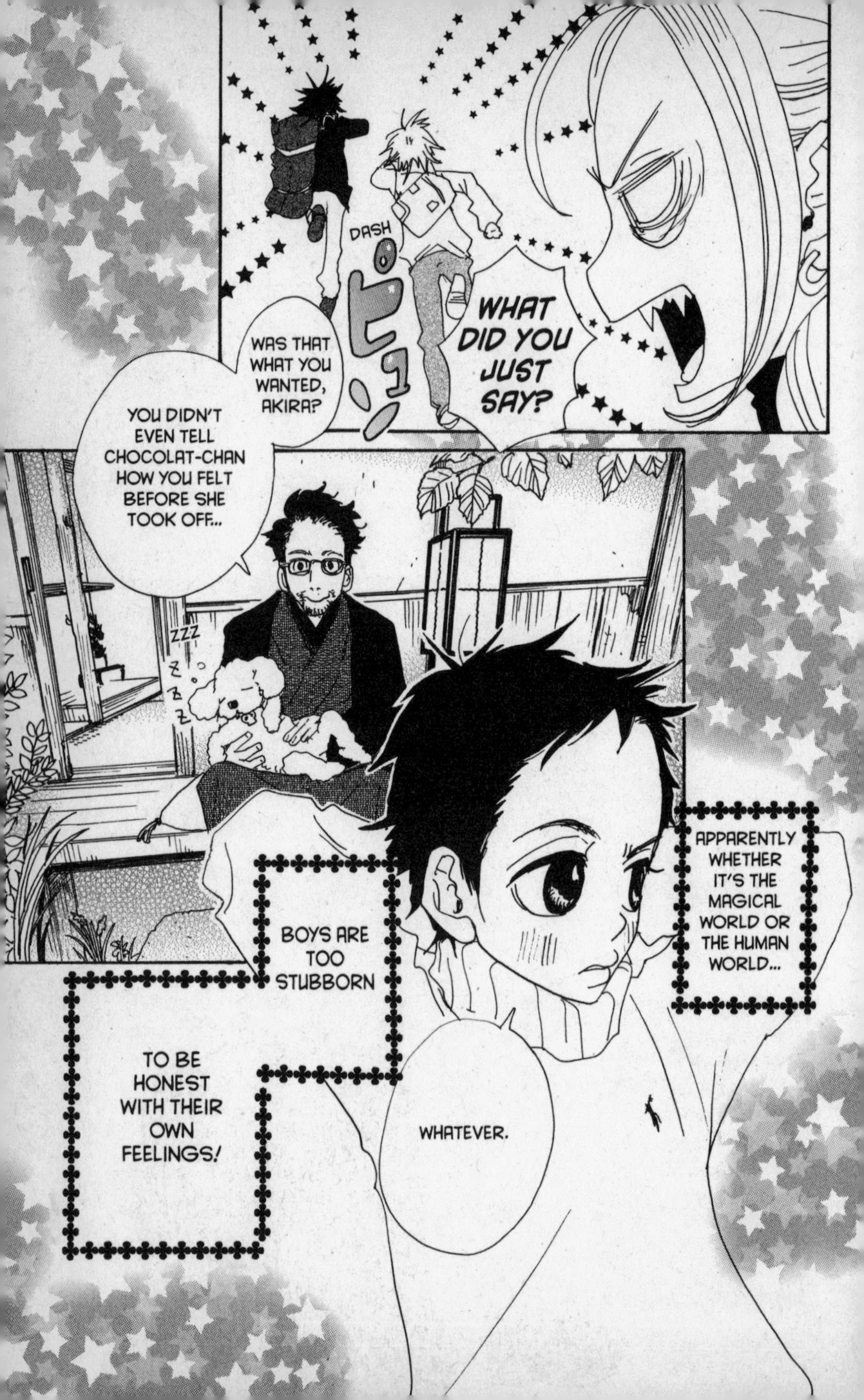
WHAT DID YOU JUST SAY?
DASH
ピュ
WAS THAT WHAT YOU WANTED, AKIRA?
YOU DIDN'T EVEN TELL CHOCOLAT-CHAN HOW YOU FELT BEFORE SHE TOOK OFF...
ZZZ
APPARENTLY WHETHER IT'S THE MAGICAL WORLD OR THE HUMAN WORLD...
BOYS ARE TOO STUBBORN
TO BE HONEST WITH THEIR OWN FEELINGS!
WHATEVER.

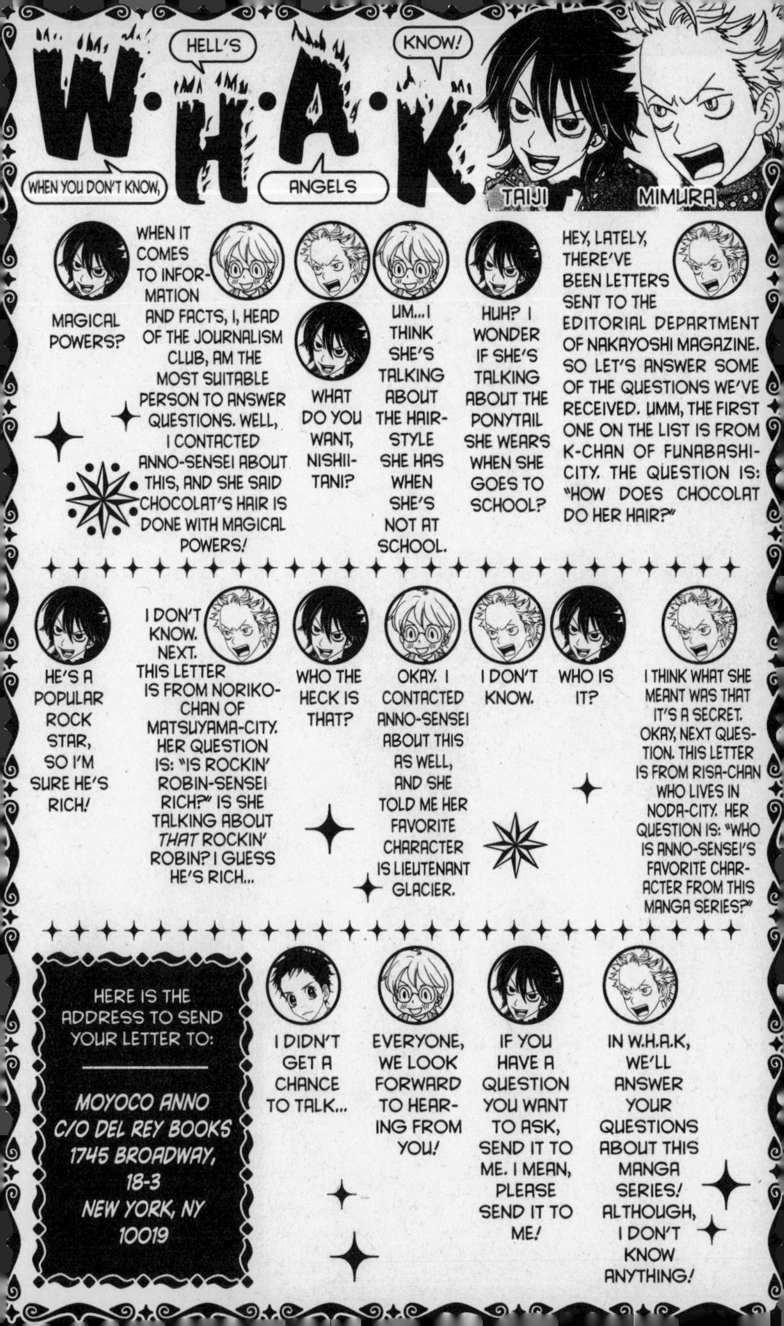
W·H·A·K
WHEN YOU DON'T KNOW,
HELL'S
ANGELS
KNOW!
TAIJI
MIMURA
HEY, LATELY, THERE'VE BEEN LETTERS SENT TO THE EDITORIAL DEPARTMENT OF NAKAYOSHI MAGAZINE. SO LET'S ANSWER SOME OF THE QUESTIONS WE'VE RECEIVED. UMM, THE FIRST ONE ON THE LIST IS FROM K-CHAN OF FUNABASHI-CITY. THE QUESTION IS: "HOW DOES CHOCOLAT DO HER HAIR?"
HUH? I WONDER IF SHE'S TALKING ABOUT THE PONYTAIL SHE WEARS WHEN SHE GOES TO SCHOOL?
UM...I THINK SHE'S TALKING ABOUT THE HAIR-STYLE SHE HAS WHEN SHE'S NOT AT SCHOOL.
WHAT DO YOU WANT, NISHII-TANI?
WHEN IT COMES TO INFOR-MATION AND FACTS, I, HEAD OF THE JOURNALISM CLUB, AM THE MOST SUITABLE PERSON TO ANSWER QUESTIONS. WELL, I CONTACTED ANNO-SENSEI ABOUT THIS, AND SHE SAID CHOCOLAT'S HAIR IS DONE WITH MAGICAL POWERS!
MAGICAL POWERS?
I THINK WHAT SHE MEANT WAS THAT IT'S A SECRET. OKAY, NEXT QUES-TION. THIS LETTER IS FROM RISA-CHAN WHO LIVES IN NODA-CITY. HER QUESTION IS: "WHO IS ANNO-SENSEI'S FAVORITE CHAR-ACTER FROM THIS MANGA SERIES?"
WHO IS IT?
I DON'T KNOW.
OKAY. I CONTACTED ANNO-SENSEI ABOUT THIS AS WELL, AND SHE TOLD ME HER FAVORITE CHARACTER IS LIEUTENANT GLACIER.
WHO THE HECK IS THAT?
I DON'T KNOW. NEXT. THIS LETTER IS FROM NORIKO-CHAN OF MATSUYAMA-CITY. HER QUESTION IS: "IS ROCKIN' ROBIN-SENSEI RICH?" IS SHE TALKING ABOUT *THAT* ROCKIN' ROBIN? I GUESS HE'S RICH...
HE'S A POPULAR ROCK STAR, SO I'M SURE HE'S RICH!
IN W.H.A.K, WE'LL ANSWER YOUR QUESTIONS ABOUT THIS MANGA SERIES! ALTHOUGH, I DON'T KNOW ANYTHING!
IF YOU HAVE A QUESTION YOU WANT TO ASK, SEND IT TO ME. I MEAN, PLEASE SEND IT TO ME!
EVERYONE, WE LOOK FORWARD TO HEAR-ING FROM YOU!
I DIDN'T GET A CHANCE TO TALK...
HERE IS THE ADDRESS TO SEND YOUR LETTER TO:
MOYOCO ANNO
C/O DEL REY BOOKS
1745 BROADWAY, 18-3
NEW YORK, NY 10019

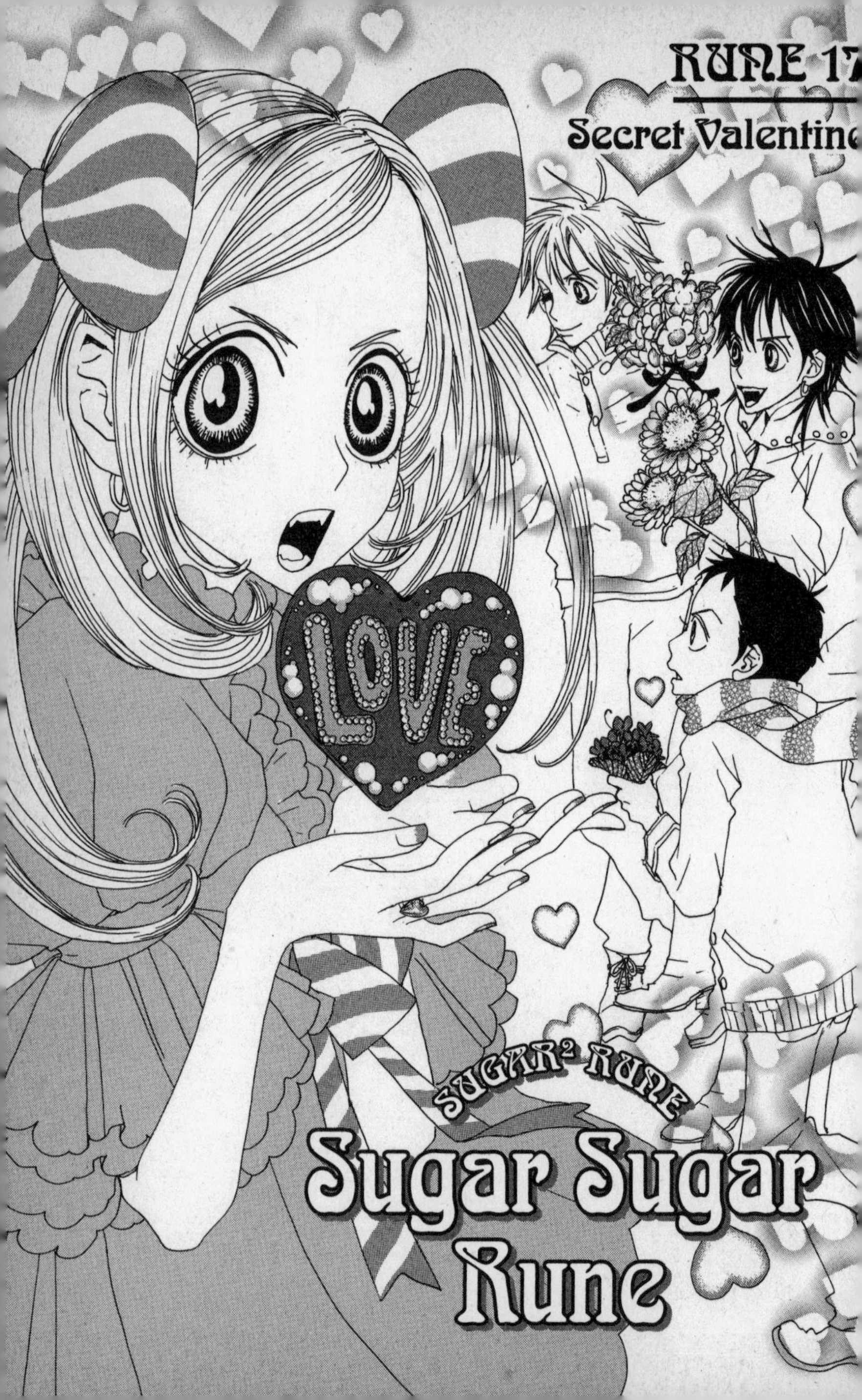
RUNE 17
Secret Valentine
LOVE
SUGAR² RUNE
Sugar Sugar Rune

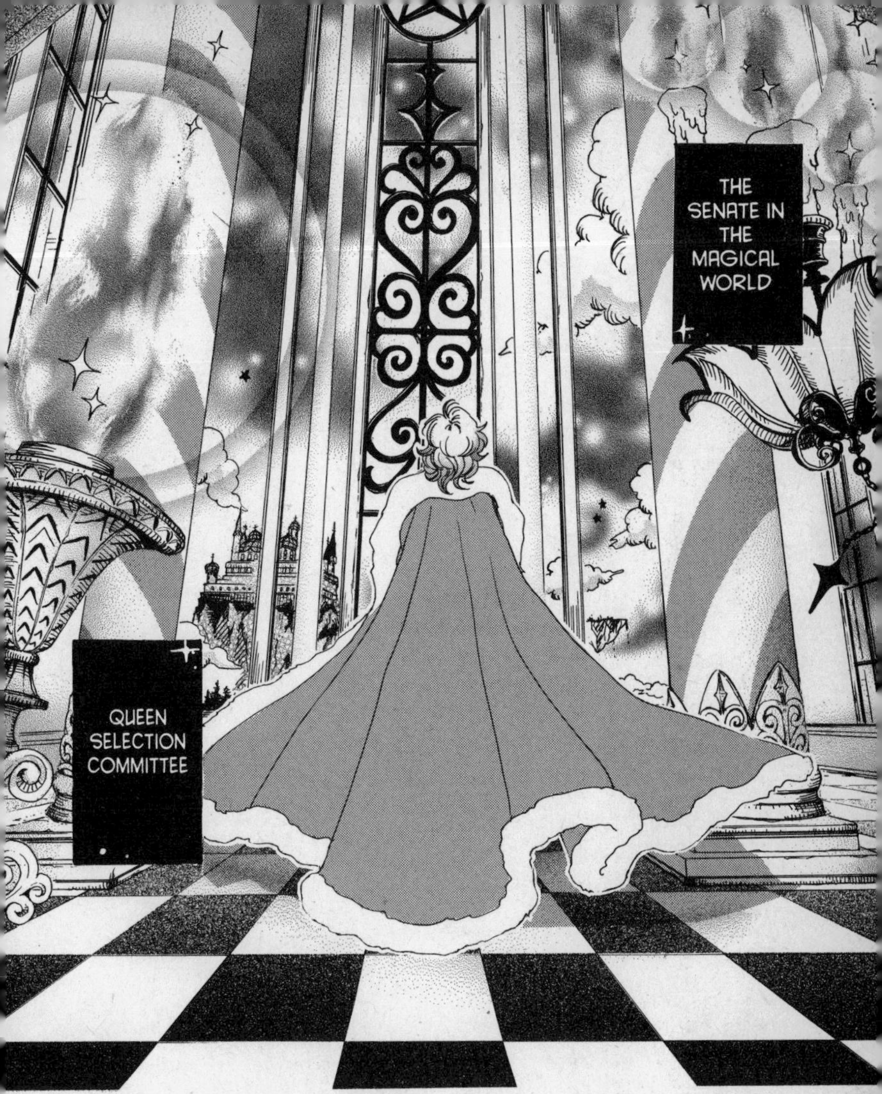
THE SENATE IN THE MAGICAL WORLD
QUEEN SELECTION COMMITTEE

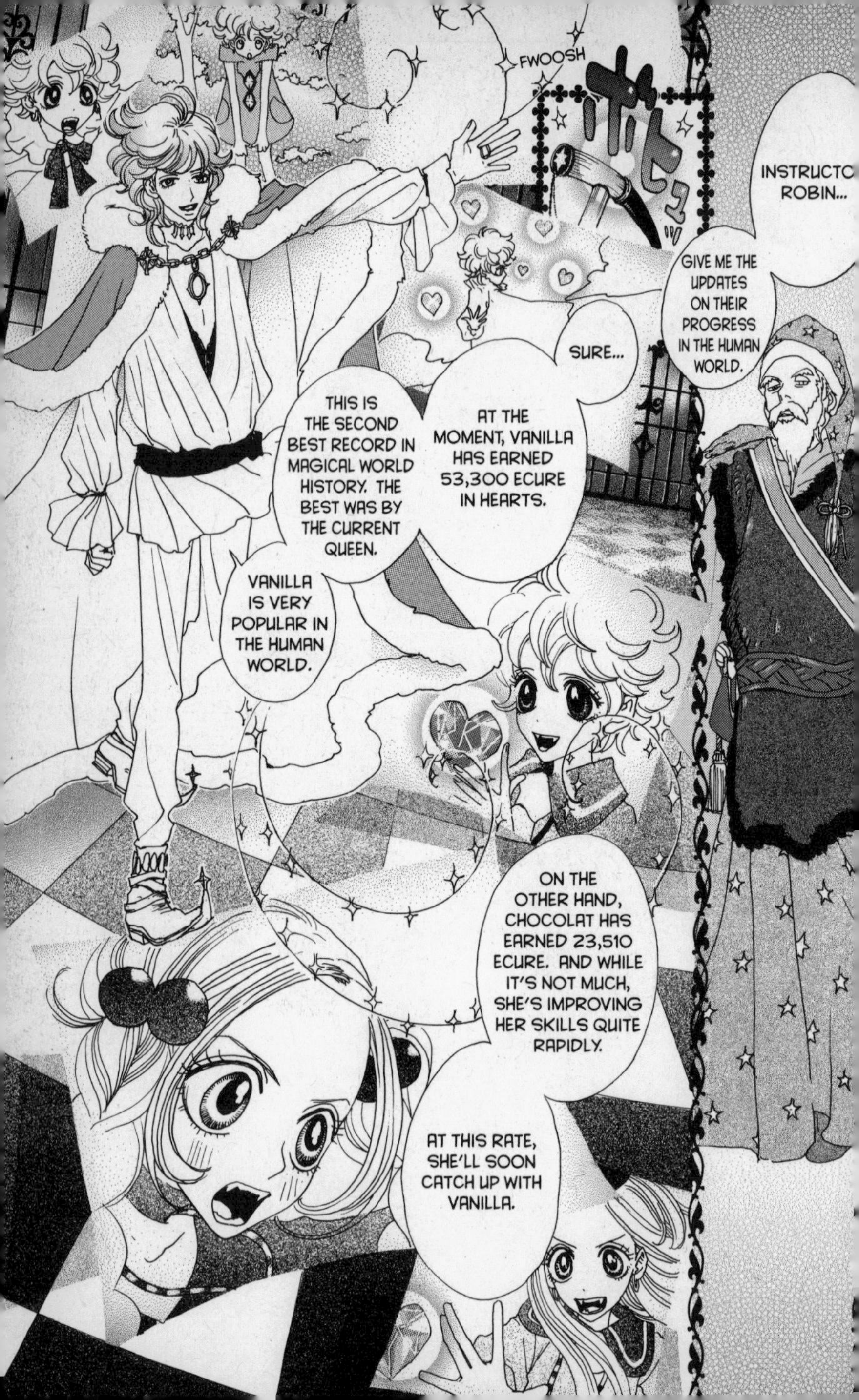

INSTRUCTO ROBIN...
GIVE ME THE UPDATES ON THEIR PROGRESS IN THE HUMAN WORLD.
FWOOSH
SURE...
AT THE MOMENT, VANILLA HAS EARNED 53,300 ECURE IN HEARTS.
THIS IS THE SECOND BEST RECORD IN MAGICAL WORLD HISTORY. THE BEST WAS BY THE CURRENT QUEEN.
VANILLA IS VERY POPULAR IN THE HUMAN WORLD.
ON THE OTHER HAND, CHOCOLAT HAS EARNED 23,510 ECURE. AND WHILE IT'S NOT MUCH, SHE'S IMPROVING HER SKILLS QUITE RAPIDLY.
AT THIS RATE, SHE'LL SOON CATCH UP WITH VANILLA.

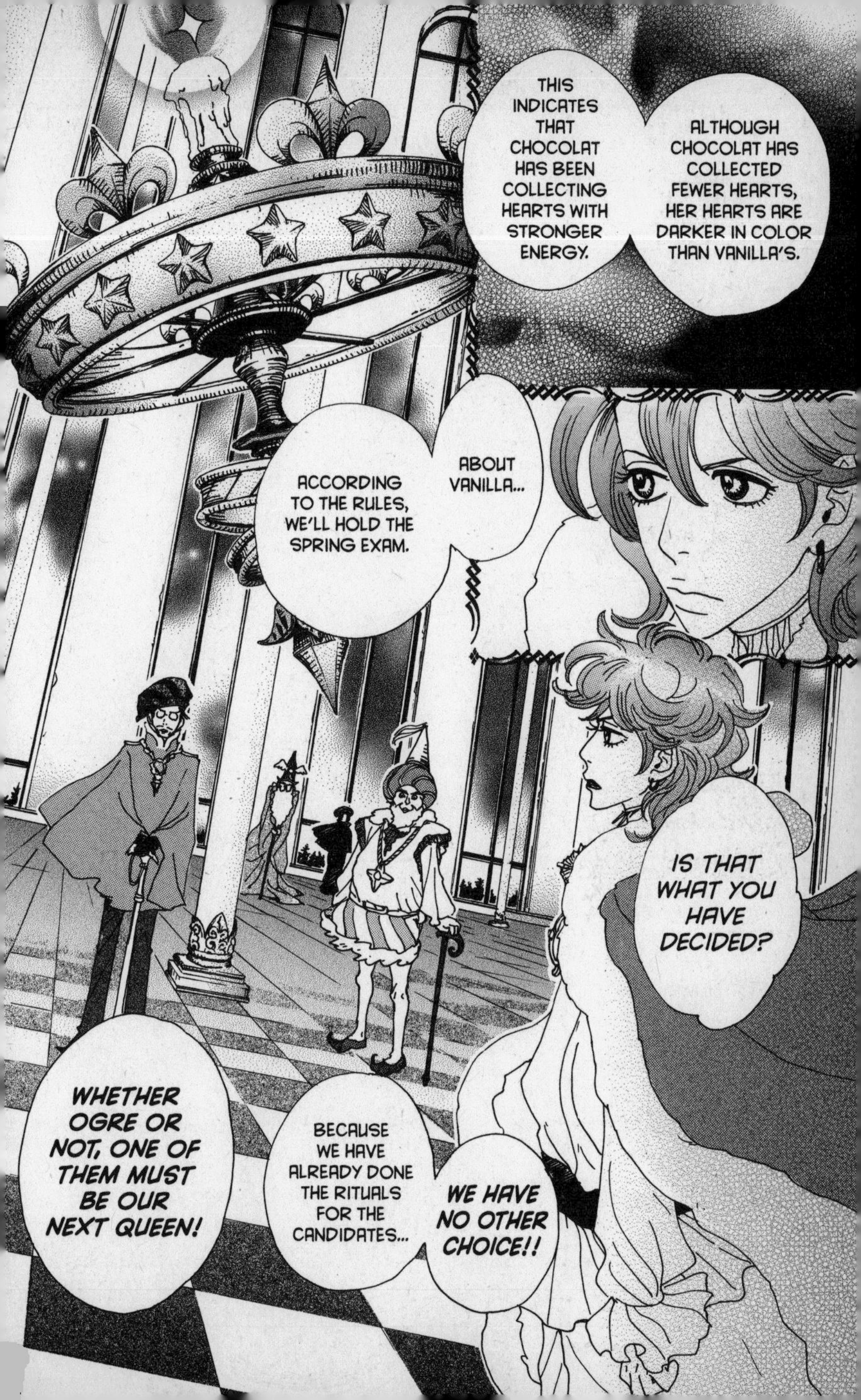
ALTHOUGH CHOCOLAT HAS COLLECTED FEWER HEARTS, HER HEARTS ARE DARKER IN COLOR THAN VANILLA'S.
THIS INDICATES THAT CHOCOLAT HAS BEEN COLLECTING HEARTS WITH STRONGER ENERGY.
ABOUT VANILLA...
ACCORDING TO THE RULES, WE'LL HOLD THE SPRING EXAM.
IS THAT WHAT YOU HAVE DECIDED?
WE HAVE NO OTHER CHOICE!!
BECAUSE WE HAVE ALREADY DONE THE RITUALS FOR THE CANDIDATES...
WHETHER OGRE OR NOT, ONE OF THEM MUST BE OUR NEXT QUEEN!

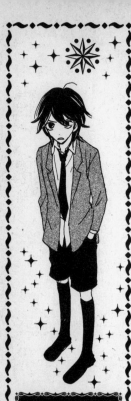

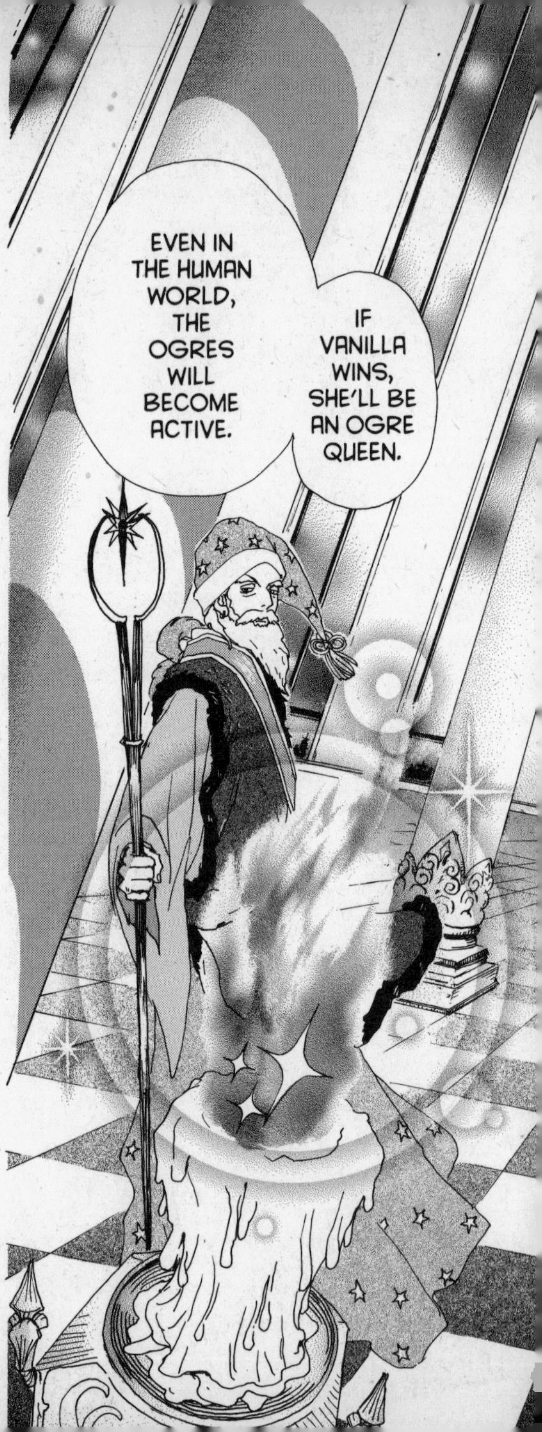
IF VANILLA WINS, SHE'LL BE AN OGRE QUEEN.
EVEN IN THE HUMAN WORLD, THE OGRES WILL BECOME ACTIVE.

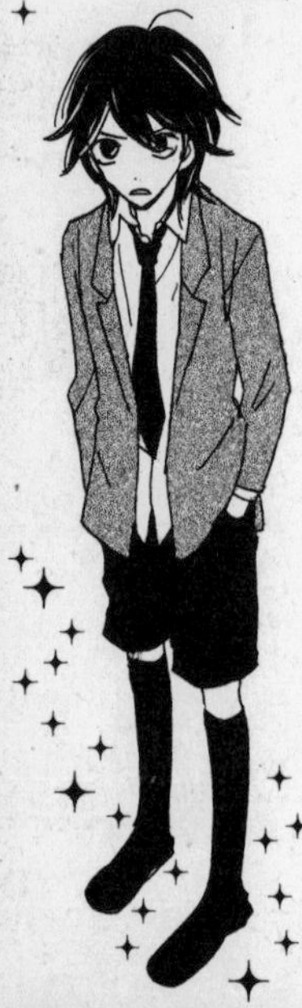

TAIJI SUGIYAMA

HEIGHT: 156 CM

AGE: 10 YEARS OLD

HOBBY: READING BOOKS

SPECIALTY: PLAYING CELLO (BUT HE'S NOT VERY GOOD)

WEAKNESS: GIRLS

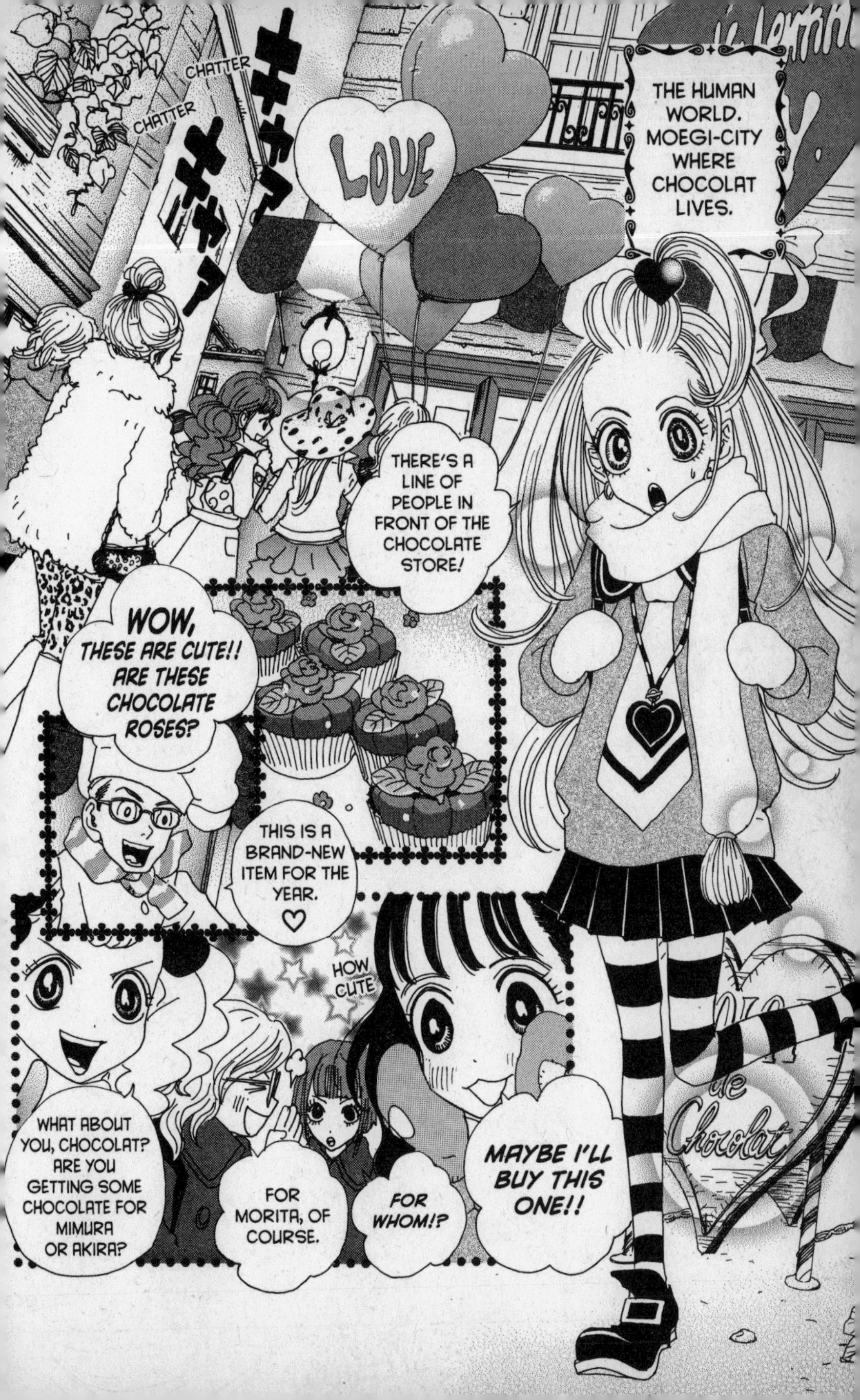
THE HUMAN WORLD. MOEGI-CITY WHERE CHOCOLAT LIVES.
CHATTER
CHATTER
LOVE
THERE'S A LINE OF PEOPLE IN FRONT OF THE CHOCOLATE STORE!
WOW, THESE ARE CUTE!! ARE THESE CHOCOLATE ROSES?
THIS IS A BRAND-NEW ITEM FOR THE YEAR. ♡
le Chocolat
HOW CUTE
MAYBE I'LL BUY THIS ONE!!
FOR WHOM!?
FOR MORITA, OF COURSE.
WHAT ABOUT YOU, CHOCOLAT? ARE YOU GETTING SOME CHOCOLATE FOR MIMURA OR AKIRA?

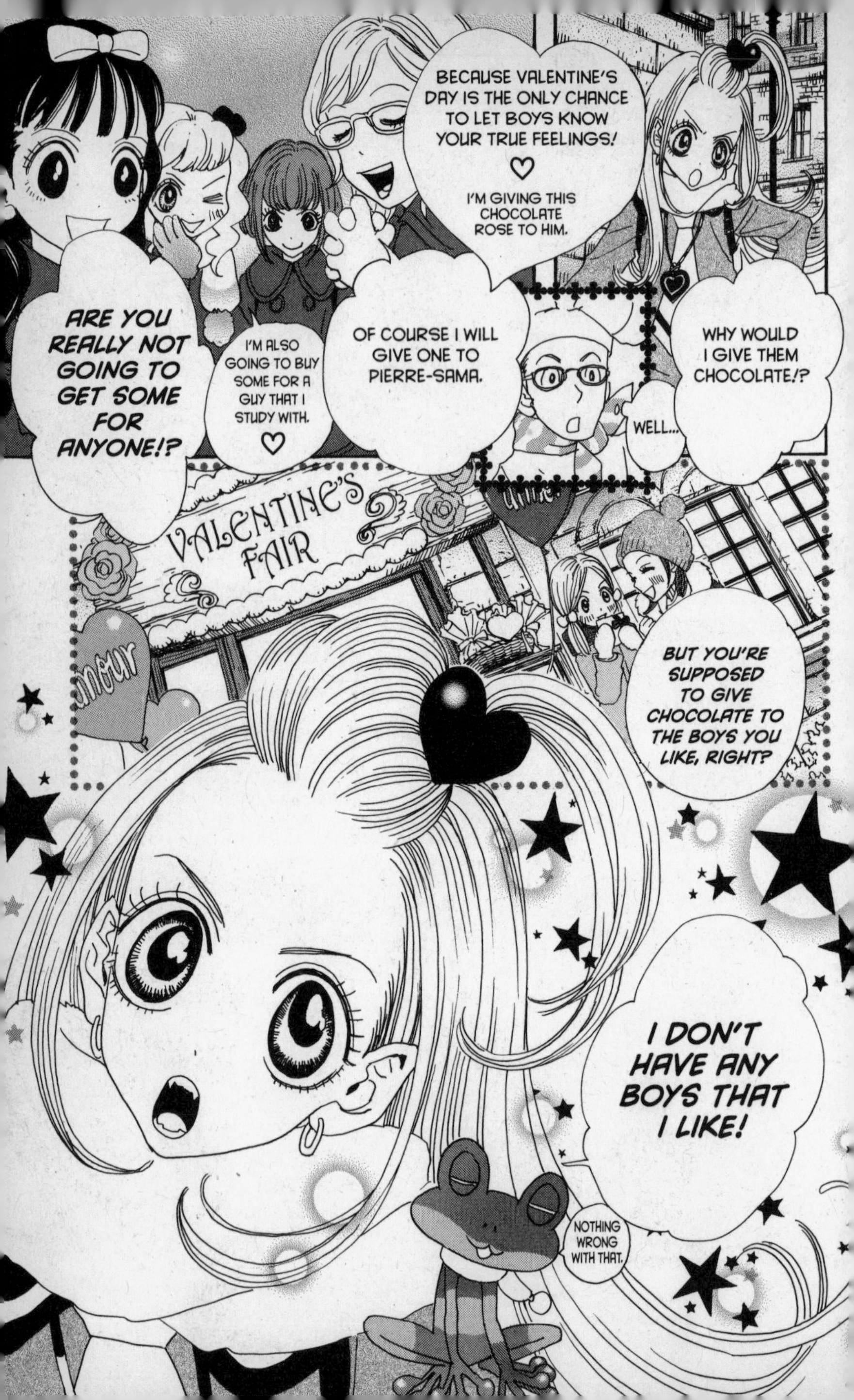
BECAUSE VALENTINE'S DAY IS THE ONLY CHANCE TO LET BOYS KNOW YOUR TRUE FEELINGS! ♡
I'M GIVING THIS CHOCOLATE ROSE TO HIM.
WHY WOULD I GIVE THEM CHOCOLATE!?
WELL...
OF COURSE I WILL GIVE ONE TO PIERRE-SAMA.
I'M ALSO GOING TO BUY SOME FOR A GUY THAT I STUDY WITH. ♡
ARE YOU REALLY NOT GOING TO GET SOME FOR ANYONE!?
VALENTINE'S FAIR
BUT YOU'RE SUPPOSED TO GIVE CHOCOLATE TO THE BOYS YOU LIKE, RIGHT?
I DON'T HAVE ANY BOYS THAT I LIKE!
NOTHING WRONG WITH THAT.

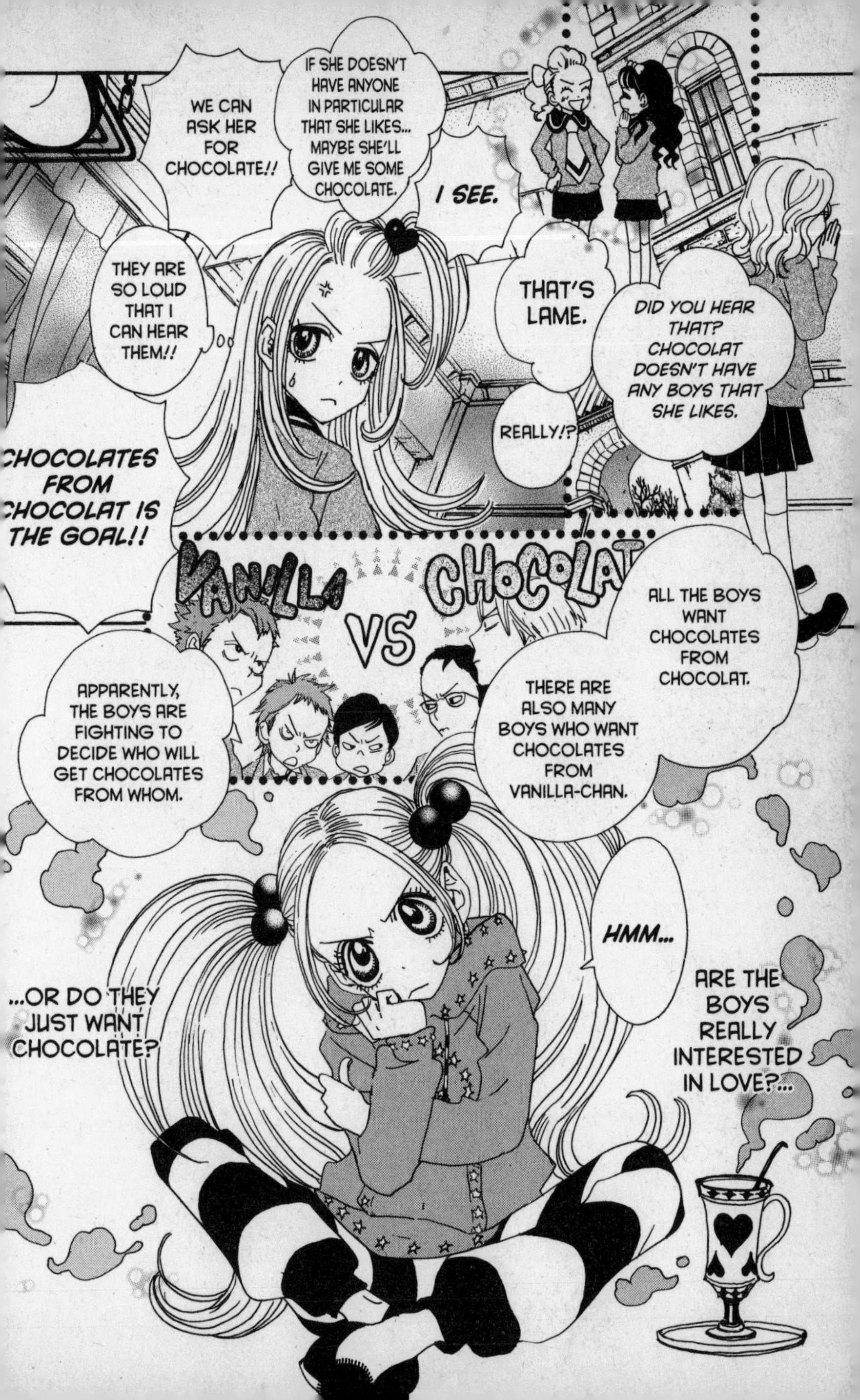
IF SHE DOESN'T HAVE ANYONE IN PARTICULAR THAT SHE LIKES... MAYBE SHE'LL GIVE ME SOME CHOCOLATE.
WE CAN ASK HER FOR CHOCOLATE!!
DID YOU HEAR THAT? CHOCOLAT DOESN'T HAVE ANY BOYS THAT SHE LIKES.
REALLY!?
THAT'S LAME.
I SEE.
THEY ARE SO LOUD THAT I CAN HEAR THEM!!
CHOCOLATES FROM CHOCOLAT IS THE GOAL!!
VANILLA VS CHOCOLAT
ALL THE BOYS WANT CHOCOLATES FROM CHOCOLAT.
THERE ARE ALSO MANY BOYS WHO WANT CHOCOLATES FROM VANILLA-CHAN.
APPARENTLY, THE BOYS ARE FIGHTING TO DECIDE WHO WILL GET CHOCOLATES FROM WHOM.
HMM...
ARE THE BOYS REALLY INTERESTED IN LOVE?...
...OR DO THEY JUST WANT CHOCOLATE?

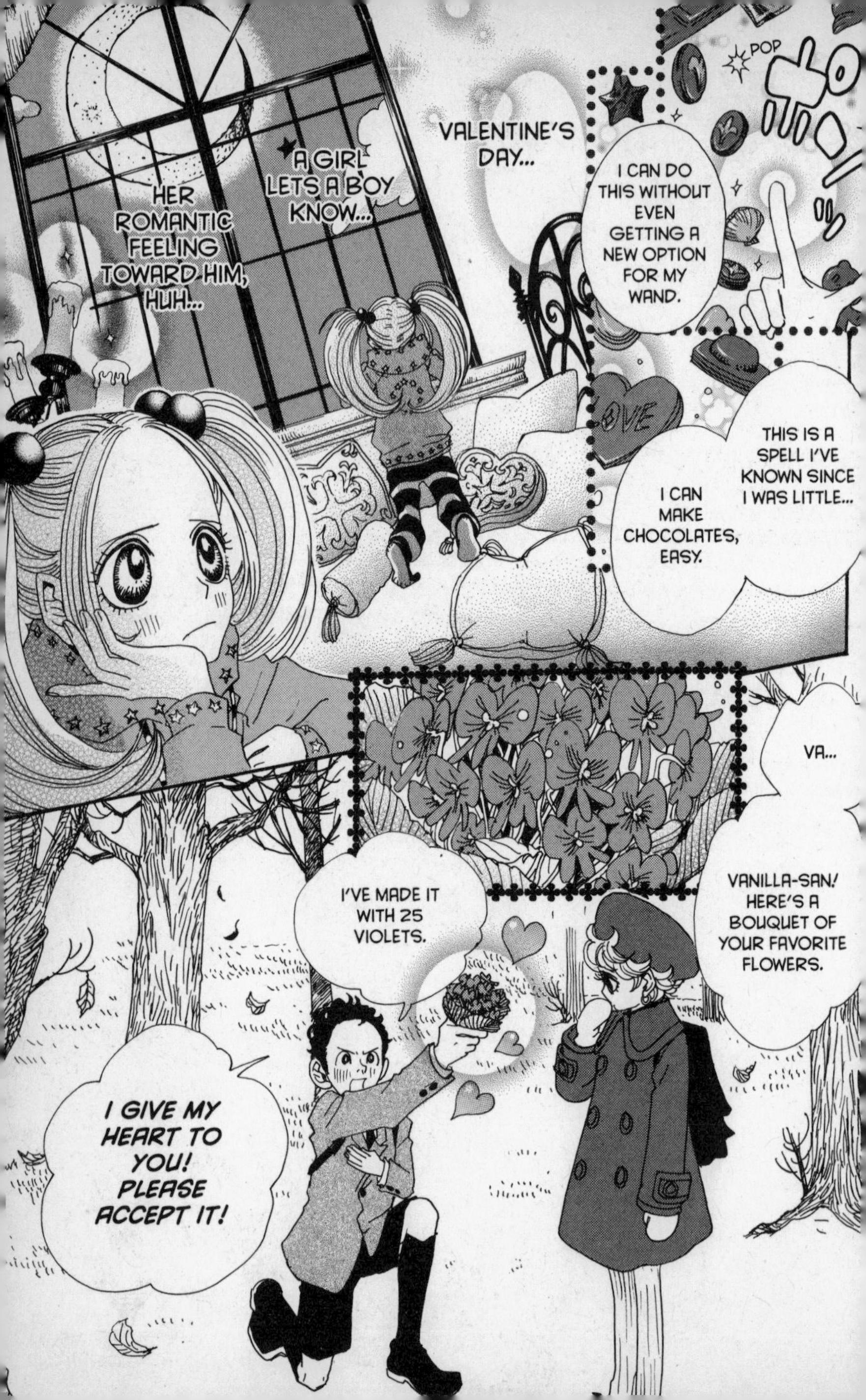
VALENTINE'S DAY...
A GIRL LETS A BOY KNOW...
HER ROMANTIC FEELING TOWARD HIM, HUH...
POP
I CAN DO THIS WITHOUT EVEN GETTING A NEW OPTION FOR MY WAND.
THIS IS A SPELL I'VE KNOWN SINCE I WAS LITTLE...
I CAN MAKE CHOCOLATES, EASY.
VA...
VANILLA-SAN! HERE'S A BOUQUET OF YOUR FAVORITE FLOWERS.
I'VE MADE IT WITH 25 VIOLETS.
I GIVE MY HEART TO YOU! PLEASE ACCEPT IT!

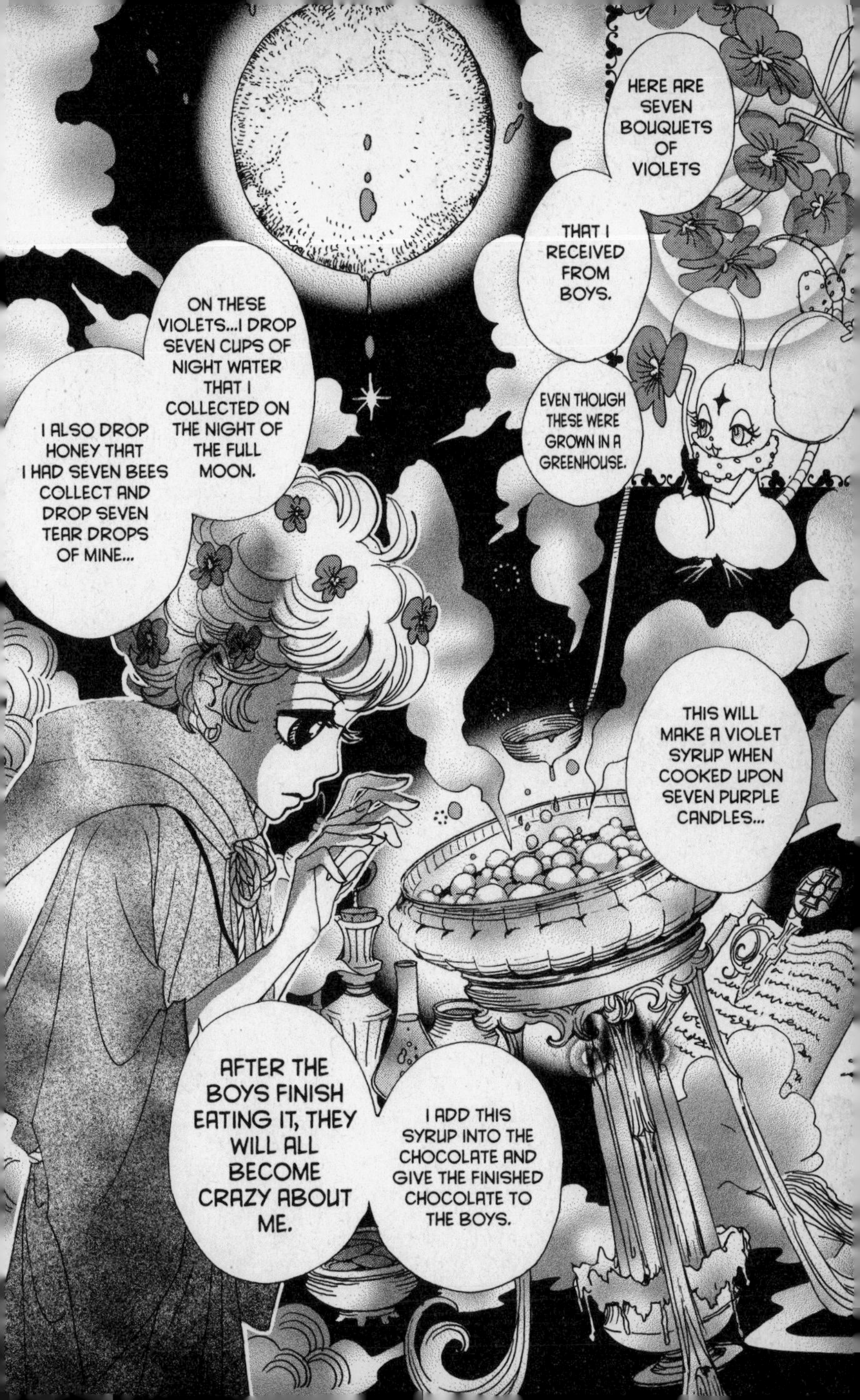
HERE ARE SEVEN BOUQUETS OF VIOLETS
THAT I RECEIVED FROM BOYS.
EVEN THOUGH THESE WERE GROWN IN A GREENHOUSE.
ON THESE VIOLETS...I DROP SEVEN CUPS OF NIGHT WATER THAT I COLLECTED ON THE NIGHT OF THE FULL MOON.
I ALSO DROP HONEY THAT I HAD SEVEN BEES COLLECT AND DROP SEVEN TEAR DROPS OF MINE...
THIS WILL MAKE A VIOLET SYRUP WHEN COOKED UPON SEVEN PURPLE CANDLES...
I ADD THIS SYRUP INTO THE CHOCOLATE AND GIVE THE FINISHED CHOCOLATE TO THE BOYS.
AFTER THE BOYS FINISH EATING IT, THEY WILL ALL BECOME CRAZY ABOUT ME.

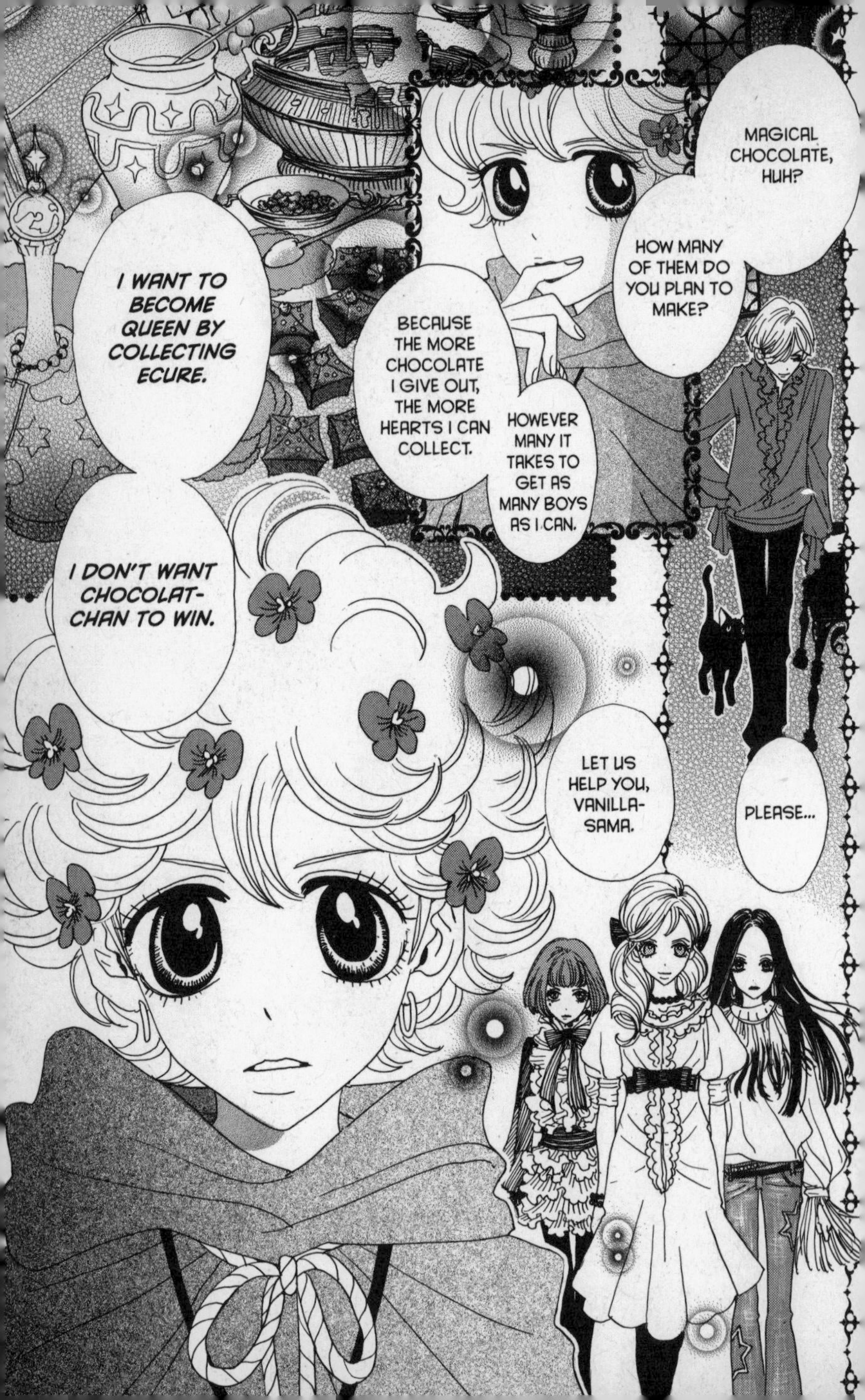
MAGICAL CHOCOLATE, HUH?
HOW MANY OF THEM DO YOU PLAN TO MAKE?
HOWEVER MANY IT TAKES TO GET AS MANY BOYS AS I CAN.
BECAUSE THE MORE CHOCOLATE I GIVE OUT, THE MORE HEARTS I CAN COLLECT.
I WANT TO BECOME QUEEN BY COLLECTING ECURE.
I DON'T WANT CHOCOLAT-CHAN TO WIN.
PLEASE...
LET US HELP YOU, VANILLA-SAMA.

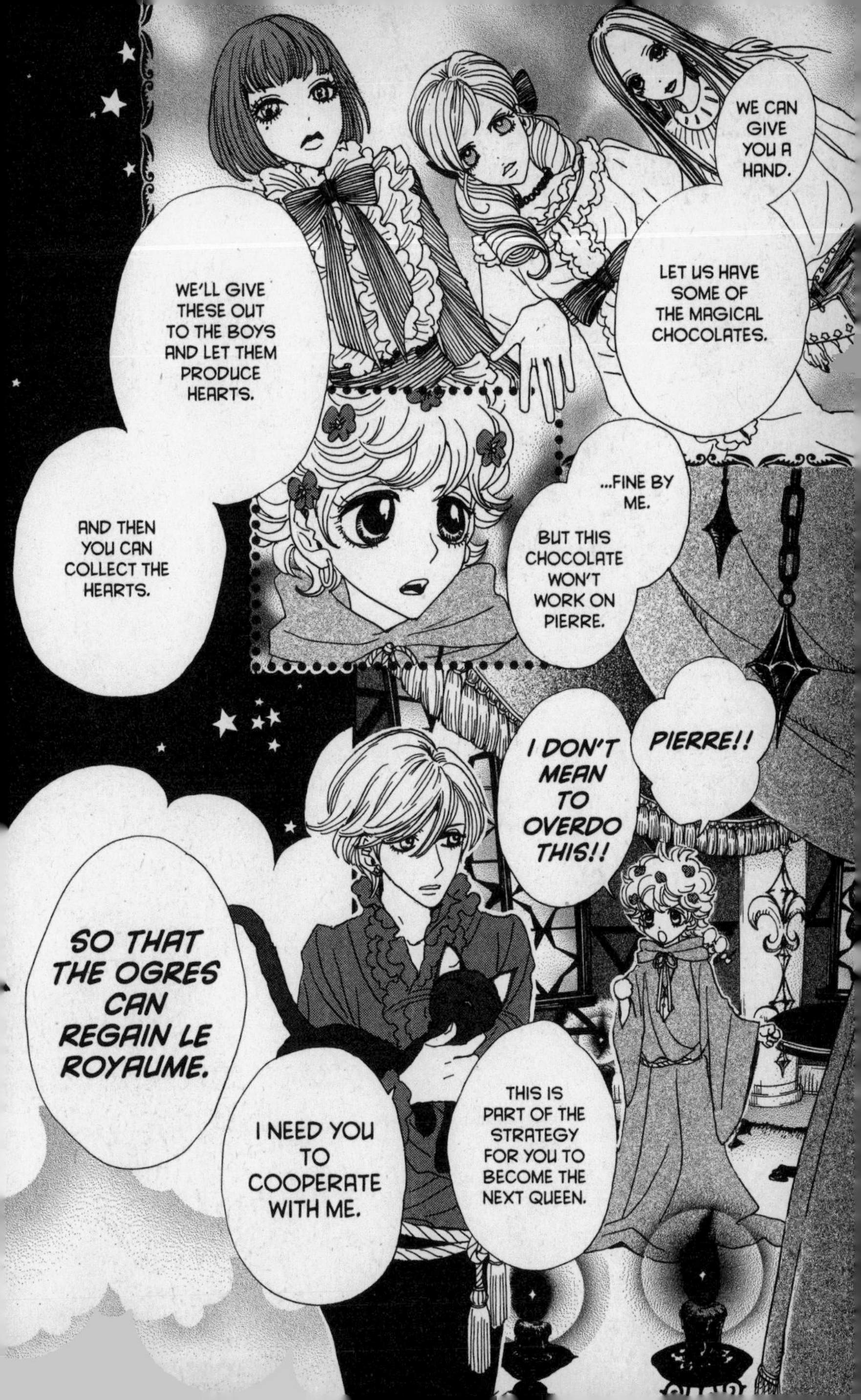
WE CAN GIVE YOU A HAND.
LET US HAVE SOME OF THE MAGICAL CHOCOLATES.
WE'LL GIVE THESE OUT TO THE BOYS AND LET THEM PRODUCE HEARTS.
AND THEN YOU CAN COLLECT THE HEARTS.
...FINE BY ME.
BUT THIS CHOCOLATE WON'T WORK ON PIERRE.
PIERRE!!
I DON'T MEAN TO OVERDO THIS!!
THIS IS PART OF THE STRATEGY FOR YOU TO BECOME THE NEXT QUEEN.
I NEED YOU TO COOPERATE WITH ME.
SO THAT THE OGRES CAN REGAIN LE ROYAUME.

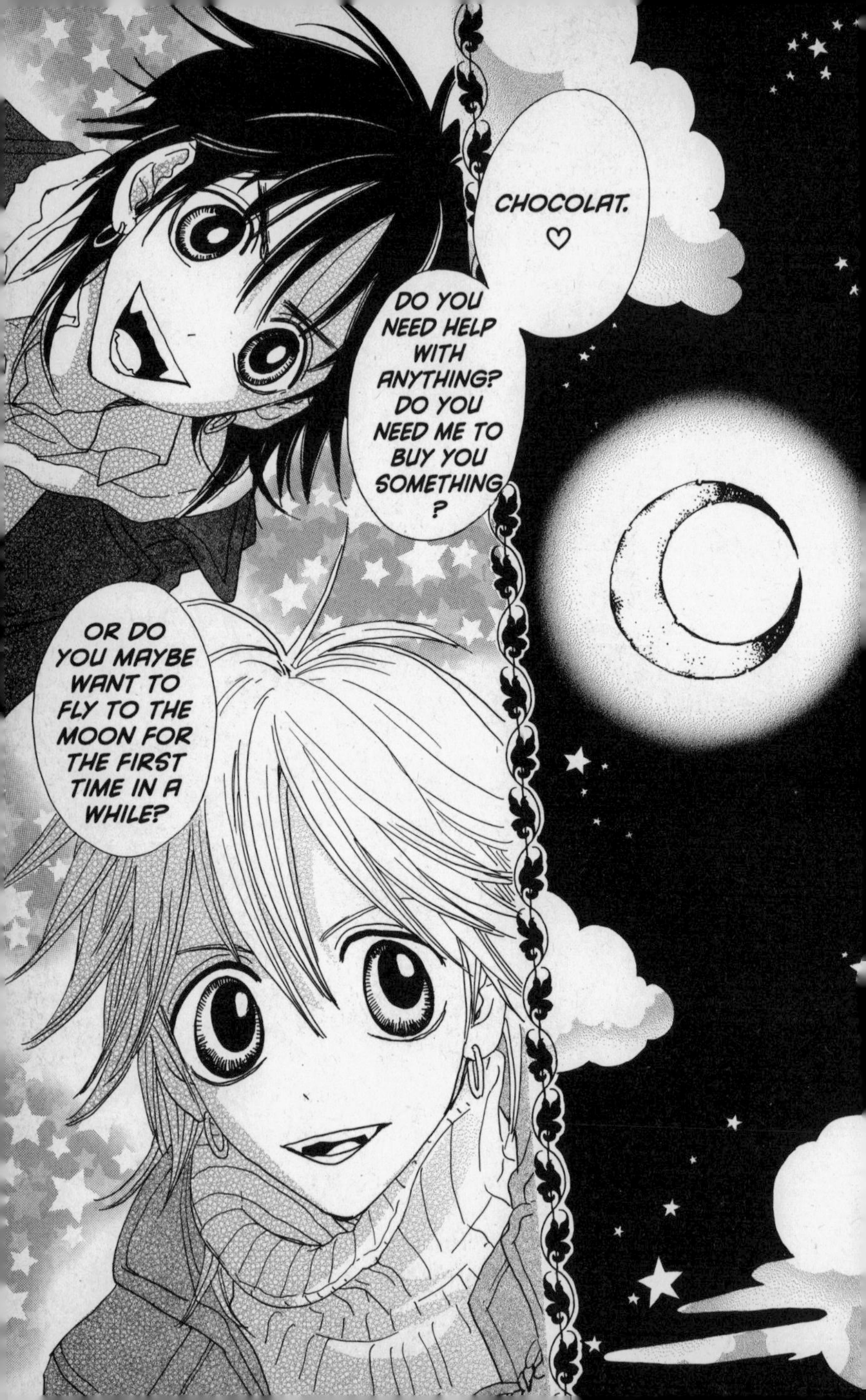
CHOCOLAT. ♡
DO YOU NEED HELP WITH ANYTHING? DO YOU NEED ME TO BUY YOU SOMETHING ?
OR DO YOU MAYBE WANT TO FLY TO THE MOON FOR THE FIRST TIME IN A WHILE?

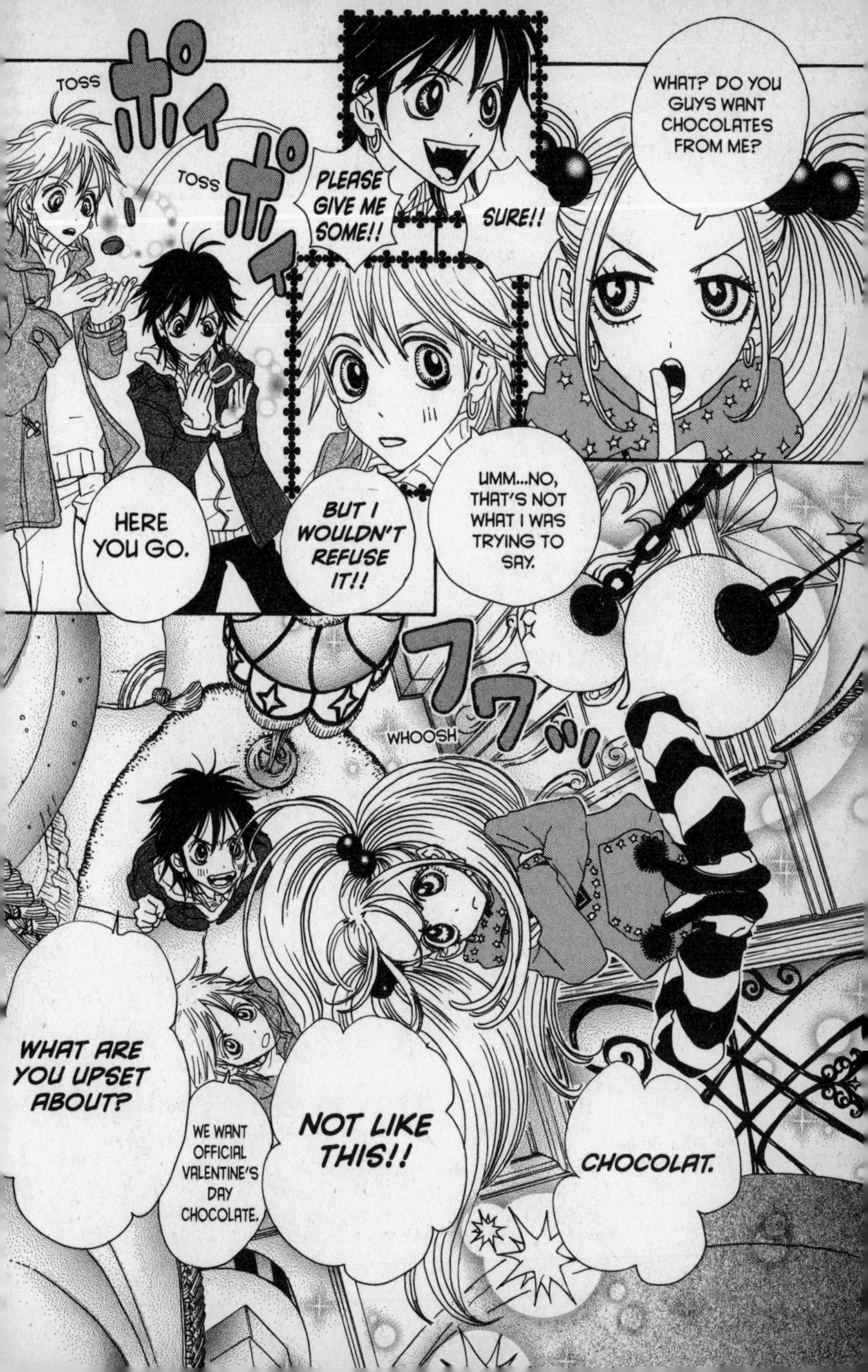
WHAT? DO YOU GUYS WANT CHOCOLATES FROM ME?
SURE!!
PLEASE GIVE ME SOME!!
UMM...NO, THAT'S NOT WHAT I WAS TRYING TO SAY.
BUT I WOULDN'T REFUSE IT!!
TOSS
TOSS
HERE YOU GO.
WHOOSH
CHOCOLAT.
NOT LIKE THIS!!
WE WANT OFFICIAL VALENTINE'S DAY CHOCOLATE.
WHAT ARE YOU UPSET ABOUT?

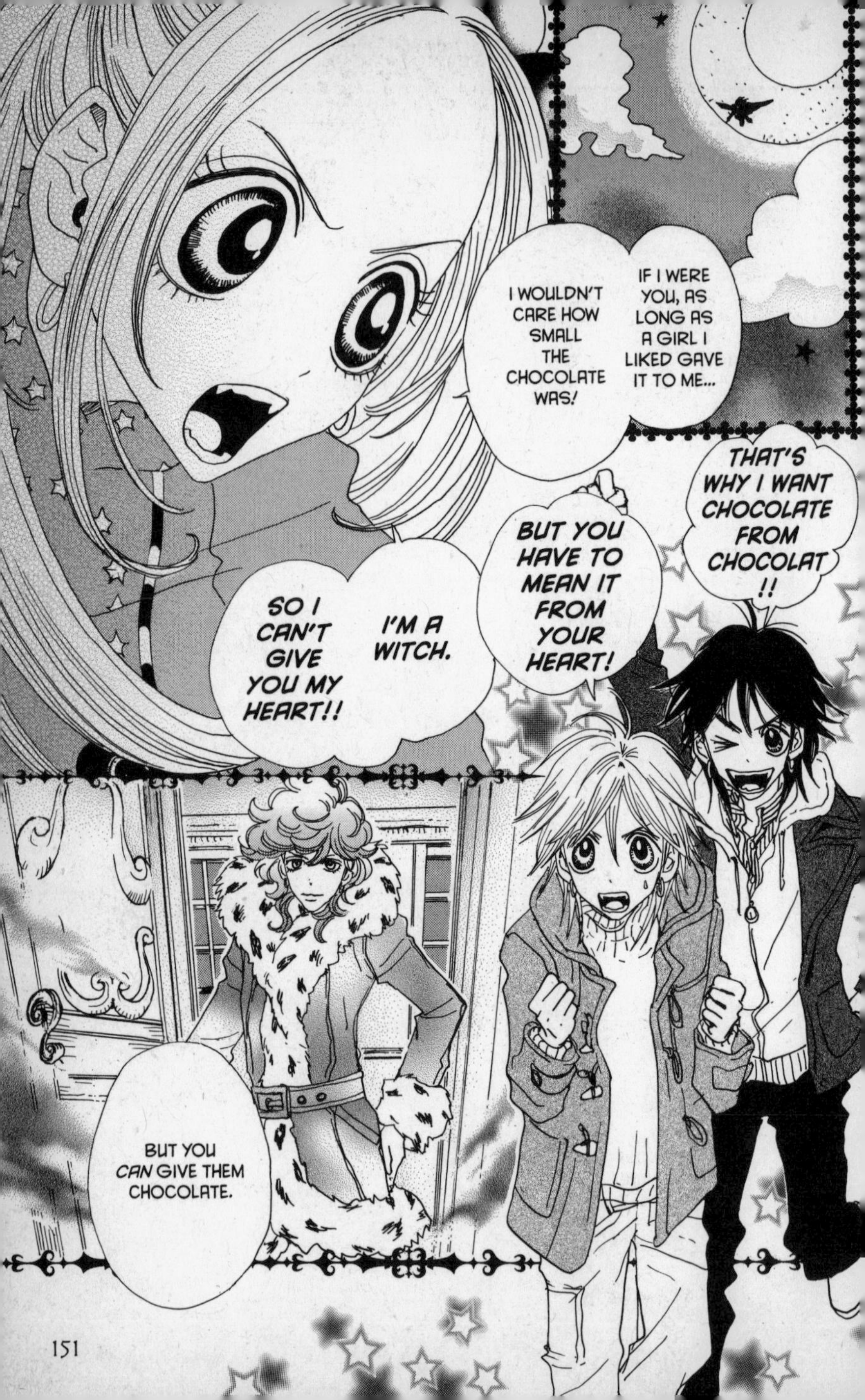
IF I WERE YOU, AS LONG AS A GIRL I LIKED GAVE IT TO ME...
I WOULDN'T CARE HOW SMALL THE CHOCOLATE WAS!
THAT'S WHY I WANT CHOCOLATE FROM CHOCOLAT!!
BUT YOU HAVE TO MEAN IT FROM YOUR HEART!
I'M A WITCH.
SO I CAN'T GIVE YOU MY HEART!!
BUT YOU *CAN* GIVE THEM CHOCOLATE.

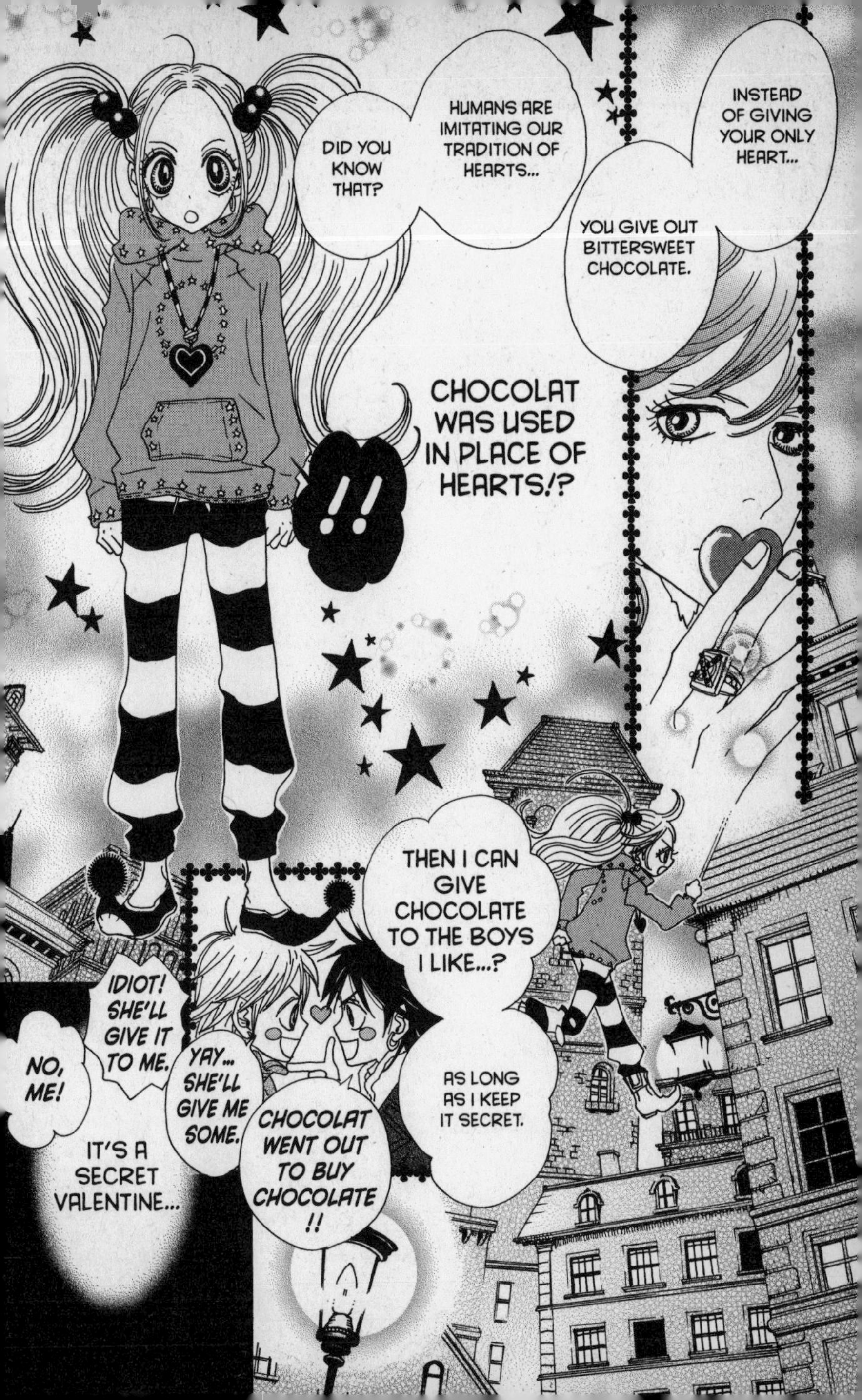
INSTEAD OF GIVING YOUR ONLY HEART...
YOU GIVE OUT BITTERSWEET CHOCOLATE.
HUMANS ARE IMITATING OUR TRADITION OF HEARTS...
DID YOU KNOW THAT?
CHOCOLAT WAS USED IN PLACE OF HEARTS!?
!!
THEN I CAN GIVE CHOCOLATE TO THE BOYS I LIKE...?
AS LONG AS I KEEP IT SECRET.
CHOCOLAT WENT OUT TO BUY CHOCOLATE !!
YAY... SHE'LL GIVE ME SOME.
IDIOT! SHE'LL GIVE IT TO ME.
NO, ME!
IT'S A SECRET VALENTINE...

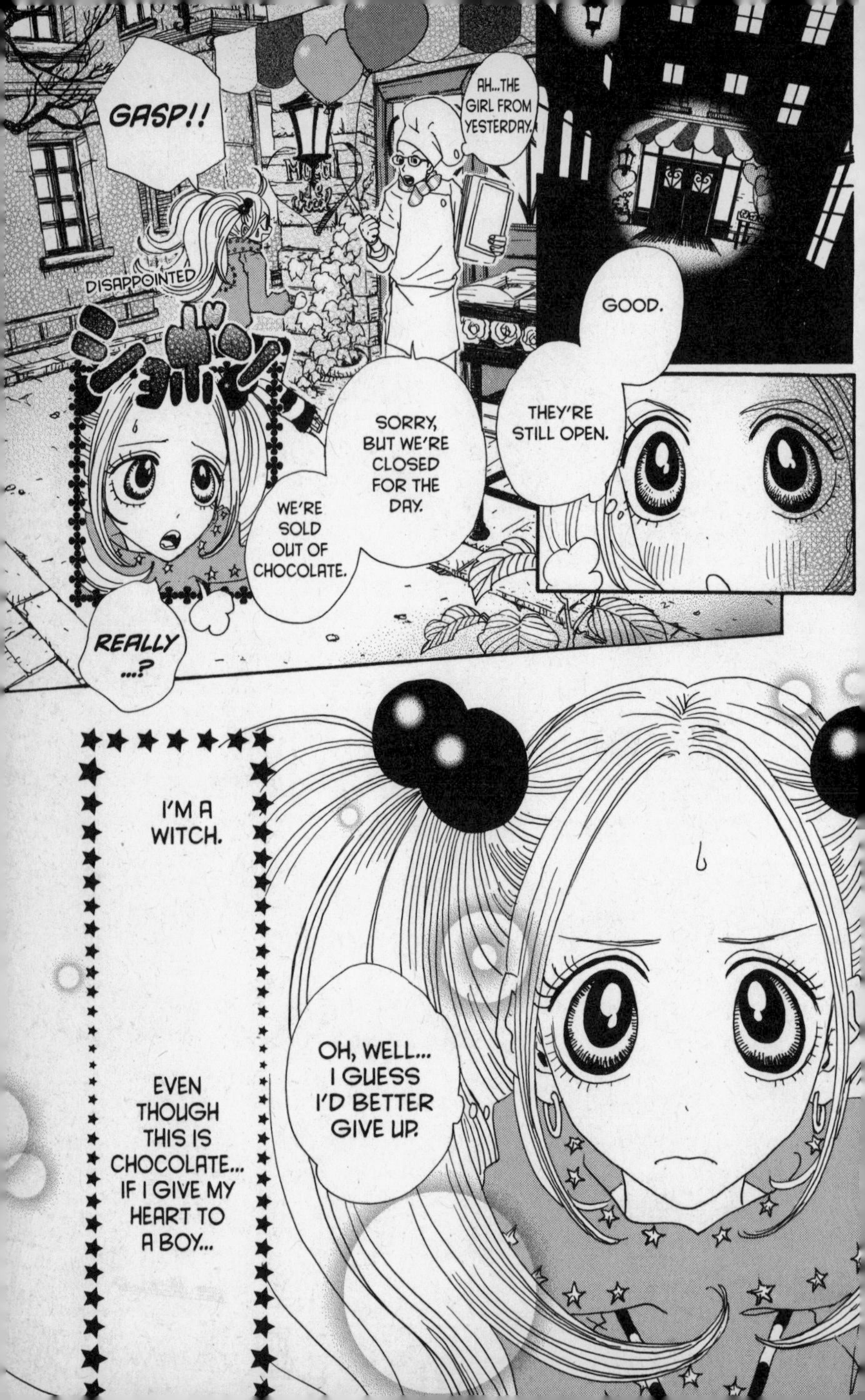
GOOD.
THEY'RE STILL OPEN.
AH...THE GIRL FROM YESTERDAY.
GASP!!
SORRY, BUT WE'RE CLOSED FOR THE DAY.
WE'RE SOLD OUT OF CHOCOLATE.
DISAPPOINTED
REALLY ...?
OH, WELL... I GUESS I'D BETTER GIVE UP.
I'M A WITCH.
EVEN THOUGH THIS IS CHOCOLATE... IF I GIVE MY HEART TO A BOY...

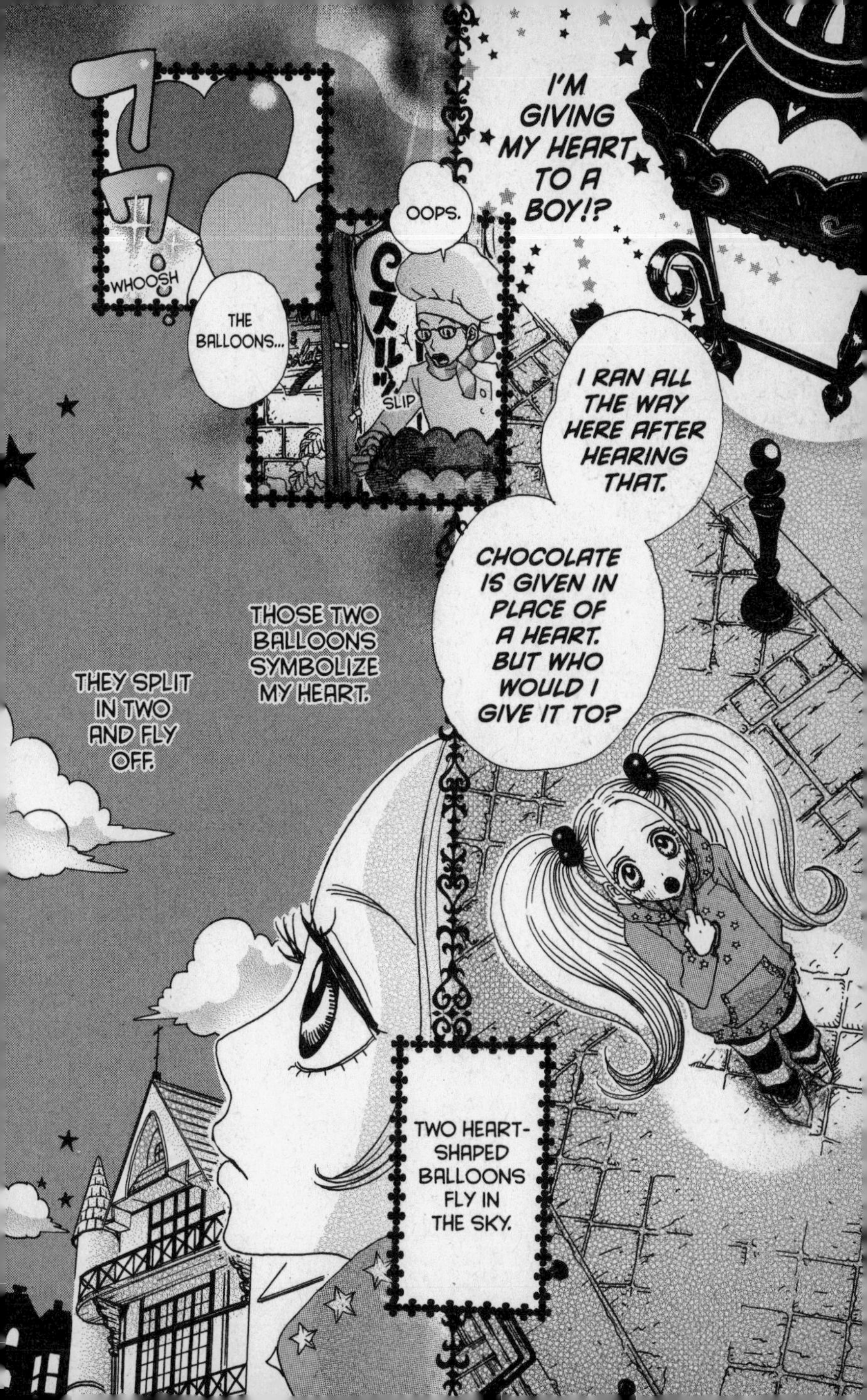
I'M GIVING MY HEART TO A BOY!?
OOPS.
SLIP
THE BALLOONS...
WHOOSH
I RAN ALL THE WAY HERE AFTER HEARING THAT.
CHOCOLATE IS GIVEN IN PLACE OF A HEART. BUT WHO WOULD I GIVE IT TO?
THOSE TWO BALLOONS SYMBOLIZE MY HEART.
THEY SPLIT IN TWO AND FLY OFF.
TWO HEART-SHAPED BALLOONS FLY IN THE SKY.

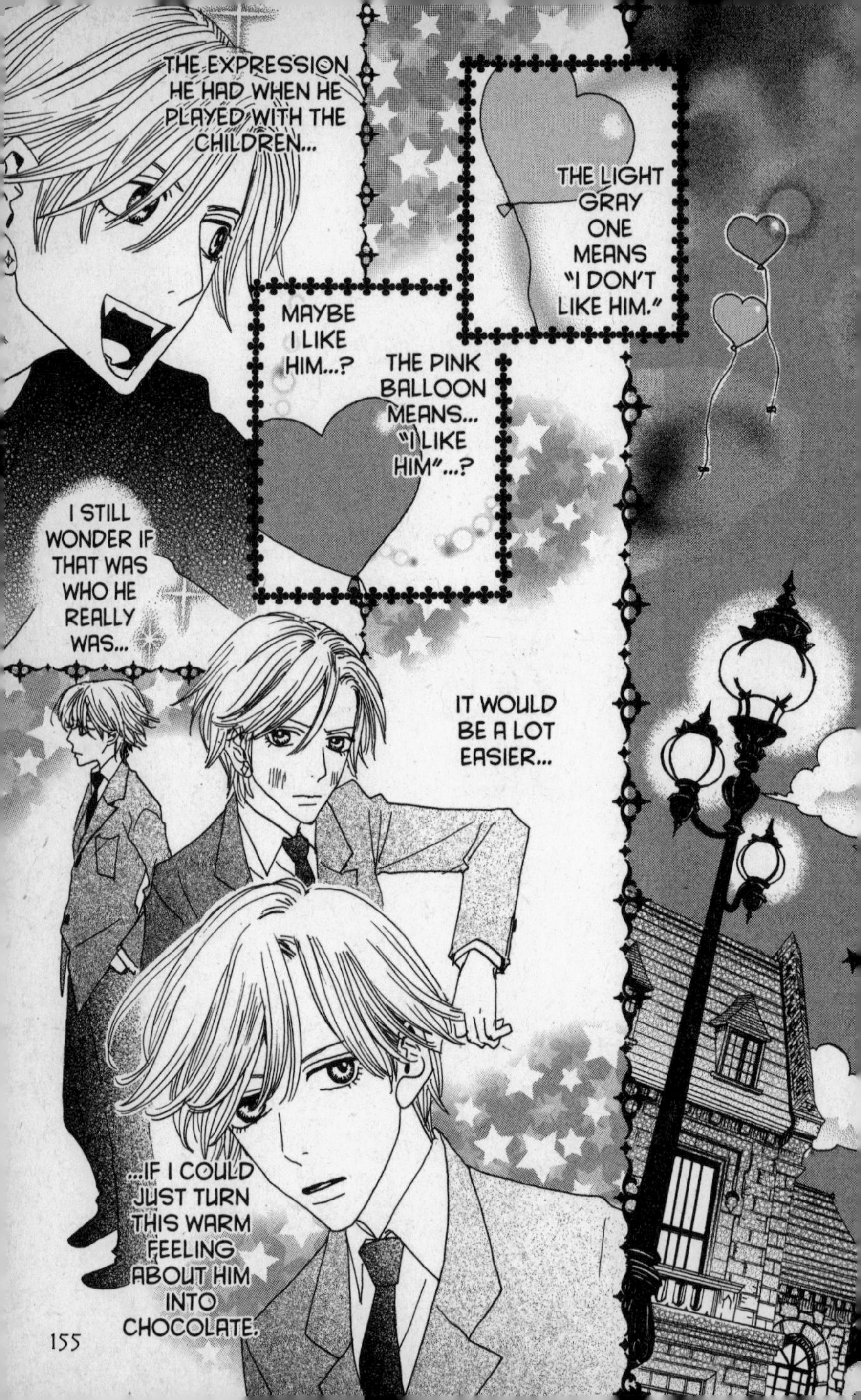
THE LIGHT GRAY ONE MEANS "I DON'T LIKE HIM."
THE EXPRESSION HE HAD WHEN HE PLAYED WITH THE CHILDREN...
THE PINK BALLOON MEANS... "I LIKE HIM"...?
MAYBE I LIKE HIM...?
I STILL WONDER IF THAT WAS WHO HE REALLY WAS...
IT WOULD BE A LOT EASIER...
...IF I COULD JUST TURN THIS WARM FEELING ABOUT HIM INTO CHOCOLATE.

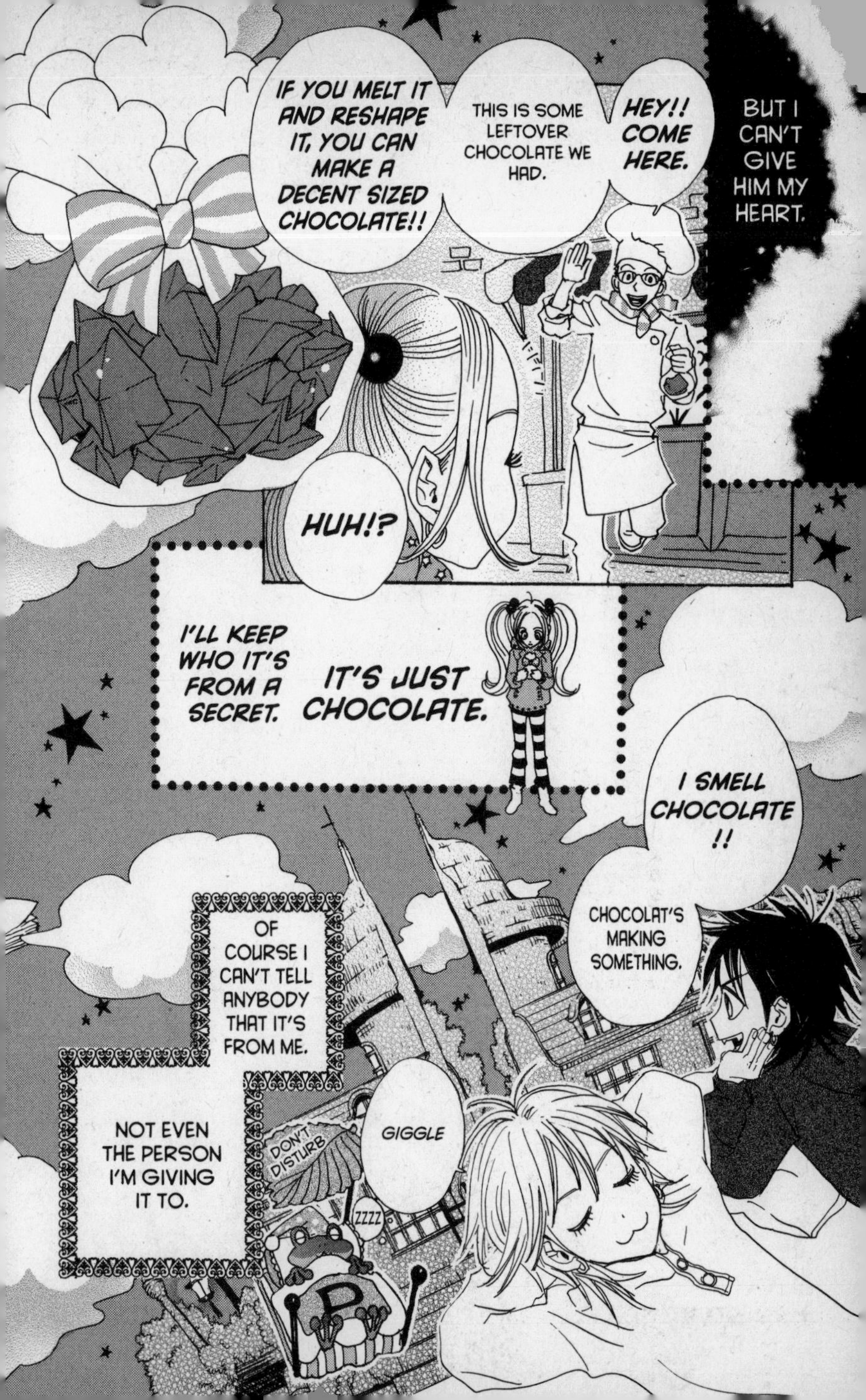
BUT I CAN'T GIVE HIM MY HEART.
HEY!! COME HERE.
THIS IS SOME LEFTOVER CHOCOLATE WE HAD.
IF YOU MELT IT AND RESHAPE IT, YOU CAN MAKE A DECENT SIZED CHOCOLATE!!
HUH!?
IT'S JUST CHOCOLATE.
I'LL KEEP WHO IT'S FROM A SECRET.
I SMELL CHOCOLATE!!
CHOCOLAT'S MAKING SOMETHING.
OF COURSE I CAN'T TELL ANYBODY THAT IT'S FROM ME.
GIGGLE
DON'T DISTURB
ZZZZ
NOT EVEN THE PERSON I'M GIVING IT TO.

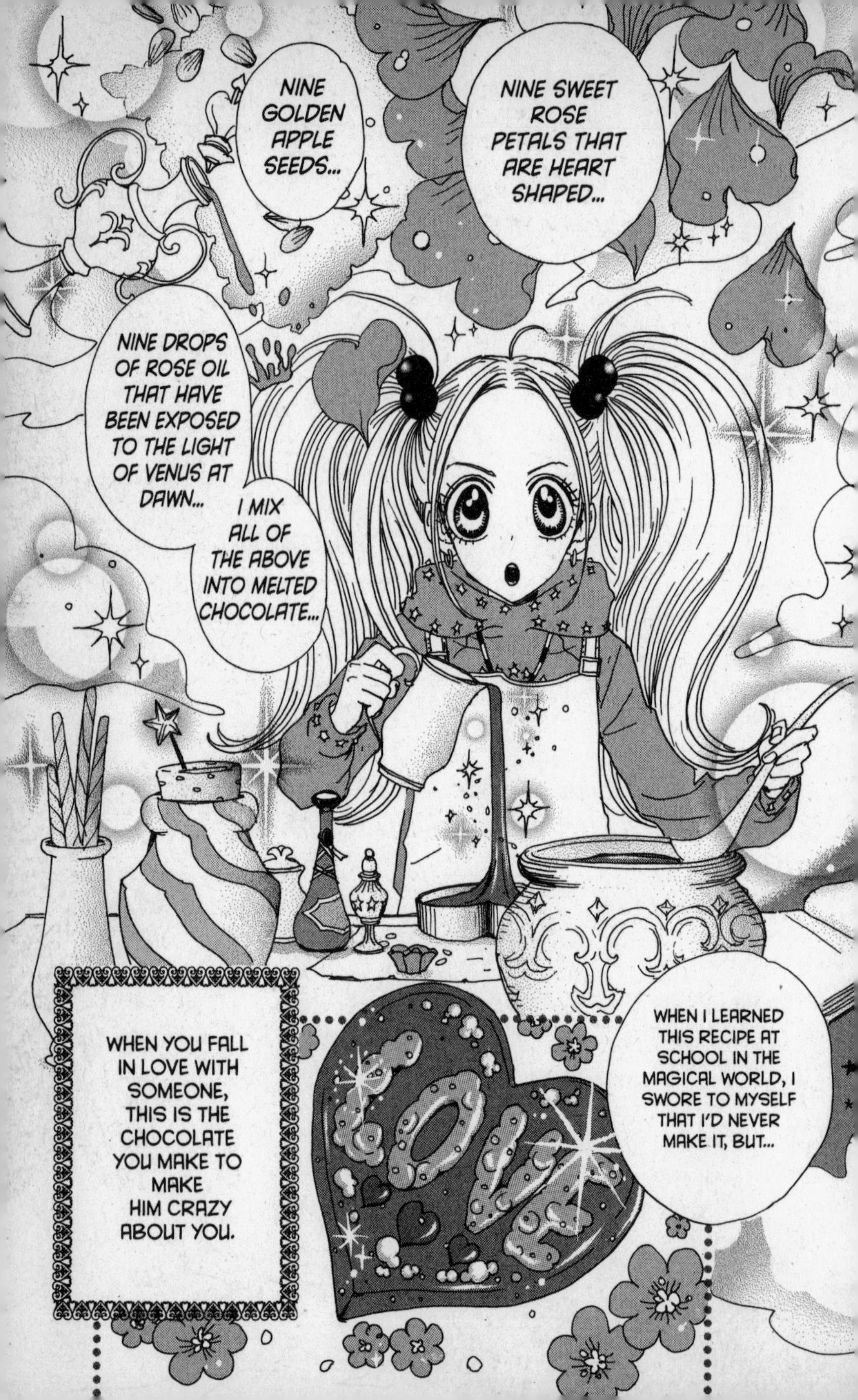
NINE SWEET ROSE PETALS THAT ARE HEART SHAPED...
NINE GOLDEN APPLE SEEDS...
NINE DROPS OF ROSE OIL THAT HAVE BEEN EXPOSED TO THE LIGHT OF VENUS AT DAWN...
I MIX ALL OF THE ABOVE INTO MELTED CHOCOLATE...
WHEN I LEARNED THIS RECIPE AT SCHOOL IN THE MAGICAL WORLD, I SWORE TO MYSELF THAT I'D NEVER MAKE IT, BUT...
WHEN YOU FALL IN LOVE WITH SOMEONE, THIS IS THE CHOCOLATE YOU MAKE TO MAKE HIM CRAZY ABOUT YOU.

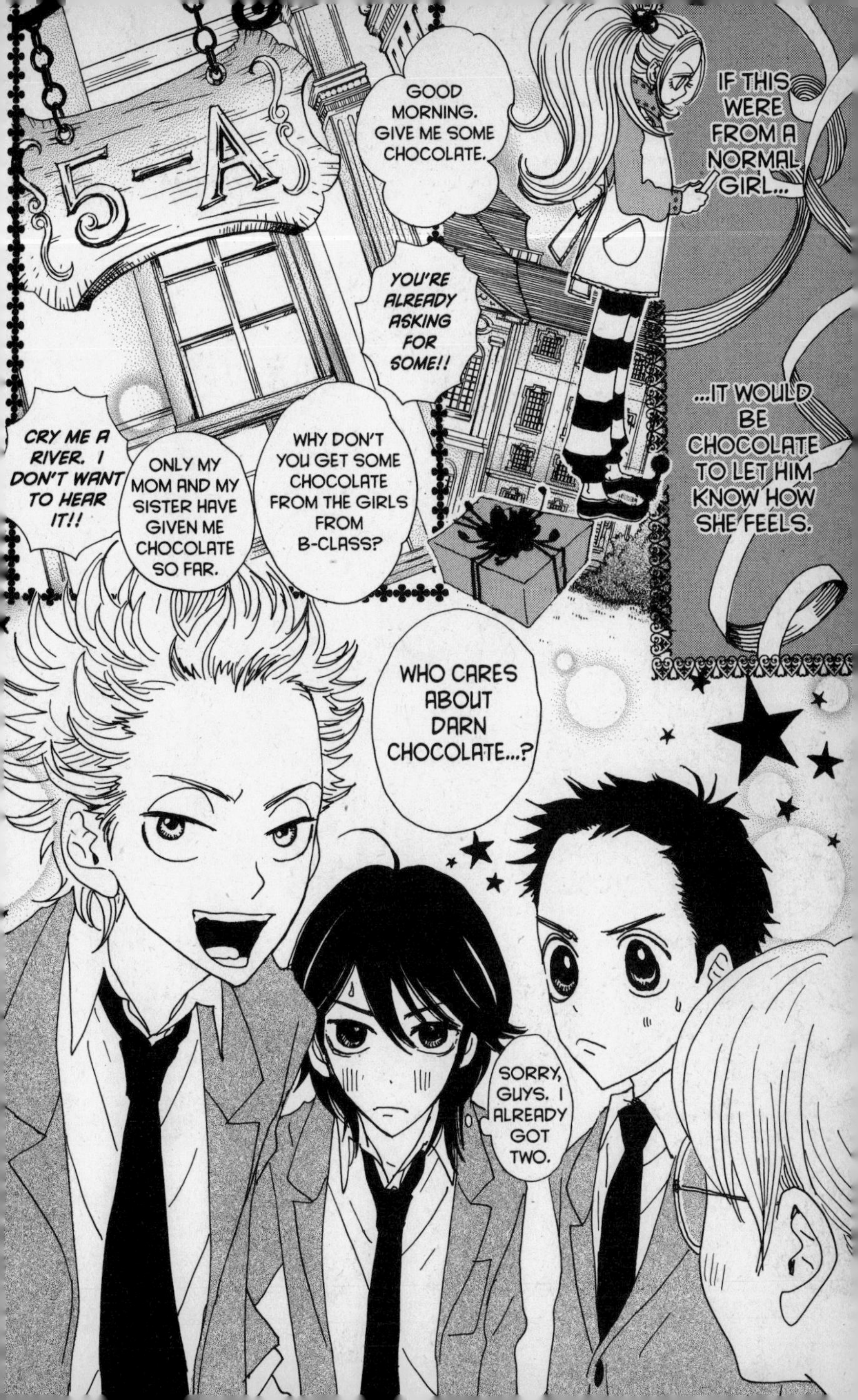
IF THIS WERE FROM A NORMAL GIRL...
...IT WOULD BE CHOCOLATE TO LET HIM KNOW HOW SHE FEELS.
5-A
GOOD MORNING. GIVE ME SOME CHOCOLATE.
YOU'RE ALREADY ASKING FOR SOME!!
WHY DON'T YOU GET SOME CHOCOLATE FROM THE GIRLS FROM B-CLASS?
ONLY MY MOM AND MY SISTER HAVE GIVEN ME CHOCOLATE SO FAR.
CRY ME A RIVER. I DON'T WANT TO HEAR IT!!
WHO CARES ABOUT DARN CHOCOLATE...?
SORRY, GUYS. I ALREADY GOT TWO.

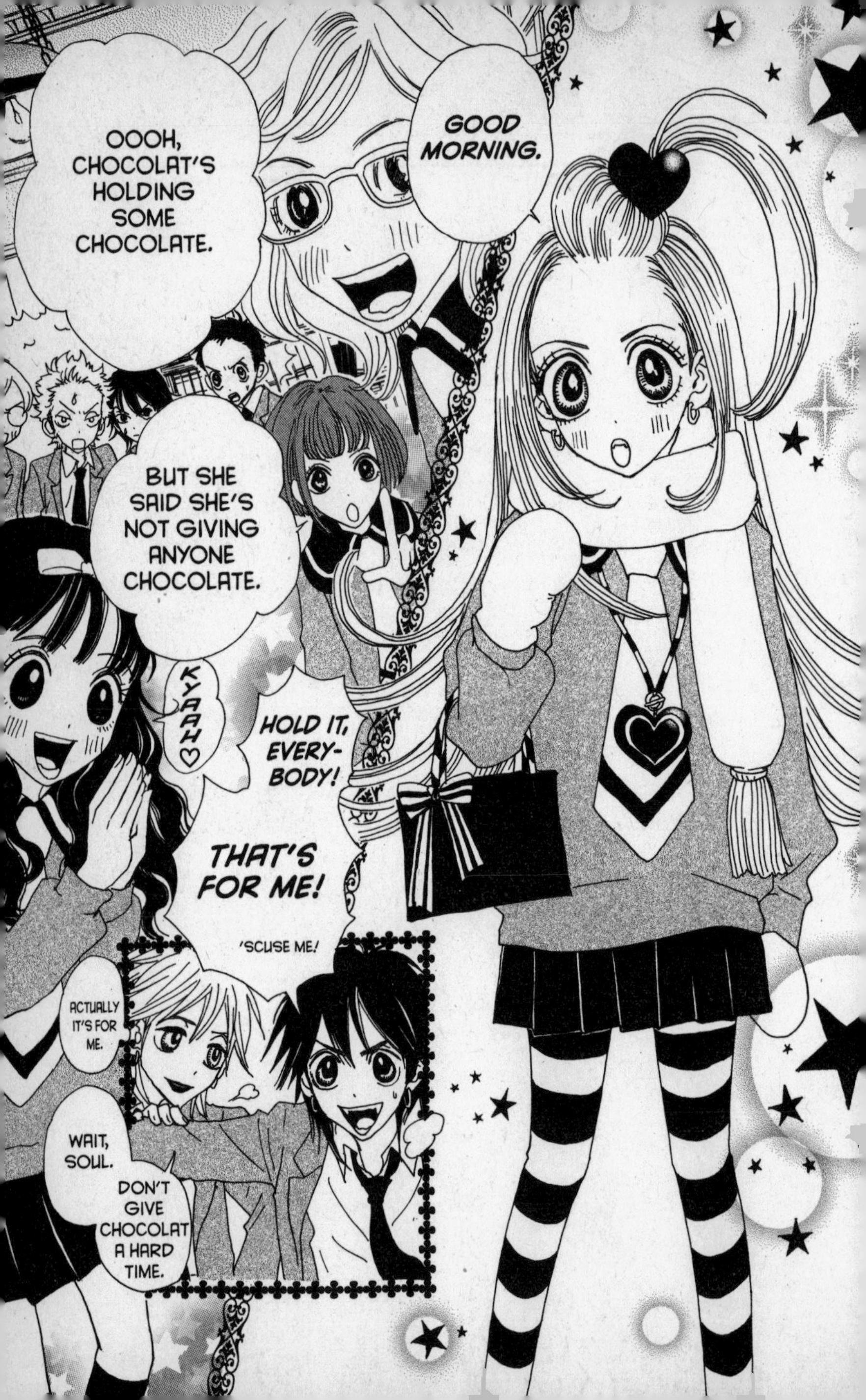
GOOD MORNING.
OOOH, CHOCOLAT'S HOLDING SOME CHOCOLATE.
BUT SHE SAID SHE'S NOT GIVING ANYONE CHOCOLATE.
KYAAH♡
HOLD IT, EVERY-BODY!
THAT'S FOR ME!
'SCUSE ME!
ACTUALLY IT'S FOR ME.
WAIT, SOUL.
DON'T GIVE CHOCOLAT A HARD TIME.

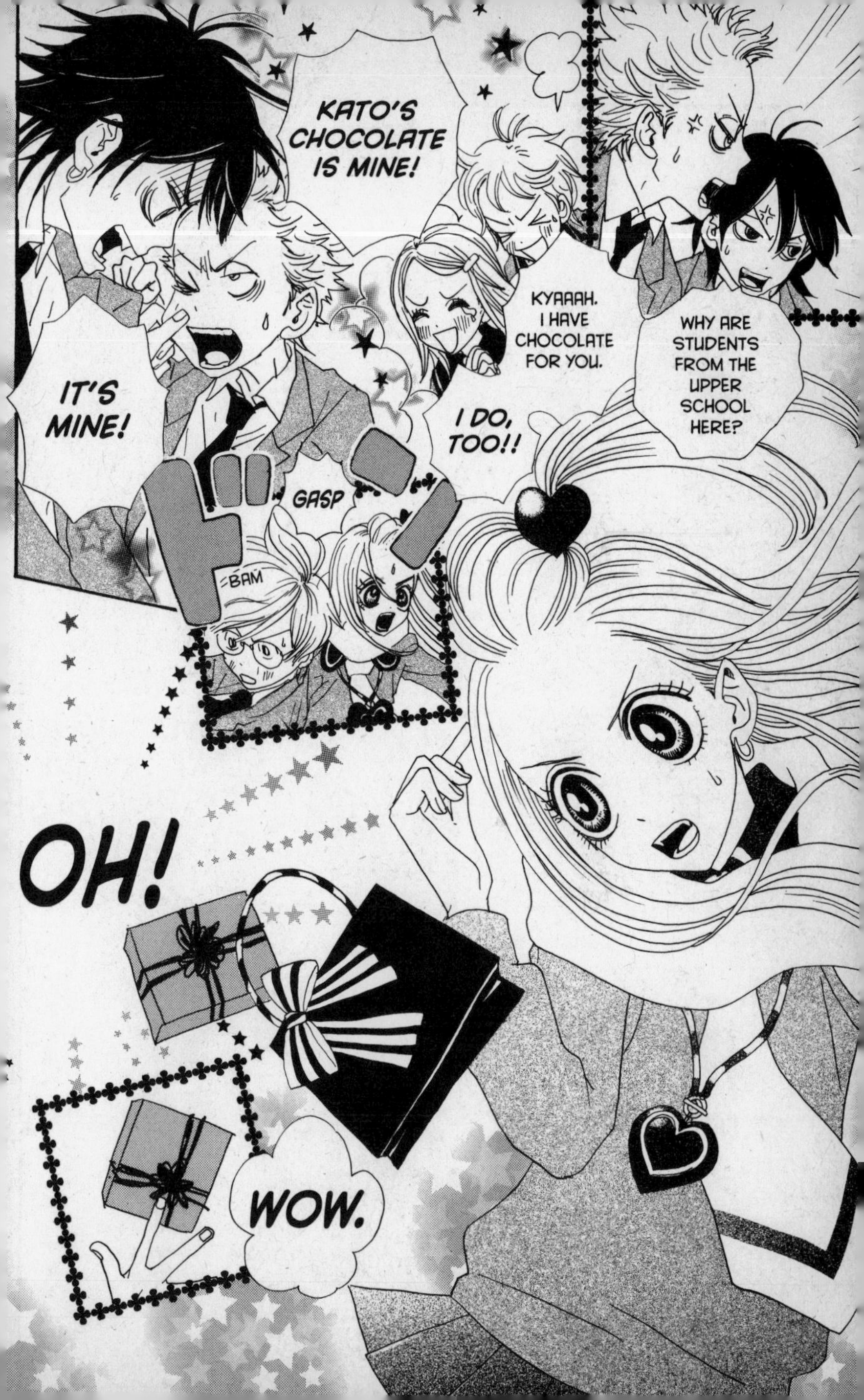
WHY ARE STUDENTS FROM THE UPPER SCHOOL HERE?
KATO'S CHOCOLATE IS MINE!
KYAAAH. I HAVE CHOCOLATE FOR YOU.
I DO, TOO!!
IT'S MINE!
GASP
BAM
OH!
WOW.

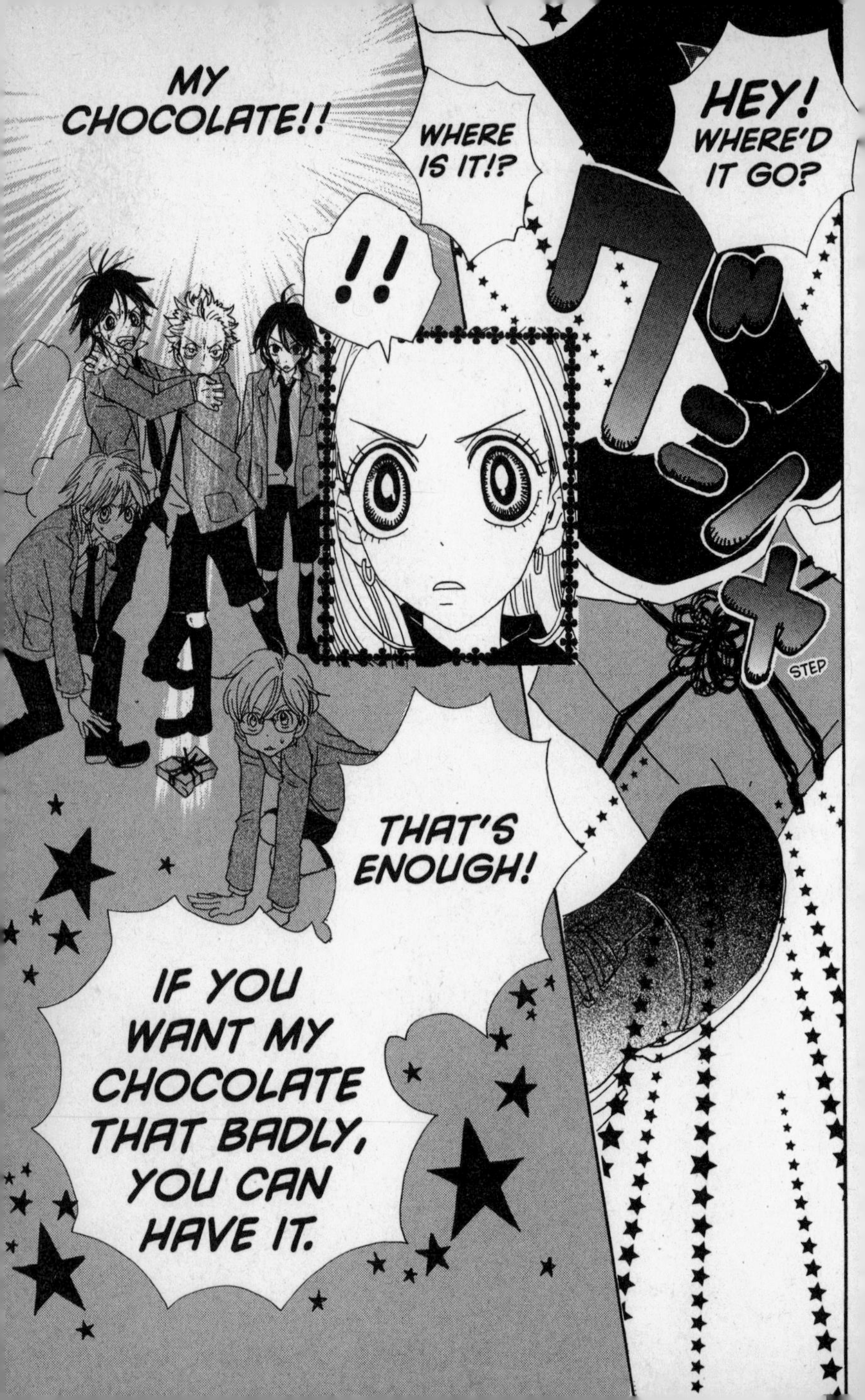
HEY! WHERE'D IT GO?
WHERE IS IT!?
MY CHOCOLATE!!
!!
STEP
THAT'S ENOUGH!
IF YOU WANT MY CHOCOLATE THAT BADLY, YOU CAN HAVE IT.

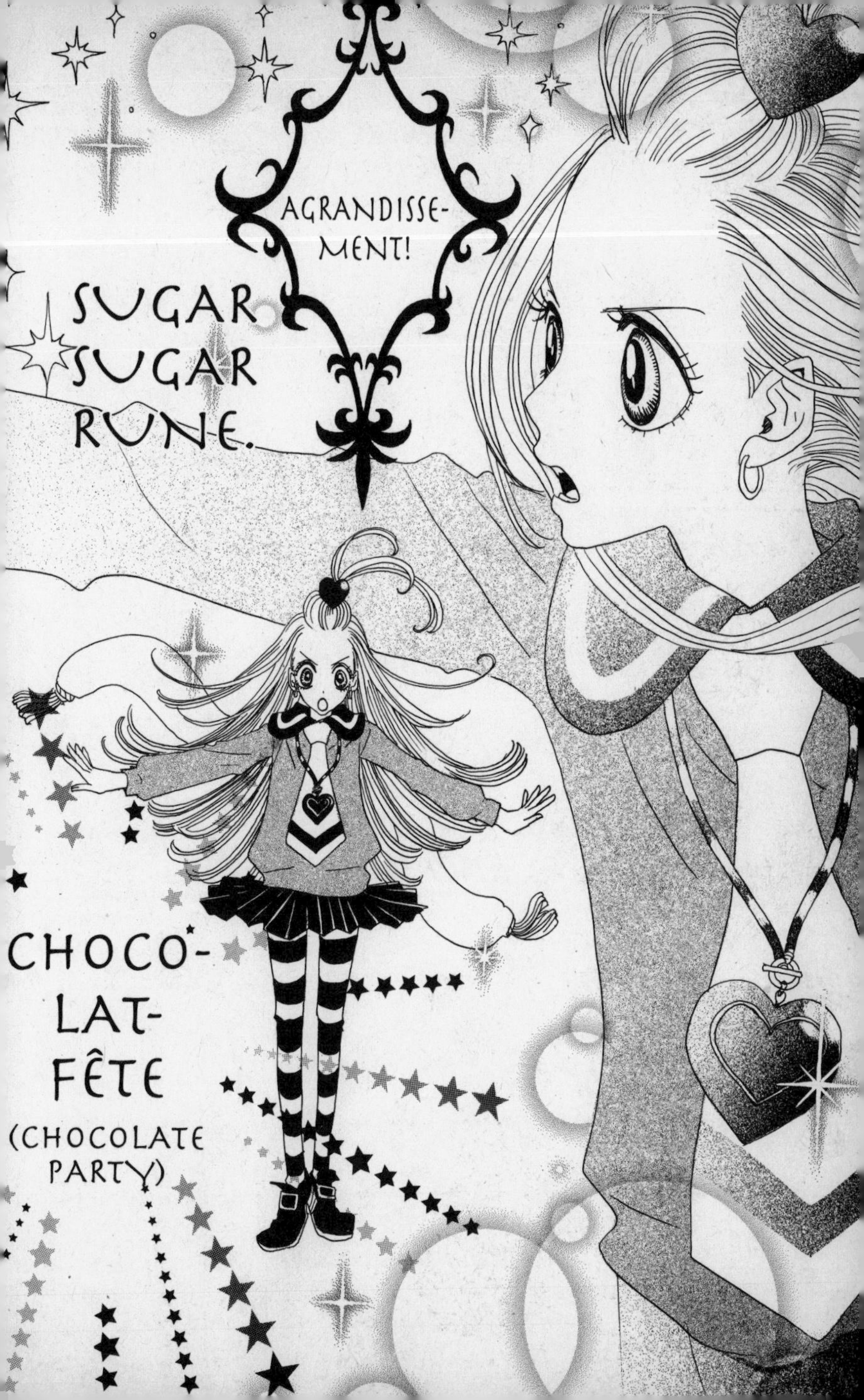
AGRANDISSE-MENT!
SUGAR SUGAR RUNE.
CHOCO-LAT-FÊTE
(CHOCOLATE PARTY)

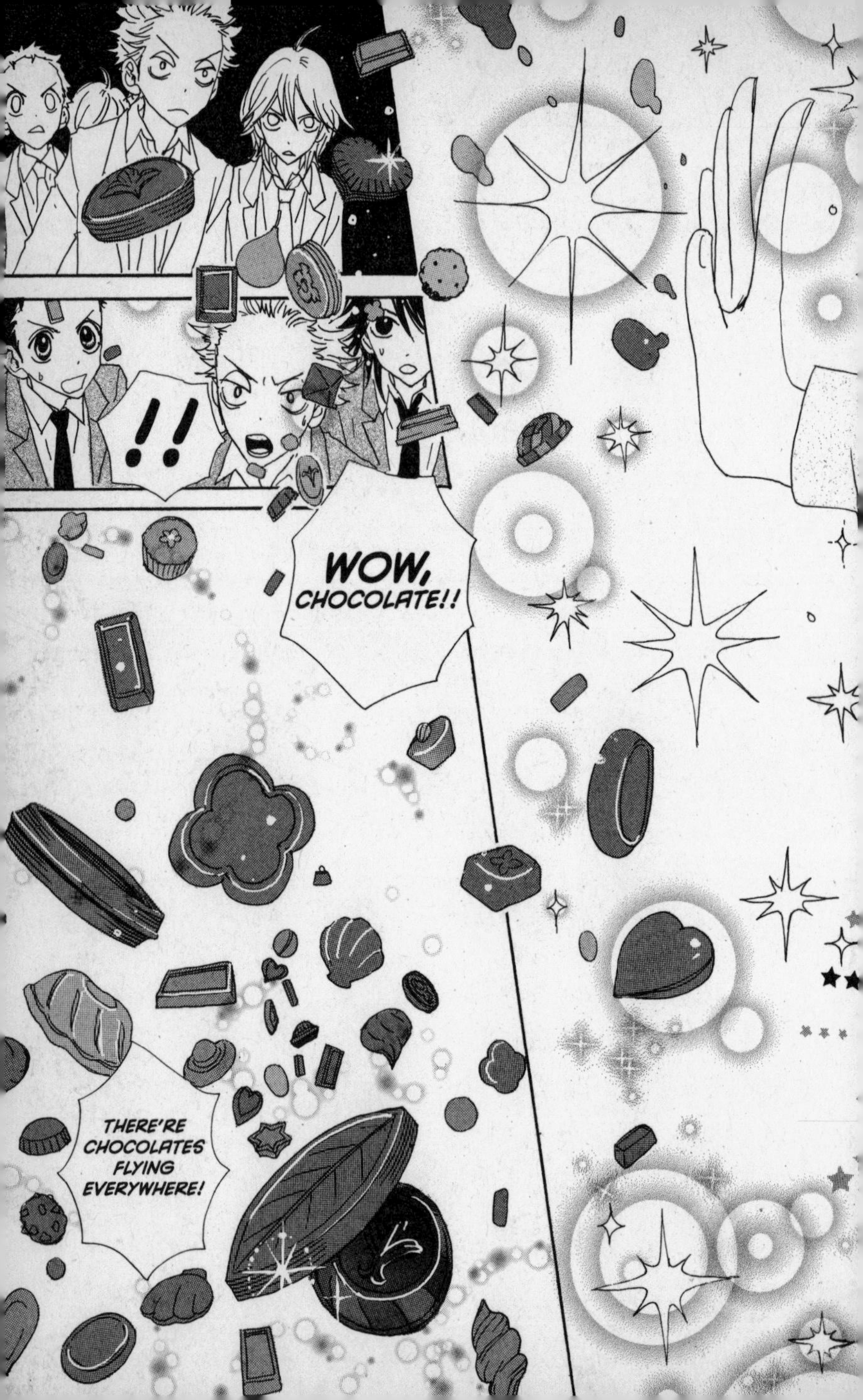
!!
WOW, CHOCOLATE!!
THERE'RE CHOCOLATES FLYING EVERYWHERE!

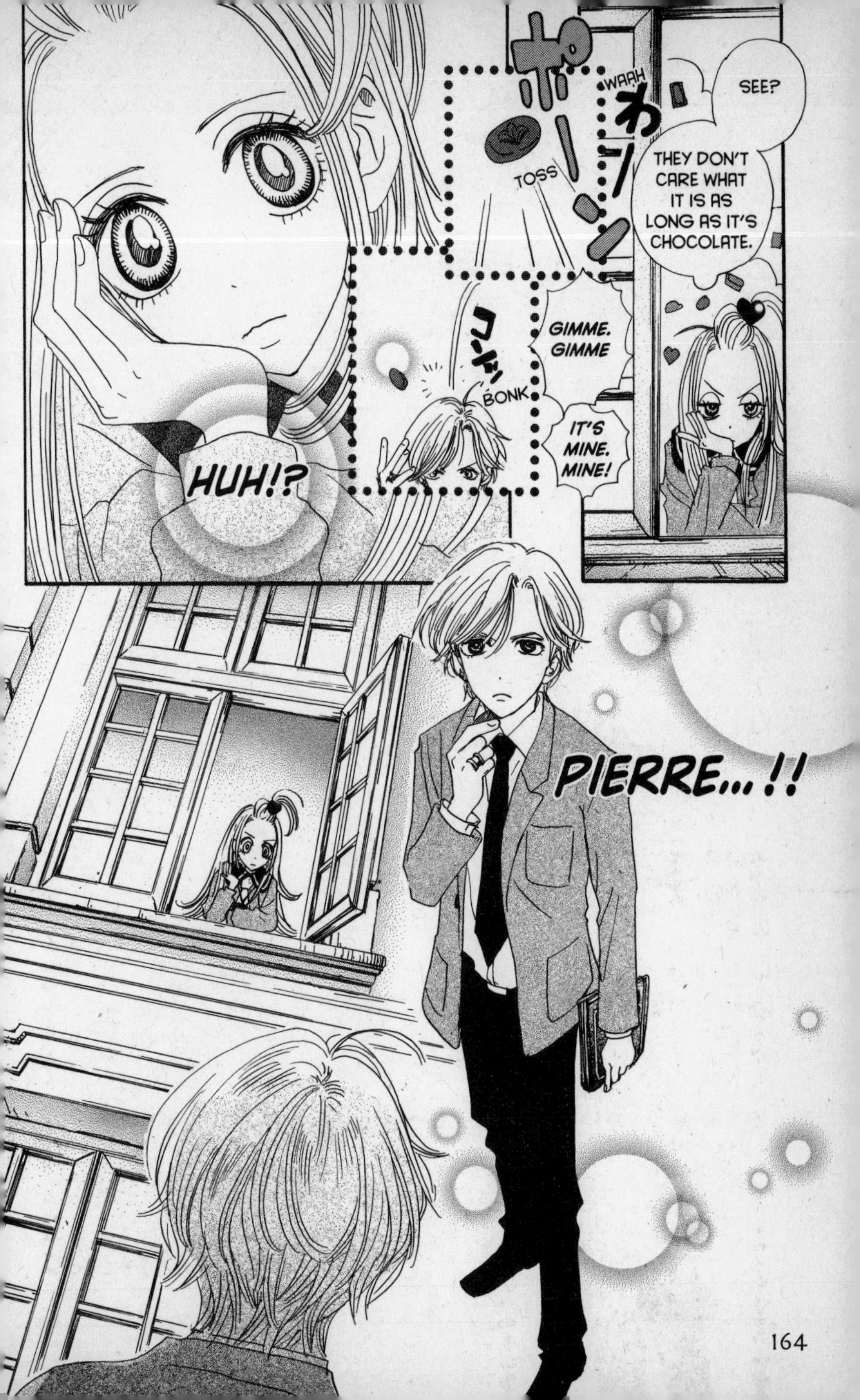
SEE?
THEY DON'T CARE WHAT IT IS AS LONG AS IT'S CHOCOLATE.
WAAH
TOSS
GIMME. GIMME
BONK
IT'S MINE. MINE!
HUH!?
PIERRE...!!

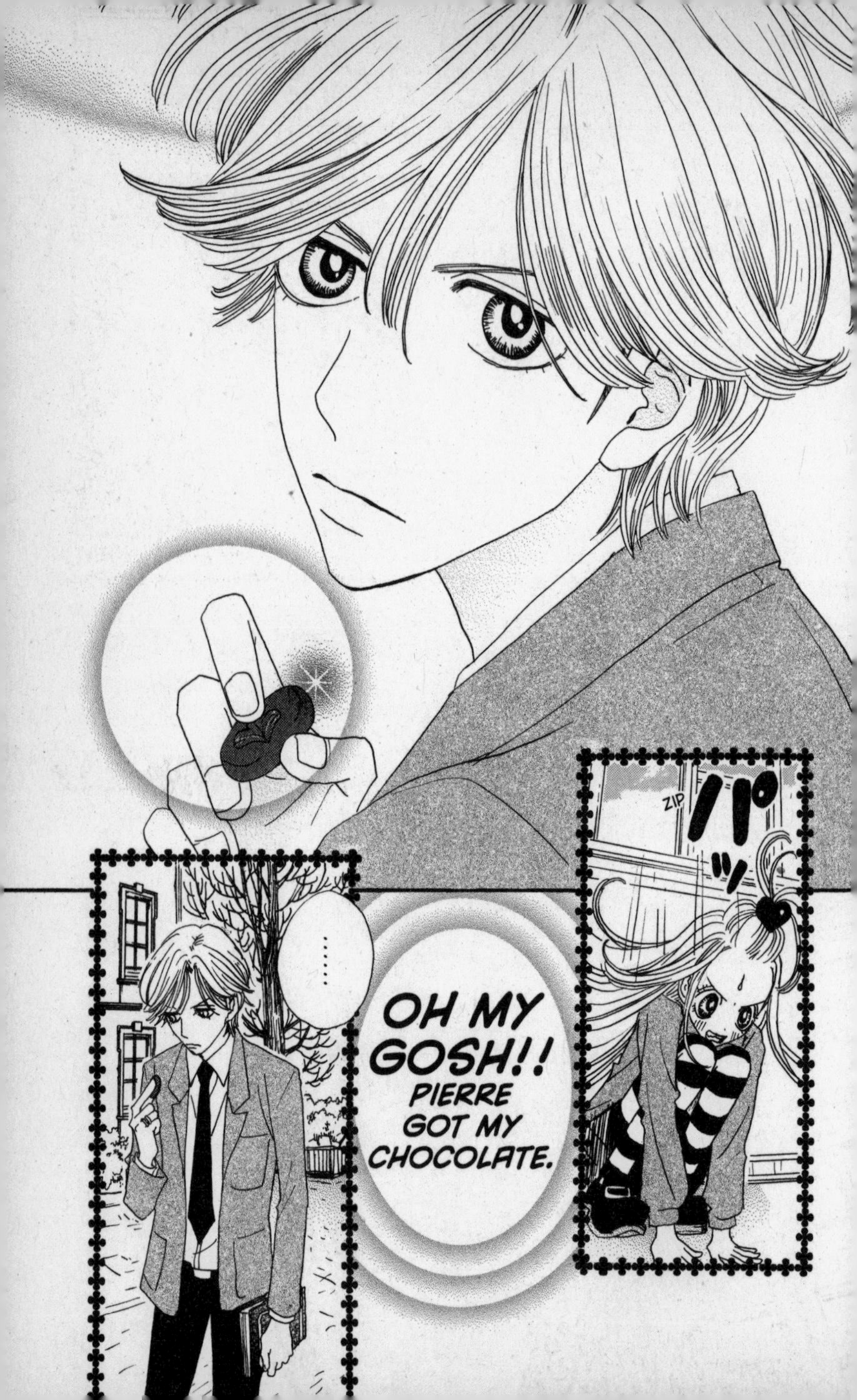
ZIP
パッ
OH MY GOSH!! PIERRE GOT MY CHOCOLATE.
......

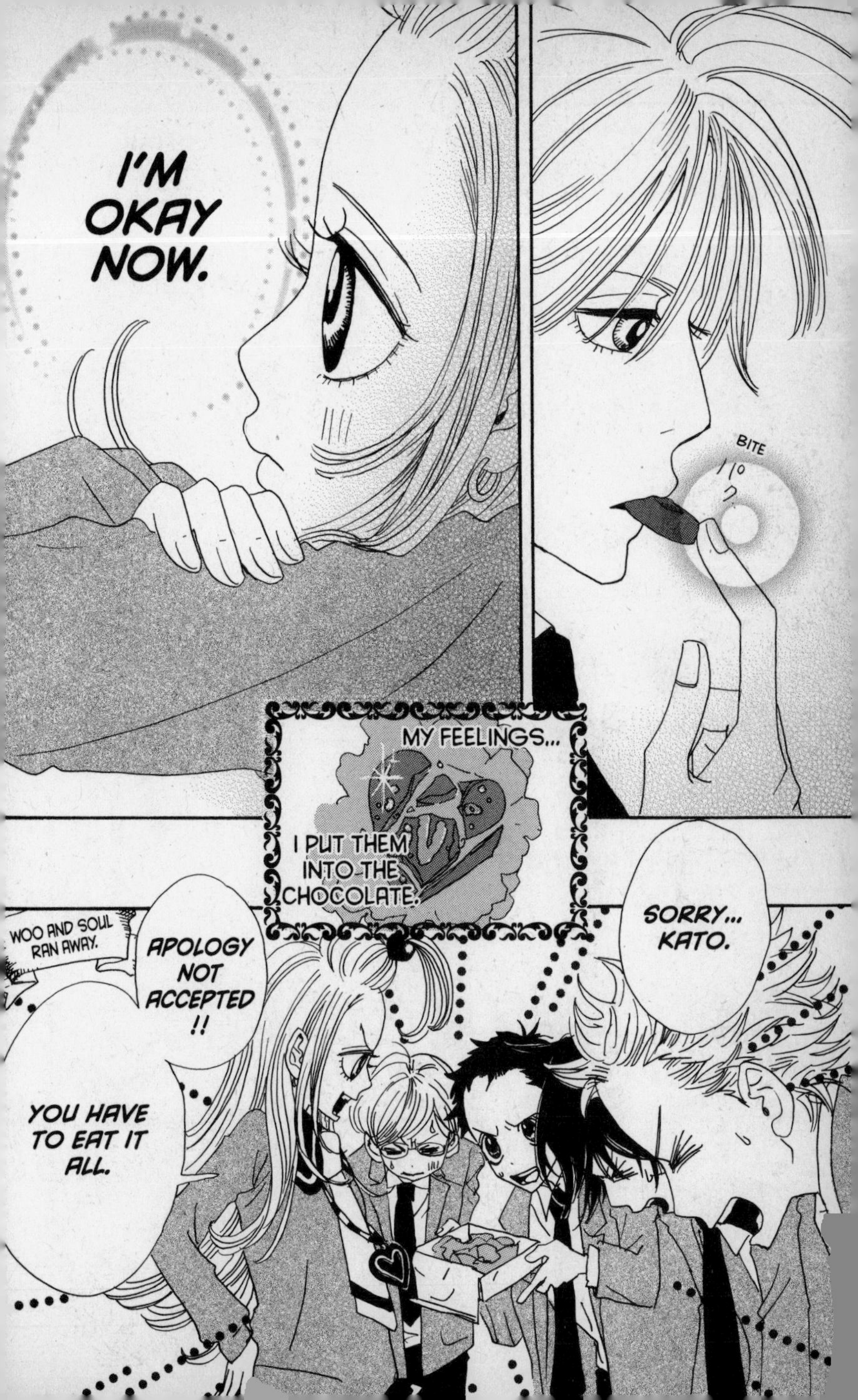
BITE
I'M OKAY NOW.
MY FEELINGS...
I PUT THEM INTO THE CHOCOLATE.
SORRY... KATO.
APOLOGY NOT ACCEPTED!!
YOU HAVE TO EAT IT ALL.
WOO AND SOUL RAN AWAY.

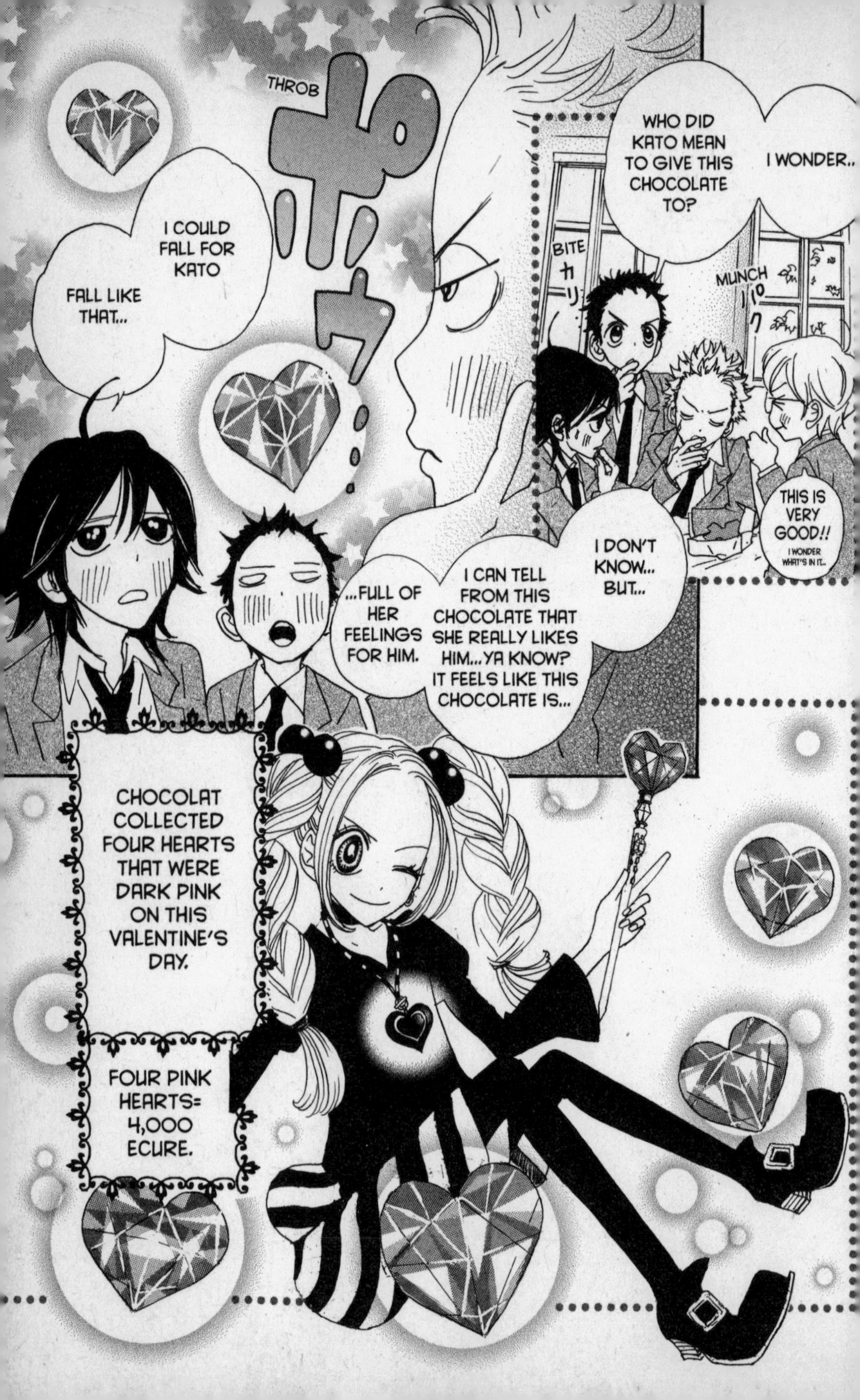
WHO DID KATO MEAN TO GIVE THIS CHOCOLATE TO?
I WONDER..
BITE
MUNCH
THIS IS VERY GOOD!!
I WONDER WHAT'S IN IT..
I DON'T KNOW... BUT...
I CAN TELL FROM THIS CHOCOLATE THAT SHE REALLY LIKES HIM...YA KNOW? IT FEELS LIKE THIS CHOCOLATE IS...
...FULL OF HER FEELINGS FOR HIM.
THROB
I COULD FALL FOR KATO
FALL LIKE THAT...
CHOCOLAT COLLECTED FOUR HEARTS THAT WERE DARK PINK ON THIS VALENTINE'S DAY.
FOUR PINK HEARTS= 4,000 ECURE.

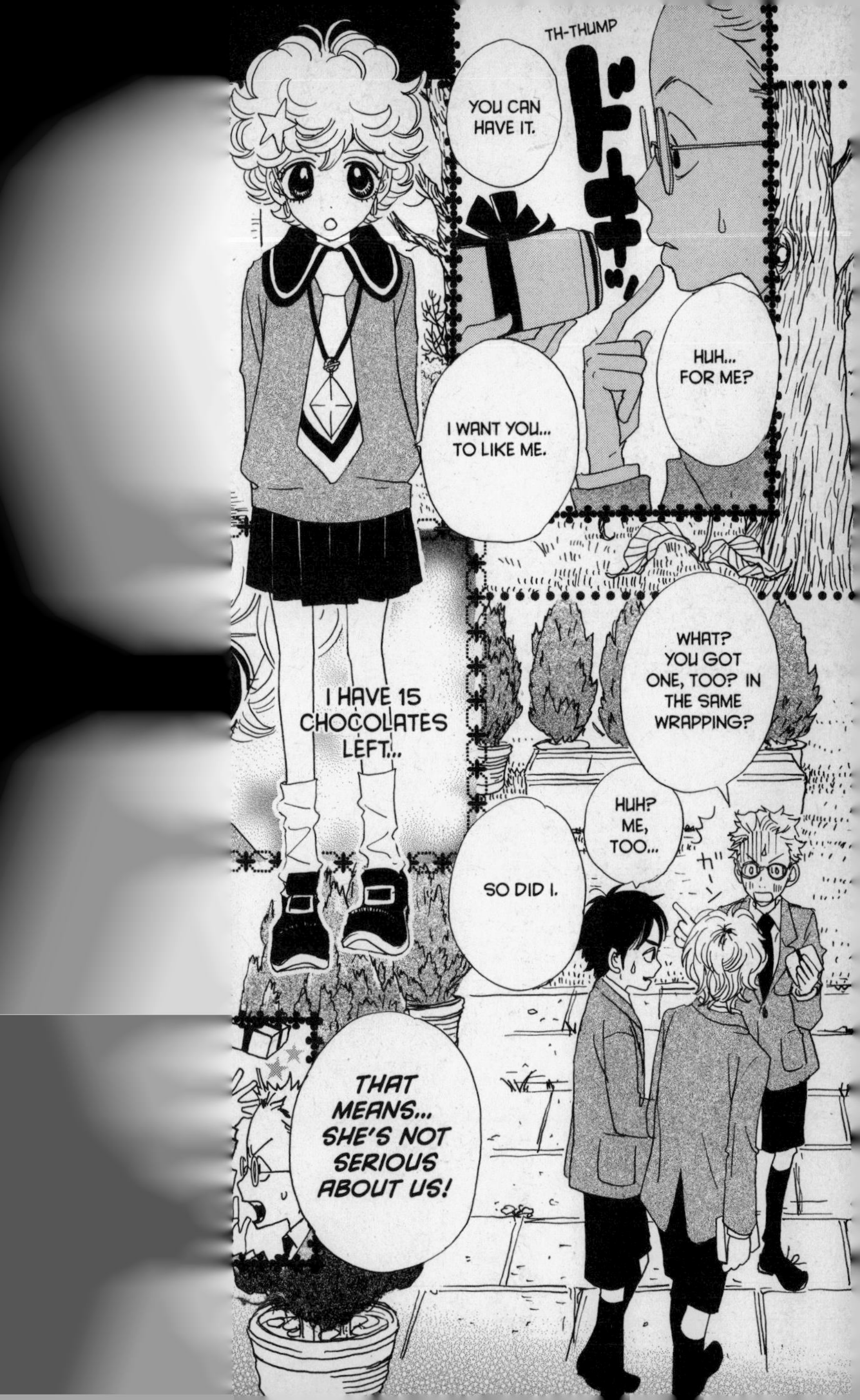
TH-THUMP
YOU CAN HAVE IT.
HUH... FOR ME?
I WANT YOU... TO LIKE ME.
WHAT? YOU GOT ONE, TOO? IN THE SAME WRAPPING?
HUH? ME, TOO...
SO DID I.
I HAVE 15 CHOCOLATES LEFT...
THAT MEANS... SHE'S NOT SERIOUS ABOUT US!

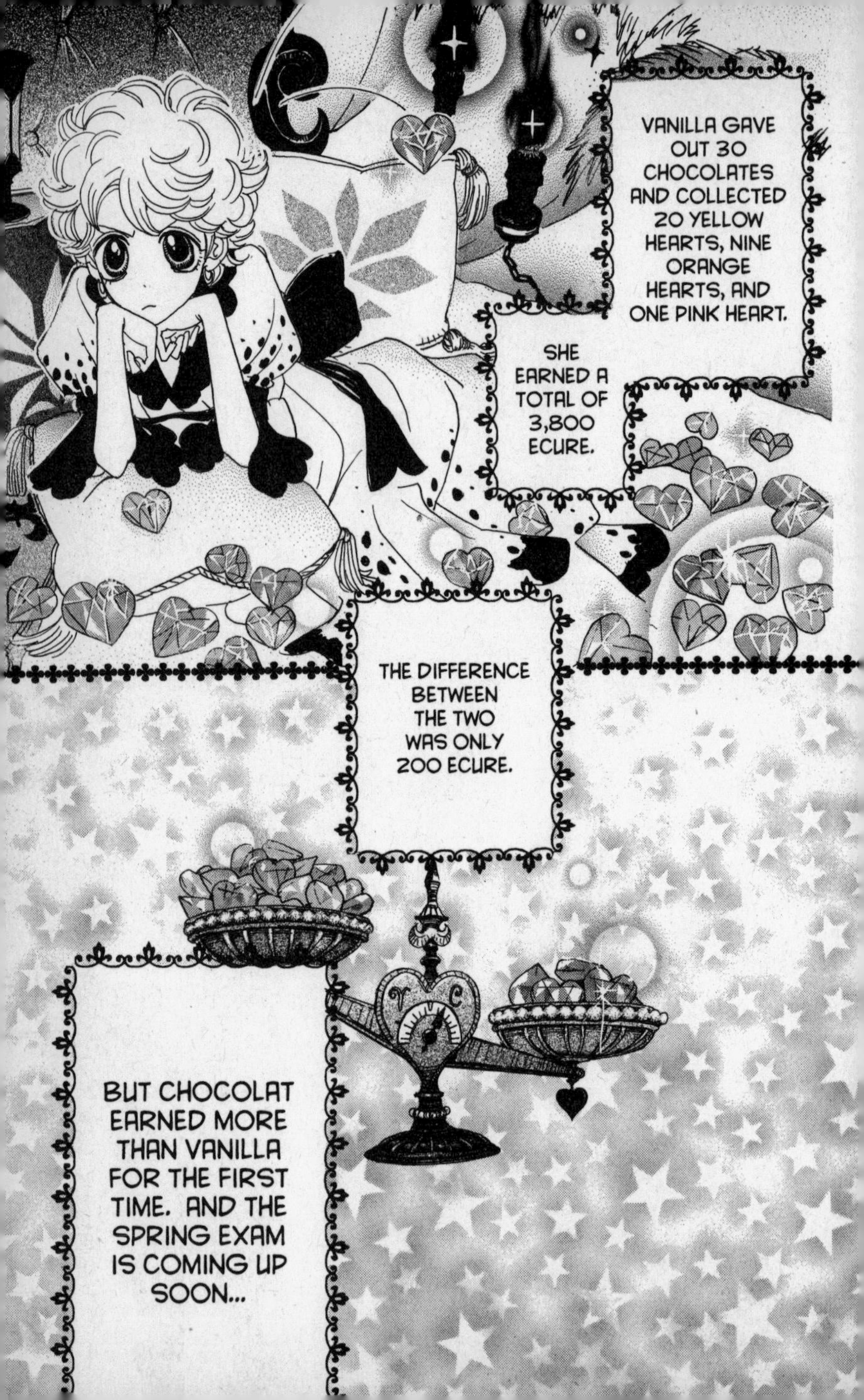
VANILLA GAVE OUT 30 CHOCOLATES AND COLLECTED 20 YELLOW HEARTS, NINE ORANGE HEARTS, AND ONE PINK HEART.
SHE EARNED A TOTAL OF 3,800 ECURE.
THE DIFFERENCE BETWEEN THE TWO WAS ONLY 200 ECURE.
BUT CHOCOLAT EARNED MORE THAN VANILLA FOR THE FIRST TIME. AND THE SPRING EXAM IS COMING UP SOON...

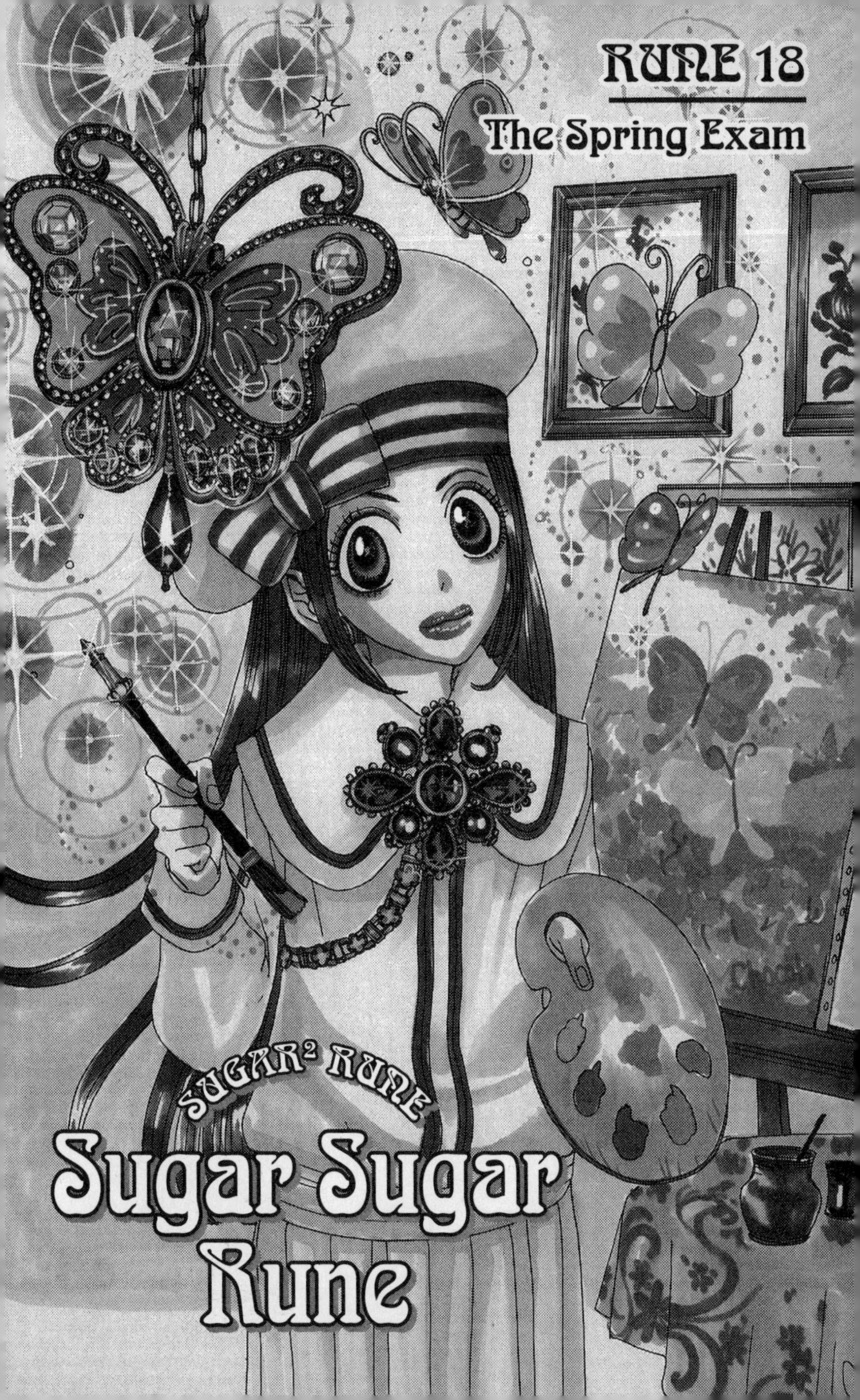
RUNE 18
The Spring Exam
SUGAR² RUNE
Sugar Sugar Rune

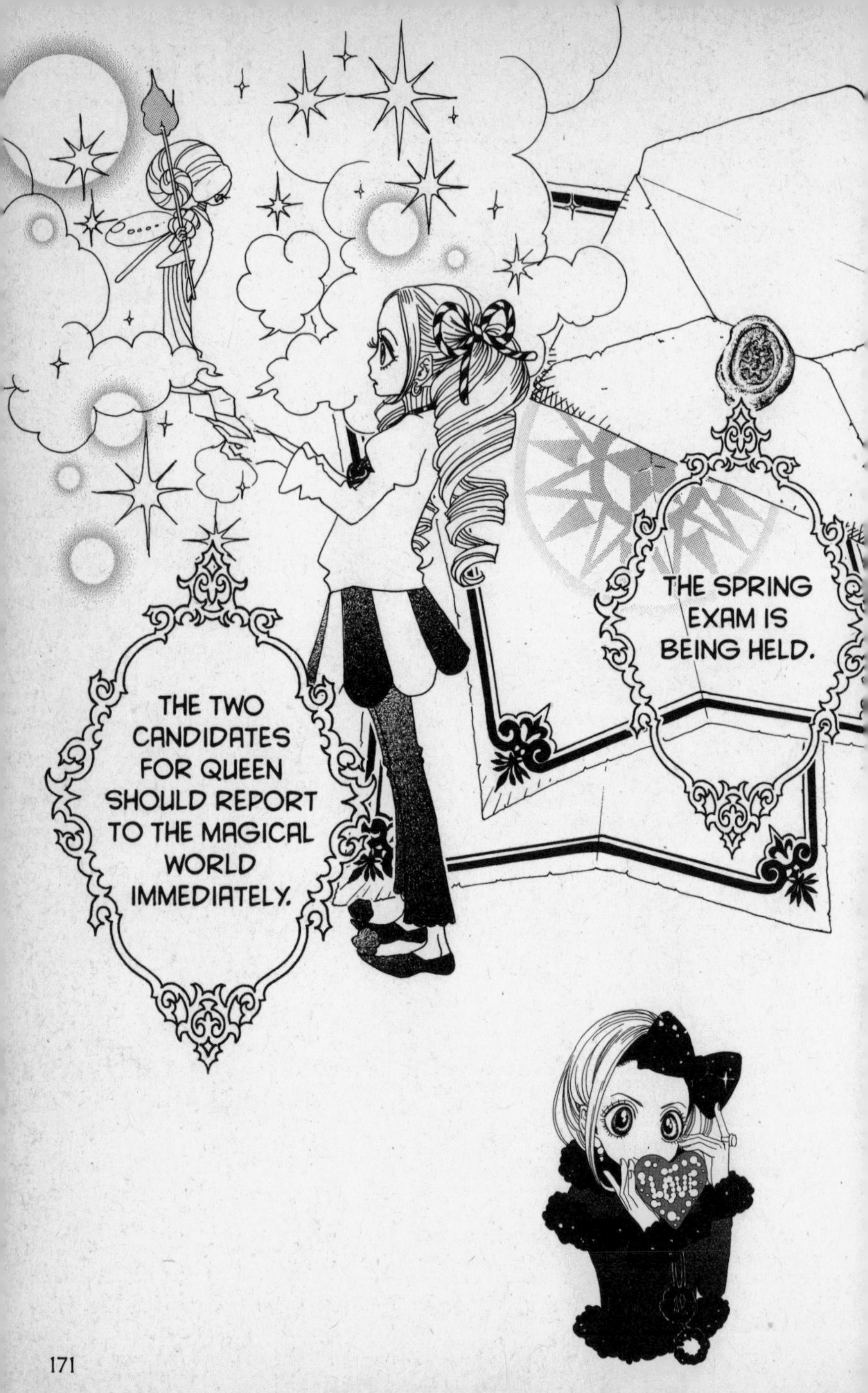
THE SPRING EXAM IS BEING HELD.
THE TWO CANDIDATES FOR QUEEN SHOULD REPORT TO THE MAGICAL WORLD IMMEDIATELY.
LOVE

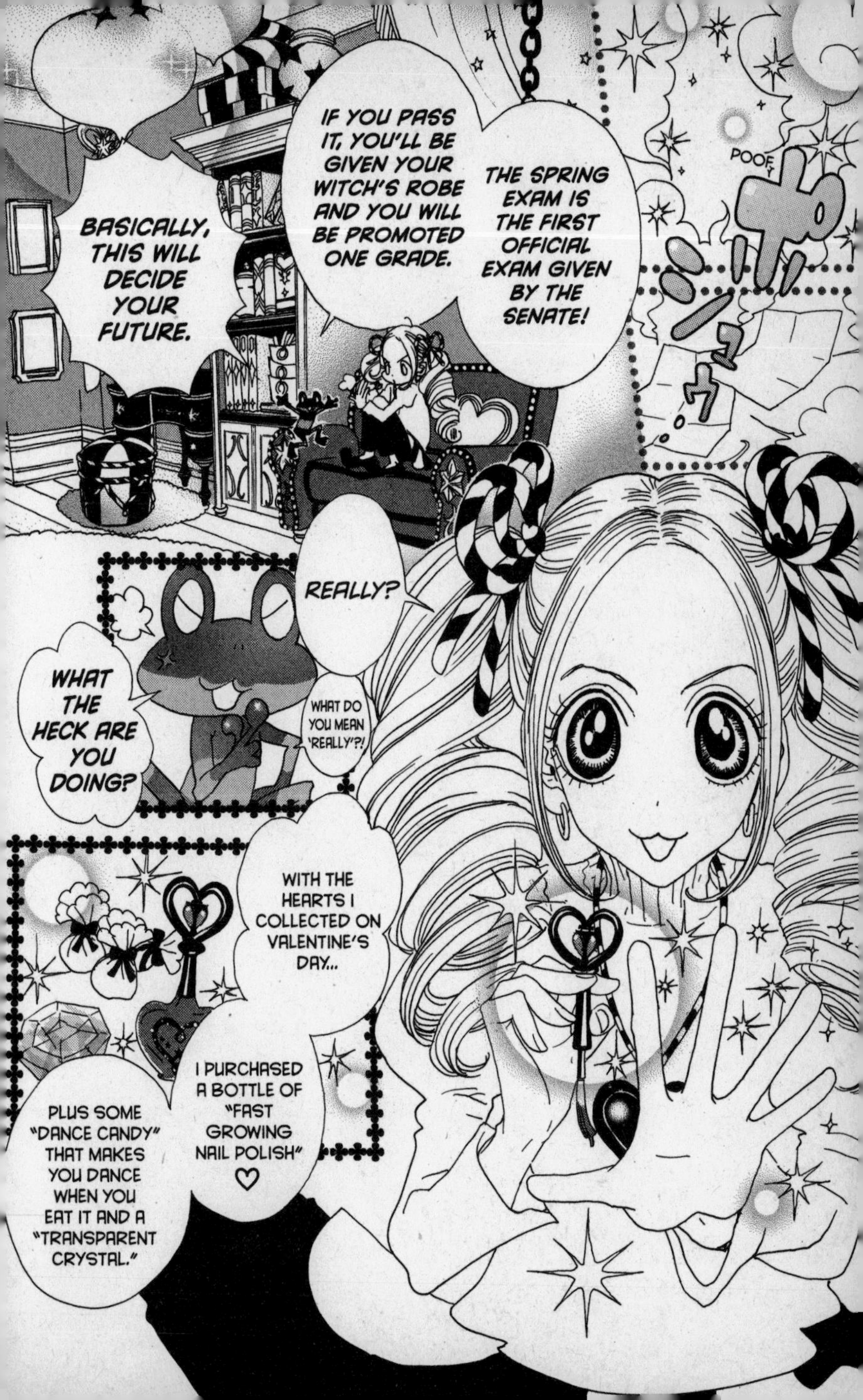
POOF
THE SPRING EXAM IS THE FIRST OFFICIAL EXAM GIVEN BY THE SENATE!
IF YOU PASS IT, YOU'LL BE GIVEN YOUR WITCH'S ROBE AND YOU WILL BE PROMOTED ONE GRADE.
BASICALLY, THIS WILL DECIDE YOUR FUTURE.
REALLY?
WHAT THE HECK ARE YOU DOING?
WHAT DO YOU MEAN 'REALLY'?!
WITH THE HEARTS I COLLECTED ON VALENTINE'S DAY...
I PURCHASED A BOTTLE OF "FAST GROWING NAIL POLISH" ♡
PLUS SOME "DANCE CANDY" THAT MAKES YOU DANCE WHEN YOU EAT IT AND A "TRANSPARENT CRYSTAL."

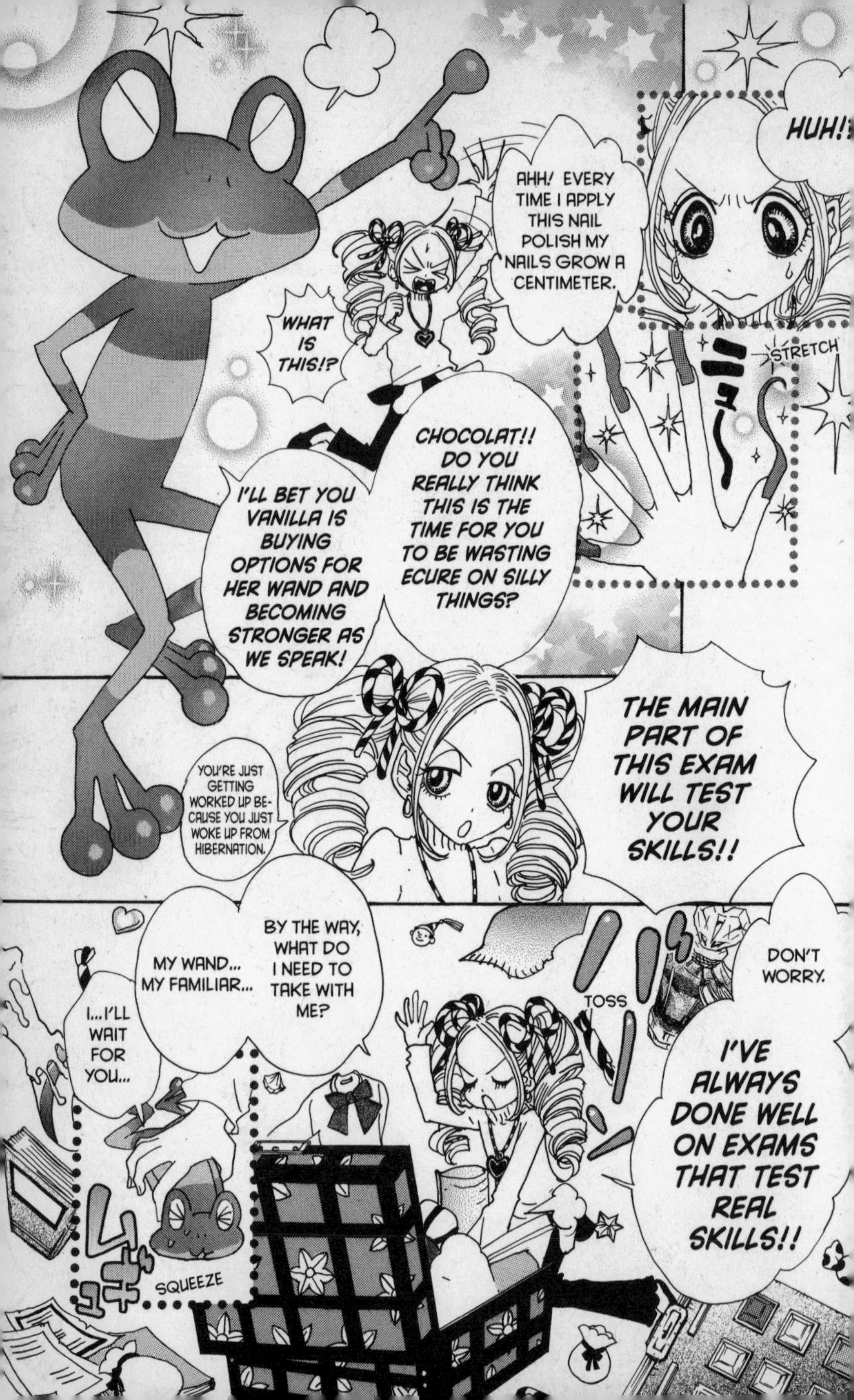
HUH!!
STRETCH
AHH! EVERY TIME I APPLY THIS NAIL POLISH MY NAILS GROW A CENTIMETER.
WHAT IS THIS!?
CHOCOLAT!! DO YOU REALLY THINK THIS IS THE TIME FOR YOU TO BE WASTING ECURE ON SILLY THINGS?
I'LL BET YOU VANILLA IS BUYING OPTIONS FOR HER WAND AND BECOMING STRONGER AS WE SPEAK!
THE MAIN PART OF THIS EXAM WILL TEST YOUR SKILLS!!
YOU'RE JUST GETTING WORKED UP BECAUSE YOU JUST WOKE UP FROM HIBERNATION.
DON'T WORRY.
I'VE ALWAYS DONE WELL ON EXAMS THAT TEST REAL SKILLS!!
TOSS
BY THE WAY, WHAT DO I NEED TO TAKE WITH ME?
MY WAND... MY FAMILIAR...
I...I'LL WAIT FOR YOU...
SQUEEZE

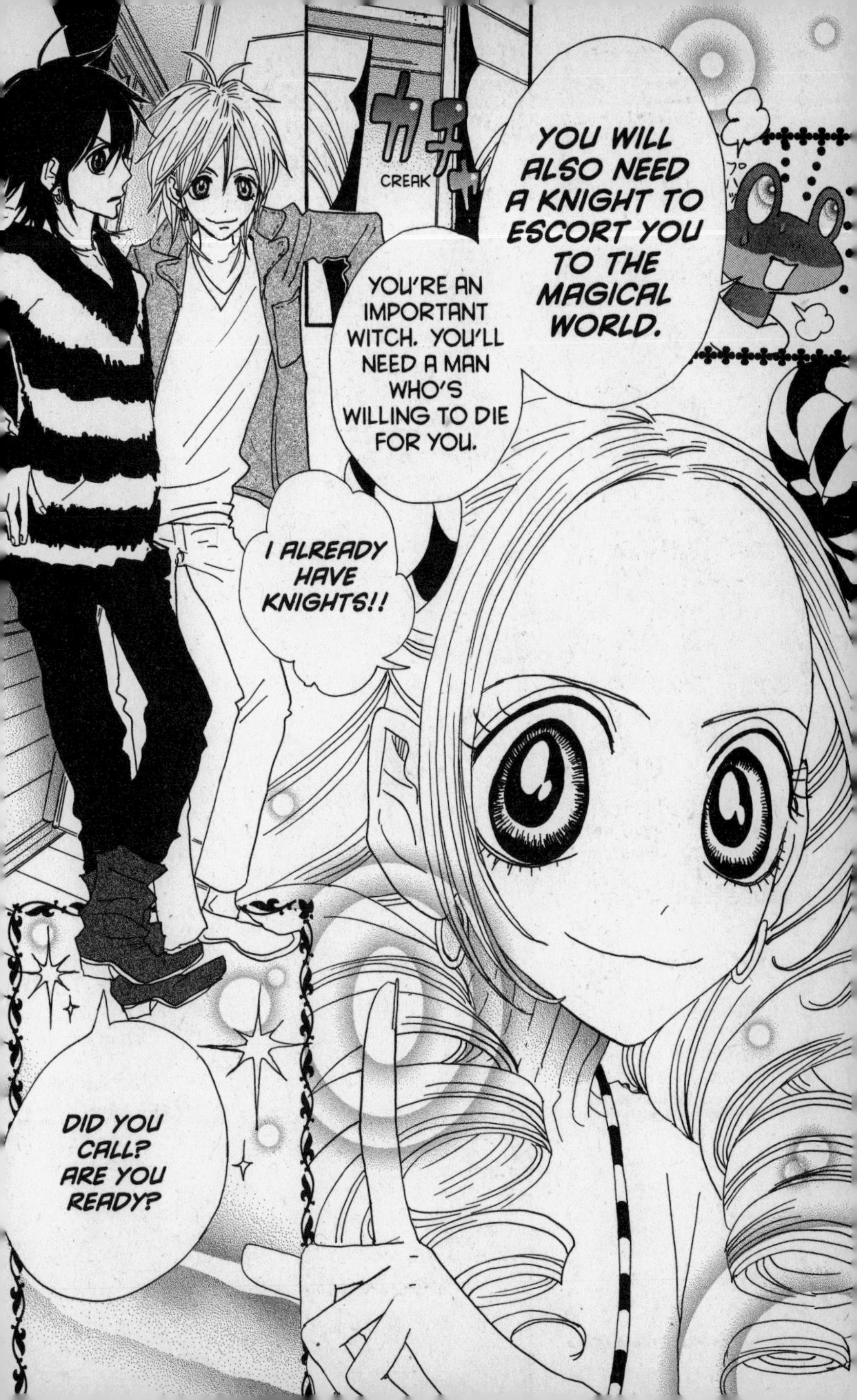
YOU WILL ALSO NEED A KNIGHT TO ESCORT YOU TO THE MAGICAL WORLD.
カチャ
CREAK
YOU'RE AN IMPORTANT WITCH. YOU'LL NEED A MAN WHO'S WILLING TO DIE FOR YOU.
I ALREADY HAVE KNIGHTS!!
DID YOU CALL? ARE YOU READY?

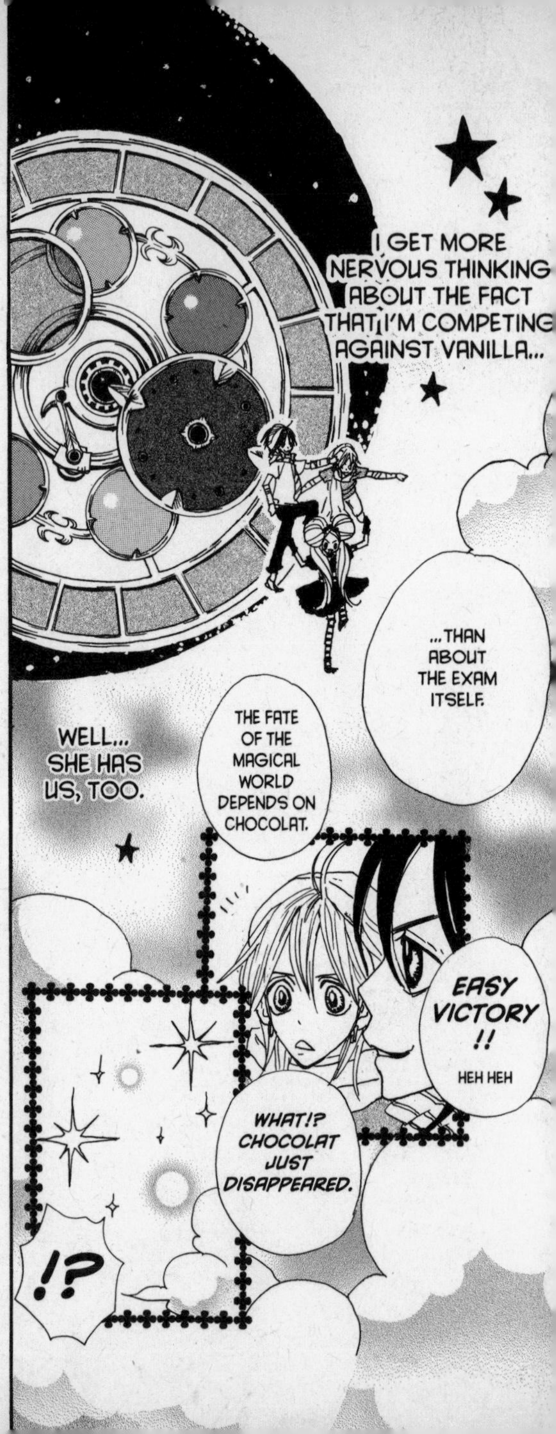
I GET MORE NERVOUS THINKING ABOUT THE FACT THAT I'M COMPETING AGAINST VANILLA...
...THAN ABOUT THE EXAM ITSELF.
THE FATE OF THE MAGICAL WORLD DEPENDS ON CHOCOLAT.
WELL... SHE HAS US, TOO.
EASY VICTORY!!
HEH HEH
WHAT!? CHOCOLAT JUST DISAPPEARED.
!?

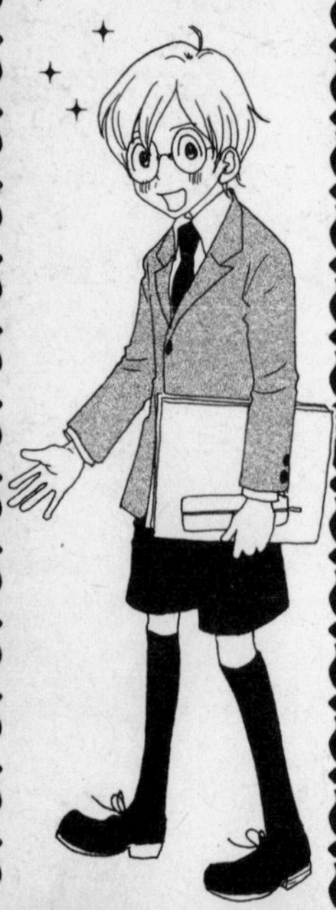

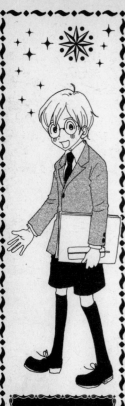

HAJIME NISHITANI

HEIGHT: 154 CM

AGE: 11 YEARS OLD

HOBBIES:
COLLECTING COINS, TAKING PHOTOGRAPHS, DOING RESEARCH

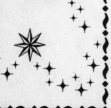

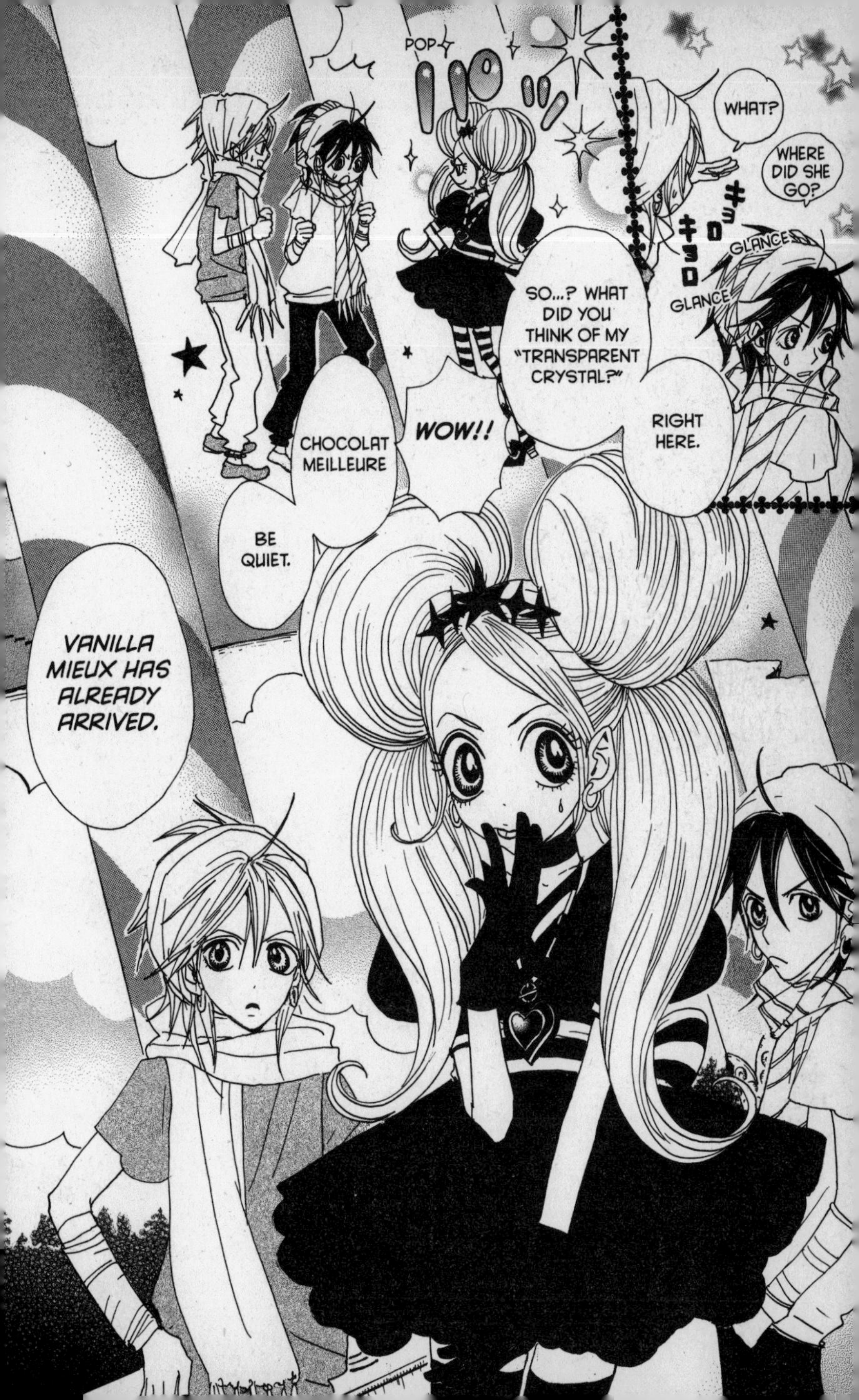
WHAT?
WHERE DID SHE GO?
キョロ
キョロ
GLANCE
GLANCE
POP
RIGHT HERE.
SO...? WHAT DID YOU THINK OF MY "TRANSPARENT CRYSTAL?"
WOW!!
CHOCOLAT MEILLEURE
BE QUIET.
VANILLA MIEUX HAS ALREADY ARRIVED.

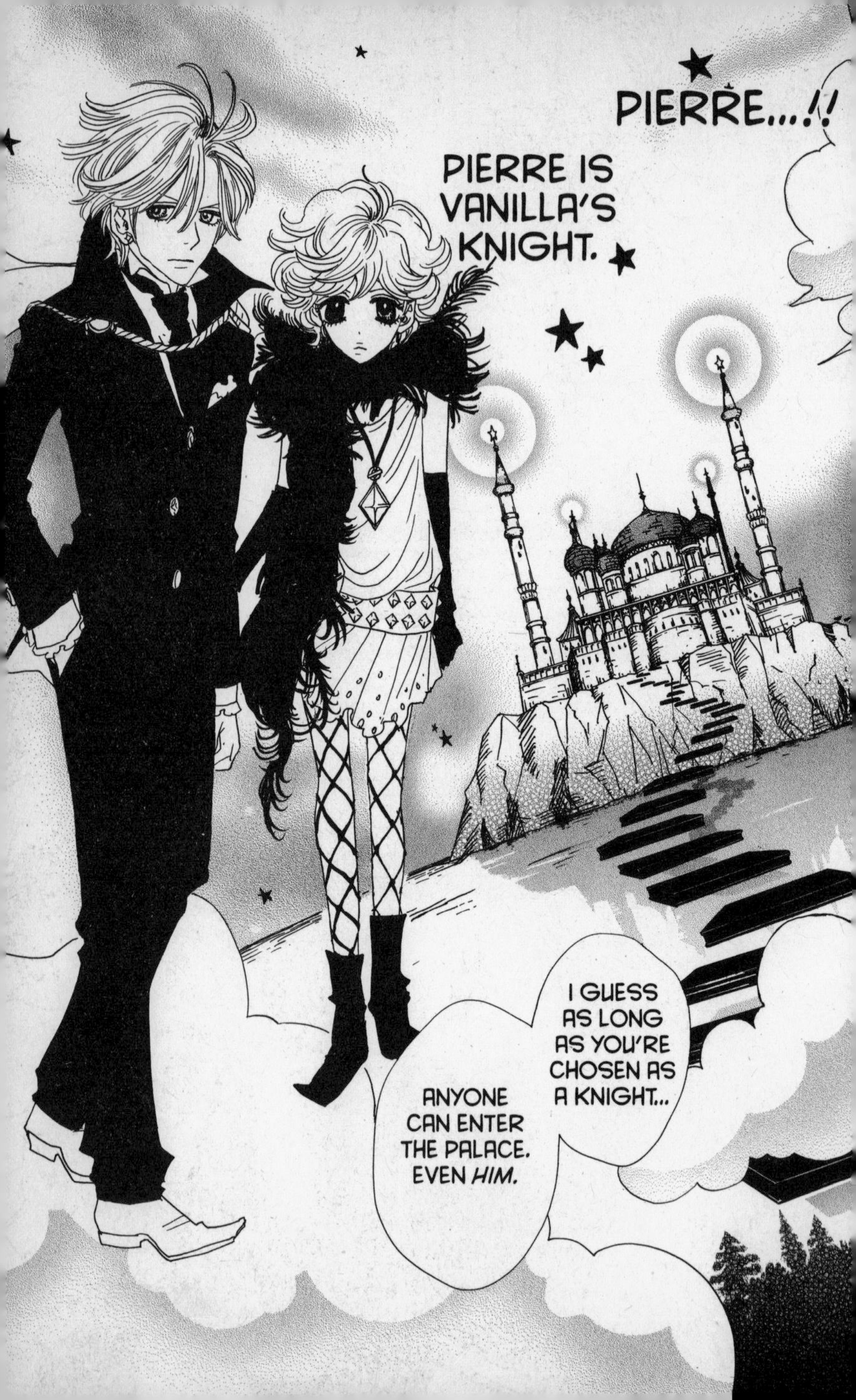
PIERRE...!!
PIERRE IS VANILLA'S KNIGHT.
I GUESS AS LONG AS YOU'RE CHOSEN AS A KNIGHT...
ANYONE CAN ENTER THE PALACE.
EVEN *HIM.*

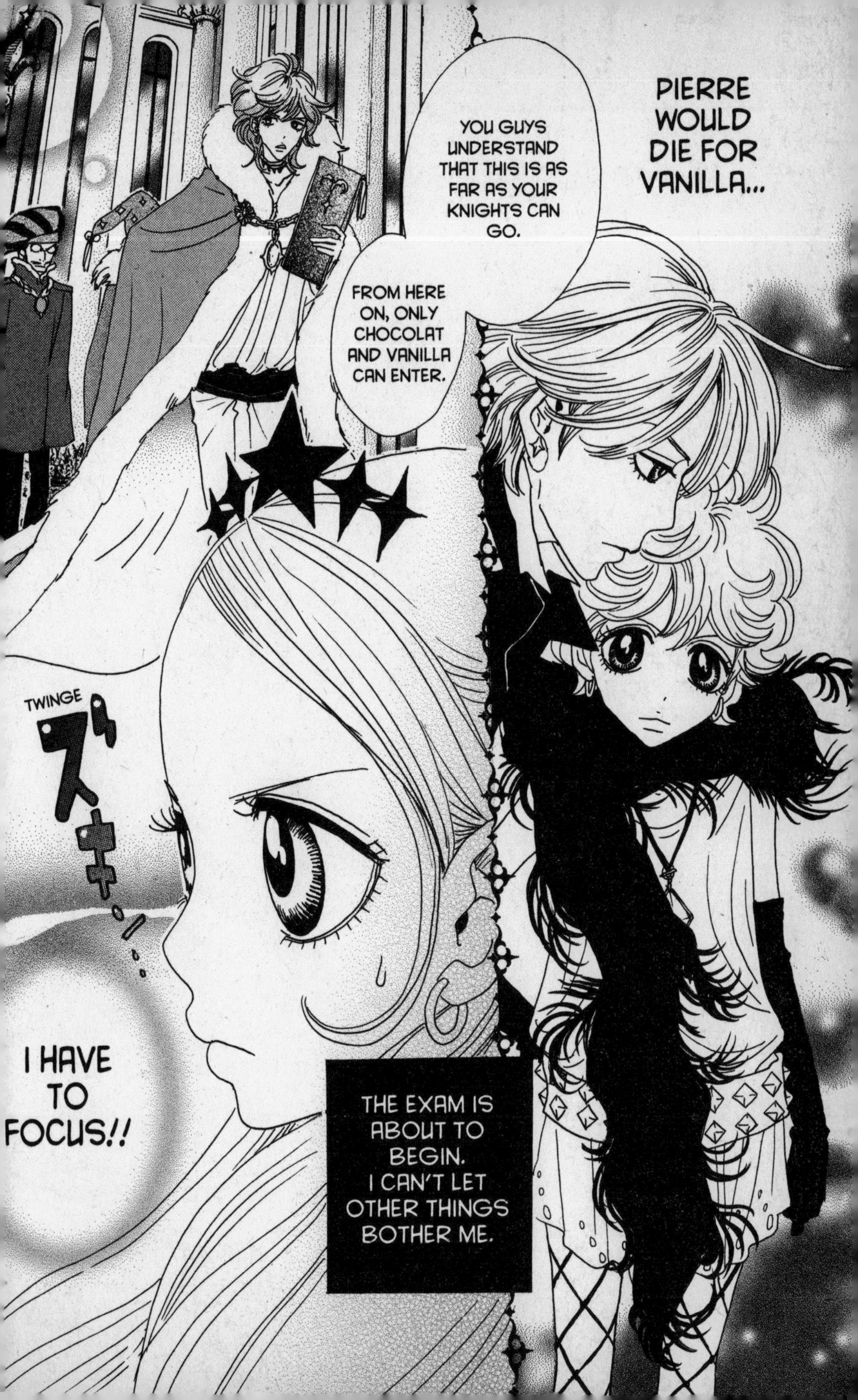
PIERRE WOULD DIE FOR VANILLA...
YOU GUYS UNDERSTAND THAT THIS IS AS FAR AS YOUR KNIGHTS CAN GO.
FROM HERE ON, ONLY CHOCOLAT AND VANILLA CAN ENTER.
TWINGE
THE EXAM IS ABOUT TO BEGIN. I CAN'T LET OTHER THINGS BOTHER ME.
I HAVE TO FOCUS!!

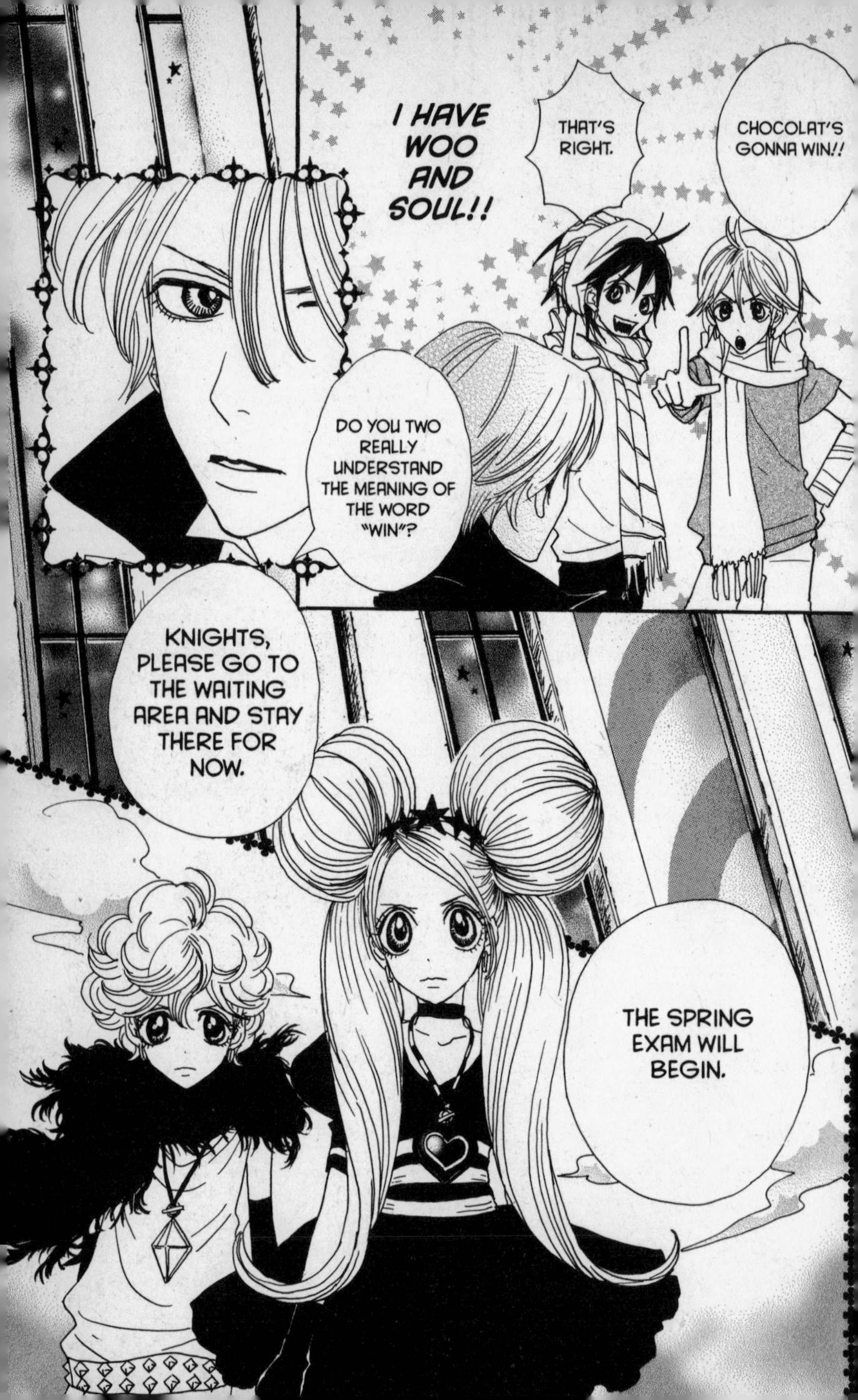
CHOCOLAT'S GONNA WIN!!
THAT'S RIGHT.
I HAVE WOO AND SOUL!!
DO YOU TWO REALLY UNDERSTAND THE MEANING OF THE WORD "WIN"?
KNIGHTS, PLEASE GO TO THE WAITING AREA AND STAY THERE FOR NOW.
THE SPRING EXAM WILL BEGIN.

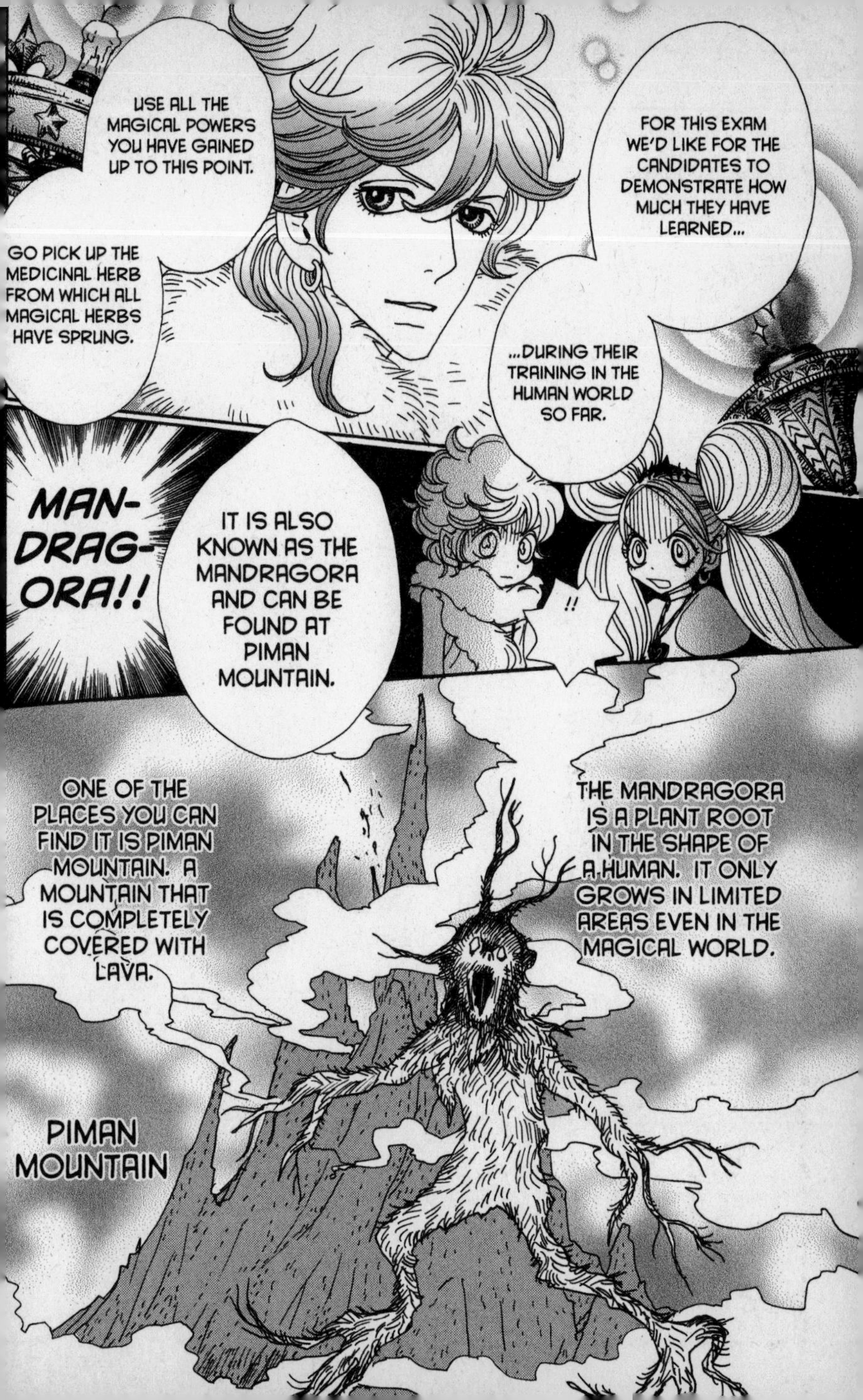
FOR THIS EXAM WE'D LIKE FOR THE CANDIDATES TO DEMONSTRATE HOW MUCH THEY HAVE LEARNED...
...DURING THEIR TRAINING IN THE HUMAN WORLD SO FAR.
USE ALL THE MAGICAL POWERS YOU HAVE GAINED UP TO THIS POINT.
GO PICK UP THE MEDICINAL HERB FROM WHICH ALL MAGICAL HERBS HAVE SPRUNG.
!!
IT IS ALSO KNOWN AS THE MANDRAGORA AND CAN BE FOUND AT PIMAN MOUNTAIN.
MAN-DRAG-ORA!!
THE MANDRAGORA IS A PLANT ROOT IN THE SHAPE OF A HUMAN. IT ONLY GROWS IN LIMITED AREAS EVEN IN THE MAGICAL WORLD.
ONE OF THE PLACES YOU CAN FIND IT IS PIMAN MOUNTAIN. A MOUNTAIN THAT IS COMPLETELY COVERED WITH LAVA.
PIMAN MOUNTAIN

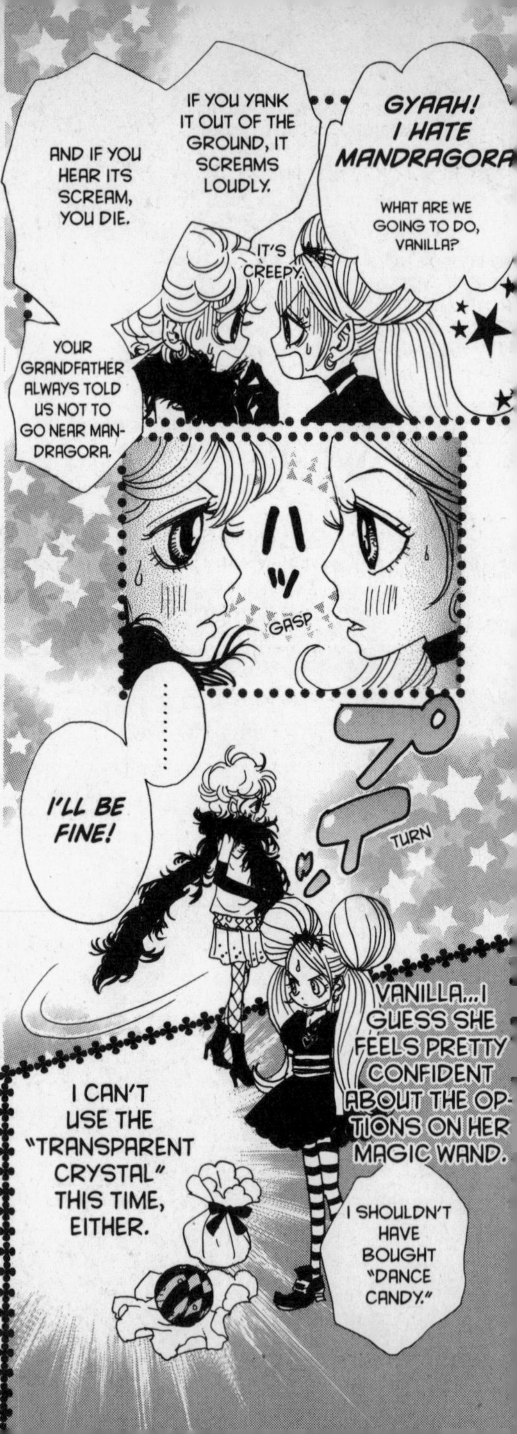
GYAAH! I HATE MANDRAGORA
WHAT ARE WE GOING TO DO, VANILLA?
IT'S CREEPY.
IF YOU YANK IT OUT OF THE GROUND, IT SCREAMS LOUDLY.
AND IF YOU HEAR ITS SCREAM, YOU DIE.
YOUR GRANDFATHER ALWAYS TOLD US NOT TO GO NEAR MAN-DRAGORA.
GASP
......
I'LL BE FINE!
TURN
VANILLA...I GUESS SHE FEELS PRETTY CONFIDENT ABOUT THE OP-TIONS ON HER MAGIC WAND.
I SHOULDN'T HAVE BOUGHT "DANCE CANDY."
I CAN'T USE THE "TRANSPARENT CRYSTAL" THIS TIME, EITHER.

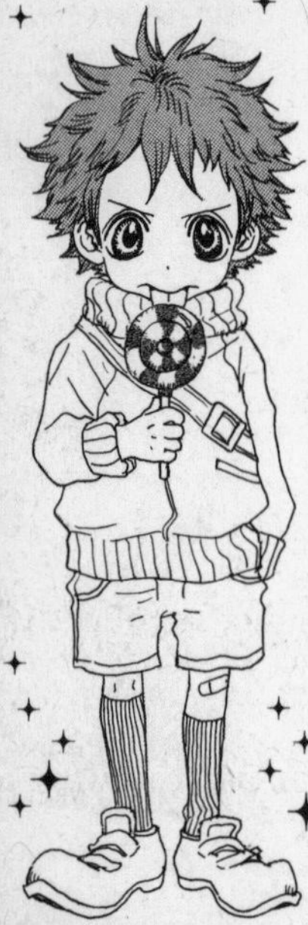

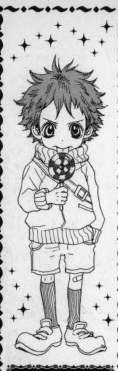

MIHARU SAKAMOTO

HEIGHT: 108 CM

AGE: 4 YEARS OLD

HOBBY: COLLECTING CHESTNUTS

SPECIALTY: UMEKEN SAMBA DANCE

OTHER: HE IS AKIRA'S COUSIN. HIS MOTHER, A FASHION PHOTOGRAPHER, IS THE YOUNGER SISTER OF AKIRA'S FATHER.

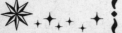

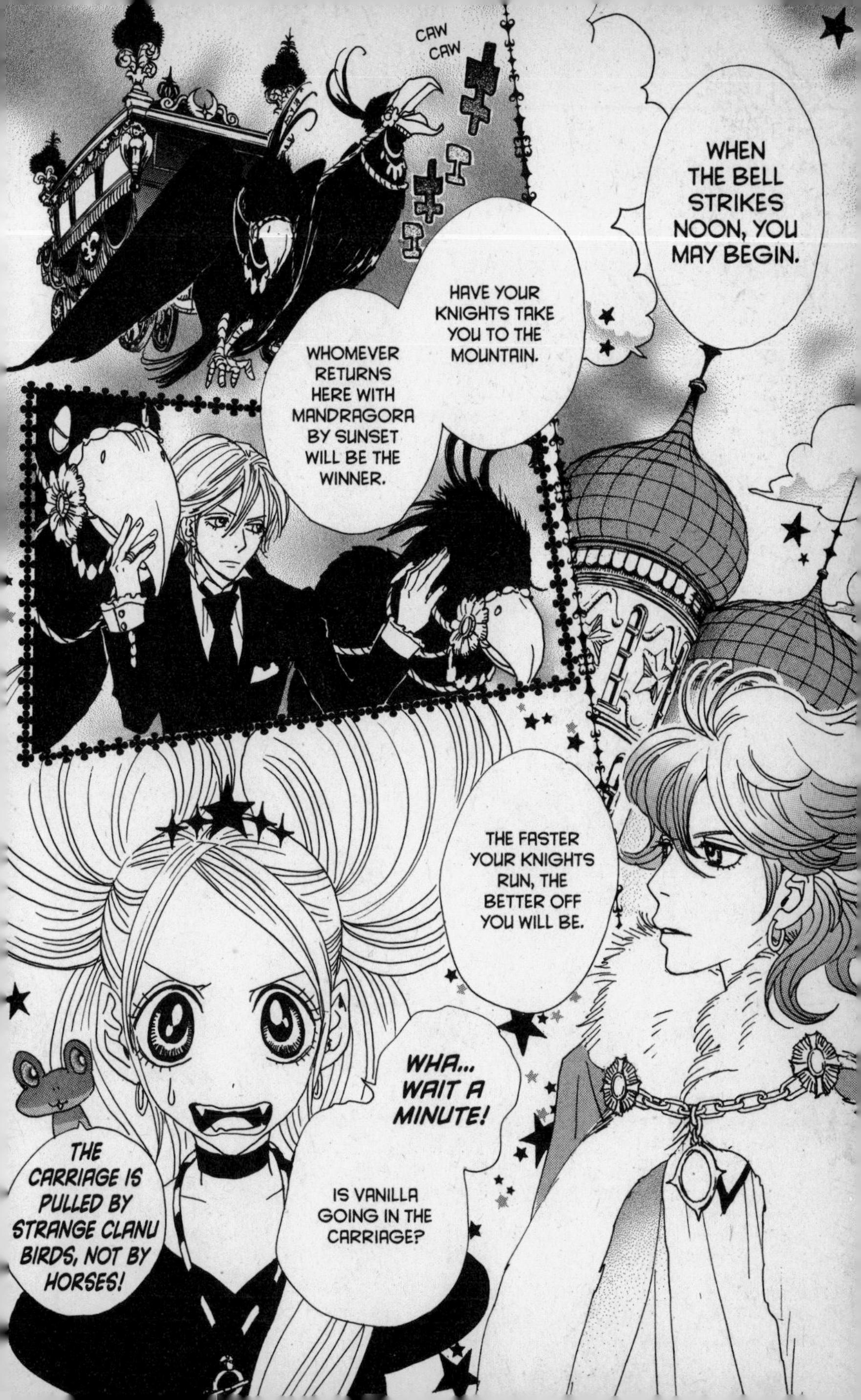
WHEN THE BELL STRIKES NOON, YOU MAY BEGIN.
CAW CAW
HAVE YOUR KNIGHTS TAKE YOU TO THE MOUNTAIN.
WHOMEVER RETURNS HERE WITH MANDRAGORA BY SUNSET WILL BE THE WINNER.
THE FASTER YOUR KNIGHTS RUN, THE BETTER OFF YOU WILL BE.
WHA... WAIT A MINUTE!
IS VANILLA GOING IN THE CARRIAGE?
THE CARRIAGE IS PULLED BY STRANGE CLANU BIRDS, NOT BY HORSES!

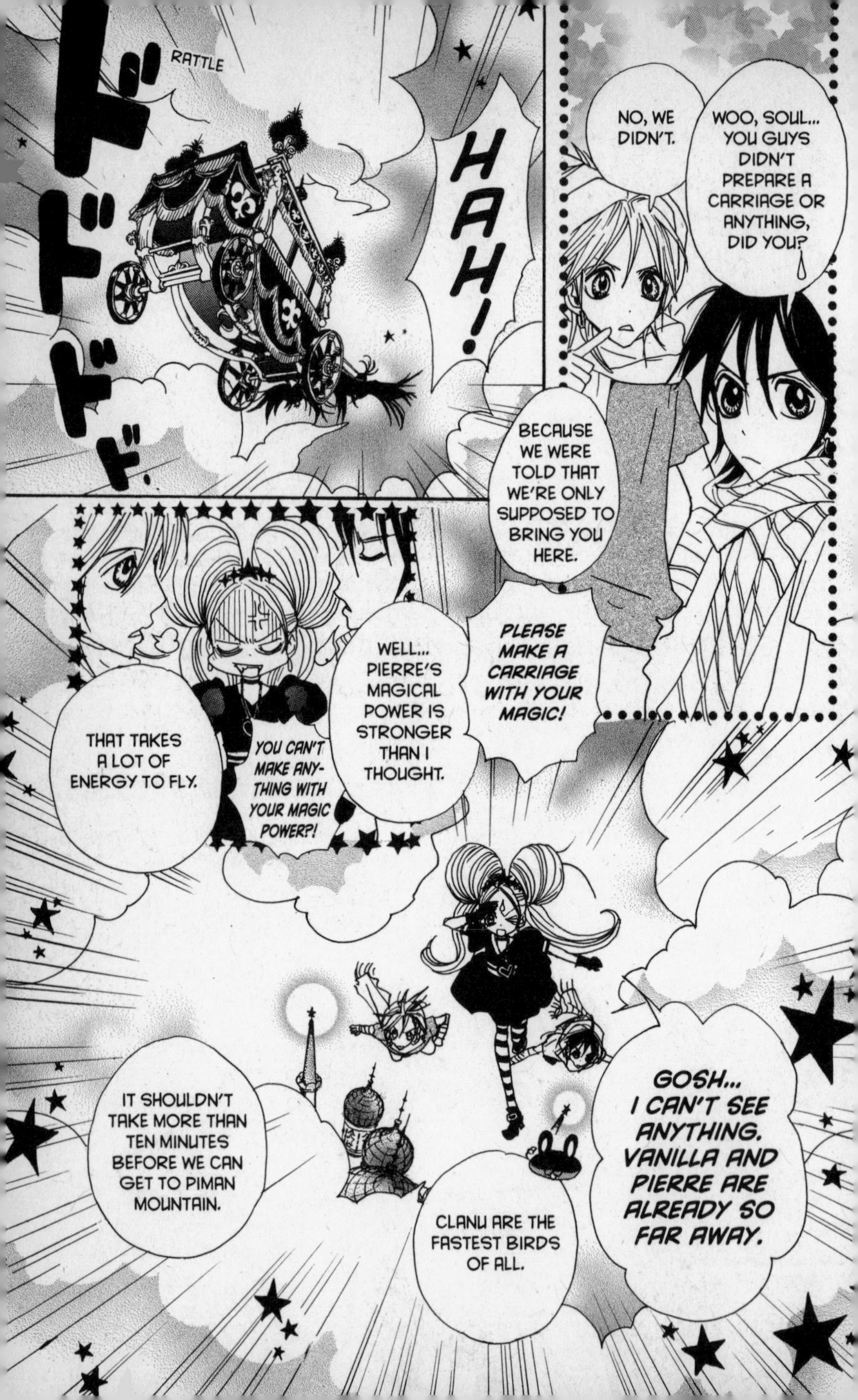
WOO, SOUL... YOU GUYS DIDN'T PREPARE A CARRIAGE OR ANYTHING, DID YOU?
NO, WE DIDN'T.
BECAUSE WE WERE TOLD THAT WE'RE ONLY SUPPOSED TO BRING YOU HERE.
HAH!
ドドドド
RATTLE
PLEASE MAKE A CARRIAGE WITH YOUR MAGIC!
WELL... PIERRE'S MAGICAL POWER IS STRONGER THAN I THOUGHT.
YOU CAN'T MAKE ANYTHING WITH YOUR MAGIC POWER?!
THAT TAKES A LOT OF ENERGY TO FLY.
GOSH... I CAN'T SEE ANYTHING. VANILLA AND PIERRE ARE ALREADY SO FAR AWAY.
CLANU ARE THE FASTEST BIRDS OF ALL.
IT SHOULDN'T TAKE MORE THAN TEN MINUTES BEFORE WE CAN GET TO PIMAN MOUNTAIN.

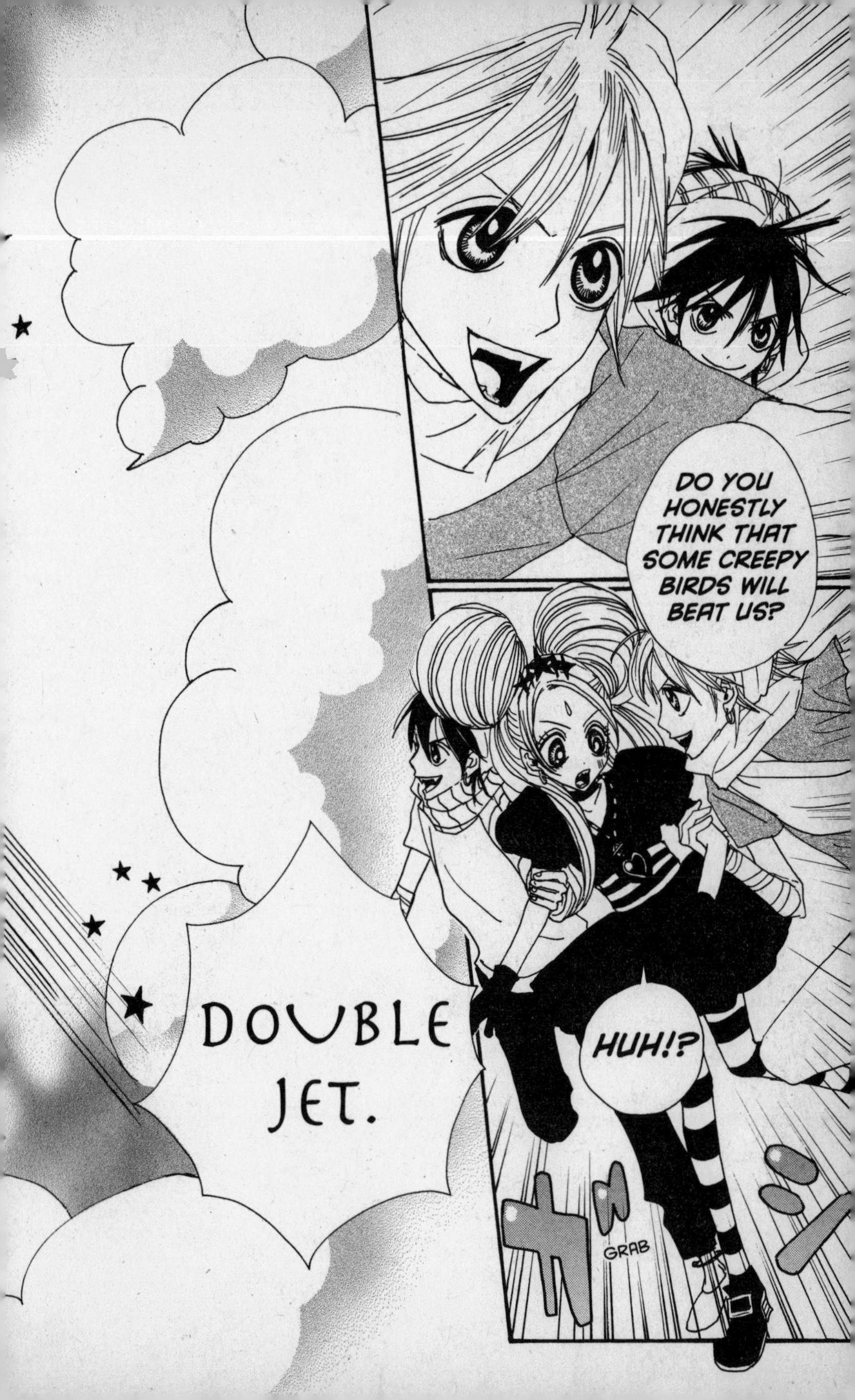
DO YOU HONESTLY THINK THAT SOME CREEPY BIRDS WILL BEAT US?
HUH!?
GRAB
DOUBLE JET.

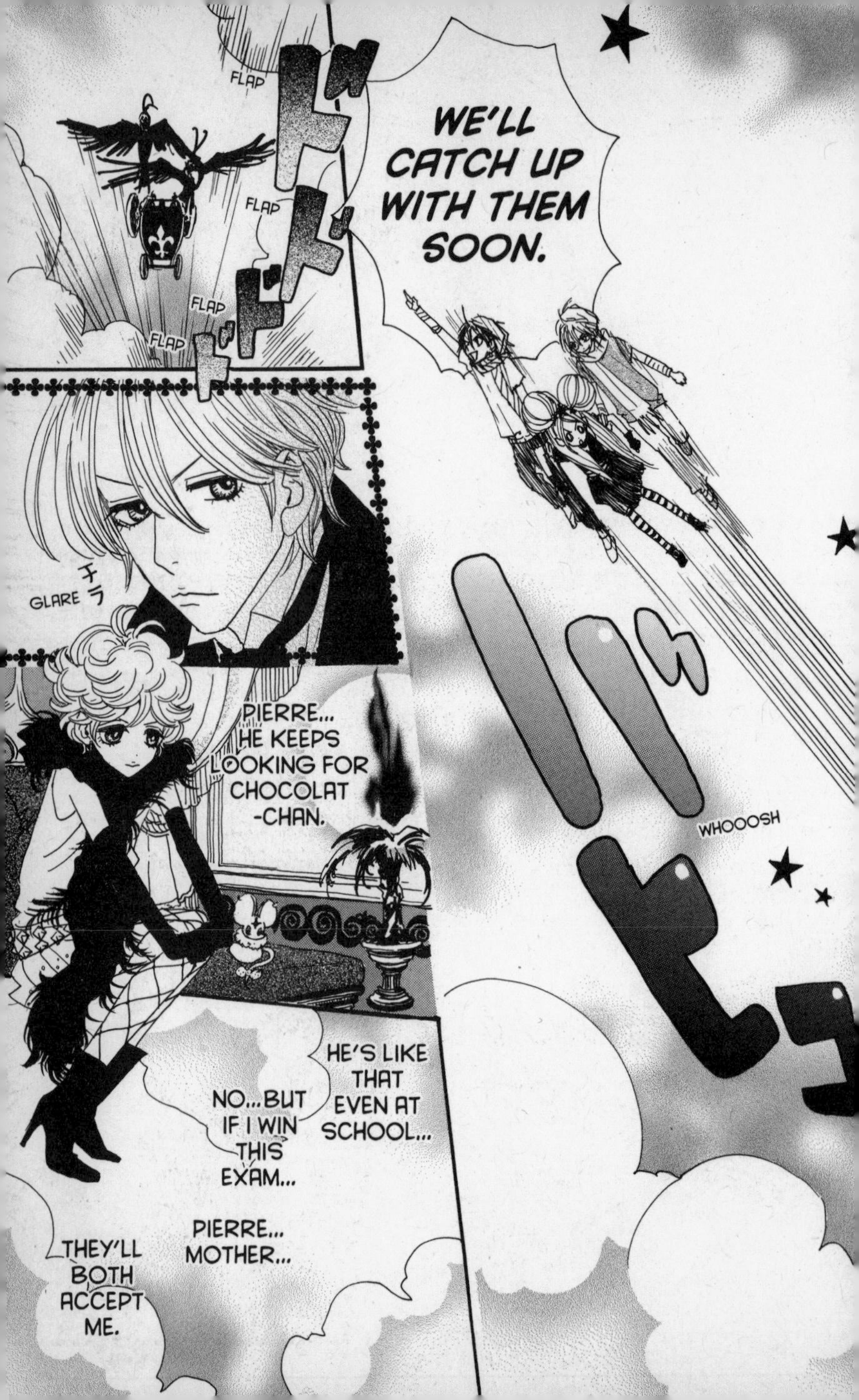
WE'LL CATCH UP WITH THEM SOON.
WHOOOSH
FLAP
FLAP
FLAP
FLAP
GLARE
チラ
PIERRE... HE KEEPS LOOKING FOR CHOCOLAT -CHAN.
HE'S LIKE THAT EVEN AT SCHOOL...
NO...BUT IF I WIN THIS EXAM...
PIERRE... MOTHER...
THEY'LL BOTH ACCEPT ME.

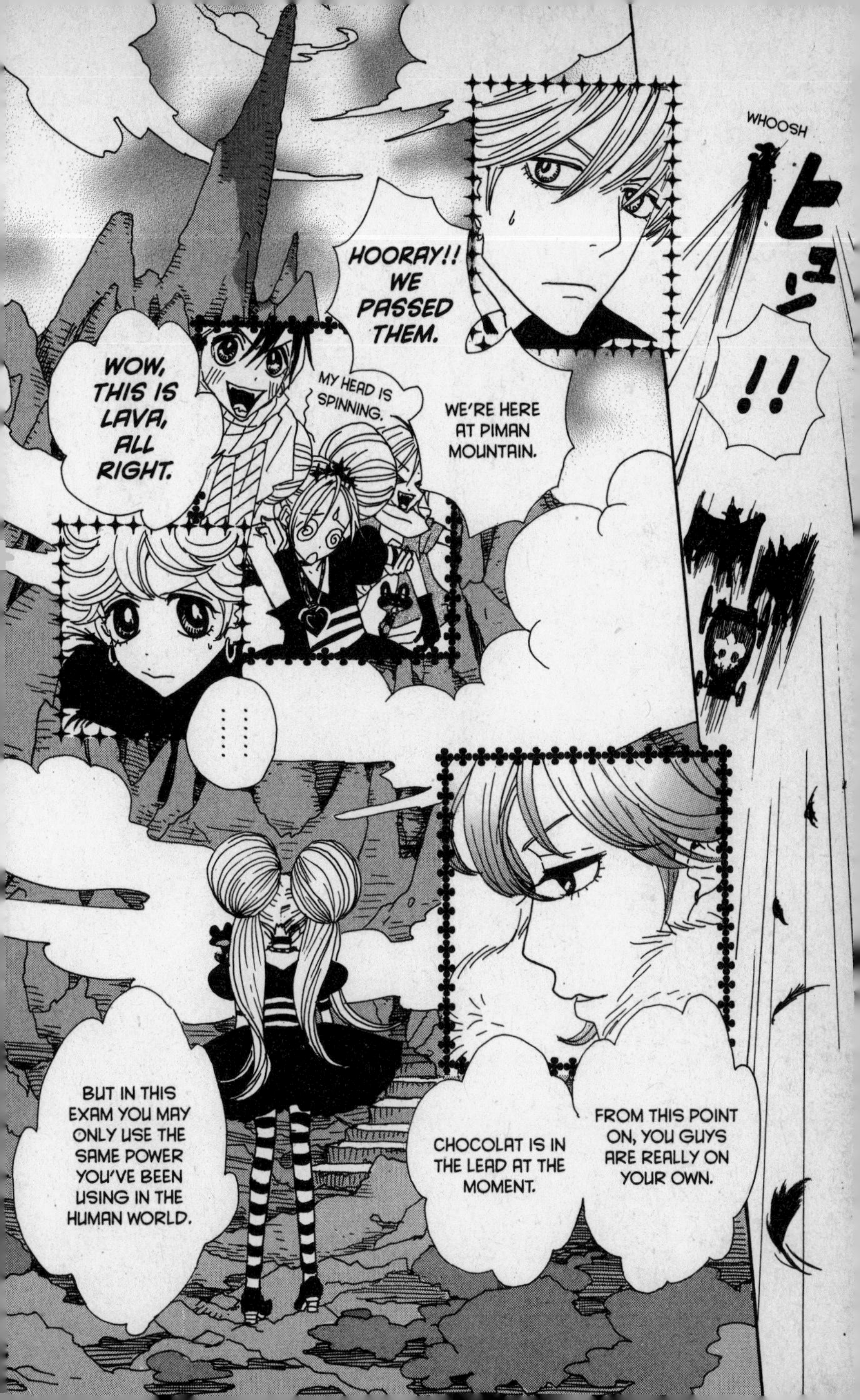
WHOOSH
ヒュッ!!
HOORAY!! WE PASSED THEM.
WE'RE HERE AT PIMAN MOUNTAIN.
MY HEAD IS SPINNING.
WOW, THIS IS LAVA, ALL RIGHT.
......
FROM THIS POINT ON, YOU GUYS ARE REALLY ON YOUR OWN.
CHOCOLAT IS IN THE LEAD AT THE MOMENT.
BUT IN THIS EXAM YOU MAY ONLY USE THE SAME POWER YOU'VE BEEN USING IN THE HUMAN WORLD.

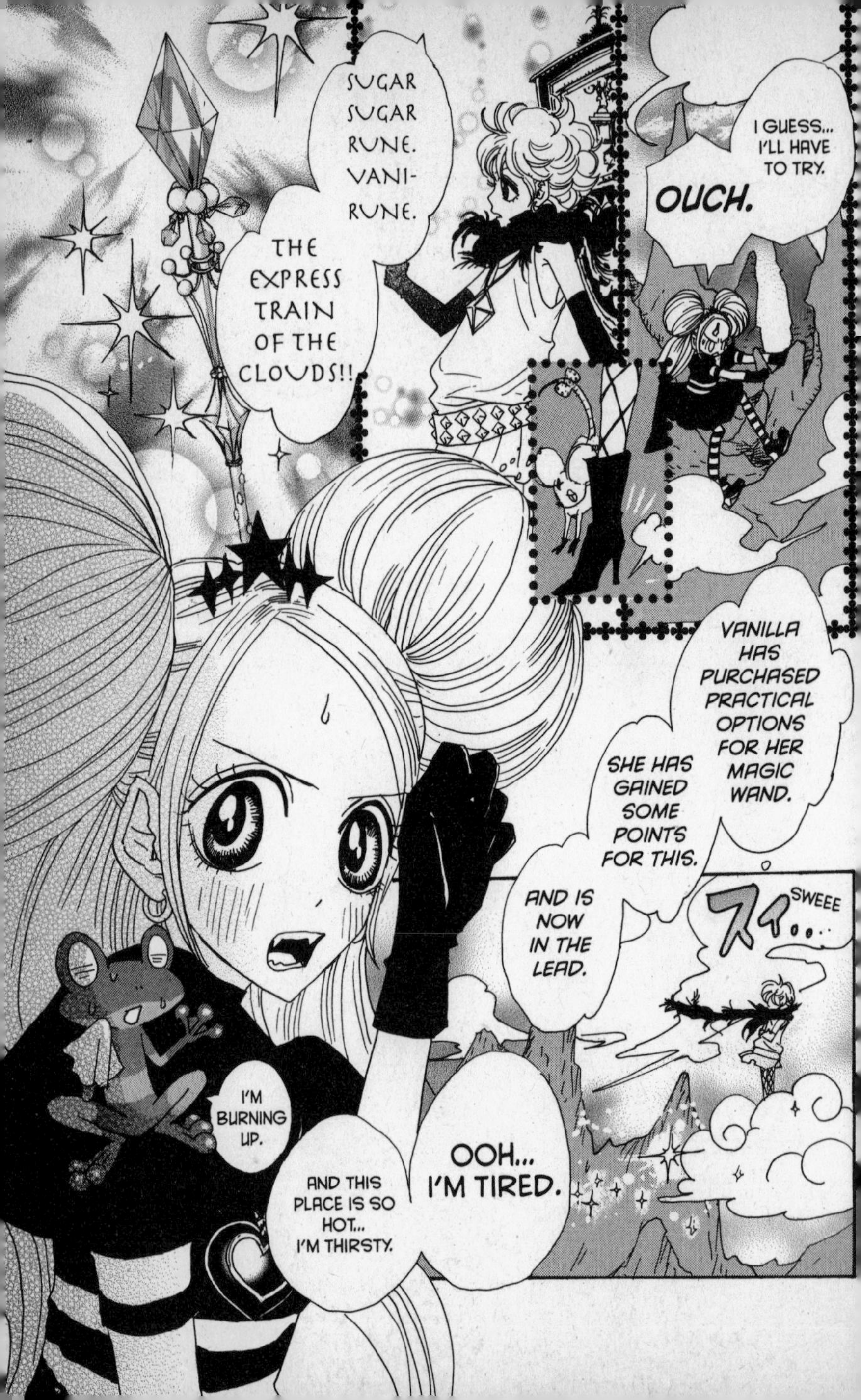
I GUESS... I'LL HAVE TO TRY.
OUCH.
SUGAR SUGAR RUNE. VANI-RUNE.
THE EXPRESS TRAIN OF THE CLOUDS!!
VANILLA HAS PURCHASED PRACTICAL OPTIONS FOR HER MAGIC WAND.
SHE HAS GAINED SOME POINTS FOR THIS.
スイ...
SWEEE
AND IS NOW IN THE LEAD.
OOH... I'M TIRED.
AND THIS PLACE IS SO HOT... I'M THIRSTY.
I'M BURNING UP.

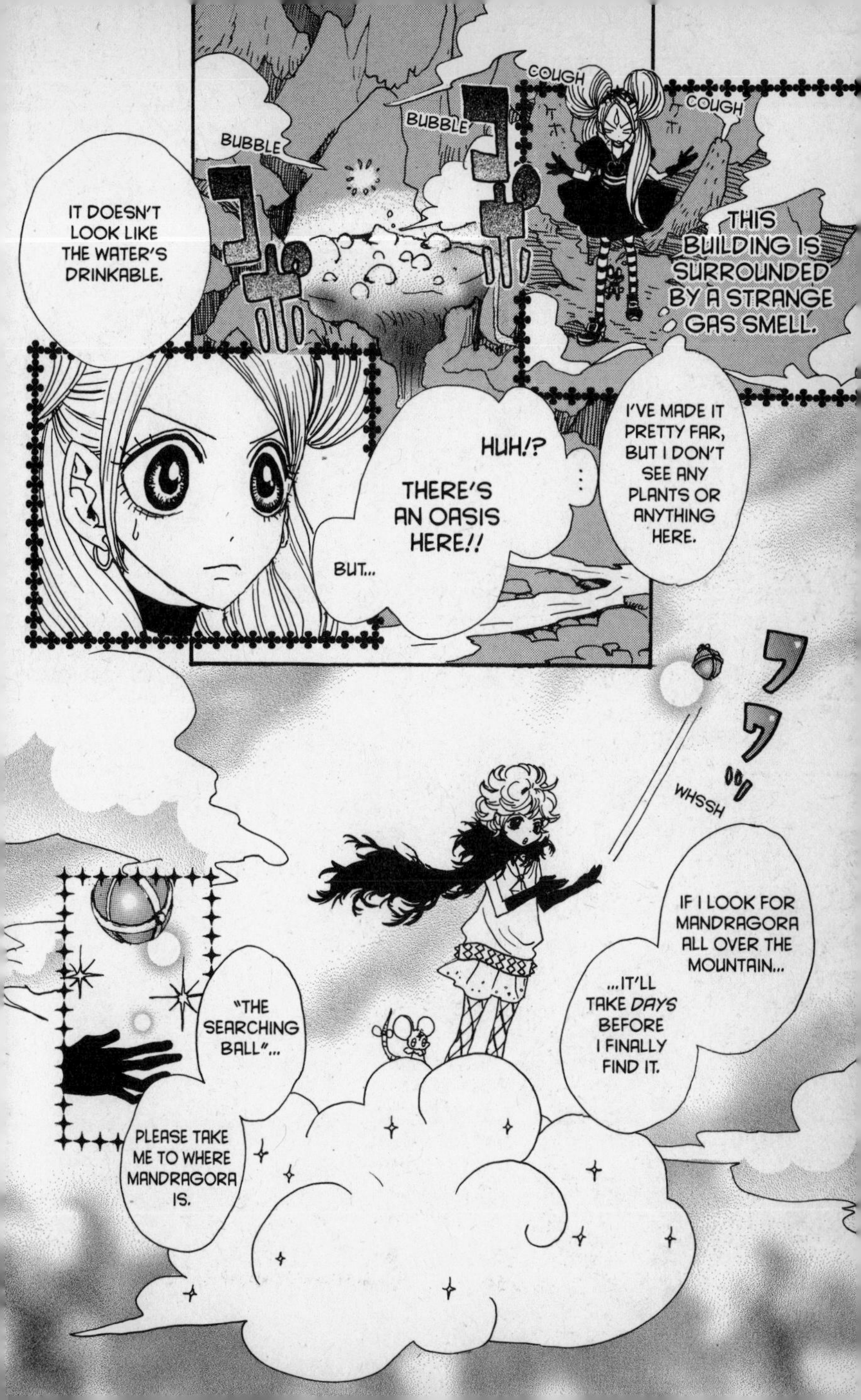
COUGH
COUGH
THIS BUILDING IS SURROUNDED BY A STRANGE GAS SMELL.
I'VE MADE IT PRETTY FAR, BUT I DON'T SEE ANY PLANTS OR ANYTHING HERE.
...
HUH!?
THERE'S AN OASIS HERE!!
BUT...
BUBBLE
BUBBLE
IT DOESN'T LOOK LIKE THE WATER'S DRINKABLE.
WHSSH
IF I LOOK FOR MANDRAGORA ALL OVER THE MOUNTAIN...
...IT'LL TAKE *DAYS* BEFORE I FINALLY FIND IT.
"THE SEARCHING BALL"...
PLEASE TAKE ME TO WHERE MANDRAGORA IS.

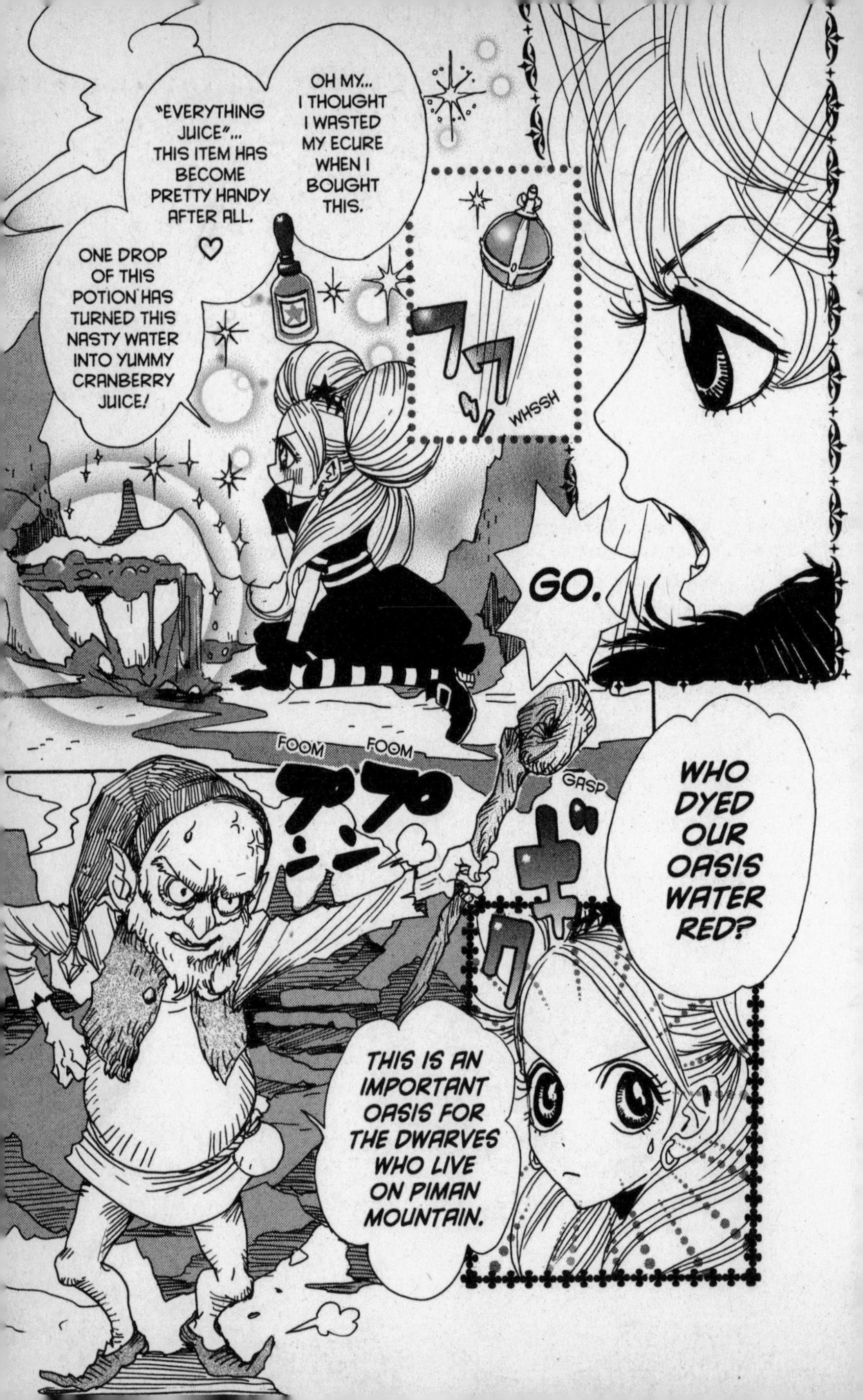
GO.
WHSSH
OH MY... I THOUGHT I WASTED MY ECURE WHEN I BOUGHT THIS.
"EVERYTHING JUICE"... THIS ITEM HAS BECOME PRETTY HANDY AFTER ALL. ♡
ONE DROP OF THIS POTION HAS TURNED THIS NASTY WATER INTO YUMMY CRANBERRY JUICE!
GASP
WHO DYED OUR OASIS WATER RED?
FOOM
FOOM
THIS IS AN IMPORTANT OASIS FOR THE DWARVES WHO LIVE ON PIMAN MOUNTAIN.

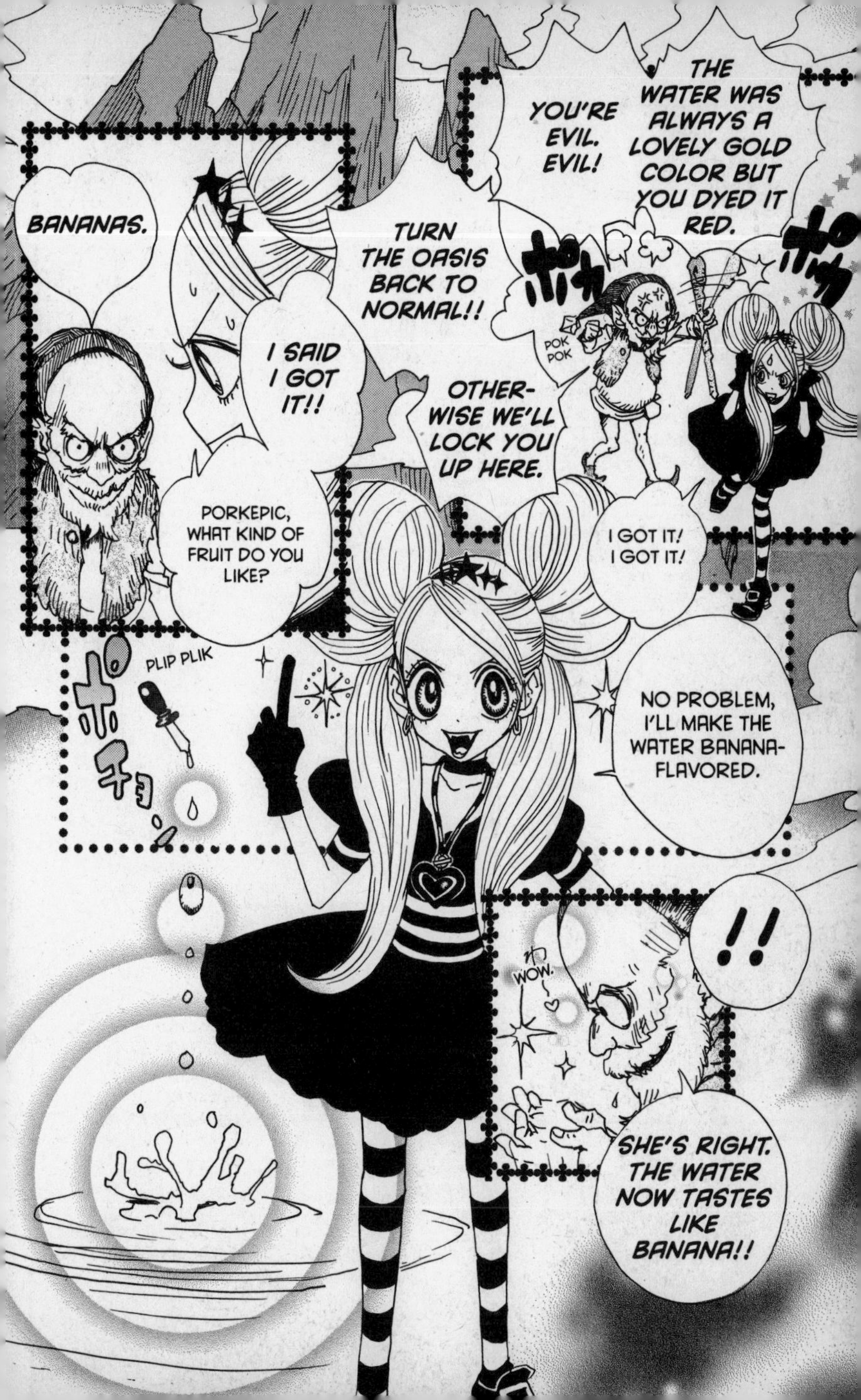
THE WATER WAS ALWAYS A LOVELY GOLD COLOR BUT YOU DYED IT RED.
YOU'RE EVIL. EVIL!
TURN THE OASIS BACK TO NORMAL!!
POK POK
OTHER-WISE WE'LL LOCK YOU UP HERE.
I GOT IT! I GOT IT!
I SAID I GOT IT!!
PORKEPIC, WHAT KIND OF FRUIT DO YOU LIKE?
BANANAS.
NO PROBLEM, I'LL MAKE THE WATER BANANA-FLAVORED.
PLIP PLIK
!!
WOW.
SHE'S RIGHT. THE WATER NOW TASTES LIKE BANANA!!

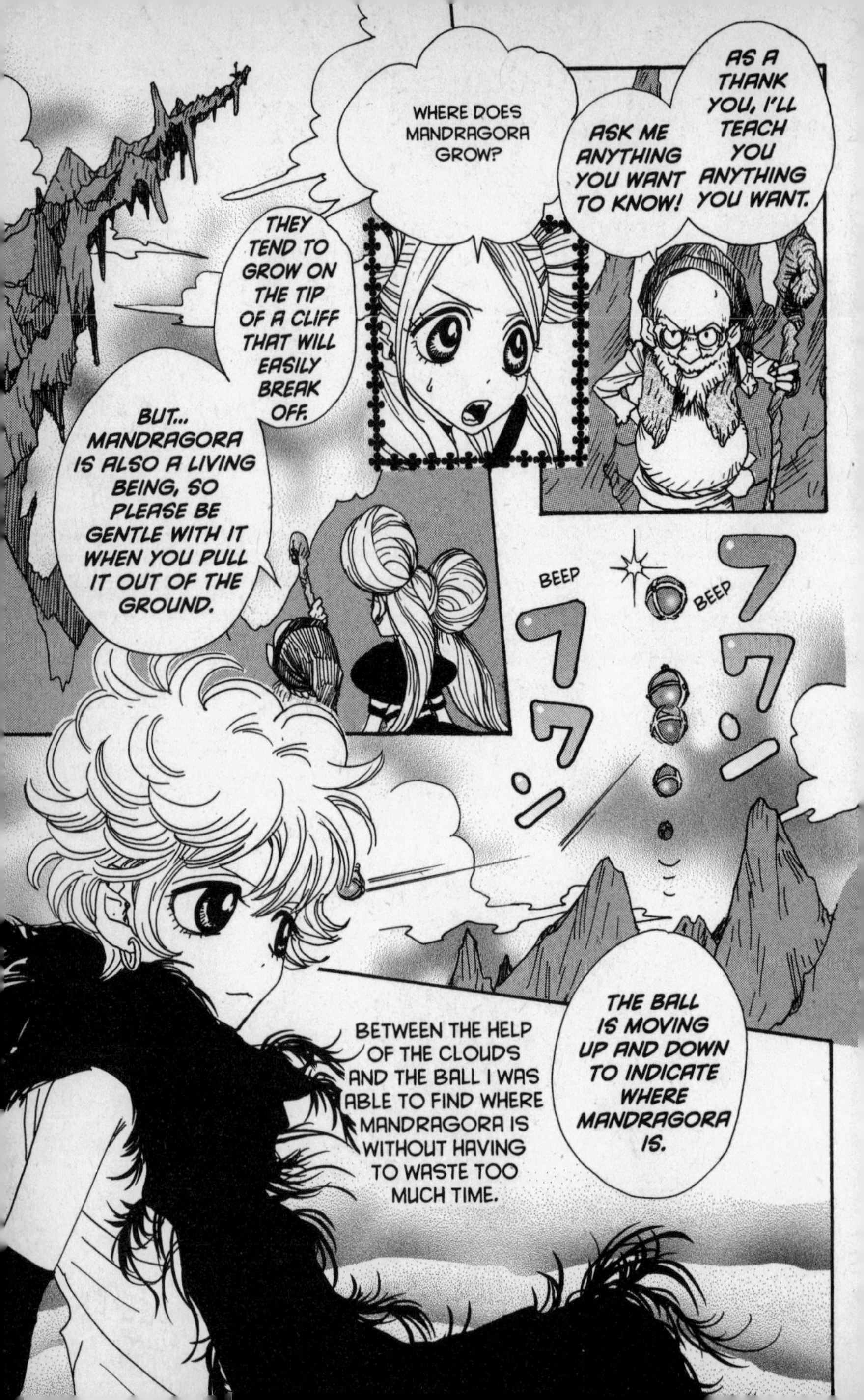
AS A THANK YOU, I'LL TEACH YOU ANYTHING YOU WANT.
ASK ME ANYTHING YOU WANT TO KNOW!
WHERE DOES MANDRAGORA GROW?
THEY TEND TO GROW ON THE TIP OF A CLIFF THAT WILL EASILY BREAK OFF.
BUT... MANDRAGORA IS ALSO A LIVING BEING, SO PLEASE BE GENTLE WITH IT WHEN YOU PULL IT OUT OF THE GROUND.
BEEP
BEEP
THE BALL IS MOVING UP AND DOWN TO INDICATE WHERE MANDRAGORA IS.
BETWEEN THE HELP OF THE CLOUDS AND THE BALL I WAS ABLE TO FIND WHERE MANDRAGORA IS WITHOUT HAVING TO WASTE TOO MUCH TIME.

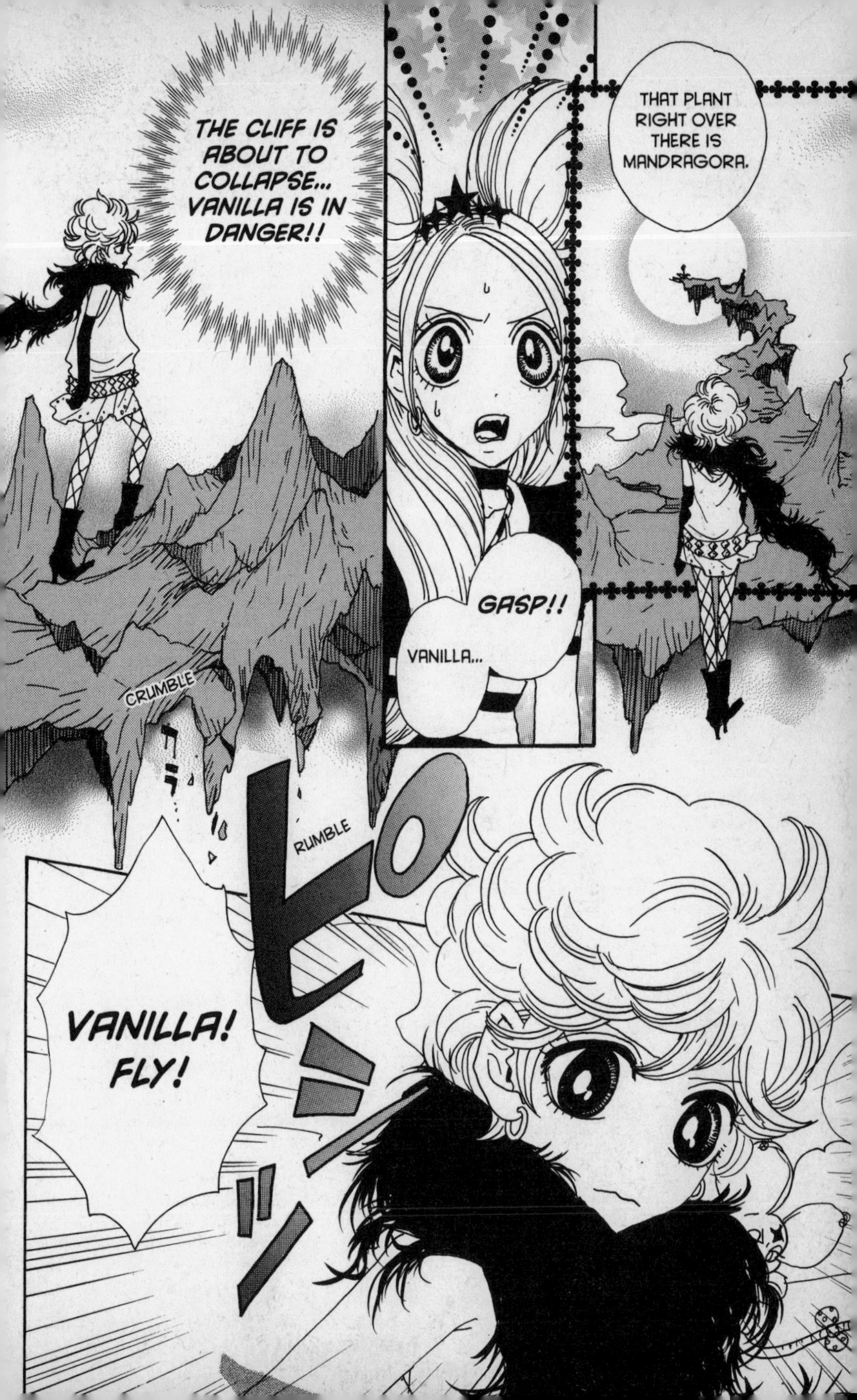
THAT PLANT RIGHT OVER THERE IS MANDRAGORA.
GASP!!
VANILLA...
THE CLIFF IS ABOUT TO COLLAPSE... VANILLA IS IN DANGER!!
CRUMBLE
RUMBLE
VANILLA! FLY!

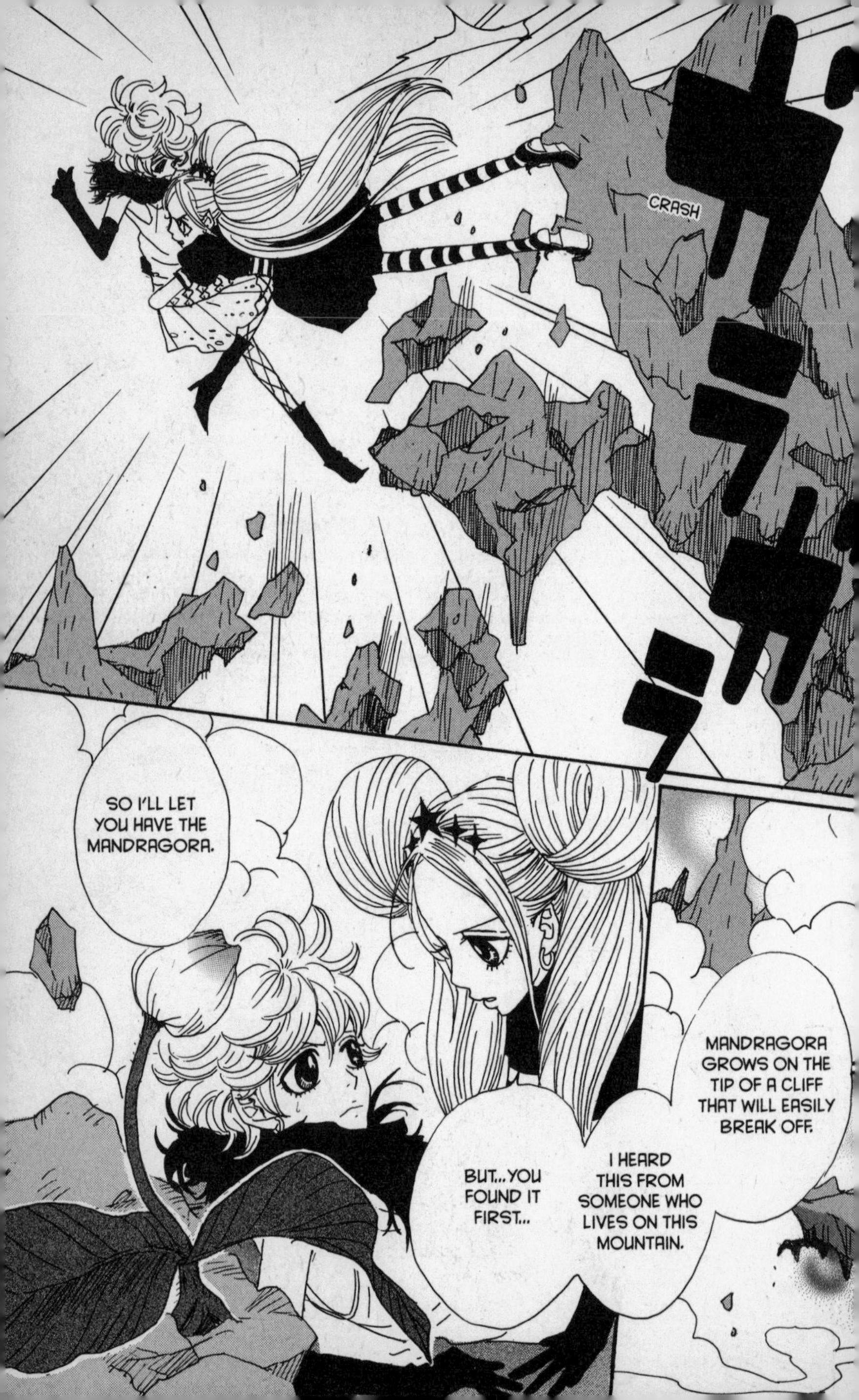
CRASH
MANDRAGORA GROWS ON THE TIP OF A CLIFF THAT WILL EASILY BREAK OFF.
I HEARD THIS FROM SOMEONE WHO LIVES ON THIS MOUNTAIN.
BUT...YOU FOUND IT FIRST...
SO I'LL LET YOU HAVE THE MANDRAGORA.

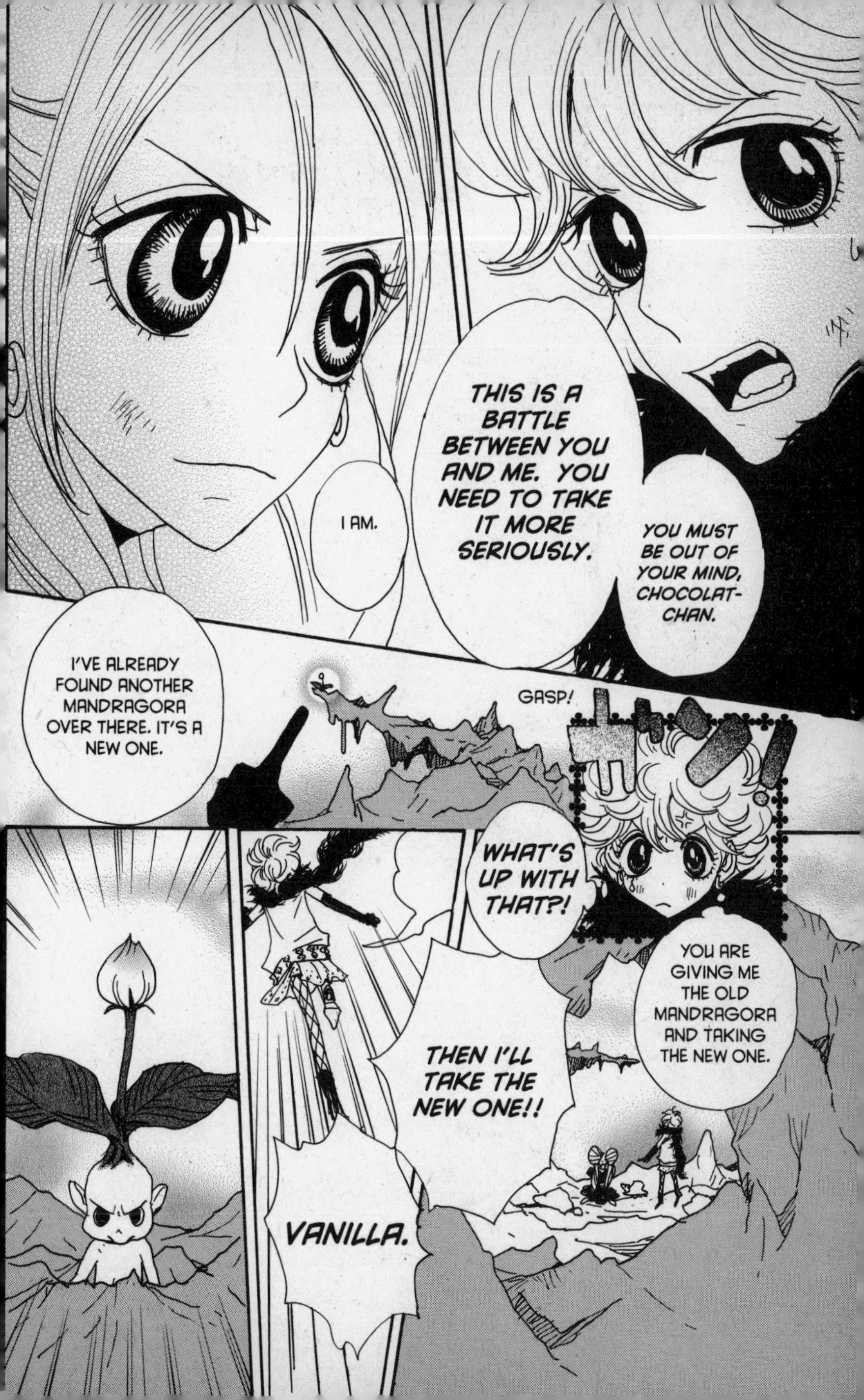
YOU MUST BE OUT OF YOUR MIND, CHOCOLAT-CHAN.
THIS IS A BATTLE BETWEEN YOU AND ME. YOU NEED TO TAKE IT MORE SERIOUSLY.
I AM.
I'VE ALREADY FOUND ANOTHER MANDRAGORA OVER THERE. IT'S A NEW ONE.
GASP!
WHAT'S UP WITH THAT?!
YOU ARE GIVING ME THE OLD MANDRAGORA AND TAKING THE NEW ONE.
THEN I'LL TAKE THE NEW ONE!!
VANILLA.

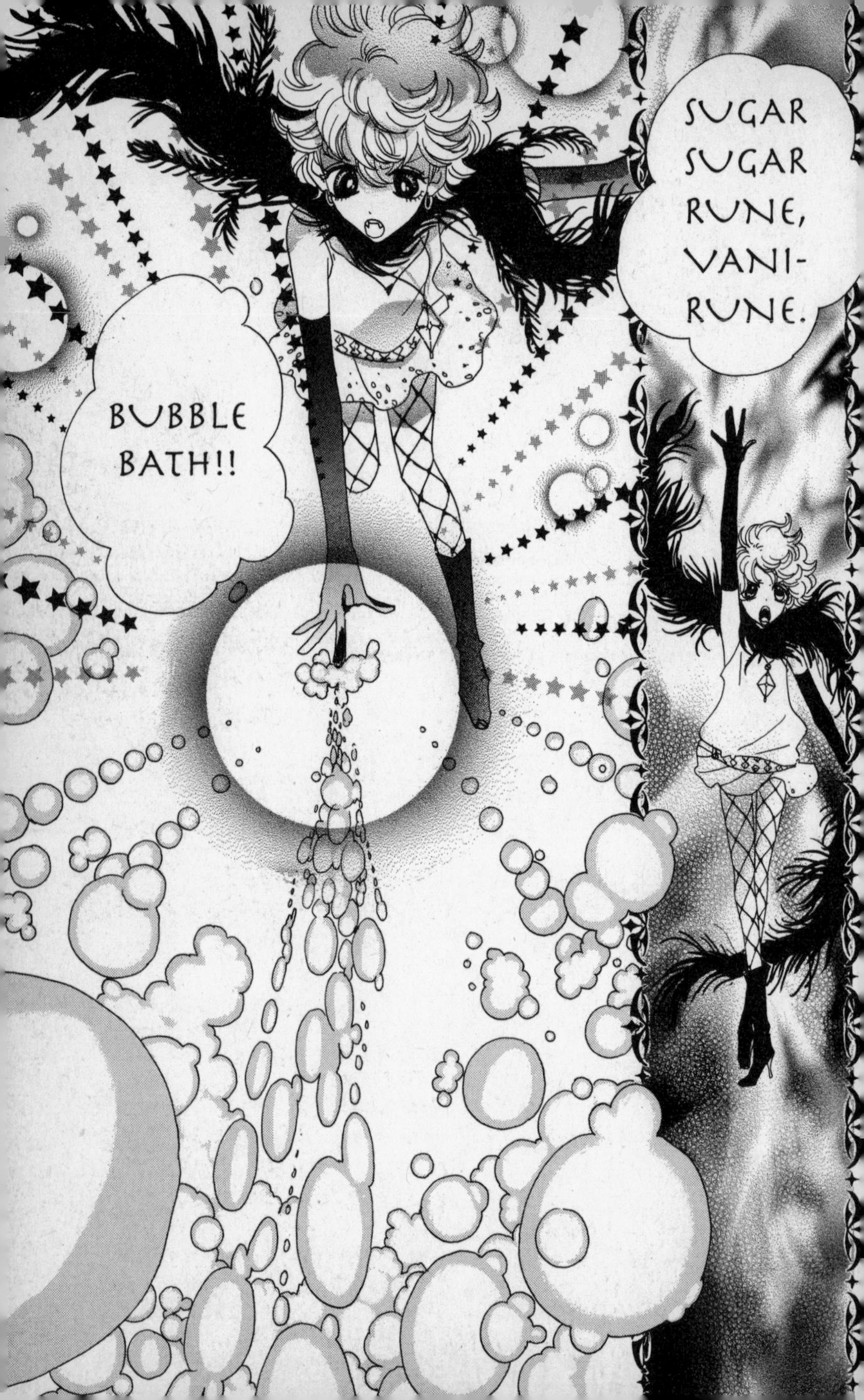
SUGAR SUGAR RUNE, VANI-RUNE.
BUBBLE BATH!!

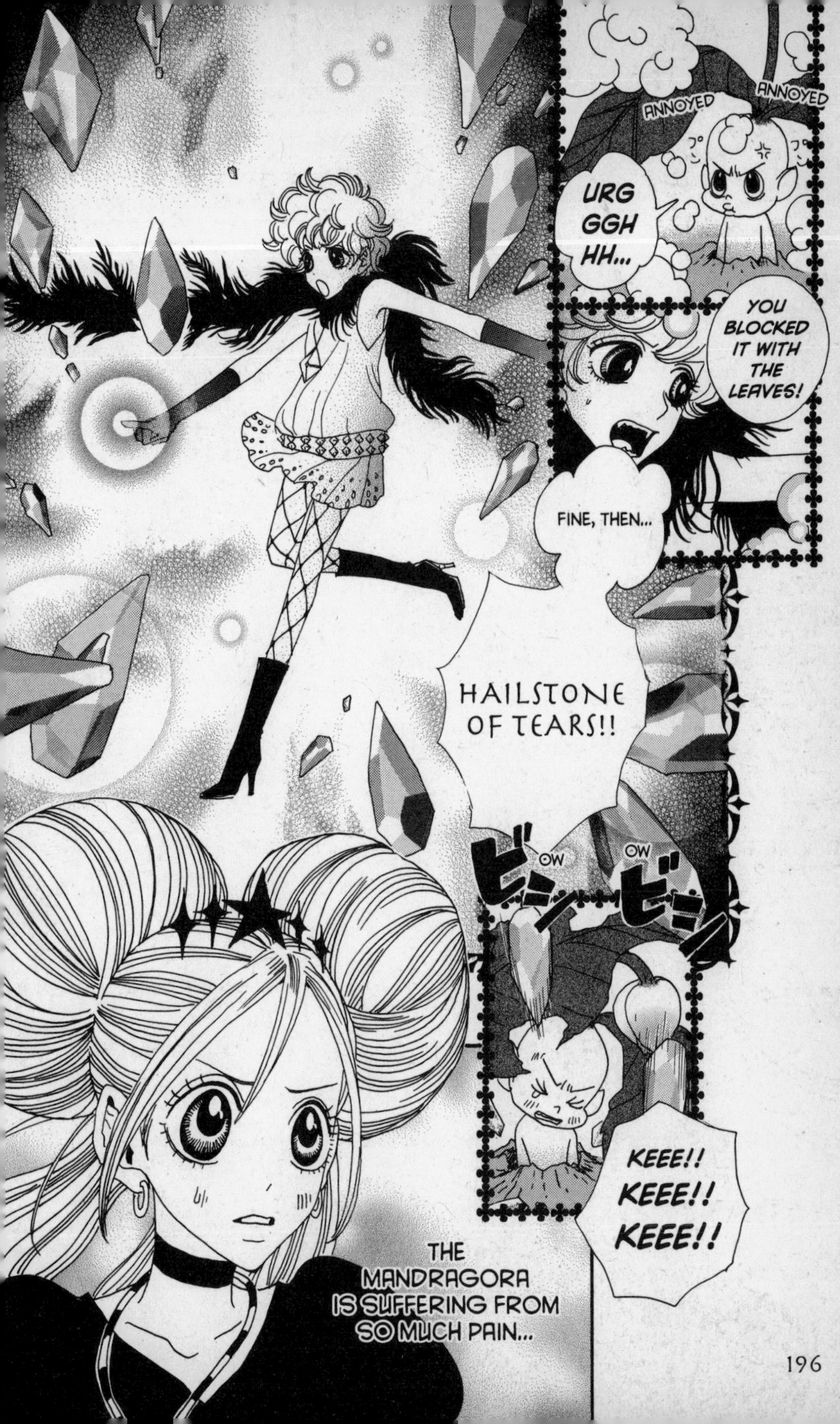
ANNOYED
ANNOYED
URGGGHHH...
YOU BLOCKED IT WITH THE LEAVES!
FINE, THEN...
HAILSTONE OF TEARS!!
OW
OW
KEEE!! KEEE!! KEEE!!
THE MANDRAGORA IS SUFFERING FROM SO MUCH PAIN...

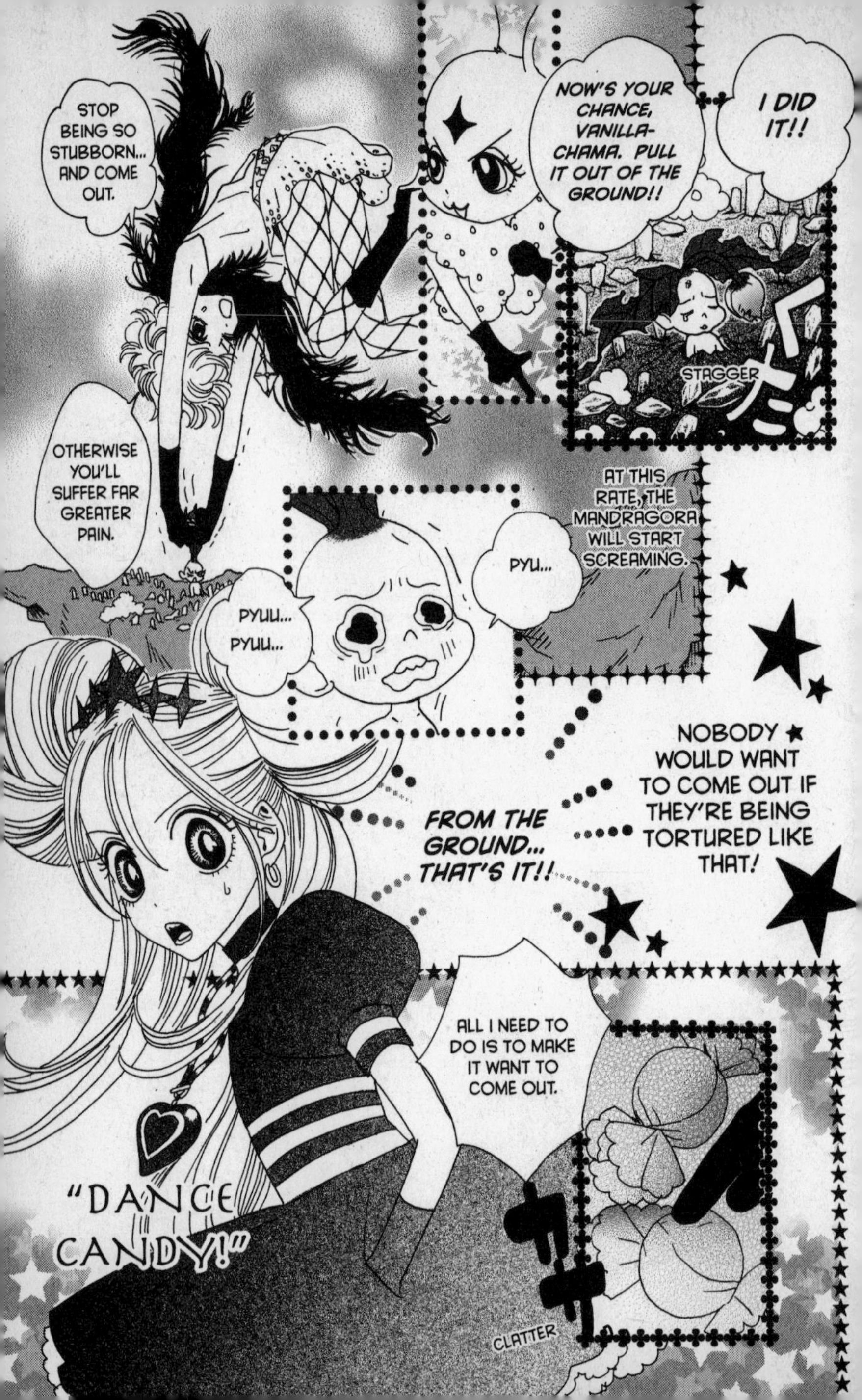
I DID IT!!
STAGGER
NOW'S YOUR CHANCE, VANILLA-CHAMA. PULL IT OUT OF THE GROUND!!
STOP BEING SO STUBBORN... AND COME OUT.
OTHERWISE YOU'LL SUFFER FAR GREATER PAIN.
AT THIS RATE, THE MANDRAGORA WILL START SCREAMING.
PYU...
PYUU... PYUU...
NOBODY ★ WOULD WANT TO COME OUT IF THEY'RE BEING TORTURED LIKE THAT!
FROM THE GROUND... THAT'S IT!!
ALL I NEED TO DO IS TO MAKE IT WANT TO COME OUT.
CLATTER
"DANCE CANDY!"

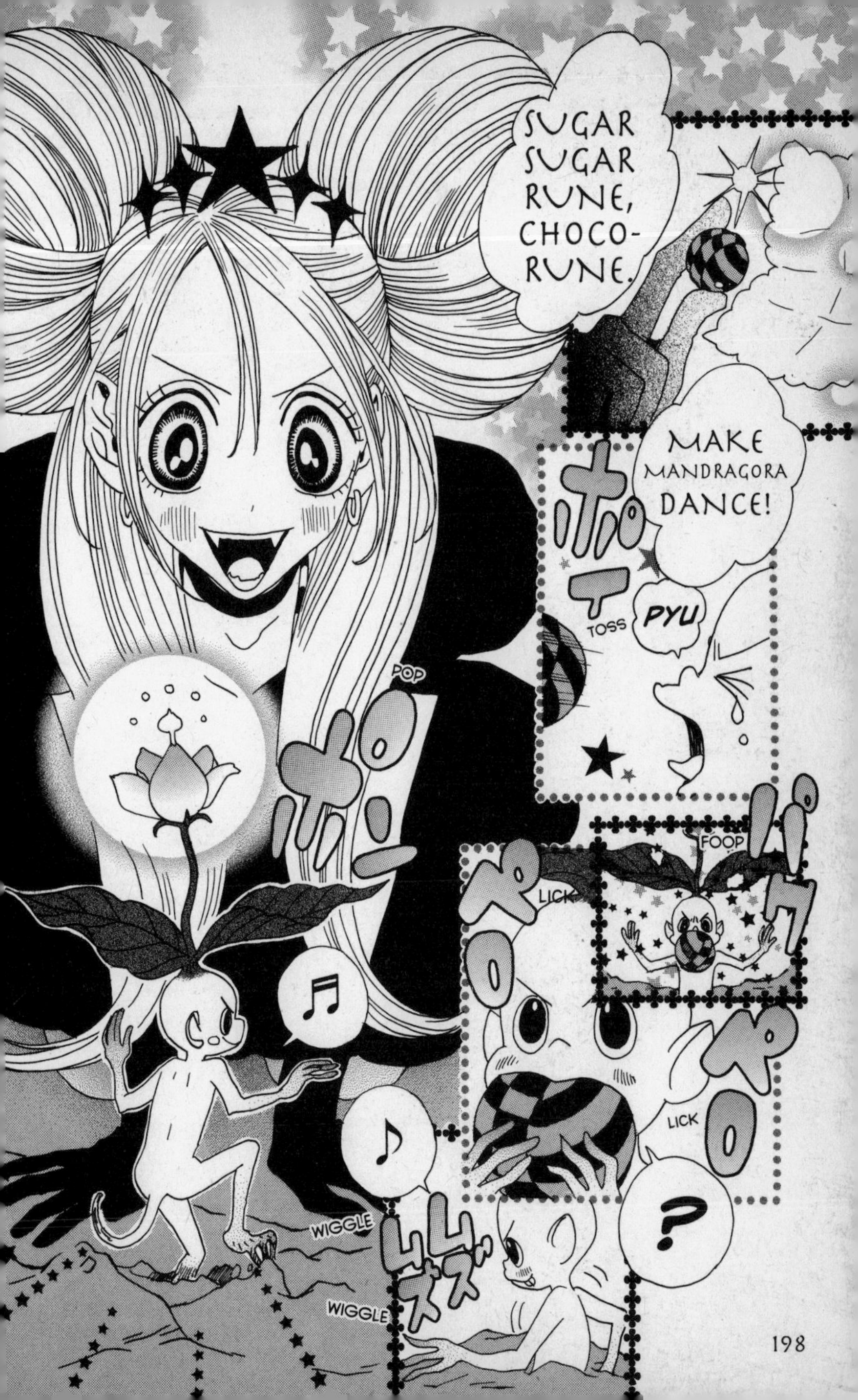
SUGAR SUGAR RUNE, CHOCO-RUNE.
MAKE MANDRAGORA DANCE!
PYU
TOSS
POP
FOOP
LICK
LICK
?
WIGGLE
WIGGLE

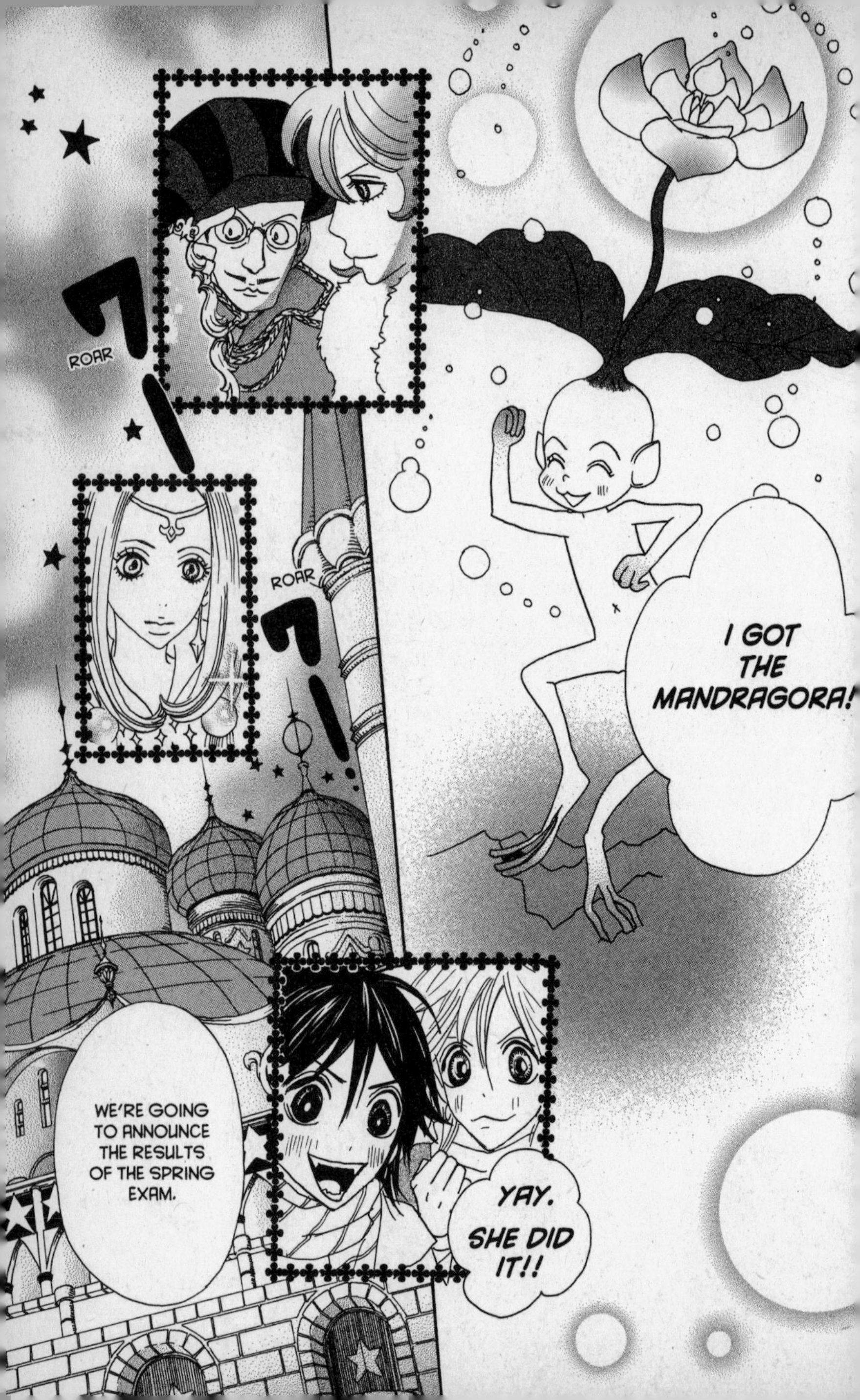
I GOT THE MANDRAGORA!
ROAR
ROAR
YAY. SHE DID IT!!
WE'RE GOING TO ANNOUNCE THE RESULTS OF THE SPRING EXAM.

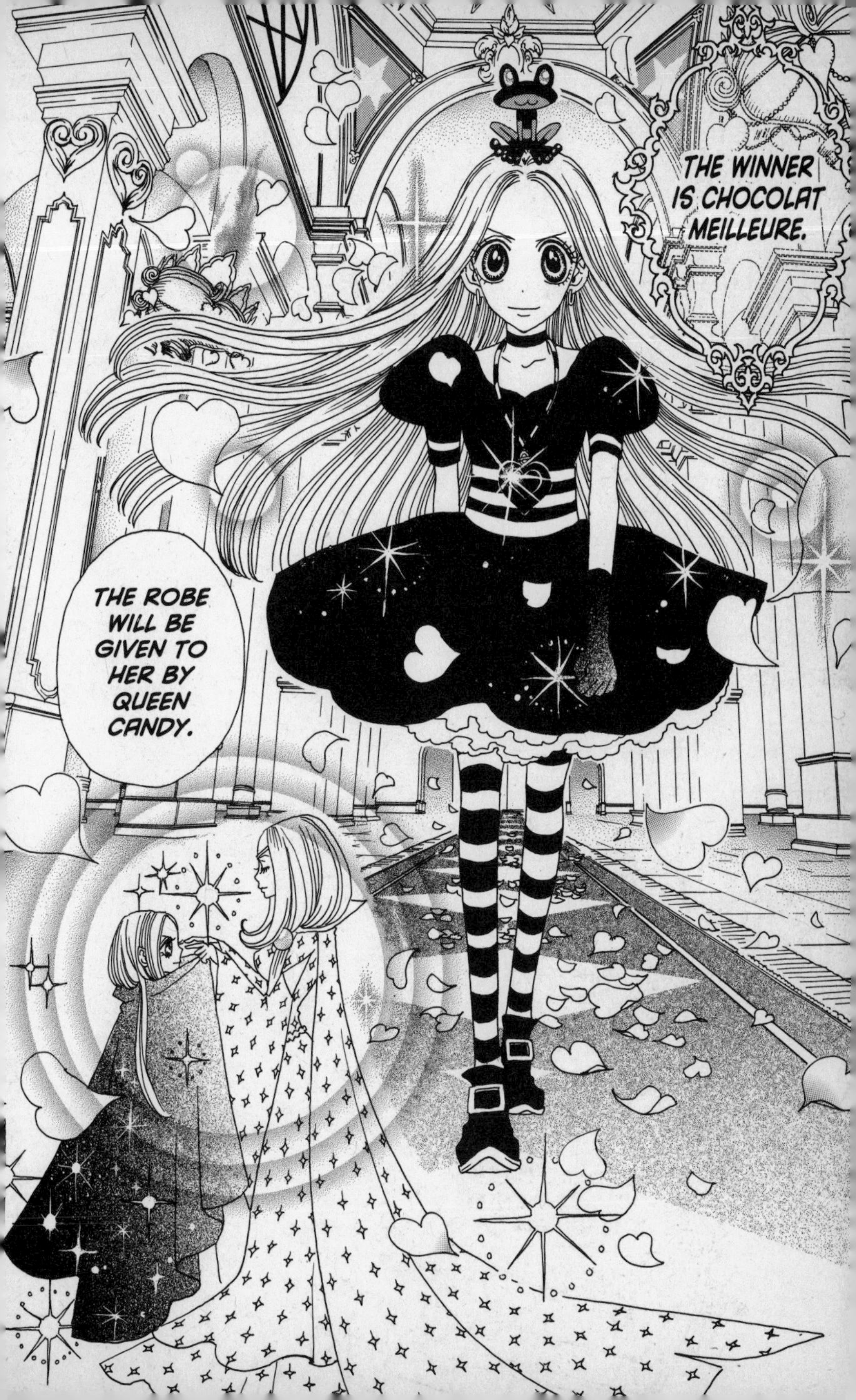
THE WINNER IS CHOCOLAT MEILLEURE.
THE ROBE WILL BE GIVEN TO HER BY QUEEN CANDY.

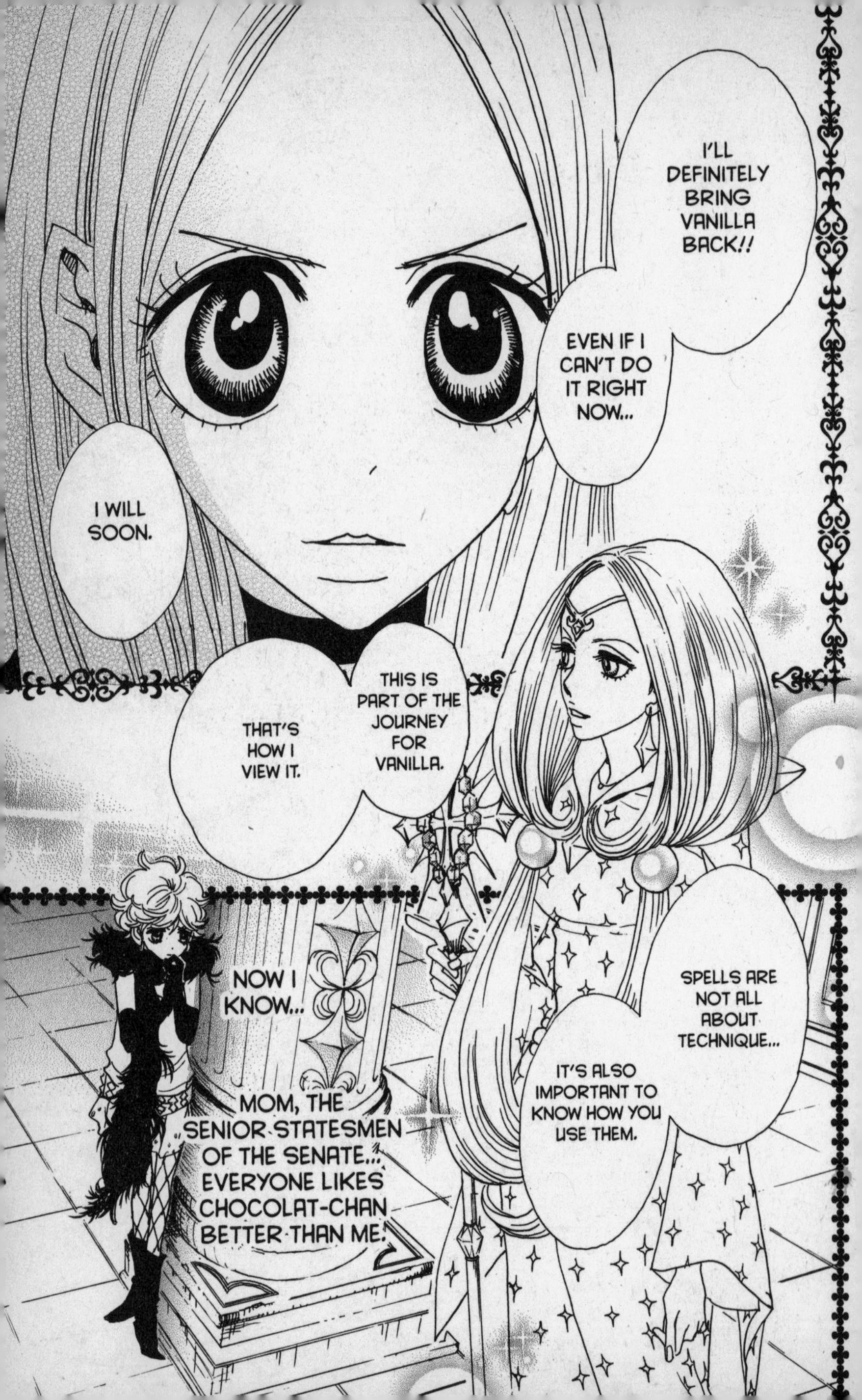
I'LL DEFINITELY BRING VANILLA BACK!!
EVEN IF I CAN'T DO IT RIGHT NOW...
I WILL SOON.
THIS IS PART OF THE JOURNEY FOR VANILLA.
THAT'S HOW I VIEW IT.
SPELLS ARE NOT ALL ABOUT TECHNIQUE...
IT'S ALSO IMPORTANT TO KNOW HOW YOU USE THEM.
NOW I KNOW...
MOM, THE SENIOR STATESMEN OF THE SENATE... EVERYONE LIKES CHOCOLAT-CHAN BETTER THAN ME.

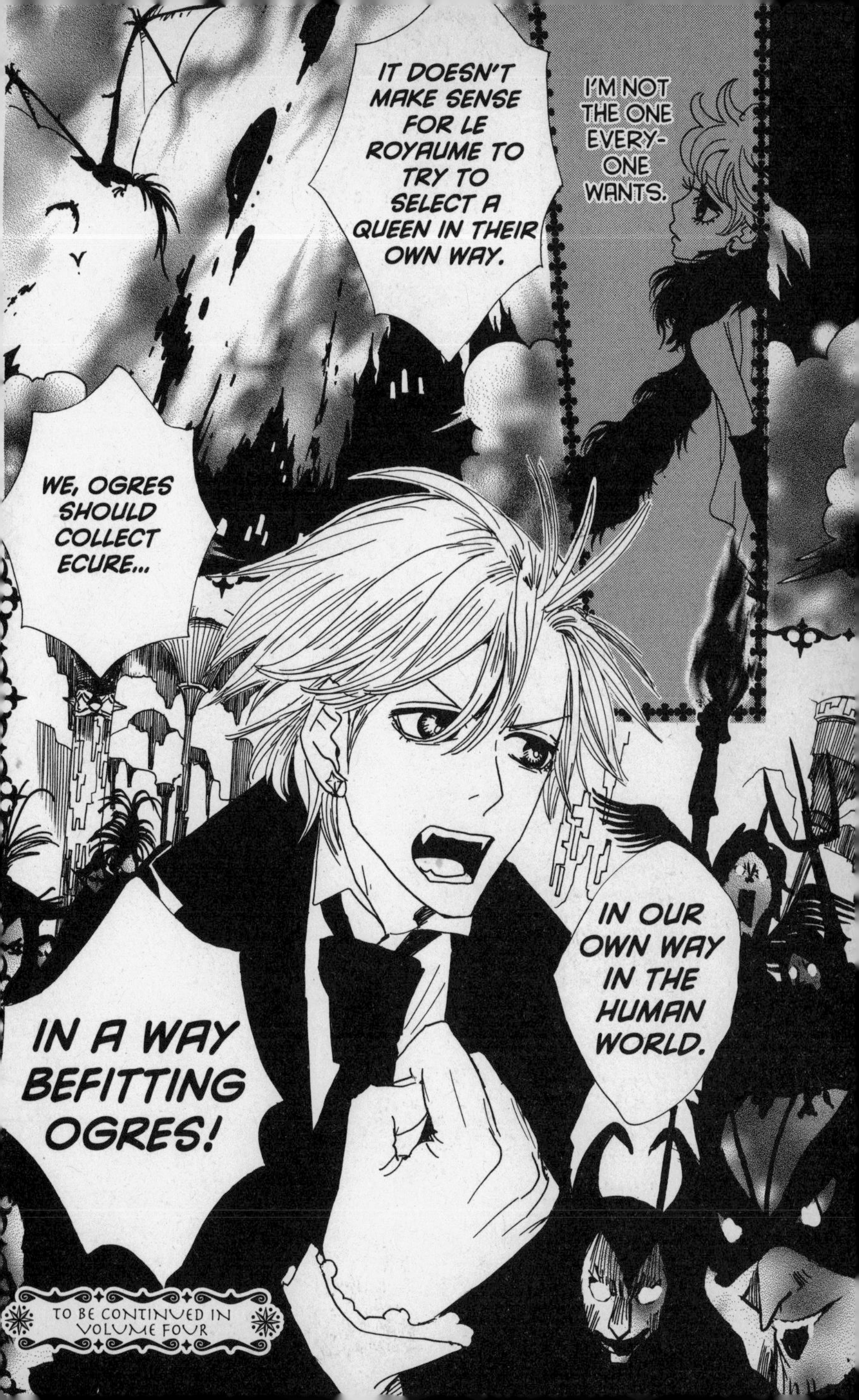
I'M NOT THE ONE EVERY-ONE WANTS.
IT DOESN'T MAKE SENSE FOR LE ROYAUME TO TRY TO SELECT A QUEEN IN THEIR OWN WAY.
WE, OGRES SHOULD COLLECT ECURE...
IN OUR OWN WAY IN THE HUMAN WORLD.
IN A WAY BEFITTING OGRES!
TO BE CONTINUED IN VOLUME FOUR

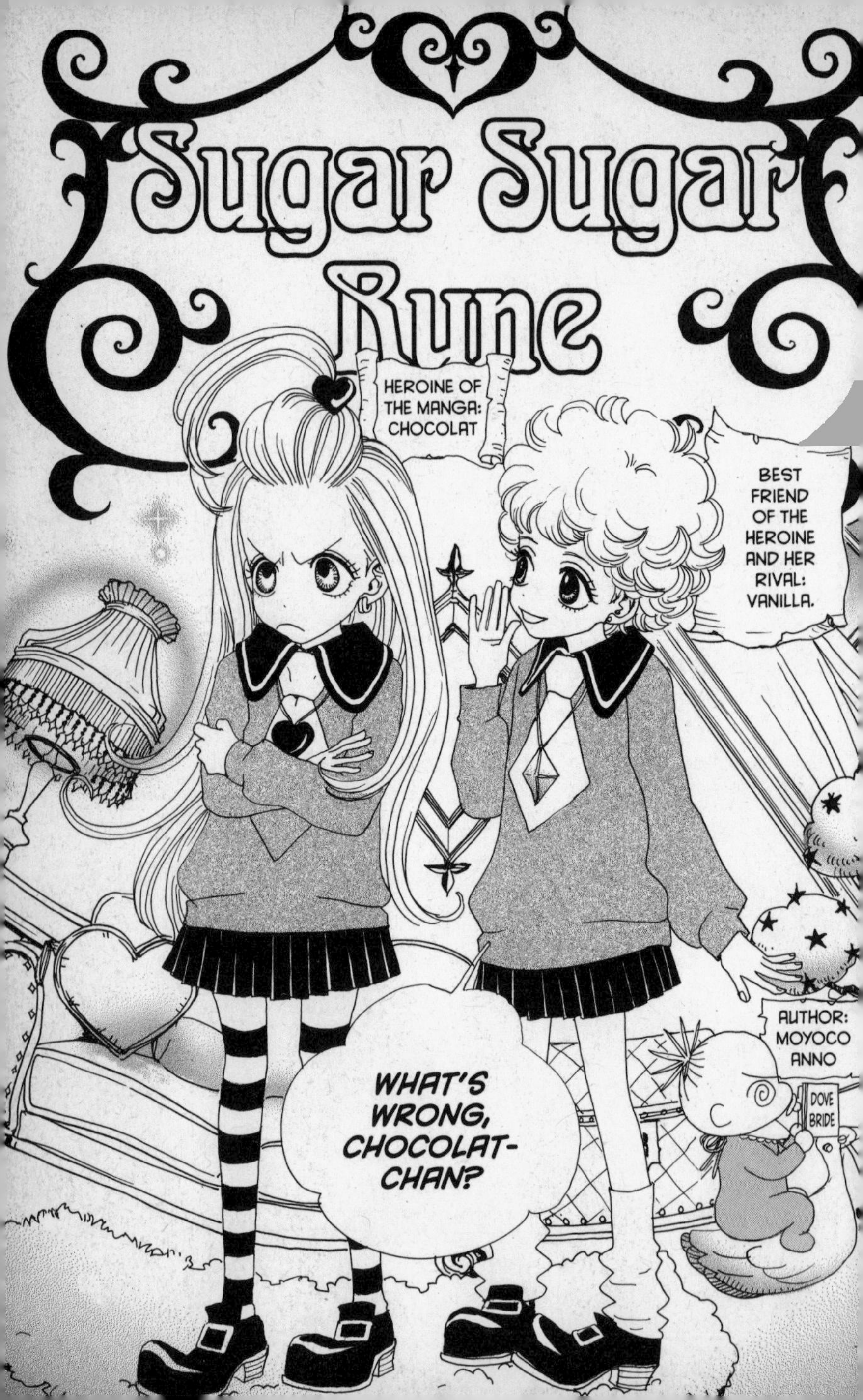
Sugar Sugar Rune
HEROINE OF THE MANGA: CHOCOLAT
BEST FRIEND OF THE HEROINE AND HER RIVAL: VANILLA.
AUTHOR: MOYOCO ANNO
DOVE BRIDE
WHAT'S WRONG, CHOCOLAT-CHAN?

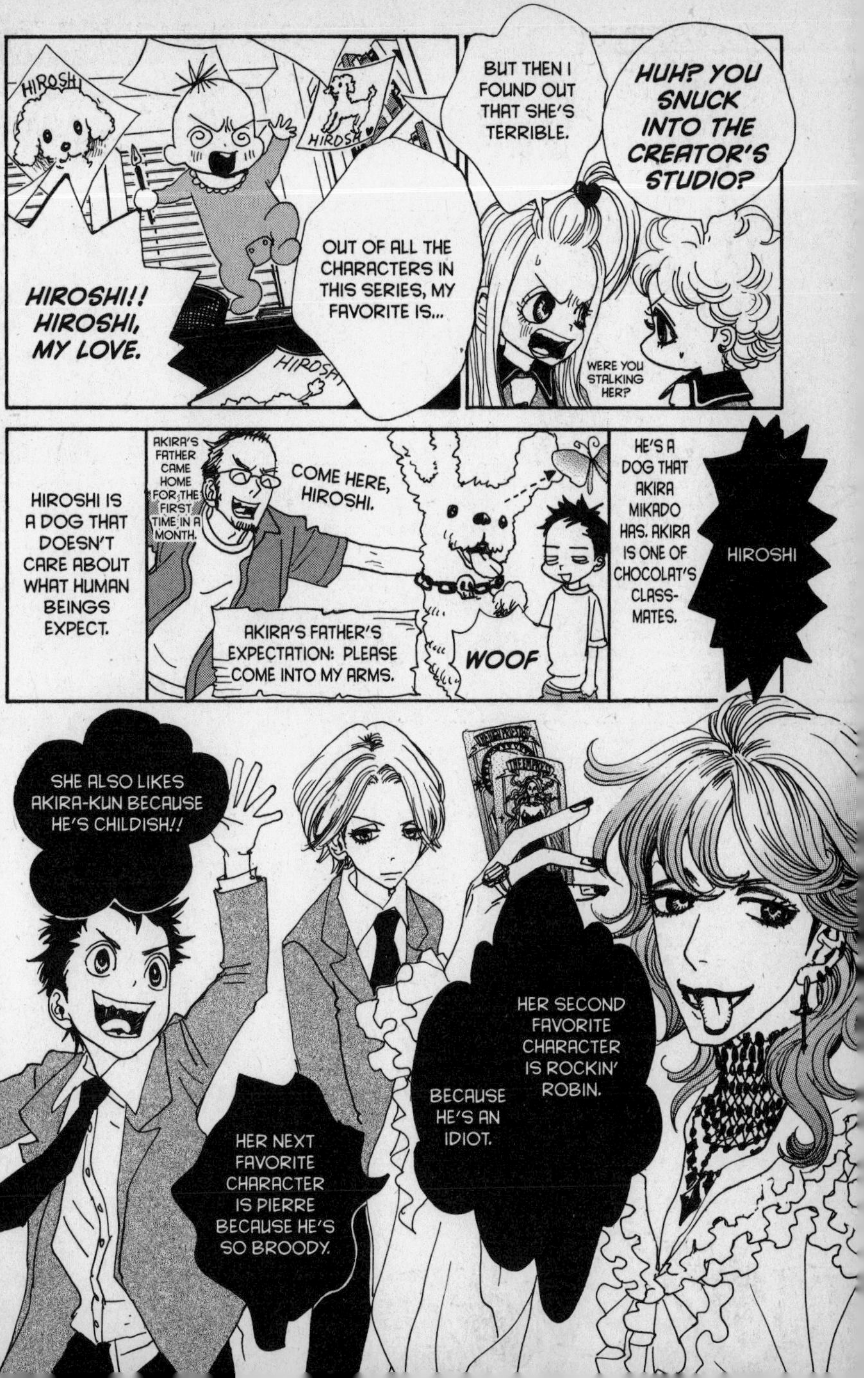
HUH? YOU SNUCK INTO THE CREATOR'S STUDIO?
BUT THEN I FOUND OUT THAT SHE'S TERRIBLE.
WERE YOU STALKING HER?
HIROSHI
HIROSHI ♥
OUT OF ALL THE CHARACTERS IN THIS SERIES, MY FAVORITE IS...
HIROSHI!! HIROSHI, MY LOVE.
HIROSHI
HIROSHI
HE'S A DOG THAT AKIRA MIKADO HAS. AKIRA IS ONE OF CHOCOLAT'S CLASS-MATES.
AKIRA'S FATHER CAME HOME FOR THE FIRST TIME IN A MONTH.
COME HERE, HIROSHI.
AKIRA'S FATHER'S EXPECTATION: PLEASE COME INTO MY ARMS.
WOOF
HIROSHI IS A DOG THAT DOESN'T CARE ABOUT WHAT HUMAN BEINGS EXPECT.
HER SECOND FAVORITE CHARACTER IS ROCKIN' ROBIN.
BECAUSE HE'S AN IDIOT.
HER NEXT FAVORITE CHARACTER IS PIERRE BECAUSE HE'S SO BROODY.
SHE ALSO LIKES AKIRA-KUN BECAUSE HE'S CHILDISH!!

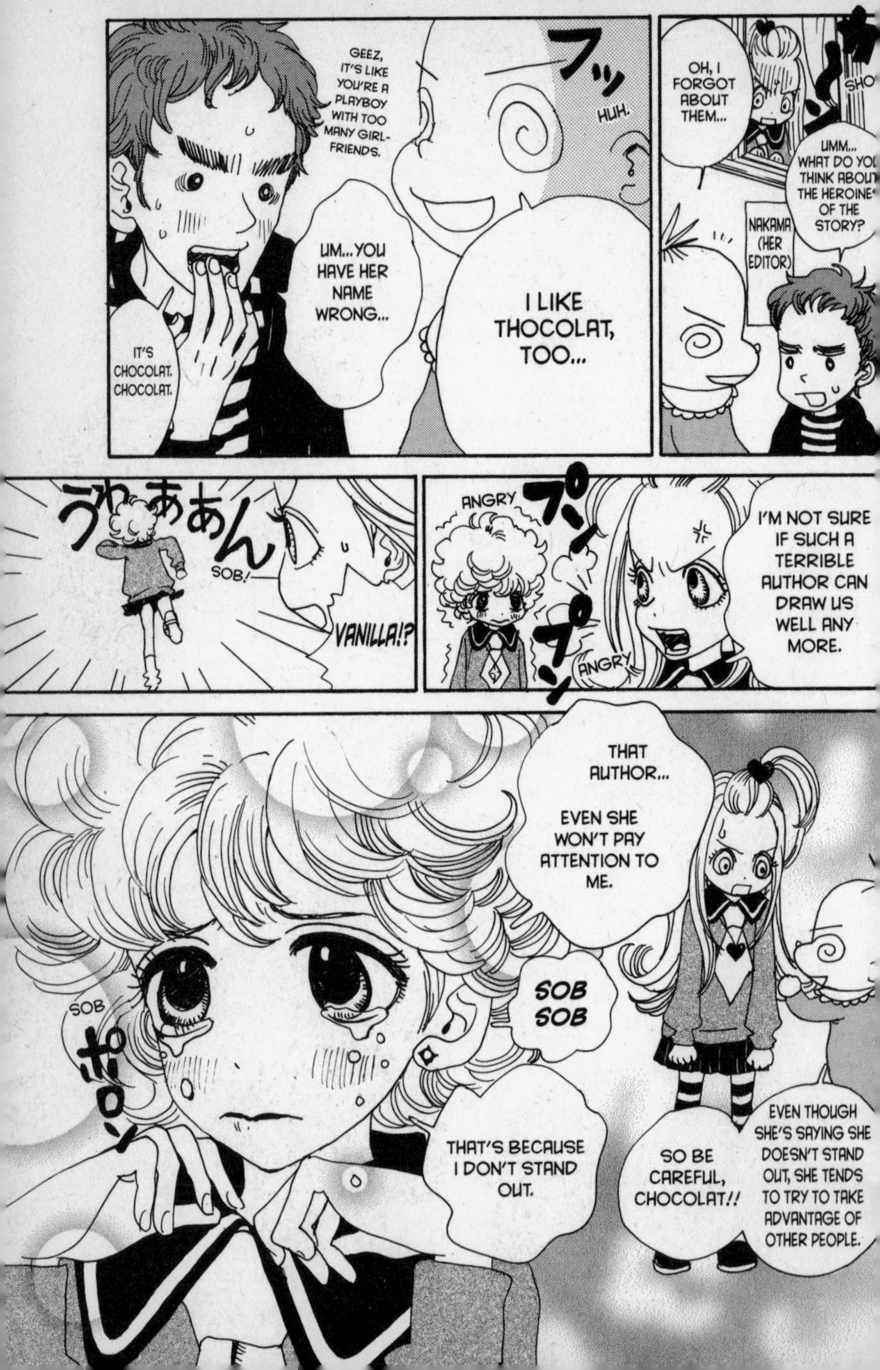

OH, I FORGOT ABOUT THEM...
SHO
UMM... WHAT DO YO THINK ABOUT THE HEROINE OF THE STORY?
NAKAMA (HER EDITOR)
フッ
HUH.
I LIKE THOCOLAT, TOO...
GEEZ, IT'S LIKE YOU'RE A PLAYBOY WITH TOO MANY GIRL-FRIENDS.
UM...YOU HAVE HER NAME WRONG...
IT'S CHOCOLAT. CHOCOLAT.
I'M NOT SURE IF SUCH A TERRIBLE AUTHOR CAN DRAW US WELL ANY MORE.
プンプン
ANGRY
ANGRY
VANILLA!?
うわあああん
SOB!
THAT AUTHOR... EVEN SHE WON'T PAY ATTENTION TO ME.
EVEN THOUGH SHE'S SAYING SHE DOESN'T STAND OUT, SHE TENDS TO TRY TO TAKE ADVANTAGE OF OTHER PEOPLE.
SO BE CAREFUL, CHOCOLAT!!
SOB SOB
THAT'S BECAUSE I DON'T STAND OUT.
SOB

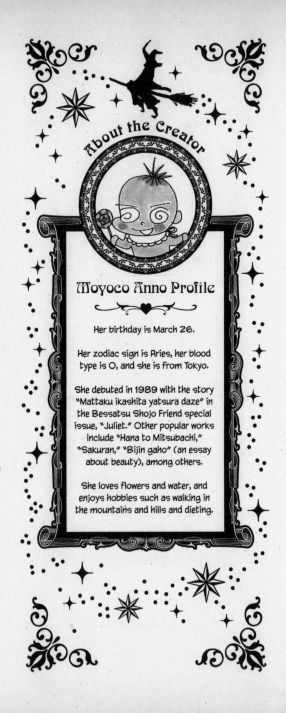

About the Creator

Moyoco Anno Profile

Her birthday is March 26.

Her zodiac sign is Aries, her blood type is O, and she is from Tokyo.

She debuted in 1989 with the story "Mattaku ikashita yatsura daze" in the Bessatsu Shojo Friend special issue, "Juliet." Other popular works include "Hana to Mitsubachi," "Sakuran," "Bijin gaho" (an essay about beauty), among others.

She loves flowers and water, and enjoys hobbies such as walking in the mountains and hills and dieting.

TRANSLATION NOTES

For your edification and reading pleasure, here are notes to explain some of the cultural and story references from our translation of *Sugar Sugar Rune 3*.

PAGE 4,
THE SPELLING OF CHOCOLAT'S NAME

"Chocolat" is the French word for chocolate. Sometimes the Japanese prefer to use French words, particularly if they wish to imply the person or thing named is expensive or fragile. In this case, "chocolat" is meant to connote expensive, gourmet chocolate.

PAGE 4,
CHOCOLAT'S FULL NAME

Chocolat's full name is Chocolat Meilleure. "Meilleure" means "best" in French.

PAGE 4,
CHOCOLAT'S ASSUMED NAME, CHOCOLAT KATO

In Japanese, names are spoken in this order: surname and then given name. So Chocolat's full name would be spoken in Japanese as Kato Chocolat. In the Japanese language, usage of different Chinese characters can end up producing the same sound. In the case of the characters in the original Japanese manga, Kato Shokora (Kato Chocolat) means "sugar-added chocolate" when completely different Chinese characters are used.

PAGE 4,
VANILLA'S FULL NAME

Vanilla's full name is Vanilla Mieux. "Mieux" means "better" in French.

PAGE 4,
VANILLA'S ASSUMED NAME, VANILLA ICE

Vanilla's Japanese name while she is in the Human World is Vanilla Ice. In Japan, there is an ice cream, which sometimes comes in a bar, called Vanilla Ice. It is popular among kids.

Page 4, What's a Familiar?

A familiar is a magical creature who serves a witch or wizard.

Page 5, Chocolat's Grandfather's Name

Chocolat's grandfather's first name, Corne, comes from the French term "corne-horn," which means "hard skin."

Page 5, What Are Ecure?

Ecure is a form of currency used in the Magical World.

Page 8, Le Royaume

Le royaume is French for "kingdom."

Page 17, The Ice Prince's Name

The Ice Prince's name, Glacé, means "ice" in French.

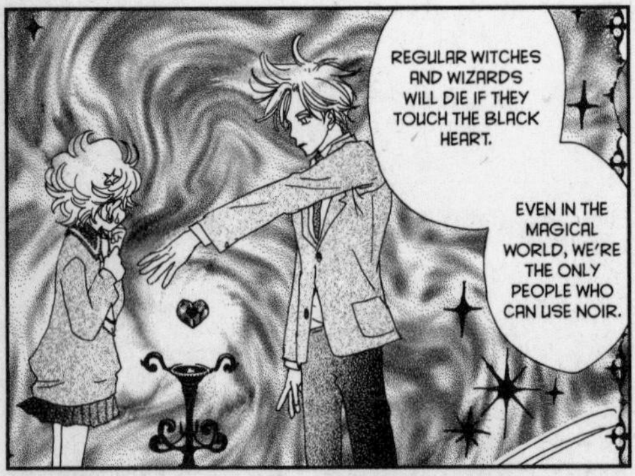
REGULAR WITCHES AND WIZARDS WILL DIE IF THEY TOUCH THE BLACK HEART.
EVEN IN THE MAGICAL WORLD, WE'RE THE ONLY PEOPLE WHO CAN USE NOIR.

Page 72, What Is Noir?

Noir means black in French.
In the story, it refers to black hearts—hearts colored by the emotion of hatred.

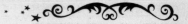

PAGE 80, WHY DOES THE STUDENT REFER TO VANILLA AS VANILLA-TAN?

VANILLA-TAN IS MISSING...
WE'VE BEEN LOOKING FOR HER, TOO.

-Tan is an honorific similar to –chan. -Tan is usually used by small children or when addressing someone very young.

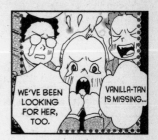

PAGE 110, WHY DOES THE MAGICAL WORLD MAIL ORDER DELIVERY MAN TALK FUNNY?

This delivery man speaks with a Kansai accent. We have tried to capture the feeling of his accent in English.

WHY ARE ALL OF YOU CLIMBING ON MY FAMILY'S TREE?
ARE YOU GUYS AKIRA'S FRIENDS? PERFECT.
WE'RE MAKING RICE CAKES RIGHT NOW.
COME DOWN FROM THE TREES AND JOIN US.
WARM
WARM

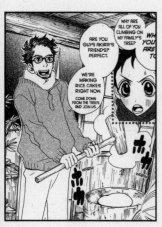

PAGES 117 AND 118, WHAT IS AKIRA'S FATHER MAKING WOO AND SOUL DO?

Akira's father is pounding steamed rice into the dough used to make rice cakes. The Japanese term for this is *mochi tsuki*, and this term is used later by Soul.

PAGE 117, WHY DOES MIHARU REFER TO HIMSELF AS MI-KUN?

Mi-kun is a childish way of saying Miharu-kun.

PAGE 121, *HATSUMOUDE*

Hatsumoude is the first shrine visit of the year. After the clock strikes midnight on January 1, people gather at the shrines to pray and make resolutions for a healthy and successful new year.

PAGE 125,
DAIKICHI AND OMIKUJI

Daikichi means very good luck and *omikuji* is a written fortune. Here the
written fortune *(omikuji)* Miharu drew predicted very good luck for the
year. After drawing one's fortune, it's traditional to tie it to a tree branch.

PAGE 125,
WHAT DOES AKIRA'S FATHER MEAN WHEN
HE MENTIONS THE DOG AND THE STICK?

He's referring to a Japanese proverb: *Inu mo arukeba bòuni ataru*. This literally means
"When a dog walks, it runs across a stick." This proverb has two meanings. The first is: If
you're too forward, you're likely to meet with disaster. The second is: Every dog has its day.
Here Akira's father is implying the second meaning as Miharu got *daikichi* in his *omikuji*.

PAGE 125,
WHAT'S THE CARD GAME THEY'RE PLAYING?

Hyakunin Issyu is a Japanese New Year's card game in which the players
try to match the first and second halves of each of the One Hundred Tanka
(short verse) Poems by One Hundred Celebrated Poets.

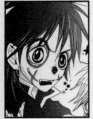

PAGE 125,
WHAT'S THE GAME CHOCOLAT AND THE BOYS ARE
PLAYING, AND WHY IS SOUL'S FACE PAINTED?

Here Chocolat and Akira are playing *hanetsuki*. *Hanetsuki* is a Japanese game
similar to badminton. Traditionally, it's played on New Year's. The *hagoita* that
Chocolat refers to is a rectangular wooden paddle. The loser in *hanetsuki* draws
marks on his or her face with *sumi* (India) ink.

PAGE 129,
JAPANESE BUDDHIST ALTAR

After a person's death, the family selects a household Buddhist altar, which is
made of rare foreign wood. A picture of Miharu's father, who is deceased, is
displayed in the Buddhist altar along with incense for the offering. Part of the
Buddhist tradition is to ring the metal prayer bowl (which is not shown in this
panel) with a special stick while burning incense and praying.

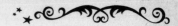

PAGE 131, AGRANDISSEMENT

Chocolat uses this magic word to make things grow larger. It's French for "expansion."

PAGE 136, W.H.A.K.

The original acronym was made by taking the first letter of the Japanese text, which is literally translated as "If you need something answered, ask the Hell's Angels." For layout purposes, the translation was altered to "When you don't know, Hell's Angels know!"

WOW, THESE ARE CUTE!! ARE THESE CHOCOLATE ROSES?
THIS IS A BRAND-NEW ITEM FOR THE YEAR. ♡

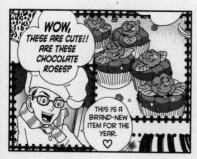

PAGE 142, VALENTINE'S DAY IN JAPAN

Valentine's Day (February 14) in Japan is one of the most exciting yet nerve-racking days of the year for many Japanese schoolgirls and a busy time for buying chocolate. On this day, a woman can give chocolate to a man she likes to let him know she's interested in him. The gifts of chocolate can be divided into two types. *Giri choco* (obligatory chocolate) is the chocolate you give to your superior or co-workers. *Honmei choco* is the chocolate you give to someone you love. It's common for a woman to buy twenty to thirty boxes of chocolate for Valentine's Day to cover her needs for giving both *giri choco* and *honmei choco*. Many department stores prepare fun and elaborate chocolate Valentine's gifts as Valentine's Day approaches. Chocolate companies in Japan sell more chocolate in the week before Valentine's Day than they do all year. White Day, which is exactly one month after Valentine's Day, is the day for men to return the favor by giving women candies.

PAGE 181, UMEKEN SAMBA DANCE

Umeken Samba may be a play on the name of an actual dance. The *Matsuken Samba* is a playful samba dance performed by actor Matsuken (Ken Matsudaira).

PAGE 197, WHY DID BLANCA CALL HER VANILLA-CHAMA?

Since Blanca is a magical mouse, she has a mouse accent, which sounds a little like baby talk. She means to say "sama," but it sounds like "chama" with her accent.

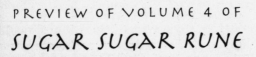

PREVIEW OF VOLUME 4 OF
SUGAR SUGAR RUNE

We are pleased to present you with a preview of the next
volume of *Sugar Sugar Rune*. Volume 4 is not yet available
in English, so for now you'll have to make do with Japanese!

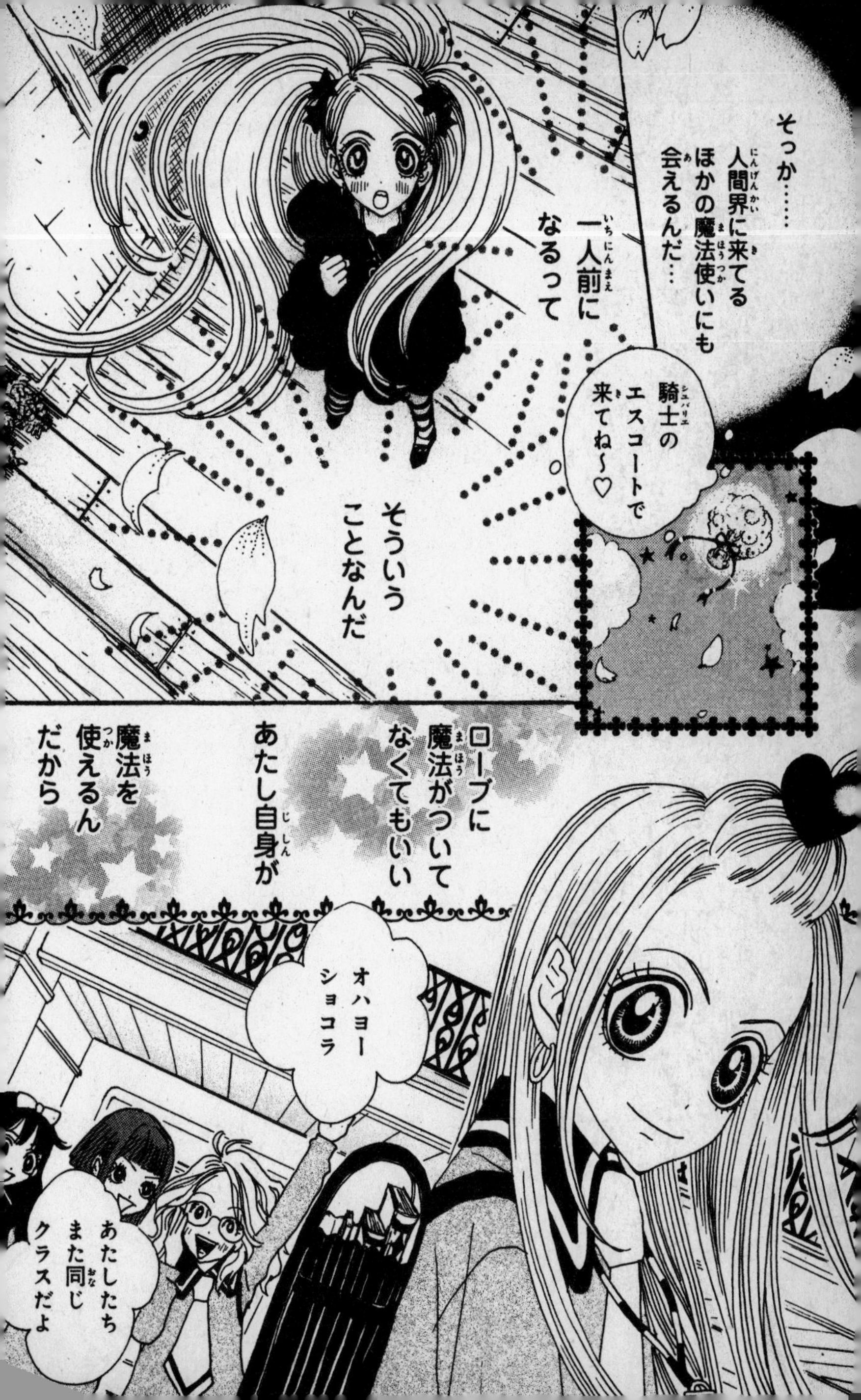
そっか……
人間界に来てるほかの魔法使いにも会えるんだ…
騎士のエスコートで来てね～♡
一人前になるって
そういうことなんだ
ローブに魔法がついてなくてもいい
あたし自身が
魔法を使えるんだから
オハヨーショコラ
あたしたちまた同じクラスだよ

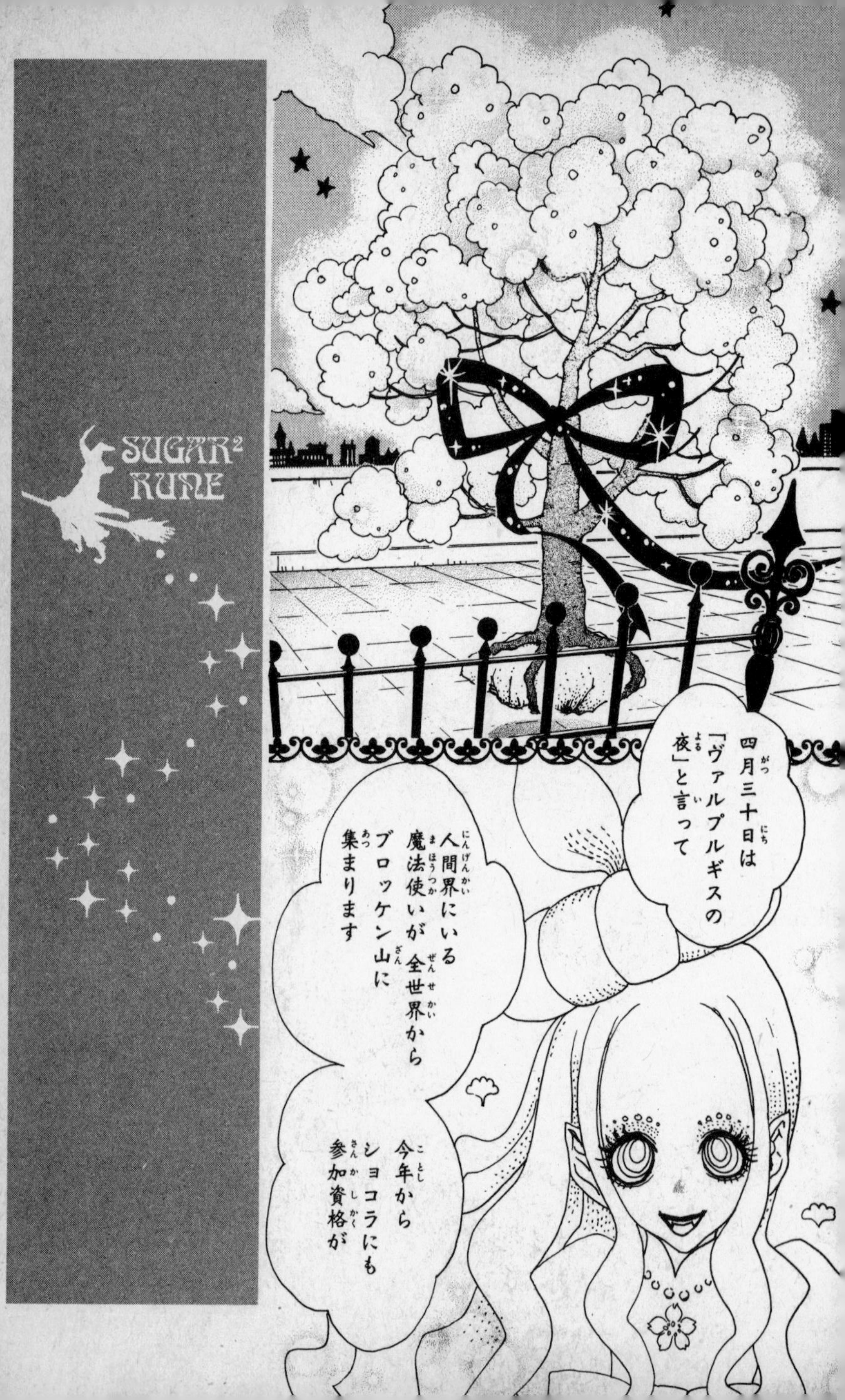
SUGAR² RUNE
四月三十日は「ヴァルプルギスの夜」と言って
人間界にいる魔法使いが全世界からブロッケン山に集まります
今年からショコラにも参加資格が

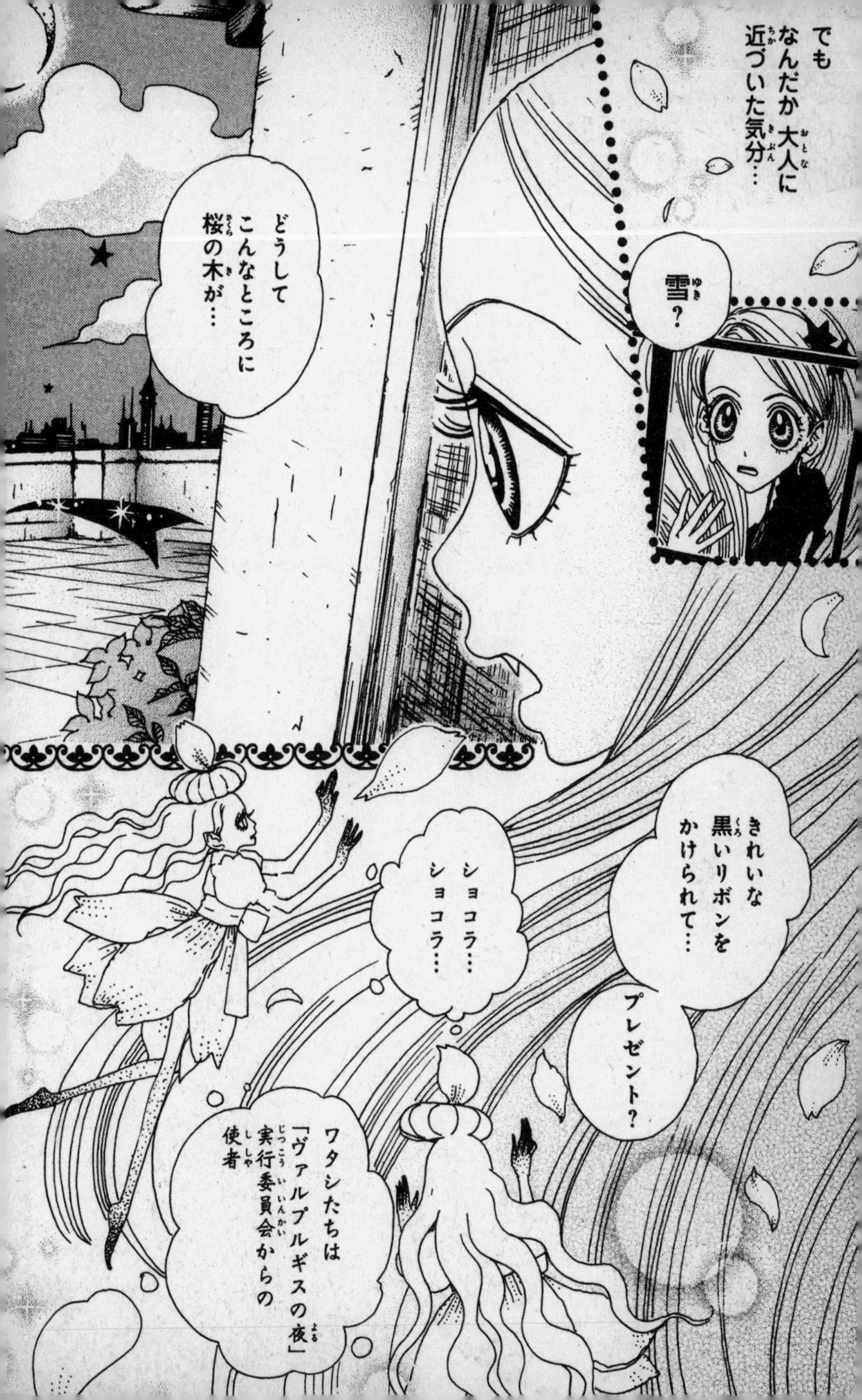
でもなんだか大人に近づいた気分…
雪？
どうしてこんなところに桜の木が…
きれいな黒いリボンをかけられて…
プレゼント？
ショコラ…ショコラ…
ワタシたちは「ヴァルプルギスの夜」実行委員会からの使者

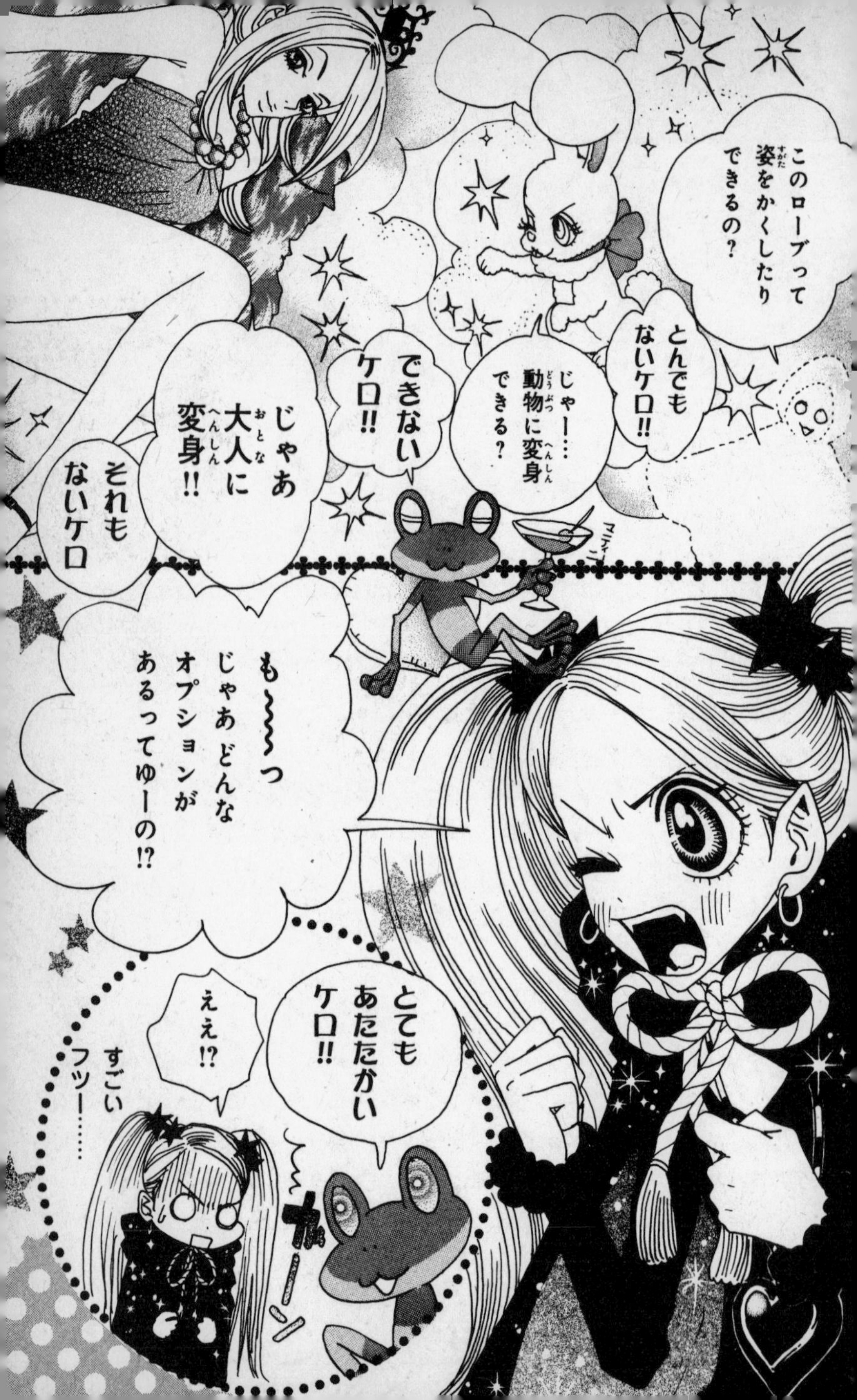
このローブって姿をかくしたりできるの？
とんでもないケロ!!
じゃー…動物に変身できる？
できないケロ!!
マティーニ
じゃあ大人に変身!!
それもないケロ
も〜〜っじゃあどんなオプションがあるってゆーの!?
とてもあたたかいケロ!!
ええ!?
すごいフツー……

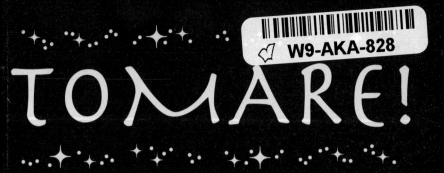

TOMARE!

W9-AKA-828

STOP!

YOU'RE GOING THE WRONG WAY!

MANGA IS A COMPLETELY DIFFERENT TYPE
OF READING EXPERIENCE.

TO START AT THE BEGINNING,
GO TO THE END!

THAT'S RIGHT!

AUTHENTIC MANGA IS READ THE TRADITIONAL
JAPANESE WAY—FROM RIGHT TO LEFT. EXACTLY THE OPPOSITE
OF HOW AMERICAN BOOKS ARE READ. IT'S EASY TO FOLLOW:
JUST GO TO THE OTHER END OF THE BOOK, AND READ EACH
PAGE—AND EACH PANEL—FROM RIGHT SIDE TO LEFT SIDE,
STARTING AT THE TOP RIGHT. NOW YOU'RE EXPERIENCING
MANGA AS IT WAS MEANT TO BE.